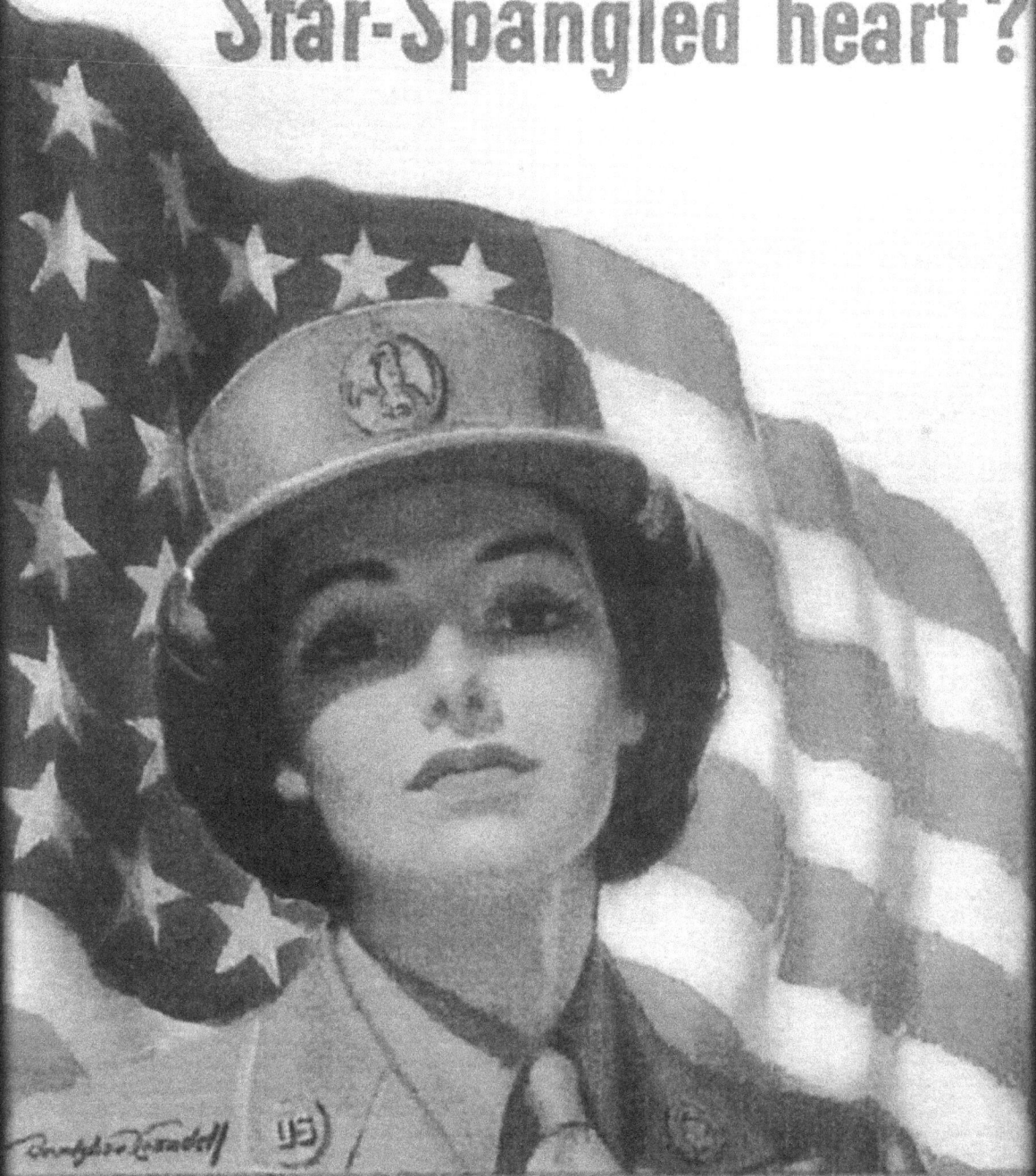

TURNER PUBLISHING COMPANY
PADUCAH, KENTUCKY

Other Books Published by Jackson County Historical Society

By Loren W. Noblitt, Ph.D.
Noblesse Oblige (Noblitt)
Mit Complementen Abweisen (Kamman)
Tides of Life (Hendershot)
Torchbearers of America (Walls)
Compsite History of Jackson County – 2 Volumes
Autobiography of John Reno
Tragic Destiny
Echoes from the Hills around Starve Hollow
A Digest of Pioneer Settlers of Jackson County
A History of Blish Milling Company
Underground RR Through Jackson County
Myth or Reality (Aquilla Rogers)Halfway to Freedom
Gen. Morgan and His Confederate Raiders
One Hundred Years of Christian Worship
A History of Jackson County Churches
Records of Pioneer Weddings
Quaker Patriots of the Revolution
Sleep Gallant Soldier, Sleep
Stack Arms
Call to Arms
A History of the Shields Family
Military Records of the War Between the States
"D" Day Assault on Omaha Beach – World War II

By Richard D. Benton
Voices of Vietnam

By Marcia Walker
A Millenium Moment

RECALL

RECORDS
OF
JACKSON COUNTY VETERANS
1776 - 2004

Jackson County Historical Society
207 East Walnut Street – Box 215
Brownstown, IN 47220-1514

Turner®
PUBLISHING COMPANY

412 Broadway • P.O. Box 3101
Paducah, Kentucky 42002-3101
(270) 443-0121
www.turnerpublishing.com

Turner Publishing Company Staff:
Randy Baumgardner, Editor
Peter Zuniga, Designer

All photographs presented herein are from
the people who donated them for the purpose of inclusion
in this volume

Library of Congress Control Number: 2004112331

ISBN 978-1-63026-958-6

Limited Edition.

LET US NOT FORGET....

Everyone seems to repeat there shall be wars and rumors of war, few believe those nations will one day be rebuked; and the time will come when they shall turn their swords into ploughshares, and their spears into pruninghooks, and there will be no more war, nations will prepare for war no more because their stockpiles of weapons will have been destroyed.

Matt 24: 6-7   Micah 4:3   Psalm 46:4

DEDICATION

Young men and women in the prime of their lives are called to defend the freedoms of this nation. They set forth with courage and dreams that they will also be able to enjoy the liberties defined in the Declaration of Independence. In the spirit of 1776 many are sacrificed as the price we pay for our freedom. For their service to this country, the members of the Jackson County Historical Society are pleased to pay tribute to all veterans dead and alive who possess county connections.

IN MEMORY OF EACH COMRADE

Many lights shine above our heads ever so bright
They are special stars firmly fixed in my heart,
Because in our conflicts for freedom and right
They represent all who valiantly did their part!

They are stars of service shining ever so bright
They stand as beacons of right so firm and true,
Their rays of light shine during each dark night
They are the stars with colors of twinkling blue!

To God in Heaven, the Creator of all, we bow
It is daily we offer to Him our needs in prayer,
Whatever dangers or suffering may come now
We will rest securely in His wonderful care!

The stars in the blue yonder under His vast dome
Through countless ages ever constant and true,
Those stars in our hearts and lights of our homes
Shine forever comrades and always just for you!

Loren W. Noblitt, Ph.D.
Secretary and Compiler
Jackson County Historian: 1991 - 1998

EMPSON
AN AMERICAN FAMILY OF MILITARY VETERANS
1768-2004

Cornelius, a nine year-old lad arrived in America aboard the *"Tannerheist"* with his father, Daniel Empson, when they landed at Perth Amboy in East Jersey September 23, 1768. Ship records fail to list other passengers from Ireland, but everyone was fleeing to escape the famine at home. Both father and son migrated into the Virginia Colony and settled near Front Royal. When Daniel died in 1777, just after the new American Flag with its circle of 13 stars was hoisted aloft, the 18 year-old Cornelius Empson enlisted in the Continental Army and served under General Anthony Wayne during the Battle of Brandywine Creek. Cornelius Empson was then assigned to the Pennsylvania Frontier Rangers. He served under Captain Jacob Henderschatte commanding the 2nd Battalion in 1779 and 1780. While on leave he was married but his wife died March 1, 1779 while delivering a baby named John Empson. Records show he returned to duty and participated in the Battle of Yorktown in 1781.

Following the war, Cornelius Empson was married to Hannah Oldham in 1793 and almost immediately, the couple moved down the Ohio River following others into the beautiful lands of Kentucky. When they struck out across country, they met James Smith, a circuit-riding minister. The Empson family followed him into Bourbon County in 1794. It was preacher Smith who induced Cornelius Empson to attend his church services before the veteran left to serve in the War of 1812, It was during those services where his son, John Empson was converted to faith. He was later married to Suzannah Prather in 1804. So strong did his faith become that he uttered a single Bible verse when his own son, Azariah Empson, was born in 1808. Preacher Smith entered that verse in his diary:

…I have placed my Spirit upon your son so that he might live, and I shall lead him to a land where he may prosper greatly…

John Empson later moved his family to Indiana where he homesteaded 160 acres of land in Jackson County. In 1827 they moved upstream and settled in Jackson County. In 1827 they moved upstream and settled in Grassy Fork Township. It was there along the Muscatatuck River where Azariah Empson married Martha Holmes in 1831. A year later that newly-married groom was placed on stand-by status when he volunteered to serve in the Black Hawk War. As his farmland holdings grew to more than 700 acres, so did his family multiply! Eleven children were born to Azariah and Martha Empson, including a son named Daniel Empson who arrived to greet his family in 1839. He continued to live on the family farm even after his brother William Empson enlisted in the 137th Regiment of Indiana Volunteers. In October 1861, Daniel Empson walked to Seymour and enlisted in the 50th Regiment of Indiana Volunteers. After moving southward, his unit was charged to hold the Green River Bridge. Defeated in battle, the men were captured, returned to Indianapolis and later paroled to fight once again.

The regiment was re-activated and the men were assigned to capture Little Rock. Not long after that Daniel Empson was discharged January 6, 1865 and returned home to the family farm. He married Sarah Waskom and them were born nine children. Somewhere along the line Robert (Bud) Empson enlisted in the United States Navy in 1900 and served two months during the Spanish-American War. It seems he remained in the service through World War I. There is no doubt the military heritage of the Empson family had been made secure. Other Empson boys who served their country included Dan, Leroy, Francis and Harold Empson who were all members of the Armed Forces during World War II. Yet another brother was destined to serve in World War II. Howard Empson joined the Air Force during the Korean Police Action, and by the time the Vietnam Conflict broke out, other Empson young men served their country. Included were Thomas, Bobby, Larry, and John Empson who became veterans. Then came Stephan Empson who served in the Navy during the Persian Gulf War. Currently serving in the military forces is the great-great-granddaughter of the Empson family forbear, Jillian Richards, who is completing her training in the Army and looking forward to her first airborne jump.

The military records of the Empson family represent the highest form of patriotism during its 225 years of life! Indeed, Empson sons and daughters have answered the call to duty from 1777 to 2004. They deserve to be saluted with well-deserved honor and respect. The compiler of these records pays his sincere tribute to each of them, along with every other veteran included in this volume!

CONTENTS

A PECULIAR ORDER FOR THE VETERANS BOOK
WITH
AN UNSIGNED MILITARY RECORD
OF AN
UNIDENTIFIED JACKSON COUNTY VETERAN

One young man from the wrong side of the tracks in Seymour, Indiana, was a freshman student at Indiana Central College in the fall of 1941. Many people yet alive today know that was the time of suspense when Pearl Harbor was attacked. Even in classes we were bombarded with the slogan to "Remember Pearl Harbor." But, there were several in class who didn't know where the target of the Japanese planes was located. This young man was one of those backward students, so he decided to enlist in the Army so he could find out more about that so-called "dastardly and unprovoked attack on the United States."

After his basic training he was sent to Bowman Field for more training but he was unaware of what kind it was to be. Within three months he was shipped overseas and landed in England thinking he was to be some kind of clerk. Instead, he cleaned latrines, drove army trucks and drilled for hours with a rifle he would never be able to fire! It was several months before that young man understood he was no longer a useless college student. He was now a legitimate soldier intent on doing his part to preserve the "American way of life with freedom."

The young man was about to see his first action, and it surely came on June 6, 1944. He didn't learn it was called "D" Day until he was wounded and recuperating in a French field hospital. And be never expected to be returned to action again! But he was sent to his unit and survived the sustained advances through Luxembourg and into the Axis homelands of Germany. Much later he remembered the "Battle of the Bulge" as the bloodiest of all the fighting. Even later than that he learned that was Hitler's last gasp, but the advance continued!

He recently received a framed plaque from the government of France! Fifty-nine years after the fact he was being offered belated "thanks" for liberating their country. That young man, older and wiser than ever, certainly appreciated the sentiments, but he proclaimed the United States was really not much different than when he left. He said he could go wherever he wanted, do whatever he wanted, say whatever he wanted to say. But now, he was physically unable to do much of anything; all he could do was sit in his rocker and thank God that Tyranny was defeated! With that unseen belief in the Almighty power, he had decided that it was the veterans, and not the government who preserved the freedom of the press, It was the veterans, not the poet who ensured freedom of speech. It was the veterans, not the protesters, who made certain the right to assemble. The veterans, not the politicians preserved the right to vote. The veterans made certain people could worship as they pleased. The American spirit was worth fighting for! And he was only happy that he had been part of God's action!

LONG MAY SHE WAVE

THE SYMBOL OF AMERICAN FREEDOM

Jackson County Veterans Defended our Country and its Flag
1776-2004

18 December 2003

Dr. Loren W. Noblitt, Secretary
Re: "RECALL - Records of Jackson County Veterans"
Jackson County Historical Society
207 East Walnut Street - Box 215
Brownstown, IN 47220-1514

Dear Dr. Noblitt:

It is my pleasure to endorse this very important and worthwhile project to preserve the memories of Jackson County Veterans. I believe the published book will document some of the best and brightest history of the country. Often times the most treasured memories die with the ones who lived them.

With the memories captured on the written pages, our children and grandchildren and all of those who follow will be able to read about the valor, courage and sacrifices each veteran offered while defending our freedom. The sentiments which spring forth from the memories of our veterans is far too important to let them got away from us.

I salute you and the members of the Veterans Recall Committee for attempting this project sponsored by the Jackson County Historical Society. It is quite fitting to recognize and document the deeds of our local men and women who served us. Perhaps, it might offer future generations a better idea of what and how things happened.

Mike Fink

ABOUT THE COMPILER

Loren W. Noblitt, ScD., L.L.D., J.D., Ph.D
Jackson County Historian: 1991–1998

Dr. Loren W. Noblitt, Secretary of Jackson County Historical Society, was requested to compile a volume depicting tributes to the military veterans of the county. Emphasis was to be placed on the records of anyone who answered the call to defend the American freedoms. Every veteran with Jackson County connection who served this nation at any time and in any war from 1776 to 2004 may have his biographical records included in this memorial book honoring those who served.

The compiler is the author of three dozen books on Jackson County and its development. The current effort merely continues the annual publications for the society. The compiler is a retired educator with more than forty years of experience in the public schools. He has taught students of every age group, from the elementary grades, secondary classes and college students at the graduate level, various aspects of American history and political jurisprudence.

The oldest son of Rev. Loren S. and Minnie Walls Noblitt, a very young lad relocated from New Jersey and received his elementary instruction in Indianapolis. He attended Shortridge High School but at the end of one year transferred to Western Military Academy in Alton, Illinois. He later attended Morgan Prep School in Tennessee on a football scholarship. He finally returned home to Ogilville and graduated from Columbus High School with the class of 1940. He enrolled at Indiana Central College but withdrew after one semester when he was employed by Arvin Industries producing bomb casings for the war effort.

In mid-August 1942 he enlisted in the Army Airborne Command. He survived nine campaigns In North Africa, the Middle East, Sicily, Anzio, Rome-Foggio, Normandy, Central France, the Rhineland, but was wounded during the paratroop drop to capture the Nijmagen Bridge in Holland. After returning home he was discharged in 1945 and resumed his quest for an education.

As a Garriott Fellow, he received his undergraduate degree in 1949. He earned his MS degree from Butler University, and continued graduate study under the GI Bill which permitted him to earn multiple doctoral degrees. He was later named the national "teacher of the year" and listed in the "California Who's Who" for his extended research on the American Constitution. He is the author of several books and hundreds of school district policies. As the recipient of local, state and national distinction, Loren W. Noblitt was appointed Superintendent of Schools in Visalia, California.

He returned to Brownstown for his retirement years with his wife Kathryn. He later was named the "citizen of the year" for his involvement in community affairs. He participates in veterans affairs, serves as President of the Library Board of Trustees and continues as Secretary of the Historical Society and teaching of adult Bible Classes. They are the parents of two married daughters and have four grandchildren.

Compiler's Disclaimer

Whenever wars are fought, most youthful men become instant patriots and answer the call to arms. They leave their homes and peaceful lives with courage and hope. Most are willing and ready to defend their way of life from tyranny.

The sacrifice of those young warriors in battle always solidifies the American will to remain free at any cost, and that includes death. The public will never surrender their historical heritage of liberty!

When the fighting comes to an end, the wartime survivors certainly owe their fellow servicemen a debt of gratitude. Those who died had kept the faith and shed their blood for them. Military death is always the cost of freedom!

The accounts depicted in this delayed tribute to Jackson County veterans represent only a few of those who stepped forward to defend the United States from being overrun by an enemy. Most of the soldiers possess no right to be called heroes, but there are always a few who deserve that status because of their courageous deeds of valor. The others carried out what was expected of them. They sought only victory because they wanted to go home and enjoy the peace they helped ensure.

Memories of those military experiences often became faded with time for some. There are others who recall the terrible acts of war vividly long after the events!

Jackson County veterans, no matter the war period from 1776 to 2004 should understand the cost of liberty always comes with a high price.

Loren W. Noblitt, Ph.D.
County Historian: 1991-1998
Secretary

401 East Walnut Street
Brownstown, IN 47220
November 11, 2003

MEMORIAL MONUMENT
HONORS
REVOLUTIONARY WAR VETERANS BURIED IN JACKSON COUNTY

THE BLACK MARBLE MONUMENT

A marble monument erected jointly by the Sons of the American Revolution and the Jackson County Historical Society now stands mutely to honor all 34 Revolutionary War Veterans who are buried within the boundaries of the county. Keeping eternal watch high above the sacred plot may be seen a replica of the Betsy Ross Flag presented to General George Washington. That impressive monument forms the centerpiece for the Colonel John Ketcham Pioneer Village under construction and located just across the street from the county courthouse annex.

Jackson County Veterans Memorial

Courthouse Square

Brownstown, Indiana

Dedicated To Servicemen Killed On Foreign Soil

World War I

Akers, Stanley Garland
Allman, Fred
Arbuckle, Walter
Brewer, Francis Marvin
Burbrink, Frank W.
Caseboldt, Robert Sanford
Cobb, Henry Elkanah
Cox, James Colvin
Fountain, Virgil
Gossman, Vance Harold
Graves, Michael Charles
Greenlee, Orvil Edgar
Hackman, Hubert
Hagan, Martin A.
Hartwell, Chester A.
Huckleberry, Lebert
Leslie, Harry Alexander
Lewis, Albert May
Lockhart, Clarence
Lubker, Fred R.
Lucas, James
Mitchell, Carl
Mount, Leslie Lewis
Myers, William Joseph
Pruden, James Harold
Schill, Joseph E.
Stewart, James B.
Tabor, Louis Jackson
Thompson, Charles W.
Wilson, Arvie R.
Zimmerman, Edward Peter

World War II

Ault, Jesse J.
Baker, Carl R.
Baker, Charles R.
Baker, Feltner
Barkadale, Thomas L.
Bechtel, Newton H.
Beldon, James F.
Blackwell, Marion F.
Blair, William A.
Bobb, Virgil F.
Brown, George A.
Brown, Melvin M.
Brown, Oren E.
Cline, Gilbert
Cockerum, Kenneth E.
Cole, Morris A.
Cook, Keith E.
Cottingham, Robert H.
Crawford, Fred
Davers, Clyde
Davis, Roy J.
Eisele, Luther D.
Findley, Curtis E.
Fish, Eathel I.
Fleetwood, Donald
Fleetwood, Verlas W.
Fleetwood, Robert
Fox, Carl D.
Frost, Charles O.
Frost, Owen
Gambrel, John Richard
Green, Avery
Gresham, Hershel R.
Gumm, Wesley W.
Hanncock, Loren W.
Harbaugh, Ronald C.
Hattabaugh, Paul E.
Harington, Max
Hubbard, Billie E.
Hovener, Lawrence
Heckman, Omer H.
Henderson, Warren N.
Hunnicutt, William O.
Jordan, Robert C., III
Keller, Donald W.
Kriete, Howard W.
Kriete, James F.
Landau, William
Larkin, George N.
Lewis, Albert M.
Lewis, Frank W.
Loper, Glenn E.
McConnell, Clarence H.
McKain, William
McKinney, Robert D.
McMillan, James W.
Mackey, Willard A.
Martin, William A. Jr.
Mikeles, Donald
Mitchell, Richard L.
Moore, Donald L.
Moore, Marshall E.
Morgan, Franklin L.
Morgan, Kenneth E.
Nicholson, Woodrow W.
Norris, Max
Nowling, James E.
Oberring, Albert J.
Pfaffenberger, Forrest W.
Peek, Howard H.
Poore, Kelso M.
Pruitt, James G.
Putman, John C.
Ranabauer, Howard B.
Reynolds, Clinton O.
Reynolds, Wilford
Richardson, Billy
Rigel, Raymond L.
Ritter, Chester W.
Rose, Herschel A.
Ross, Glen E.
Rudolph, Ferrell
Sapp, Robert B.
Schwalbach, James E.
Smith, George O.
Speer, Robert E.
Spray, Dallas C. Jr.
Stahl, Robert E. Jr.
Steinkamp, Ralph F. Jr.
Steltenpohl, Melvin W.
Stewart, Roger
Sutton, John G.
Sweany, Albert E.
Thomas, Max V.
Tidd, Winfred A.
Tinch, James E.
Trapp, William H.
Trapp, Ermil R.
Tudor, Max G.
Vance, Harold "Pete"
Waldkoetter, Walter
Walker, Donald A.
Weddel, Clayton C.
Wells, Charles R.
Wheeler, Herbert H.
White, Johnny
White, Robert
Whitsett, Archie Jr.
Wieneke, Harold M.
Williams, Marlin N.
Wonning, Earl H.
Wood, Earl H.
Woodson, George M.
Wright, Albert J.

Korean Conflict

Acton, Floyd Neal
Bevers, Lyneul
Brock, Joseph Henderson
Edmonds, Clarence Richard
Farley, James E.
Hawn, Roscoe L.
Holmes, John Ray Shields
Kurtz, Albert Joseph
McKain, Marshall Floyd
Rosemeyr, Earl George
Sutton, Walter John

Conflict in Vietnam

Branaman, Kenneth Merle
Carmichael, Dale Eugene
Clark, Gary Lee
Clevenger, William Henry
Daulton, William Manson
Goen, Martin Douglas
Guthrie, Thomas Leon
Harrell, James Elmore
Haws, Homer Howard
Laraway, William Dean
Miller, David K.
Reynolds, Jackie Dean
Rothring, Howard Earl Jr.
Stevens, Thomas Arthur Jr.

REVOLUTIONARY WAR VETERANS
AT REST IN
JACKSON COUNTY

JACKSON CO. VETERANS – MAY 1994

WHO'S WHO

AMONG

JACKSON COUNTY VETERANS

1776-2004

A TRIBUTE TO THOSE WHO SERVED

Ste MERE EGLISE
Target point for the Airborne parachute invasion to create a shield to protect the assault forces landing on Normandy.

GEN. DWIGHT D. EISENHOWER
High Command
Official Send Off for "D" Day
June 6, 1944

ARMY AIRBORNE COMMAND
316th TROOP CARRIER GROUP
COTTESMORE, ENGLAND
June 3, 1944
C-47 Planes ready for "D" Day paratrooper assault on Normandy

NORMANDY

6 JUNE 1944

OMAHA BEACH

"H" HOUR PLUS 60 MINUTES
Tank #9 on the beach
Company A - 741st Battalion
16th Regiment - 1st Infantry Division

MARKET – GARDEN AIRBORNE ASSAULT
NIJMEGEN BRIDGE IN HOLLAND
17 September 1944

C-47 Troop Carrier Plane
flak-damage
crash-landed at Cottesmore, England
17 September 1944

C-47 Troop Carrier Plane
Ground crew inspection
nose damage beyond repair
18 September 1944

Trustworthy Pilot
Flew flak damaged plane
home to base at Cottesmore, England
18, September 1944

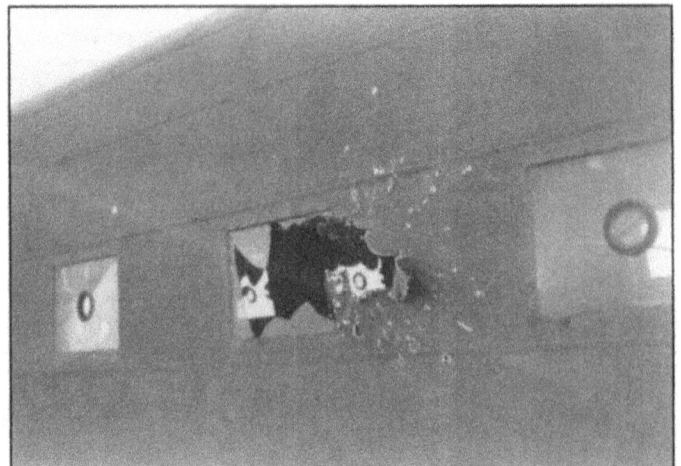

C-47 Troop Carried Plane
flak damage
located just above paratrooper heads
17 September 1944

MARKET-GARDEN AIRBORNE MISSION
Nijmegen Bridge
17 September 1944

316th Troop Carrier Group
44th Squadron
Photograph by U.S. Army Signal Corps - "Stars and Stripes"

SP 4 Samuel Spray
US Army
1970-1972

Mike Fink
US Navy
1965-68 and 1974-92

Pfc. John Nolting
US Army
4th Infantry Division

CAPTAIN MANDY LANE BANTHER

Seymour, Indiana
First Woman Graduate (1993) of West Point Military Academy
Deployed to Iraq with the 211th MP Battalion

SGT. DONALD WOLTERS
507TH MAINTENANCE COMPANY
Killed in Action
Nasiriyah, Iraq
Posthumously
Awarded a Bronze State

THE REVOLUTIONARY WAR

1776-1783

Minuteman

American Officer

The Liberty Bell
at Philadelphia

British Soldier

Minuteman at Lexington

British Officer

Hessian Soldier

MINUTEMEN AT LEXINGTON

Come Jolly Sons of Liberty…
Come all with hearts United,
Our motto "we dare to be free"
Never easily are we affrighted!

Oppression we shall subdue…
Now is the time to act or never,
Each man rings the motto true
Slavery from a king now sever!

Paul Revere

French Officer

INDEPENDENCE WON

Virginia Militiaman

VETERANS OF THE REVOLUTIONARY WAR
1776-1783
BURIED IN JACKSON COUNTY

The marble monument erected jointly by the Sons of the American Revolution *and the* Jackson County Historical Society *honors the 34 patriot veterans later buried in Jackson County, Indiana. Keeping eternal watch above the sacred plot is a replica of the* Betsy Ross Flag *presented to George Washington on June 14, 1777. The impressive monument forms the centerpiece for the John Ketcham Pioneer Village now under construction at the Jackson County Historical Society Grounds located in Brownstown, Indiana. Names of those Revolutionary veterans are listed alphabetically below:*

Thomas Alexander	Philip Langdon
John Alsup	Samuel Lee
Samuel Applegate	Vincent Lockman
David Benton	John McCormick
Henry Boas	Richard Medlock
Christian Branaman	Benjamin Newkirk
Francis Burrell	John Patterson
Michael Byarley	Asahel Phelps
William Chambers	Thomas Prather
Buckner Daniel	Daniel Ross
Levi Davis	John Russell
Michael Downing	Benjamin Scott
John Edwards	Leonard Shuemaker
Lt. James Guffy	Robert M. Smith
Charles Hagan	James Sparks
David Johnson	James Thompson
George Keiphert	Obadiah Walker

Earliest Revolutionary War Veterans

February 25, 1779 - September 3, 1783

Lands Deeded By The Virginia Legislature

In

The Clark Grant Of Indiana

Officers And Soldiers

George Rogers Clark, Brigadier General
John Frederick Montgomery, Lt. Colonel

Major Joseph Bowman   Major William Lynn   Major Thomas Quick

Captains

John Bailey	Richard Brashear	Robert George	William Herrod	Leonard Helms
Abraham Keller	Richard McCarthy	James Rogers	Isaak Ruddick	James Shelby
John Thurston	Isaac Taylor	John Williams	Edward Worthington	Jacob Vanmeter

Lieutenants

Isaac Bowman	Joseph Calvert	Martin Varney	Abraham Chaplane	Richard Clark
Valentine Dalton	James Davis	Henry Floyd	John Gerault	Harold Harrison
Michael Perault	James Merriweather	Fred Clifton	James Robertson	Levi Todd
John Robert Swan	Lawrence Slaughter	Jarred Williams	Thomas Wilson	Wm. Greathuse

Sergeants

John Brand	Wm. Merriweather	William Pritchard	James Brown	Michael Miles
William Rubey	Will Crump	John Moore	Samuel Syrode	Henry Dewitt
Charles Morgan	Beverly Trent	William Elms	John Greer	John Vaughn
James Irby	Edward Parker	John Walker	Isaac Keller	Robert Patterson
John Williams	Thomas Key	Buckner Pittman	Davis Floyd, Sr.	James Bigger

Privates

David Allen	William Chapman	Richard Chenowit	Joseph Anderson	James Flunn
Dominick Flanagan	John Ash	Andrew Clark	Floyd Isham	Martin Asher
George Clark	William Foster	David Bailey	Thomas Clifton	William Freeman
Robert Barnett	William Cofer	Will Flogget	Thomas Batten	Dennis Chohet
Stephen Frost	James Baxter	Cornelius Copland	Henry Funk	Wm. Buckley
Harman Consule	Robert Garriott	Samuel Bell	Richard Cox	Gagnia Thems
James Bentley	Jacob Coger	Gasper Gayler	John Bentley	Peter Coger
George Gilmore	Elisha Bethany	Noah Craze	Michael Glass	James Bigger
Will Crosley	David Glenn	Chas Bolderjack	James Curry	Francis Gadfry
Sam Blackford	Richard Curtiss	William Goodwin	Henry Blankenship	Ashael Davis

Recruits Continued

RECRUITS

Booton, Travis
Booton, William
Bowean, Ebenezer
Boyles, John
Bryant, James
Bulger, Edward
Burk, Nicholas
Bush, William
Cameron, Angus
Camp, Reuben
Campbell, John
Camper, Tilman
Conore, Andrew
Hatten, Christopher
Hayes, Thomas
Henry, David
Henry, Hugh
Henry, Isaac
Hebry, John
Higgins, Barney
Holms, James
Honaker, Henry
Honaker, Thomas
Hooper, Thomas
House, Andrew
Hughes, John
Humphries, Samuel
Isaacs, John
James, Abraham
January, James
Jerrald, James
Johnson, John
Johnston, Edward
Jones, Charles
Jones, David
Jones, John
Jones, Mathew
Joynes, John
Kendall, Benjamin
Kenton, Simon
Key, George Francis
Leare, William
Lemon, John
Levingston, George
Lindsey, Arthur
Lockhart, Pleasant
Lunsford, George
Lovell, Richard
Lunsford, Mason
Lunsford, Moses
Lusado, Abraham
Lutterell, Richard
McBride, Isaac
McDermet, Francis
McIntyre, Alexander

Davis, Robert
Dawson, James
Doherty, Frederick
Doherty, Neal
Doran, Patrick
Dudley, Aemistead
Duff, John
Elms, John
Elms, James
Evans, Charles
Farris, Isaac
Foar, Edmund
Finley, Samuel
McManus, George
McManus, John Sr.
McManus, John Jr.
McMullin, Samuel
McNutt, James
Mayfield, Micah
Mahoney, Flores
Manifee, Jonas
Marr, Patrick
Martin, Charles
Mershorn, Nate
Miller, Abraham
Montgomery, John
Monroe, John
Moore, John
Moore, Thomas
Murphy, John
Murry, Edward
Myers, William
Nelson, Enoch
Newton, Peter
Noblett, Isaak
Oakley, John
Oreer, Daniel
Oreer, Jesse
Orcer, William
Osburn, Ebenezer
Oundsley, Charles
Pagen, David
Paintree, John
Patten, James
Paul, John
Peters, John
Phelps, Josiah
Pickens, Samuel
Prather, Henry
Priest, Peter
Pniitt, Josiah
Purcell, William
Ray, William
Ruddle, Cornelius
Ross, Joseph

Greathouse, William
Green, John
Grimes, John
Guthrie, William
Gwinn, William
Hacker, John
Hammet, James
Hardin, Francis
Harland, Silas
Harris, James
Harris, John
Harris, Samuel, Sr.
Harris, Samuel, Jr.
Sarine, John
Sartine, Page
Saunders, John
Severn, Ebenezer
Severn, Peter
Shepherd, Peter
Shepherd, George
Sitzer, John
Simpton, Thomas
Stack, William
Slack, Edward
Smith, George
Smith, William
Sworden, Jonathon
Snow, George
Spear, Jacob
Spilman, James
Stevens, Shep
Spillman, Francis
Stephanson, Samuel
Swan, William
Swearington, Van
Talley, John
Taylor, Abraham
Teall, Levi
Thompson, William
Thornton, Joseph
Tygert, Daniel
Taylor, William
Vance, Hanley
Vanmeter, Isaac
Vershimer, George
Walker, Thomas
Watkins, Samuel
Walen, Barney
White, Layton
White, Randall
Whitecotton, John
Whitley, William
Williams, Daniel
Wood, James
Zackledge, William

Other Revolutionary War Veterans
With Connections To
Jackson County Through Their Descendants

John B. Abel – Maryland
James Alexander – Pennsylvania
Samuel Baker - Connecticut
William Beasley - Virginia
George Boone - Pennsylvania
William Bond - Virginia
Andrew Burrell - Virginia
Francis Burrell – Virginia
James Christie - Virginia
Arnold Custer - Virginia
Enoch Davis - New Jersey
John Fislar - New Jersey
John Gayle - Virginia
Thomas Graves - Virginia
Higgeson Grubbs – Virginia
Daniel Guthrie - Pennsylvania

John Hayes – Pennsylvania
John Hancock – Virginia
James Harris - Virginia
Asahel Haskins - Massachusetts
George Helman - New Jersey
George Huckelberry - Pennsylvania
Barnett Odol - NC
Archibald Johnson – NC
Daniel Joseph – Virginia
Thomas Little - Virginia
John Locke – Maryland
David McClure – Connecticut
Francis Miloren – Virginia
Jethro New – Delaware
Michael Niphes - New Jersey
Seth Payne – Connecticut

Nathan Robertson – Maryland
Barry Scott – Virginia
Nate Scudder - New Jersey
Abel Shields – NC
John Shields – NC
Richard Shores - Pennsylvania
Joshua Taylor - Virginia
Peter Vandeveer - New Jersey
David Vawter - Virginia
William Vermilya - New York
John Wakefield - Pennsylvania
Harman Wayman - Virginia
Abner Wilson - Virginia
John Witherspoon - New Jersey

Other Revolutionary War Veterans
With
Jackson County Connections

DAVID BENTON, Revolution, Continental Army, 1780-1782, born near Salisbury, Connecticut at the end of the French and Indian War in 1763. He was thus a contemporary of Aquilla Rogers and later both men became early settlers in Jackson County. By 1779 he was living in Sheffield, Massachusetts and the next year he enlisted in Captain Warren's Company of John Brown's Regiment. Following six months of service he was transferred to a Marine 16-gun brig. Eventually, he was captured and held prisoner until 1782.

On the eve of George Washington's inaugural as the first president of the United States in 1789, David Benton became the very first settler in Seneca, N.Y. Thirty years later in 1819 he and his family migrated westward and settled in Jackson County. He died March 7, 1845 and was buried at Brownstown.

HENRY (BOAZ) BOAS, Revolutionary War, 1st Battalion - Pennsylvania Frontier Guards, 1776-1777, born in the Province of Hesse on October 30, 1760 and, as a young boy emigrated along with his parents to the new world. The family settled in Lancaster County, PA and, later on July 1, 1776 this sixteen-year-old boy enlisted as a private in the militia. Much later he remembered some of the officers for whom he had served, including General Hand, Colonel Hains and Ensign James Turner.

Within the period of his initial enlistment, Henry Boas fought in a "severe" battle on Long Island. His unit was later marched to White Plains and placed under the command of the Continental Army led by General Putnam. Later the Continental soldiers advanced in an attack on Trenton. It was there his unit captured "900 Hessian prisoners" on Christmas

Day in 1776. Henry Boas was discharged a few days later on New Year's Day in 1777,

Henry Boas, his wife Dorothy and children resided in Maryland and in 1791 they migrated to Kentucky. Twenty years later in 1819 they moved on to Brownstown. On June 7, 1832 the federal Congress approved pensions be paid Revolutionary War veterans. He applied through the court system in Jackson County and was awarded a small allotment which he used to help raise his family which included five children. Elizabeth married James Mitchell and the daughter married Thomas Carr and provided the heritage for the Jackson County descendants.

Henry Boas died March 4, 1838 and his wife one year later. Both were buried in the Brown Cemetery located north of Sparksville. Current residents locally who are descendants include the Boas, Carr and Freeman families.

JOHN FLAVEL CARR, SR., Revolutionary War, 1st Pennsylvania Battalion, 1778-1783, John F. Carr and his wife, Margaret (Peggy) Ewing Carr, migrated across the Atlantic Ocean from Ballyahinch County sometime before the Revolutionary War and settled in Westmoreland County. He then served the American cause for freedom by enlisting in Captain John Nelson's Company of riflemen who were the sharp shooters of the 1st Pennsylvania Battalion. Just after George Washington was inaugurated President, John F. Carr, a Revolutionary War veteran, died and was buried near Lancaster, Pennsylvania.

ROBERT COCHRAN, Revolution, Continental Army, Major, a firm supporter of American freedom from British tyranny, was a longtime resident of Vermont. In 1771 he and his friend, Ethan Allen,

defended the settlers around Green Mountain. As Captain of a military contingent of soldiers, he led his company on an expedition against Fort Ticonderoga in 1775. When the Continental Army was formed he enlisted with the rank of Major. His company was assigned to guard the Mohawk Valley, and so successful was their defense that he was promoted to Lt. Colonel by the Continental Congress in 1779. He was discharged November 3, 1783,

Robert Cochran's daughter, Jennet was married to Asahel Haskin who also served the cause as a private. He was discharged in 1790. Their great-granddaughter, Florence Haskin Wiseman, became a resident in Vallonia in 1930.

JONAS CRANE, Revolution, Courtland Battalion, Thomas Williams Regiment, 1780-1781, a son of Benjamin and Phoebe Martin Crane, can trace his lineage to Robert Treat, Governor of Connecticut. Jonas Crane was born in Essex County, NJ on May 20, 1756. He was later married to Abigail Kitchell whose father served in the Continental Army during the Revolutionary War. He joined the New Jersey Militia and served as a private assigned to Captain Thomas Williams Regiment. His first action came during the Battle for Newark, and he survived successive campaigns throughout the remainder of the war. He was discharged in mid-January 1781.

Migrating westward, Jonas Crane eventually settled east of Brownstown. His homestead was situated along the river and covered hundreds of acres all the way to top of Crane Hill. He died the last week in August, and his will was probated in February 1841. Toward the end of the year his will was probated to Thomas Kitchell and his children. It is believed Jonas Crane was buried in Crane Cemetery, but his head stone has never been located.

JOSEPH CUMMINGS, Revolution, 1776-1782, a son of Malachi and Verlinsa Burke, was born February 11, 1762 in Virginia. He left the plantation in Fauquier County and enlisted in the Colonial Militia. Along with his Virginia neighbors he went ahead and was stationed in Richmond. He was one of the guards charged with the Redcoat prisoners taken at Yorktown.

He was discharged in 1782 and they became parents of 11 children. Joseph Cummings died at Sparta, Tennessee in 1859. Malachi Cummings, one of his children, named after his grandfather bore several children, one of whom later settled in Jackson County, Indiana.

MICHAEL DOWNING, Revolutionary War Veteran Buried in Jackson County, Veteran of the War of 1812, born in the County of Cork, Ireland on December 18, 1760. His lineage verifies he was Scotch-Irish by descent. In 1776 as a young lad, he enlisted in the Continental Army and was assigned to the regiments fighting under General Anthony Wayne.

Surviving the fight for American freedom, he served his country during the War of 1812, and he survived the dastardly massacre at Pigeon Roost. His military discharge, dated August 2, 1815, stated he was 5 feet 6 inches tall, with dark complexion, gray eyes, dark hair and had a defect in his sight. Records show he served eleven years for his home lands.

Michael Downing was buried in the Pioneer Cemetery near Mt. Sidney in Grassy Fork Township. The inscription on his tombstone reads "Mich'L Downing. Va Mil Rev War." He did not have a middle initial.

He was married to Mary Anne Wells, but her last name was actually spelled Walls. Little information exists about them!

JOHN EDWARDS, American Revolution, Lancaster County PA Frontier Guard, Brodhead's Regiment, born in Wales in 1761. He was an only child, and when he was still an infant, his parents sailed for America. His father died during the voyage and the mother and child located in Pennsylvania. When John was about seven years old, his mother died and the boy was bound out by the court to a family that so mistreated him, neighbors took him from them and found him a home with a family whose name is not known.

One day, at the age of 17 years, he was out looking after some cattle, when a party of Revolutionary soldiers came along. John went with them to Lancaster, Pennsylvania, where he enlisted in June 1778, and he served as a Drummer Boy in two companies of Colonel Brodhead's Regiment—first in Captain Van Swearingens' Company, then in Captain Clark's, until his discharge in October 1783, two years after the end of the Revolutionary War. He did not return to Pennsylvania, but located in Fayette County, Kentucky, where he married Mary Jackson, a first cousin of President Andrew Jackson, on March 29, 1790. He was at that time 29 years of age and she was 20.

They located in Boonesborough, Kentucky and lived there for several years in the historic fort, where some of their children were born. Later, they located near Somerset, Pulaski County, Kentucky. They were the parents of twelve children.

Pension was allowed to John Edwards on his application executed October 30, 1818, while a resident of Pulaski County, Kentucky. The annual allowance was $96.00.

Because they were opposed to slavery, the family moved to Indiana and located in Jackson County, between Kurtz and Clearspring. John Edwards, died on April 18, 1836 at the age of 75 and his wife Mary Jackson Edwards died in January 1846 at the age of 76. She left nine surviving children. Both John and Mary are buried in a small burial lot on what was their farm property. A small government tombstone marks their grave and honors him as a Revolutionary War Soldier. They have many direct descendants living in Jackson and surrounding counties.

DANIEL GUTHRIE SR., Revolution, Continental Army, 1778-1783, born in 1737 in Pennsylvania. He and his wife, Jane, became parents of 8 children. As a loyal subject of the king, he offered his services during the French and Indian War as a private of the Johnson's Company in General Braddock's Army.

By 1774 the Guthrie family was living in Bedford County, PA. Daniel joined the Frontier Rangers to defend the fort commanded by Captain Henderschott during the revolution. He later joined his brother at Yorktown and witnessed the British surrender.

By 1809 Daniel Guthrie, along with William Flinn, were living in Kentucky and enumerated in the census of Shelby County. Four years later in 1813 they had already erected Flinn's Fort, later known as Leesville then located in Jackson County.

SHADRACK PIERSON, Revolution, Continental Army, one of triplet sons, was born to Abraham and Sarah Pierson in 1754. Ten years after the close of the French and Indian War, he was married to Rachel Clinch. By 1775 they were living in Culpepper County, VA. On Christmas Day in 1776 he enlisted in the Continental Army and was assigned to Captain Deputy's company. During the winter months at Valley Forge his feet were frozen. He was discharged but remained a cripple for the rest of his life,

In 1794 Shadrack and Rachel Clinch Pierson became parents of a son named James W. Pierson. He married Lucretia Morgan, a 2nd cousin of John Hunt Morgan. In 1822 the newlyweds settled at Slade Ford near Crothersville. It was there where he built the 1st mill in Vernon Township.

Much later in 1863, Morgan's Raiders swept through the region where his cousin lived. Confiscation of the Pierson horses was carried out without signs of any remorse.

FRENCH & INDIAN WAR AND THE REVOLUTIONARY WAR

FREDERICK EVERHART, Private, Colonial Frontier Volunteers, Lancaster County, Pennsylvania,1749, Sergeant, Muster Roll, Company "A" - Colonial Frontier Volunteers, Northampton County, 1749-1751, fought under Captain Johann van Etten, Revolutionary War, 1777-1781.

Frederick Everhardt was born in the colony of Pennsylvania sometime in 1733 to Germanic immigrants invited to settle in the new world by William Penn. Toward the end of the French and Indian War, this young man enrolled as a Private as one of the colonial frontier guards. In 1749 he was assigned to the Northampton County rangers under the command of Major Jacob Heynderschatte who made his headquarters at Fort Bedford. His frontier service was concluded in 1763.

After the Declaration of Independence was signed to break all ties with England, Frederick Everhardt enlisted in the Continental Army under Captain Johan van Etten. After the Battle Brandwine Creek, he changed the spelling of his name to just Frederick Everhart, which was duly entered into the official Records of the United States Army.

JOHN GAYLE, SR., Revolution, Eccleston's Company – 2nd Maryland Regiment, 1777-1783, was born May 19, 1749 in Columbia, MD. He was called to take up arms against the British and he served the American cause as a lieutenant under Colonel Thomas Price. For his extraordinary deeds of bravery, he was promoted several times, and finally achieved the rank of captain.

After being captured August 22, 1777, he escaped and returned to duty. He was then assigned as Aide de Camp to General Grist in 1780, and continued his service until 1783 when he was discharged.

John Gayle, Sr. died in 1825 and was buried in Culpepper County, Virginia. His son was born in 1777 and later moved west to Owen County, KY in 1806. He married Malinda Brassfield and they were parents of 10 children.

One of their sons, James Gayle, later married Sally Green and one of their sons became the father of Sara Green who married Paul Gates of Jackson County. Mrs. Gates was active in the organization of the Vallonia DAR.

JACOB HENDERSHOT, Revolution, Bedford County Militia - Continental Army, 1770-1781. The genealogical lineage of the Hendershot family may be traced from 1681 to Michael and Anna Schneider Heynderschotte. The forebears left Eichmuhl in Bavaria and fled northward along the Rhine River. They joined others from the Patalinate who were destined to settle in Pennsylvania. They were among 2000 other German-speaking refugees aboard ten vessels which landed at Grandbys' Point in 1710.

The von Heynderschottee people settled in New Jersey and made their home along the Millstone Creek. By 1750 the spelling of family name had been changed. Several brothers moved to the rolling hills of Pennsylvania and made their homes in Lancaster County. At least three of those Hendershot brothers fought in the Revolutionary War.

Captain Jacob Hendershot was the Provost at Fort Bedford, but he was released and ordered to duty at Yorktown in 1781. He was an eye-witness to the surrender of Cornwallis, and he heard the military band play the *"World Turned Upside Down."* One of his descendants, Christian and Henrietta Bledsoe Hendershot was able to join others heading downstream on the Ohio River. They finally reached the falls and then Driftwood Township. It was there

where he helped Joseph Herman Nenntrupp erect the first trading post in Jackson County in 1827.

GEORGE HUCKLEBERRY, Revolution, German Recruit - Heidelberg County Frontier Militia, Private, a native of the Province of Hannover, was born May 17, 1752 and arrived in the new world in 1768 as a 13-year-old lad just after the French and Indian War ended. Along with his father he settled in Westmoreland County, PA and joined the Frontier Militia in 1777 as a private in Stovall's Company. After he received his honorable discharge in 1782 he was married to Rosanna Wise and in 1821 they were living in Jackson County.

They became parents of three daughters and one descendant named Laura Kathryn Hancock who was born in Seymour. Later she was married to John G. Laupus. Two of their three sons were veterans of the armed Forces during World War II.

SAMUEL JONATHON LEE, 1763-1840, born Feb. 17, 1763 in Richmond County, Virginia later migrated to Hardy County where he made his home. When he turned 18 years of age, he enlisted in the Continental Army on March 1, 1781. As a private in the Revolutionary War he served in Captain Anderson's Company for six months before receiving a furlough. He returned to action but was assigned to Captain Neale's Virginia Militia.

After September 14, 1781 he served as a substitute for his father when the siege of Yorktown opened. After the surrender of Cornwallis, he guarded the prisoners assigned to the compound located at Winchester. Six years later he was living once again in Hardy County, and the tax list for 1787 shows Samuel Lee's tax was paid in full by his father, William Byrd Lee. Seven years later in 1790, Samuel Lee was listed in the original federal census but he then moved to Kentucky.

Marriage bonds, signed by his father William Lee, were recorded July 15, 1798 in Mercer County, Kentucky. Those papers show the bride was Olive Willis. Six known children were born to the couple, and in 1808 Samuel bought the property of his deceased father. The Bill of Sale was recorded in Shelby County and reveals Samuel Lee's mother's name was Caty.

In 1813 Samuel J. Lee was married to Margaret Mitchell while living in Mercer County, KY. Shortly there after he was allowed a pension (S38138) executed May 19, 1834 when he was living in Spencer County. Later Samuel requested his pension be transferred to Warrick County, Indiana. Evidently, he moved to Jackson County and died before the transfer.

Records compiled in "Revolutionary War Soldiers Buried in Indiana," the census of 1840 lists Samuel J. Lee, age 77 years, living with John L. Young near the Muscatatuck in Jackson County. Samuel's brother is buried in the Mill Creek Cemetery located in Washington County.

Records compiled in "Revolutionary Soldiers Buried in Indiana" refer to the census of 1840 listing Samuel Lee, age 77 years, as living with John Young near the Muscatatuck River. Samuel Lee is one of 34 Revolutionary War veterans whose name is inscribed on the Marble Monument honoring those buried in Jackson County.

VINCENT LOCKMAN, Revolution, Hogan's Company - St. Mary's Regiment, Private. born December 20, 1760 in Surry County, NC, was married to Christian Hogan at the village of Annapolis in 1778. The next day he enlisted in the Continental Army. Upon receiving his discharge, the couple moved westward. By 1799 the

young couple had migrated into Shelby County, KY.

Sometime later they settled among others and settled near Medora in Jackson County. Indeed, they were among the earliest residents. He died in 1843 and was buried in the Heighten Hill Cemetery.

Among their descendants could be found Paul Ferrell Lockman born in 1890. He later married Goldie Mae Johnson and to them was born Dorothy Lockman. She later married Charles Benton Greger in 1936 and they became parents of a son named Charles Robert Greger born August 14, 1943 in Brownstown.

HENRY L. MILLER, Revolution, Rockbridge County, VA Frontier Militia, Private, was a German-speaking immigrant from the Province of Hesse. He arrived to the new world with his widowed mother. They disembarked at Gatlen's Point located near Philadelphia in 1771.

Five years later they were living in Rockbridge where the young lad enlisted in the Frontier Militia. Some time later he was transferred to Holton's Company and assigned to General Washington's staff. He was standing at attention when the new American Flag presented to the general by the Betsy Ross sewing circle, was first hoisted aloft in 1777.

A daughter of Henry Miller was later married to Adam Zollman; one of his descendants was named Ina Hamilton, born August 28, 1891 at Medora. She was married to Elmer N. Kestner in 1915 and later destined to be the only woman from Jackson County to serve as Clerk of the Grand Jury in 1948. Elmer and Ina Kestner became parents of four children born in Jackson County.

JETHRO A. NEW, Revolution, Dollman's Company - 2nd Delaware Regiment, Sergeant, born at Kent, DE on Sept. 20, 1757, was later married to Sarah Bowman. He enlisted as a private in the 2nd Delaware Regiment commanded by Colonel O'Neal and assigned as his personal aide. Promoted, Sgt. Jethro New was present at the execution of Major Andre. Later, he was captured by the British, stripped, tied to his horse and dragged behind the cavalry for miles. He escaped and became a personal guard for General Washington where he witnessed the surrender at Yorktown. By 1820 Jethro and Sarah Bowman New were residents of Scott County. He died in 1827 while fishing in the Muscatatuck. Among the descendants was Fern Herrod who later married Ivan C. Morgan, the founder of Morgan Packing Company in 1900.

SHADRACK PIERSON, Revolution. Continental Army, one of triplet sons, was born to Abraham and Sarah Pierson in 1754. Ten years after the close of the French & Indian War, he was married to Rachel Clinch. By 1775 they were living in Culpepper County, VA. On Christmas Day in 1776 he enlisted in the Continental Army and was assigned to Captain Deputy's company. During the winter months at Valley Forge his feet were frozen. He was discharged but remained a cripple for the rest of his life.

In 1794 Shadrack and Rachel Clinch Pierson became parents of a son named James W. Pierson. He married Lucretia Morgan, a 2nd cousin of John Hunt Morgan. In 1822 the newly-weds settled at Slade Ford near Crothersville. It was there where he built the 1st mill in Vernon Township.

Much later in 1863, Morgan's Raiders swept through the region where his cousin lived. Confiscation of the Pierson horses was carried out with no signs of any remorse.

JACOB ROBBINS, Revolution, Rowan County Frontier Militia, born in 1738 as one of three brothers who left their native Wales and reached Rowan County, NC in 1758. A few years later Jacob left his wife Mary, and reported to the local militia to defend his new homestead.

Both Jacob and his son William fought in the Battle of Guilford Couthouse during the Revolutionary War. Upon the close of hostilities the entire Robbins clan migrated into Virginia. In 1793 those intra-related families were living in Henry County, KY. It was Thomas, born in 1784 who moved across the Ohio River and served in the Mounted Rangers stationed near Corydon during the War of 1812. He and Jacob migrated into Jackson County.

SOLOMON RUDDICK, Revolution, Grayson County Frontier Militia, 1776-1781, Solomon Ruddick, a son of William and Anna Cox Ruddick, was born in Virginia in 1753. Both parents were devout Quakers and when Solomon married Anna Redsaul without approval, he was an outcast. A short time later, Anna abandoned her husband and ran away with a Tory. Solomon Ruddick and his brother broke their Quaker heritage when they volunteered to serve in the Grayson County Militia during the Revolutionary War.

By 1800 Solomon Ruddick had married a second time to Amy Elliott. He and his family migrated from Virginia into Kentucky and settled not far from Cane Ridge. In 1814 he followed his sons when they all moved across the Ohio River into Jackson County. He died in 1825 and was buried in the Quaker Cemetery

NATHANIEL SCUDDER, Revolution, 1st Regiment of Monmouth County, New Jersey, Colonel, born 1733 in Long Island, later graduated from Princeton College in 1751. He became a medical doctor and settled in Monmouth County, NJ. In 1776 he was a member of the Continental Congress who voted to approve the Articles of Confederation. He was appointed a Colonel but was later killed while leading his command during the Battle of Black Point in 1781.

After he was buried with high military honors, his son John Scudder was elected surgeon of his father's Regiment. Long after the war he was elected to Congress in 1810. By 1821 he was a resident of Washington County where he died in 1836. He was buried in the old Presbyterian Cemetery in Salem.

Among the descendants of his family lineage was Louise Thomas who became residents of Jackson County. She was married to Harry M. Palmer in 1916. They became parents of three sons, two of whom enlisted in the military service right after the destruction at Pearl Harbor.

JAMES SPARKS, Revolutionary War Veteran, Allegheny County Militia - Pennsylvania Frontier Guards, 1777-1781, James Sparks was born in 1744 in the midlands of New Jersey and died May 25, 1834 while living in Carr Township of Jackson County. In 1833 he applied for his military pension due for his services in the American Revolution. His application stated that he was living in Allegheny County, PA and was a member of the militia commended by Captain John Crow and later Captain Hertt.

Years later James Sparks remembered that "throughout the war he kept himself in a constant state of readiness for service." He was unable to recall the number of service tours he had, but his records indicate he served a total of 3 years and 4 months defending the frontier from Indians and the British "redcoat" soldiers. His description of the battle near Lake Erie stated that "many of the redskins were killed and the blood of the enemy colored the water in the creeks around the lake."

James Sparks was stationed for a time at Fort Pitt and one time his unit was dispatched to relieve the troops "besieged at Fort Lawrence near the Muskingham River fork." He recalled the troops suffered much and lived on "roots and roasted hides." While not serving as a soldier, he led pack horses carrying provisions across the mountains to both Fort Pitt and Fort McIntosh.

In 1781 James Sparks and family migrated to Kentucky and soon after they arrived, he volunteered to serve in the rangers against the Indians. Nearly twenty years later the entire family moved to Knox County, IN, but they soon returned across the Ohio River back into Kentucky. It was 1822 when James Sparks moved north again and settled near the present site of Sparksville where he lived with his son, Stephen Sparks, until he died in 1834. He was buried in the Brown Cemetery located north of Sparksville.

Members of the Carr and Freeman families currently living in Jackson County are known descendants of James Sparks.

MANLOVE AND CELIA HAZZARD WALLS, The American Revolution, Continental Patriots. Manlove Walls was born May 8, 1760 in Sussex County, Delaware. He was a son of William and Mabel Brown Walls who could trace their English lineage to Henry Hazzard, a Puritan dissenter from Durham in the British Isles.

When King George III dispatched his redcoat troops to Massachusetts some of them were stationed near his home in Sussex County. He watched with horror as they confiscated everything the Walls family owned. He cringed when he had to bury his parents in private and at night. He knew not where to run, but he escaped Delaware and found safety in Philadelphia.

He would join the Continental Army in 1776; he waited for someone to ring the Liberty Bell. Suddenly, he was surrounded by the Quakers born and reared in the tradition of peace. They would help him defeat the widespread tyranny! He found a childhood friend and she tailored a blue coat so he could join other patriots. It fit him well and he waved a kiss to her. That 13 year-old Quaker girl had been a member of a sewing circle which had completed its task.

They all smiled when Betsy Ross presented the original American Flag to George Washington. The General nodded and Manlove Walls stepped forward, saluted briskly and raised that flag before the troops at Brandywine Creek. They came to attention and presented arms as that flag with its 13 stars waved in the breeze.

A new nation had been born! Later in 1787 Manlove married Celia Hazzard Walls and while they were exchanging their vows, they learned a new Constitution guaranteed freedom for all. In 1814 that couple with their children was living in Orange County and now enjoying the freedoms of their convictions.

One of their descendants later became the compiler of these records giving tribute to the "Who's Who Among Jackson County Military Veterans." Thanks be to God Almighty!

ISAAC WHEELER, Revolution, Dolittle Regiment - Continental Army, 1779-1782, was born of Puritan stock April 14, 1754 at Concord in Maine. Some twenty years later he was married to Marianna Rugg in 1774. When fighting broke out against the British, Isaac Wheeler enlisted as a private and assigned to serve under Lt. Edward Hale during the Battle of Lexington and Concord. His unit commander was Captain Adams Wells of the Doolittle Regiment.

In 1780 Isaac Wheeler was promoted and commissioned Captain of the 7th Militia. He was discharged in 1782 and became the father of four children, each of whom eventually settled in Jackson County. One of the grandsons, David Wheeler, was born in 1818 and became the pride and joy of Isaac Wheeler. The old grandfather died February 26, 1833, but none of his descendants were able to be present at the funeral.

The Revolutionary War Veteran was buried in Tioga County near the Village of Charleston, Pennsylvania.

WAR OF 1812

Captain Biggers
Commander
Vallonia Regiment of Militia Rangers
1813

1812 (June 18) The United States declared war on Great Britain.
1812 (Oct. 13) British forces won the Battle of Oweenston Heights in Canada.
1813 (April 27) The Americans captured York (now Toronto), the capital of Upper Canada. They later burned some public buildings.
1813 (Sept. 10) American forces under Master-Commandant Oliver Hazard Perry won the Battle of Lake Erie.
1813 (Oct. 5) The Americans won the Battle of the Thames River in Moraviantown, an Indian village in Canada.
1814 (Aug. 24) British troops invaded Washington, D.C., and burned the Capitol and the White House.
1814 (Sept. 11) American forces won the Battle of Lake Champlain.
1814 (Dec. 24) The Americans and the British signed a peace treaty in Ghent, Belgium.
1815 (Jan. 8) American forces won the Battle of New Orleans. News of the peace treaty did not reach the United States until after this battle.

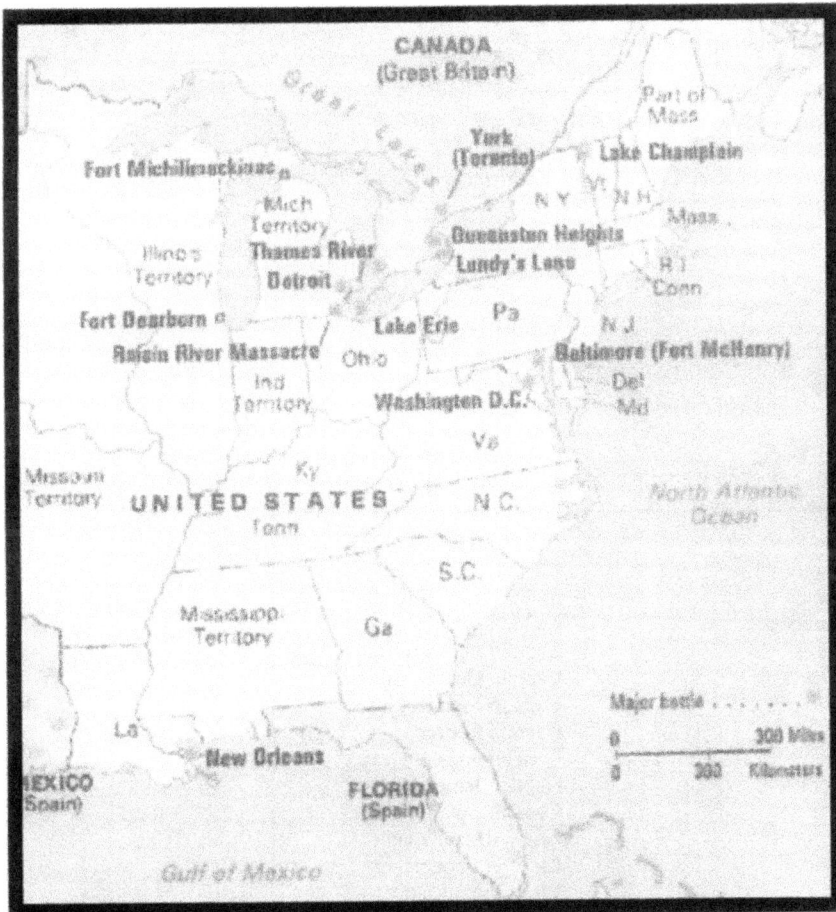

John Ketcham
1782-1865
Jackson County Pioneer
J.A. Brodheker

THE SECOND WAR FOR INDEPENDENCE

THE FRONTIER SETTLEMENTS AROUND VALLONIA
1805–1816

**RESTORED
FORT ALEXANDER AT VALLONIA
FRONTIER RANGER POST
SEPTEMBER 30, 1811**

The area which later formed Jackson County in 1816 was at one time the keystone of the frontier line of defense for the early pioneers who settled north of the Muscatatuck River. Fort Alexander at Vallonia was the post erected in 1811 for the Indiana Territorial Rangers who were charged to safeguard the frontier settlers from the Indians allied with the British. Following the destruction of the Indian Confederation by Governor Harrison at the Battle of Tippecanoe on November 7, 1812, the Ranger post became known only as Fort Vallonia. It has carried that identification ever since.

INDIANA FRONTIER MILITIA

JACKSON COUNTY CONTINGENT
CREATED APRIL 26, 1817

17TH REGIMENT

Colonel Jesse Durham	Colonel Samuel Milroy
Lt. Col. Alexander Craig	Lt. Col. John Clark
Major Richard Beem	Major Henry Dewalt
Captain Mordicai Ruddick	Captain John Henderson
Captain Stephen Sparks	Captain James Higgins
Captain James B. Rogers	Captain George Golsby
Captain Andrew Hollen	Captain John Robinson
Captain Isaac Scott	Captain George Hattabaugh
Captain John Harmer	Captain Samuel Gray
Captain William Ruddick	Captain James Marrs
Captain James Nicholson	Captain Adam Barnett
Lt. Samuel Cox	Lt. Matthew Wood
Lt. William Henderson	Lt. John Shoemaker
Lt. Michael Beem	Lt. William Lindsey
Lt. John Ritter	Lt. Isaac Rogers
Lt. Solomon Ruddick	Lt. Gabriel Jones
Lt. Joseph Drybread	Lt. Edward Crabb
Lt. Abraham Henderson	Lt. Benjamin Wilson

GENERAL JACOB JENNINGS BROWN, Namesake of Brownstown, Indiana, Jackson County Seat of Justice, The genealogical records of General Jacob Brown may be traced from long before the Revolutionary War commencing around 1700 when John William Brown settled near Buck Valley in Penn's Woods, later to be identified as the Commonwealth of Pennsylvania.

Joseph Brown, one of the sons of John William Brown served during the Revolutionary War with the 147th New York Fugeliers. His son, Samuel Brown, was married to Abigail White in 1773 and they became the parents of five sons including Jacob Jennings Brown.

Jacob Jennings Brown was born in 1775 and later became a General of the Pennsylvania Rangers during the War of 1812. He was married to Effie Ruth in Brownsville, New York. Brownstown, the first county seat of Jackson County was named after Jacob Jennings Brown in 1815 by John Ketcham who sold the land on which the Courthouse would later stand.

Although General Brown never visited Indiana, one of his sons, Jacob Frank Brown was born in 1808 and thirty years later was married to Lettie Ann Day. Five brothers all migrated west and settled near Courtland in Jackson County. Plat maps show the land records in Jackson County indicating the names of the owners of records as early as 1858.

COLONEL JOHN KETCHAM, 1782-1865, followed Aquilla and Rebecca Rogers into the area north of the Muscatatuck River. The latter erected the first log cabin in 1805 and it was located in the region later known as Jackson County. The former, the founder of Brownstown in 1811, had gained his reputation by Indian hunting escapades as a young man. Indeed, his father was the hero of an escape from Indian capture.

John Ketcham accumulated various titles during his lifetime and they can make any man jealous of his accomplishments. He was crowned colonel, appointed an honorable judge, succeeded as a self-taught surveyor and building contractor. He was also the first trustee of Indiana University. But his most prized title was that of being an elector for Andrew Jackson.

John was just two years old when his father migrated into Shelby County, Kentucky in 1784. Eight years later his father was captured by a band of Ottawa Indians but, after only a few days march, he escaped. Sometime in 1803 James Rogers stood in for him as best man when he married Elizabeth Pearcy. Eventually in 1811, they moved across the great river into Indiana Territory and were among the early settlers who depended on the government for protection.

Temporary forts were erected along a line from south of Vallonia and running through Brownstown and on toward the east. Fort Alexander at Vallonia was manned by less than 100 rangers who formed the territorial militia. After the defeat of the Indians at the Battle of Tippecanoe in 1811, the fort back home was known only as Fort Vallonia.

In 1816 Colonel John Ketcham sold his Jackson County land grant to the County government for a permanent "seat of government." The sale of his 153 acres of land for $8.00 per acre made his re-location to Monroe County possible, His grist mill built on Clear Creek was known far and wide. He was appointed a trustee of "Indiana Seminary" which became dedicated later as Indiana University. Indeed, the stone for the early buildings was quarried from Ketcham's original homestead.

WILLIAM LEWIS, War of 1812, 22nd Infantry - 3rd New York Regiment, Platters Company, the great-grandfather of Jackson County Attorney John M. Lewis, enlisted in the American army from the County of Seneca, New York.

Born in 1783 on the eve of the Treaty of Paris ending the Revolution, this lad from the great city finished his military service as a sergeant.

Following his discharge, he was married in Steuben County, NY to Sarah Miller in 1820. Their son, John M. Lewis, was born two years later in Jennings County. He was the one who later built the toll bridge across the Muscatatuck River at Newry in 1852.

ABRAHAM MILLER, War of 1812, Indiana Territorial Militia, was born as an orphan following his father's death during the Revolutionary War. As a young boy he came west with others who floated down the Ohio River into Kentucky. He was raised by the Heavenhill family in Nelson County.

In 1794 he enlisted in the Kentucky Mounted Militia and fought as one of 1,500 volunteers under General Anthony Wayne at Fallen Timbers. They defeated the Indians along the Maumee River and returned to Kentucky.

In 1803 he married Ann Margaret Mueller at Shepardsville, Bullit County. Later, in 1810, he brought his family of three children on across the Ohio into Indiana Territory. He enlisted in the 2nd Regiment of Indiana Militia in 1811. Less than one year later he marched from Vallonia to Vincennes and on to Tippecanoe.

After the Indians were defeated, he made his home near the forks of the rivers near Fort Alexander located near Vallonia. Indeed, two of his children were born at the fort.

He and his wife were among the founders of the Methodist Church in Brownstown. Both buried in the old Brownstown Cemetery.

EDGAR MILLER, Civil War, Grand Army of the Republic, born after the family settled near Vallonia to Tom and Mary Harmon Miller. He was a grandson of Abraham Miller and enlisted in Company "B" of the 22nd Infantry Regiment of Indiana Volunteers. He survived the war and returned to the Vallonia area of the state. He never married and passed away December 16, 1872 and was buried in the Vallonia Cemetery.

JONAS SAMUEL SAGE, 1767-1844, According to the Revolutionary War Pension Application filed in Norwich, New York, William Sloan, born in County Armagh, Ireland in 1752, claimed he left his family Bible in Indiana with his adopted son, born to his wife of her 1st marriage. As a widower, William Sloan lived with that son, also a veteran of the Revolutionary War, in southern Indiana in an area which became Jackson County for 18 years between 1812 - 1830.

That son, Jonas Samuel Sage, was destined to volunteer his services in the Black Hawk War commencing in 1832. He bid farewell to his father when the latter decided to return to New York where he settled in Chenango County. It was from there in 1831 where he filed his pension application at age 79 years. Nothing more is known of William Sloan and the date of his death and the identity of any other children remain unknown.

But, what is known about William Sloan is that he was one of the Scotch-Irish immigrants who entered this country with his parents, George and Mary Campbell Sloan, in 1755. Twenty years later in 1774 he married a widow by the name of Sarah Sage Cornish in Berkshire County, Maine. Around 1812 he migrated with his adopted son to Indiana Territory where they settled near Beck's Mill. After the hostilities with the Indians ceased, they later moved northward across the Muscatatack River and settled near Starve Hollow around 1818.

Jonas Samuel Sage bid his father goodbye when he enlisted in the militia to fight the Black Hawk War. Following the end of that conflict, the descendants of Jonas Sage moved on to LaMoille, Illinois. It is not known just when Jonas Sage died, nor where and there is also no information of his marriage or children.

STEPHAN SPARKS, War of 1812, Captain, 17th Regiment - Indiana Militia, Jackson County, 1775-1818

ALVIN WHEELER, War of 1812, 1st Volunteer Regiment - Ohio Frontier Rangers, 1810-1812, was the son of Isaac Wheeler who was a soldier in the Revolutionary War. Alvin was born October 19, 1790 in Danbury, CT. He was later married to Sara Willey on January 19, 1817.

Alvin Wheeler served as a Drum Major as a volunteer from Ohio and, when the war was over, he migrated to and settled in Jackson County. In 1832 he was listed on the pension roll for war injuries and living near Freetown.

Alvin Wheeler died when he was 101 years old and was buried in the Freetown Cemetery West. Several descendants of his family still reside in Jackson County, one of whom is Morris W. Durham.

THE BLACK HAWK WAR
APRIL 9, 1832 - AUGUST 3, 1832

One damp and dismal day a rider pulled up his horse, jumped off and met a group of men gathered in Vallonia. He shouted out his message that the governor had called for 75 militia volunteers from Jackson County. They were to report to Salem, Illinois on April 24, 1832. Their task was to thwart the Indians who had invaded Illinois. More than 1,500 braves, women and children intended to settle and plant corn on land which could, not be sold, *and to avenge the killing of the red men.*

Their leader was Black Hawk, a chief who had sided with the British during the War of 1812. That news was more than the men could swallow!

Several men stepped forward at once and volunteered. They would join others to form a company of Rangers, and elect their own Captain.

It was to be Meedy Shields, but he was away on one of his annual trips down the Mississippi River. In an instant they elected Matthew Tanner!

He would lead them to the quartermaster's office where the men could draw ammunition, some Salted corn pork and a barrel of whiskey. Five days later the company arrived at the federal fort near Beardstown. After being sworn to federal service, they joined 1,500 regular Army troops. They marched to Prophetstown and on to Dixon's ferry across the Rock River. Every man re-enlisted for another 30 days and those from Vallonia would march beside Abraham Lincoln's company from Illinois.

It was late in July before the Sauk and Fox Tribes under Black Hawk were routed. Once defeated the chief became prisoner and was taken to President Jackson in Washington. Captain Matthew Tanner and his company of militiamen returned to Vallonia. Much later each man drew almost $100 from the federal paymaster for his wartime service.

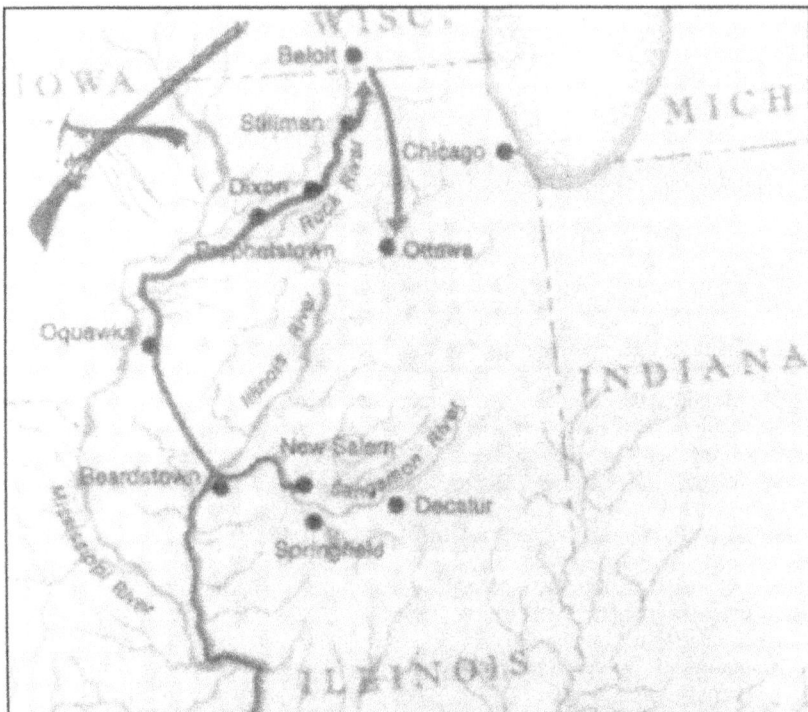

JACKSON COUNTY VOLUNTEERS

Captain Matthew Tanner
Jabez Crane
Jonah Debose
Andrew Gelwick
Jonas Sage

Azariah Empson, a newly-married 24-year-old young man, was placed on standby status and told to return to his home in Grassy Fork Township.
Meedy Shields returned from New Orleans after hostilities had ceased.

JONAS SAMUEL SAGE, 1767-1844, According to the Revolutionary War Pension Application filed in Norwich, New York, William Sloan, born in County Armagh, Ireland in 1752, claimed he left his family Bible in Indiana with his adopted son, born to his wife of her 1st marriage. As a widower, William Sloan lived with that son, also a veteran of the Revolutionary War, in southern Indiana in an area which became Jackson County for 18 years between 1812 - 1830.

That son, Jonas Samuel Sage, was destined to volunteer his services in the Black Hawk War commencing in 1832. He bid farewell to his father when the latter decided to return to New York where he settled in Chenango County. It was from there in 1831 where he filed his pension application at age 79 years. Nothing more is known of William Sloan and the date of his death and the identity of any other children remain unknown.

But, what is known about the William Sloan is that he was one of the Scotch-Irish immigrants who entered this country with his parents, George and Mary Campbell Sloan, in 1755. Twenty years later in 1774 he married a widow by the name of Sarah Sage Cornish in Berkshire County, Maine. Around 1812 he

migrated with his adopted son to Indiana Territory where they settled near Beck's Mill. After the hostilities with the Indians ceased, they later moved northward across the Muscatatuck River and settled near Starve Hollow around 1818.

Jonas Samuel Sage bid his father goodbye when he enlisted in the militia to fight the Black Hawk War. Following the end of that conflict, the descendants of Jonas Sage moved on to LaMoille, Illinois. It is not known just when Jonas Sage died, nor where, and there is also no information of his marriage or children.

THE MEXICAN WAR
MAY 13, 1846 - FEBRUARY 2, 1848

Deep-seated disputes between the United States and Mexico over the location of the southern boundary at the Rio Grande River had festered for two decades until it created a breach of relations. In 1835 Texans revolted against Mexico and then broke away from Spanish rule. The people then established a country of their own in 1846 called the Republic of Texas.

Mexico then warned the newly-elected President James Buchanan that there might be war if Texas was admitted to the Union comprising the United States. Indeed, some people considered the northern neighbor to be a super-power trying to usurp her sovereign will on Mexico.

In 1845 Texas actually became part of the United States, and that action only precipitated further disputes between the two nations. One dealt with the boundary line which had never been defined; another was the Mexican debt owed to the Americans for lives lost in the revolution, and then there was the concept *of Manifest Destiny* whereby national expansion would expand the United States *from sea to shining sea!*

Negotiations faltered because of the revolution taking place in Mexico. President James K. Polk waited no longer showing the spoils of war. He ordered old General Scott to advance with his 300 men southward toward the Rio Grande River. When they reached the river in April they were defeated by an overwhelming army of Mexicans. It was May 13, 1846 when Congress took action to declare war on Mexico to *avenge the loss of American blood* on American soil.

The government headed by old Santa Anna fell when he resigned, but the new government promptly accepted the desired terms of peace.

The Treaty of Guadelupe Hidalgo was signed on the first day of February 1848 and by the terms set forth the United States received most of the area forming new states. But then came the terrible question of whether the territory was to be free or slave. By the Compromise of 1850 the very principle of *popular sovereignty* would form the under lying cause of the American Civil War.

The Hoosier response to the Governor's call for 7,014 volunteers to fill the state's quota represented enthusiastic loyalty to the United States. But the action of Jackson County to raise a company lagged behind and when it was organized, it could not be counted as part of the state quota.

Indeed, the single company of volunteers from Jackson County came from the ranks of the local militia, and it was identified only as the *Muscatatuck River Guards.*

VETERANS OF THE MEXICAN WAR
1846-1848

Officers and enlisted personnel of the *Muscatatuck River Guards* in Jackson County,
commissioned by the Governor of Indiana on June 13, 1846 included

Captain William R. Lux
Lt. David (Button) Cody
Lt. Barton Carl Burrell

Sgt. Jesse Cox   Cpl. Ruel Stewart

Privates

John Goss	Enoch Jones
Joseph Crane	James Wilkinson
Samuel Wells	Frank Emerson
James Owens	Joseph England
Dennis Callahan	Wilbur Smith

Jesse James, the only volunteer who was killed.
Aquilla Rogers, the grandson of the first Jackson County settler.
Francis (Frank) Noblitt, who was an uncle of John Noblitt, who enlisted from Jonesville.

THE AMERICAN CIVIL WAR
1861-1865

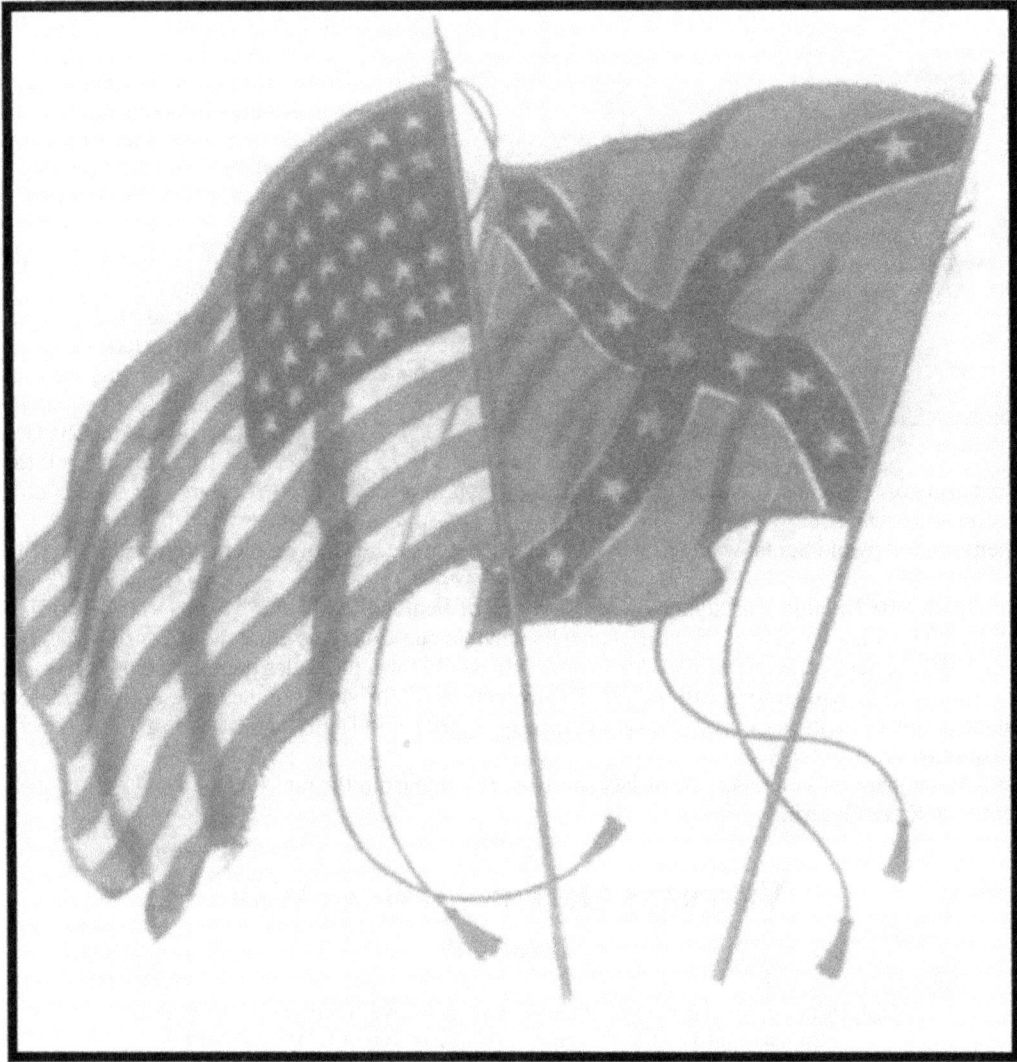

THE TRAGIC DIVISION OF NATIONAL LOYALTY
622,215 AMERICAN BOYS WERE KILLED

Mit Complementen Abweisen
A Delayed Tribute To Jackson County Veterans
American Civil War

When the Japanese bombed Pearl Harbor on December 7, 1941, one of the last surviving Confederate veterans living in Jackson County exclaimed to his offspring, *if Morgan's Raid into Grassy Fork Township had been successful, and had Captain Hines burned Hartsville College like he promised, and if Longstreet had not been late at Gettysburg, we would not be watching the boys march off to another world war...*

It probably makes little difference to most people today, but such sentiments had remained fixed in Michael Womack's mind for seventy-five years. Indeed, six of his Union brothers-in-arms also remained alive eight years later in 1949. The compiler of these records was fortunate to have interviewed two of them before he graduated from college. Those comrades of the *Grand Army of the Republic* were the last veterans of that tragic *War Between the States,* often called the American *Civil War!*

On June 13, 1949 those six old men rode in a parade around Monument Circle in Indianapolis. With their wrists extended below their blue uniformed sleeves, each one waved feebly to the crowd cheering from the sidewalk. Two of them were waving something else; they held a tiny American Flag aloft! Only one lifted yet another symbol dear to him! He waved the *Stars and Bars* high so everyone could see its colors flutter in the breeze.

Just a few hours later those old veterans of a tragic war would gather at the Claypool Hotel. Two of them would lean forward trying to hear the guest sing *Tenting Tonight in the Old Camp Ground!* Everyone knew the victorious northern army was at the point of death; the veterans were falling victims to the twin foes of age and time! The spectators sensed it was the end of a tragic era because those veterans were destined to become only names lost in history. The spirit of 1861 - 1865, with its roots planted firmly in the pioneer days, was to be buried and lost forever! All that would remain would be the records of their deeds, and their names would be destined to become blurred on the pages of some dusty governmental record.

The post-Appomattox records would verify the experiences of 200,000 Indiana Volunteers who fought bravely to preserve the Union. Most had completed their enlistment while others finished their tasks and went back home to their families. But hardly any of those veterans could forget General John Hunt Morgan and his Confederate Raid across the southern part of the state. And almost lost to history were the facts about his scouts from Jackson County!

The details of those Hoosier Rebels have been preserved, not from some old dusty journals, but by first-hand accounts extracted from letters and diaries Each preserved the personal data about the old general and his trusted horse thief, Captain Hines. He was charged to curtail the teaching of disobedience to the *Fugitive Slave Law.* All kinds of memories, including those which became fixed in folklore, were compiled later into the family heritage to confirm the records of those Confederate scouts who guided the horsemen through Jackson County. Those boys who ran south to join the Confederacy have been identified because they had elected to take up arms against their own kinfolk.

It was indeed a war where brother fought brother and father fought his sons! But it was from those eye-witness accounts which provided the last records of that tragic war.

That is why the members of the Jackson County Historical Society elected to honor the veterans of every era throughout the history of this nation. After all it has been the veterans who have guarded the American freedoms for two hundred fifty years.

Loren W. Noblitt. Ph.D.
Jackson County Historian: 1991 - 1998
Compiler of the Records for RECALL
November 11, 2003

RECORDS OF THE CIVIL WAR ROSTER
OF JACKSON COUNTY OFFICERS

Name	Location	Rank	Regiment
Fielder A. Jones	Seymour	Lt. Colonel	39th Regiment
Stephen Storey	Seymour	1st Lt.	6th Regiment
Calvin B. Trumbo	Seymour	2nd Lt.	6th Regiment
Samuel H. Charlton	Seymour	Surgeon	6th Regiment
Amos Frost	Seymour	Surgeon	6th Regiment
Horace Heffren	Jackson Co.	Lt. Colonel	50th Regiment
Palen Jackson	Millport	2nd Lt.	13th Regiment
Thomas B. Tanner	Brownstown	Lt. Colonel	22nd Regiment
Joseph A. Stillwell	Brownstown	Surgeon	22nd Regiment
William H. Ireland	Brownstown	Surgeon	22nd Regiment
Israel B. Owens	Brownstown	Captain	22nd Regiment
A.D. Sawyer	Brownstown	Captain	22nd Regiment
Matthew Tanner	Brownstown	Captain	22nd Regiment
James M. Lewis	Brownstown	1st Lt.	22nd Regiment
William H. Golden	Brownstown	1st Lt.	22nd Regiment
John Tanner	Brownstown	2nd Lt.	22nd Regiment
David Griffith	Brownstown	2nd Lt.	22nd Regiment
John H. McCormick	Seymour	1st Lt.	24th Regiment
Robert D. Callahan	Ewing	1st Lt.	24th Regiment
Arch N. Clayton	Seymour	2nd Lt.	24th Regiment
E.B. Williams	Seymour	2nd Lt.	24th Regiment
John W. Poole	Medora	2nd Lt.	25th Regiment
William H. Crenshaw	Medora	Captain	25th Regiment
John Nilson	Medora	Captain	25th Regiment
Jeffse Patterson	Medora	1st Lt.	25th Regiment
Daniel Eversole	Medora	1st Lt.	25th Regiment
Jacob Hinkle	Medora	1st Lt.	25th Regiment
Azrial W. Flinn	Medora	2nd Lt.	25th Regiment
John Daley	Houston	2nd Lt.	25th Regiment
William Proctor	Medora	2nd Lt.	38th Regiment
Charles Gordon	Seymour	Major	38th Regiment
Albert Downing	Seymour	Captain	39th Regiment
Henry C. Snyder	Jonesville	Captain	39th Regiment
Button Cody	Jonesville	Captain	39th Regiment
William Ockermann	Seymour	1st Lt.	39th Regiment
Jacob Mitchell	Seymour	Captain	39th Regiment
John Hamilton	Rockford	1st Lt.	39th Regiment
James Thompson	Seymour	1st Lt.	39th Regiment
Gabriel Woodmansee	Seymour	2nd Lt.	39th Regiment
Andrew Coleman	Seymour	2nd Lt.	39th Regiment
George Rigle	Seymour	2nd Lt.	39th Regiment
Noah S. Weddle	Carr Twnshp	2nd Lt.	140th Regiment
Frank Emerson	Brownstown	Lt. Colonel	67th Regiment
Bruce. J.W.	Owen Twnshp	2nd Lt.	39th Regiment
Robert D. Burton	Courtland	1st Lt.	67th Regiment
Samuel Beavers	Leesville	1st Lt.	50th Regiment
Andrew F. Coffey	Vallonia	Major	50th Regiment
Cleo W. Wray	Clearspring	Captain	17th Regiment
John H. Childs	Reddington	Steward	67th Regiment
John W. Goovert		2nd Lt.	67th Regiment
B.T. Dowell	Courtland	2nd Lt.	140th Regiment
Bradford Dowell	Courtland	2nd Lt.	140th Regiment
C.W. Dowell	Courtland	Major	140th Regiment
Samuel T. Weller	Vallonia	Colonel	50th Regiment
Cyrus L. Dunham	Shieldstown	Lt. Colonel	50th Regiment
John Scott	Houston	Lt. Colonel	50th Regiment
James N. Monroe	Seymour	Surgeon	50th Regiment
James C. Wells	Clearspring	Surgeon	50th Regiment
Amos Durand	Brownstown	Surgeon	50th Regiment
Andrew Burrell	Vallonia	Captain	50th Regiment
Malaich McCoy	Vallonia	Captain	50th Regiment
Thomas Boyatt	Mooney	Captain	50th Regiment
John Judy	Millport	1st Lt.	50th Regiment
Levi Davis	Medora	1st Lt.	50th Regiment
Albert Owen	Mooney	1st Lt.	50th Regiment

Frederick Killer	Vallonia	2nd Lt.	50th Regiment
Alva West	Jackson Co.	2nd Lt.	50th Regiment
Burr Peck	Medora	Captain	50th Regiment
George W. Taylor	Houston	Captain	50th Regiment
John W. Davies	Medora	1st Lt.	50th Regiment
John Bowman	Houston	1st Lt.	50th Regiment
James Johnson	Seymour	Captain	50th Regiment
Joseph McNally	Seymour	1st Lt.	50th Regiment
Patrick Honan	Seymour	1st Lt.	50th Regiment
William Newkirck	Leesville	Captain	50th Regiment
John T. Flinn	Leesville	1st Lt.	50th Regiment
Cyrus Hunter	Houston	1st Lt.	50th Regiment
George Hays	Houston	1st Lt.	50th Regiment
Richard McCounch	Seymour	Captain	50th Regiment
Francis W. Johnson	Seymour	Captain	50th Regiment
William McForgey	Seymour	Captain	50th Regiment
William Mahan	Seymour	Captain	50th Regiment
Gabriel Adams	N. Elizabeth	Captain	51st Regiment
Stephen Bowers	Brownstown		67th Regiment
Byford Long	Brownstown	Major	67th Regiment
Meredith Edmunds	Brownstown	Captain	67th Regiment
William C. Hall	Medora	2nd Lt.	67th Regiment
James W. Owen	Medora	1st Lt.	67th Regiment
Lewis W. Peck	Medora	1st Lt.	67th Regiment
Charles Prow	Seymour	Capt.	67th Regiment
John Hinderlider	Seymour	1st Lt.	67th Regiment
Nelson Crabb	Seymour	2nd Lt.	67th Regiment
George Paulson	Seymour	Captain	67th Regiment
TAzwell Vawter	Seymour	1st Lt.	67th Regiment
Albert Black	Courtland	2nd Lt.	22nd Regiment
John Stockdell	Rockford	1st Lt.	25th Regiment
Robert G. Vallahan	Leesville	Captain	25th Regiment
Robert Shilling	Vallonia	1st Lt.	39th Regiment
Henry Houston	Mooney	Captain	50th Regiment
Edward Robinson	Vallonia	Captain	50th Regiment
Edward Harrbison	Medora	2nd Lt.	50th Regiment
Ralph Applewhite	Brownstown	Captain	67th Regiment
George Carr	Medora	Lt. Colonel	93rd Regiment
Thomas Richards	Kurtz	Captain	120th Regiment
Joseph Swift	Seymour	1st Lt.	125th Regiment
B.A. Clifteon	Seymour	2nd Lt.	125th Regiment
William Crouch	Bobtown	1st Lt.	125th Regiment
William Doughtery	Brownstown	Captain	145th Regiment
William J. Boyatt	Brownstown	1st Lt.	145th Regiment

DISCHARGE ROSTER

140TH REGIMENT – INDIANA VOLUNTEERS COMPANY K

Captain William Miller,	Vallonia		
1st Lt. George Irwin,	Ewing	John Howley,	Medora
1st Lt. Lt. Noah Weddle,	Medora	David Hale,	Medora
1st Sgt. William H. Miller,	Ewing	John Humphrey,	Vallonia
Sgt. Philip S. Tuell,	Vallonia	John Jones,	Vallonia
Sgt. Eli Wray,	Medora	Absalom Matthews,	Vallonia
Cpl. William Wray,	Medora	Asa Pennock,	Courtland
Cpl. John McClary,	Medora	William Pruitt,	Little York
Cpl. John T. Eck,	Vallonia	John Randall,	Ewing
Cpl. Isaac Brown,	Vallonia	William Reno,	Rockford
Cpl. John Hazard,	Medora	William Royce,	Rockford
Thomas Anderson,	Vallonia	Joab Scott,	Medora
John W. Brown,	Medora	Samuel Tabor,	Brownstown
Owen S. Brown,	Medora	David Tuell,	Vallonia
Joshua Branch,	Vallonia	William Tilford,	Vallonia
Job Chadwick,	Vallonia	Matt Walker,	Vallonia
Oscar Davis,	Bellville	James Wright,	Medora
Samueal Dunham,	Medora	George Weddle,	Medora
William Empson,	Valonia	Orville Watson,	Vallonia
Jacob Garrett,	Little York	Daniel Womack,	Belleville

JACKSON COUNTY VOLUNTEER SERVICEMEN
DURING THE CIVIL WAR

31ST INDIANA VOLUNTEER REGIMENT
ENLISTED MEN

Company F

Adkins, Joseph	Ewing
Banks, Matthew	Brownstown
Banks, George	Brownstown
Bomgarger, Richard	Brownstown
Hughes, George	Ewing
Miller, William	Brownstown
Snyder, George	Brownstown
Snyder, Frederick	Ewing
Wirt, Coffman	Ewing

Company H

Ayers, Henry	Courtland
Clifton, Alfred	Rockford
Danatelle, Alfred	Seymour
Franklin, Samuel	Seymour
Hilner, David	Seymour
Isaacs, Francis	Courtland
Isaacs, John	Courtland
Kokenour, Jesse	Seymour
Lee, Roland	Seymour
Mahurin, Hezekiah	White Creek
Mahurin, William	Courtland
Mahurin, Thomas	Courtland
Myers, Christopher	Courtland
Meyers, Frank	Courtland
Stanfield, Alex	Seymour
Smith, Abraham	Seymour
Shutters, William	Seymour
Tidd, Thomas	Courtland

Wade, Charles	Seymour
Wyatt, William	Brownstown

Company K

Heller, August	Ewing
Pearson, Jonathon	Ewing
Prather, Uriah	Brownstown
Weddle, Hiram	Medora
Willis, Hiram	Ewing

Company J

Decker, John	Brownstown
Eichenhour, Philip	Brownstown
Geir, Lewis	Brownstown
Hooker, Jobn	Seymour
Hanschild, Fred	Tampico
Harper, Thomas	Seymour
Hess, Joseph	Brownstown
King, Victor	Seymour
Nagle, John	Seymour
Martin Simeon	Rockford
Meahl, Peter	Vallonia
Mier, Jacob	Seymour
Nierman, Henry	Brownstown
Reddick, William	Seymour
Soody, William	Brownstown
Stockamp, Peter	Rockford
Stunkel, John	Tampico
Wilson, John	Seymour

JACKSON COUNTY VOLUNTEER SERVICEMEN
DURING THE CIVIL WAR

33RD INDIANA VOLUNTEER REGIMENT
ENLISTED MEN

Bivar, Adam	Crothersville
Cox, Philip	Seymour
Coomer, George	Crothersville
Dunham, Samuel	Crothersville
Farris, Henry	Seymour
Holbrook, Rueben	Crothersville
Nolting, Henry	Rockford
Olmstead, Alonzo	Rockford
Noblitt William	Rockford (transferred to 39th Regiment)

39th Indiana Volunteer Regiment
Enlisted Men

Nading, Wesley — Jackson County
Ritchie, Charles — Jackson County
Mitchell, Jacob — Jackson County
Noblitt, William — Rockford

Winters, John	Ratcliffe, James	Sullivan, John	Crane, James	Baker, Wiley
Love, Charles	Downing, Albert	Rankin, Henry	Cooley, John	Craw, John
Hamilton, John	Jones, John	Russel, James	Anderson, John	Ash, Peter
Banks, William	Booth, David	Bohall, William	Bourman, John	Bunton, Jacob
Brooks, Luther	Compton, George	Coleman, Andrew	Clifton, Alfred	Christy, Andy
Dannettell, Mel	Doudna, Joshua	Dorrey, Cornelius	Elliott, William	Fisk, Mahlon
Flinn, Jacob	Gannon, Patrick	Gallaspy Robert	Godaker, William	Gordan, Geo
Grass, Daniel	Greer, James	Haney, George	Howard, William	Hancock, Jeff
Hagins, John	Harrod, Alonzo	Heitman, John	Holstein, Francis	Jenkins, Nate
Jones, Jacob	Jones, Thomas	Jones, Harvey	Lawson, James	Leffler, Jake
Linton, John	Lynch, Conley	Lockman, William	Lockhart, Sam	Maxwell, Jim
Moore, Nathan	Moore, Samuel	Myers, Harmon	Myers, George	McBride, S.
McCleary, Samuel	Mitchell Charles	Mitchell, George	Nading, Charles	Palmer, Jim
Paris, Clayborne	Rigle, George	Reynolds, Terrance	Robbins, Aaron	Robbins, T.
Romine, Coleman	Ross, William	Ratcliffe, William	Rucker, Nathan	Stockdell, M.
Sweeney, Harrison	Stewart, Oley	Romine, Elias	Stockdell, Riley	Crittendon, I.
Dickerson, John	Ewing, Manfred	Stewart, Blackie	Thomas, Robert	Koenig, Fred

Company K

Crane, Joseph	Ford, Benjamin	Harrison, John	Hagan, Isaiah
Love, Beaufort	Miller, James	Romine, Elias	Stoltz, Philip

Company L

Barkes, William	Barkes, Noah	Flinn, Andrew	Ratcliffe, Amos
Fisher, George	Sheppard, John		

Company M

Bryant, William	Bryant, Martin	Barnes, George	Dickerson, John
Smith, John	Stewart, Blanker	Wright, Peter	Cox, William
Crane, Abraham	Clark, John	Dunlap, John	Goins, Asbury
King, Thomas	Mace, William	Snyder, William	Tipton, William

JACKSON COUNTY VOLUNTEER SERVICEMEN DURING THE CIVIL WAR

43RD INDIANA VOLUNTEER REGIMENT

Company F

Potter, John	Medora	Carmichael, Joseph	Jackson County
Long Byford	Vallonia	Owen, Merewith	Crothersville
Wells, Philip	Clearspring	Wright, Elias	Courtland
Todd, Henry	Freetown	Russell, George	Mooney

49TH INDIANA VOLUNTEER REGIMENT

Company B

Brooks, Richard	Millport	Shields, John	Courtland
Pruett, Walker	Vallonia	Shields, Archibald	Courtland
Trueblood, Jordan	Mooney	Shields, William	Courtland
Walls, John	Ft. Ritner	Shields, Jesse	Courtland
Sommers, James	Clearspring	Shields, Caddy	Seymour

50TH INDIANA VOLUNTEER REGIMENT

Company A

Holland, William	Newkirk, John	Harbison, Edward	Durand, Amos
Judy, John	Waskom, John	Harrell, Ira	Waskom, Michael
Hunsucker, Tom	Branaman, Chris	Wells, Theodore	Briner, Andrew
England, George	Fisher, Noah	Flinn, Jesse	Gray, Joseph
Hanner, Sylvester	Humphrey, George	Humphrey, John	Jones, George
Kinworthy, John	Kindred, David	Miller, John	Nountrop, George
Nountropp, Henry	Rucker, Samuel	Ruddick, Elisha	Spurgeon, John
Spurgeon, Squire	Spurgeon, Thomas	Spurgeon, John M.	Waskom, Pierson
Empson, Daniel			

Recruits

Cummins, William	Floyd, Redmon	Hunsucker, Thomas R.	Lockman, Squire
Tate, George	Lucas, Marion	Sheppard, Allen	Sheppard, David

Company B

Davis, Levi	Critchlow, Edward	Weddell, Norman	Peck, Daniel
Weddell, Jasper	Harrell, Edmond	Biggs, Radley	Eastin, Richard
Eastin, Nicholson	Eastin, Elias	Loudermilk, Sylvester	Loudermilk, Fran
Peck, Lewis	Plummer, William	Weddell, Daniel	Weddell, Nathan
Weddell, John	Weddell, William	Winegar, Calvin	Zike, Isaac

Recruits

Hubbard, James	Hubbard, Edmond	Knott, Joseph	King, James
Lewis, John	Lewis, James	Loudermilk, William	Loudermilk, Hy
Loudermilk, Hiram	Loudermilk, Andrew	Tatlock, Thomas	Tatlock, Wesley

50TH INDIANA VOLUNTEER REGIMENT

Company K

Johnson, James
Wright, Franklin
Lewis, Andrew
Hatten, Marion
Spray, Tom
Noblitt, Woodson
Renno, William

Stotts, James
Dunlap, William
Deppert, John
Hatten, Robert
Sweany, William
Duerr, Henry
Sparks, William

Calahan, Samuel
Trueblood, Lemuel
Fosbrink, Frederick
Sage, John
Trueblood, James
Duerr, Charles
Smith, Thomas

Sparks, Evander
Mollen, Horace
Hatten, Samuel
Sage, David
Trueblood, Josiah
Floyd, John
Wies, George

Military Organization
50TH INDIANA VOLUNTEER REGIMENT

Colonel Cyrus L. Dunham, Commanding Officer

Colonel Horace Heffren
_____
Colonel H.H. Atkisson

Company A
Captain Samuel T. Wells

1st Lt. Andrew Burrell
Malachai McCoy
Thomas Boyatt
Henry Houston

97 Enlisted men

2nd Lt. Albert Owens
Levi Davis
John Leonard
John J. Judy

Company B
Captain Burr S. Peck

1st Lt. George Taylor
John Davis
Joseph McNally

102 Enlisted Men

2nd Lt. John Bowman
George Hays
W. McForgey

Company H
Captain John S. Scott

1st Lt. Cyrus Scott
Francis Johnson
Amos Durland

99 Enlisted Men

2nd Lt. Cyrus Hunter
Joseph Mahan
Ed Harbison

Company K
Captain Charles M. Gordon

1st Lt. James Mitchell
George Gordon
Richard McCormick

77 Enlisted Men

2nd Lt. John Hamilton
Jm. Thompson
Geo. Rigle

52ND INDIANA VOLUNTEER REGIMENT

Company A

Rook, David
Fenley, William
Dobson, Willis
Ard, William
Curry, James
Callahan, Jeremiah
Emery, Stephen
Gamradt, John
Hatfield, George
Hubbard, James
Lewis, Joseph
Owen, Lewis
Samparie, Henry
Wilson, William

Holt, Dewey
Weddell, J.C.
Hubbard, Aaron
Ard, Joel
Curry, Pleasant
Cunningham, William
Elkins, Granville
Gramradt, Fred
Humphries, James
Kennedy, David
McGauhey, Silas
Owen, Tom
Stockdale, Eli
Winesinger, Stephen

Hobson, James
Brown, William
Easten, Nick
Beem, Joseph
Callahan, James
Davis, Amos
Elkins, Richard
Gallion, Jacob
Hinkle, Wilson
Lewis, John W.
Matlock, James
Paris, Moses
Tadlock, Thomas
Welling, Andrew

Johnson, David
Curry, Elijah
Loudermilk, Henry
Cox, Absolem
Callahan, Moses
Eastin, Elijah
Ferguson, Lincoln
Gray, David
Hubbard, David
Lewis, James
Maxwell, Enoch
Pansey, Joseph
Tadlock, Wesley
Zimmerman, Peter

Company B

McMahan, Oliver
Bell, Michael
Black, Albert
Browning, Amzi
Cornett, Jesse
England, Christopher
Gardener, Thomas
Matlock, William
Prewitt, William
Spurgeon, Solomon
Scott, William
Tidd, George
Weekly, Joshua

Thompson, Eli
Beavers, Samuel
Brock, Jacob
Cross, Richard
Cornett, Robert
Hendry, William
Fleetwood, John
Matlock, Wells
Prewitt, Aaron
Spurgeon, John
Scott, Peter
Tidd, Peter
Zimmerman, Ben

Acton, William
Bright, John
Brock, John
Cross, James
Conrad, Francis
Lacy, John
Gardener, Jacob
McMahon, Evan
Read, James
Stewart, Robert
Scott, John
Williams, George

Zimmerman, William
Manuel, James
Acton, Wilford
Bebout, Citizen
Cross, Solomon
Dowden, Jesse
Moore, John
Gardener, John
Newby, Jeremiah
Ryan, Jesse
Stewart, Jackson
Taylor, William

Company C

Coffey, William
Slattery, Michael
Bunton, David
Cummings, Champion
Dorsett, William
Erwin, Enock
Hatten, Samuel
Johnson, Hiram
Lokhart, James
McKinney, John
Smith, Caleb
Sutherland, Fountain
Winkles, David

Sweany, William
Green, John
Bundy, Thomas
Curry, James
Deppert, John
Erb, Conrad
Hatten, Marion
Johnson, Robert
Miller, James
Oliver, Lewis
Smith, Lawrence
Squires, John
Martin, John

Boggs, Henry
Atkison, Richard
Clifton, Warren
Coloran, Patrick
Duckworth, David
Fowler, Allen
Hughes, Cyrenus
Jonker, John
Moore, John
Preggy, Henry
Smith, Samuel
Tompkins, William
Ganah, John

Maus, Peter
Bunton, Ebenezer
Calhoun, Samuel
Carter, Benjamin
Evans, Julius
Goodwin, Comador
Jones, John
Lambert, Silas
Madison, Alvin
Smith, John
Sparks, Franklin
Tape, Franklin
Young, Jacob

Company D

Gray, Isaac
Watson, Joseph

Hart, Jefferson
Whileman, Jasper

Fowler, Marion

Hinderlider, C.

MILITARY ORGANIZATION

67TH INDIANA VOLUNTEER REGIMENT
COLONEL FRANK EMERSON, COMMANDING OFFICER

Company F

Captain William Hull

1st Lt.	James Owen	2nd Lt.	Charles Prow
	Lewis Peck		Jn. Hinderlider

83 Enlisted Men

Company G

Captain Nelson Crabb

1st Lt.	Stephen Storey	2nd Lt.	Jn. McCormick
	George Poulson		Walter Tanner

94 Enlisted Men

Company E

Captain Byford Long

1st Lt. H.W. Chadwick	2nd Lt. Andy Hamilton
James Stilwell	M. Edmunds

91 Enlisted Men

Company K

Captain Ralph Applewhite

1st Lt.	Tazwell Vawter	2nd Lt.	Gabe Robinson
	Stephen Bowers		Robt. Callahan

99 Enlisted Men

JACKSON COUNTY SOLDIERS
140TH INDIANA VOLUNTEERS
REGIMENTAL ORGANIZATION

Colonel Thomas J. Brady, Commander
Muncie

Lt. Colonel David T. Mitchell
Leesville

Major Charles A. Pendergrast
Findley's Mill

Eli M. Dale, Adjutant
Guthrie Creek

Jacob S. Geyer, Chaplain
Goss Mill

John B. Routh, Quartermaster
Muncie

JACKSON COUNTY ROSTER

Company K

Captain William R. Miller
Vallonia

1st Lt. George M. Irwin
Ewing

2nd Lt. Noah S. Weddle
Weddleville

NON-COMMISSIONED OFFICERS

1st Sgt. Will H. Miller, Ewing
Sgt. Philip S. Tuell, Vallonia
Sgt. Eli Wray, Medora
Cpl. William T. Wray, Medora
Cpl. John B. McClary, Medora
Cpl. John S. Eck, Vallonia

Cpl. Isaac Dunn, Vallonia
Cpl. Hiram T. Stapp, Medora
Cpl. James Eaton, Pleasantville
Cpl. John M. Sanger, Tampico
Cpl. John Hazzard, Reddington
Mus. William Craft, Vallonia

ENLISTED MEN

Thomas Anderson, Vallonia
Jacob Arnold, Little York
John W. Brown, Medora
Owen S. Brown, Medora
Joshua Branch, Vallonia
Oscar Davis, Bellsville
Samuel Durham, Medora
Milton Hecock, Vallonia
John L. Howey, Medora
David Hale, Medora
John Humphrey, Vallonia
James Bryant, Little York
William Burton, Rockford
Job Chadwick, Vallonia
Samuel Crockett, Little York
Charles Carter, Little York

William Fullbright, Vallonia
Jacob Garrett, Little York
John Jones, Vallonia
George Langham, Vallonia
Absalom Matthews, Vallonia
Jackson McKinney, Rockford
Enos Pickering, Losantville
Asa Pennock, Courtland
William Pruitt, Little York
James Reynolds, Spraytown
John Randall, Ewing
William Reno (Renno) Rockford
William H. Royce, Rockford
Thomas A. Steele, Alfordsville
Zechariah Smith, Little York
Joab Scott, Medora

Samuel Tabor, Brownstown
David Tuell, Vallonia
Jacob Deppert, Reddington
William Tilford, Vallonia
William Walters, Acme
Matthew Walker, Vallonia
Henry Wolters, Courtland
John Winengo, Medora
James P. Wright, Medora
George Weddle, Medora
Aquilla Wilcoxon, Leesville
Oliver Watson, Vallonia
John Zager, Rockford
B.T. Dowell, Freetown
Bradford Dowell, Freetown
Charles Dowell, Freetown

...two Illinois and two Indiana (17th and 140th) Regiments of mounted cavalry constituted the very first Brigade of the Second Division. Those four lead Regiments earned the revered name of Lightening Brigade. Commanded by Colonel John Wilder, the officers and men deserved to rank along side of the Iron Brigade and the Stonewall Brigade and there can be no doubt these were among the finest fighting units of both armies...
Stephen Z. Stover
Union Cavalry
Commanding

Special Field Order #56
April 17, 1865
...all officers and men of this command are hereby informed of the assassination and death of our beloved President Abraham Lincoln at Fords Theater in Washington. All units will stand down to participate in the Grand Review of the 23rd Corps (of which the 17th and 140th Indiana Regiments are now a part) to be carried out at Raleigh on the 21st day of April 1865...
William T. Sherman
General
Commanding

THE CIVIL WAR ROLL OF HONOR

JACKSON COUNTY

Name	Place	Name	Place	Name	Place
Abel, George	Rockford	Goen, Reuben	Medora	Patterson, Jesse	Medora
Allen, Joshua	Mooney	Gosvener, Jackson	Houston	Perry, John	Sparksville
Allsup, James	Sparksville	Graves, Stephen	Crothersville	Perry, Matthew	Seymour
Applegate, Hezekiah	Pleasant Grove	Griffin, Ebanezer	Sparksville	Phipps, James	Seymour
Armstrong, Thomas	Tampico	Hancock, Jefferson	Norman	Pitts, Benjamin	Vallonia
Balser, Thomas	Crothersville	Harper, Issac	Mooney	Poole, John	Medora
Banks, Andrew	Brownstown	Hawn, Harrison	Tampico	Ratcliffe, James	Freetown
Banks, George	Brownstown	Herron, William	Sparksville	Reading, Alfred	Rockford
Barnett, David	Spraytown	Holstein, Francis	Uniontown	Reed, Harrison	Rockford
Barringer, James	Retreat	Hooker, Henry	Seymour	Reed, Warren	Rockford
Beadle, Omer	Norman	Howard, William	Rockford	Ren, Josiah	Medora
Blair, James	Crothersville	Hunter, Cyrus	Houston	Rhinehart, Philip	Dudleytown
Boehler, John	Acme	Isaacs, John	Courtland	Robinson, John	Medora
Booth, David	Acme	Johnson, George	Vallonia	Rose, William	Seymour
Booth, Harrison	Rockford	Keach, Alexander	Tampico	Ross, James	Farmington
Booth, William	Courtland	Keef, Patrick	Bobtown	Ross, William	Dudleytown
Brown, John	Bobtown	Killey, John	Crothersville	Salmons, William	Uniontown
Burge, Solon	Freetown	King, Joseph	Medora	Scott, William	Medora
Burgen, Pleasant	Acme	Lane, Benjamin	Houston	Sheppard, Daniel	Crothersville
Burrell, Simeon	Medora	Leffler, Jacob	Seymour	Shoemaker, Daniel	Crothersville
Burton, William	Rockford	Lennox, James	Brownstown	Smith, Rueben	Tampico
Bustoff, Frederick	Seymour	Lockhart, Andrew	Rockford	Smith, Simeon	Brownstone
Cameron, Richard	Sparksville	Lockhart, James	Rockford	Snyder, Abraham	Brownstown
Chritchlow, John	Medora	Lockman, Erasmus	Uniontown	Snyder, Luther	Brownstown
Clampett, David	Mooney	Marling, Spencer	Retreat	Soondy, William	Brownstown
Clark, Michael	Mooney	Marling, Walter	Retreat	Spall, Samuel	Retreat
Cockerham, William	Dudleytown	Matthew Rea	Medora	Starr, William	Houston
Compton, George	Uniontown	Maxwell, James	Vallonia	Stewart, John	Houston
Crane, Jonas	Seymour	McBride, Samuel	Vallonia	Stockdell, John	Seymour
Cross, John	Acme	McConnell, John	Dudleytown	Summa, David	Reddington
Cummings, William	Mooney	McCrary, William	Tampico	Tabor, Samuel	Brownstown
Davenport, Henry	Medora	McKinney, Jackson	Rockford	Thomas, William	Medora
Davis, Drewey	Houston	McVanway, John	Medora	Thompson, Richard	Vallonia
Day, George	Spraytown	Mier, Jacob	Seymour	Thompson, William	Courtland
Deppert, John	Seymour	Miner, Robert	Medora	Tobias, James	Crothersville
Diggs, William	Reddington	Mize, Joseph	Brownstone	Tobias, William	Dudleytown
Digmore, Nathaniel	Medora	Montgomery, William	Crothersville	Toppe, Henry	Dudleytown
Dotson, James	Medora	Moore, Wesley	Brownstone	Turner, Benjamin	Acme
Douglass, William	Rockford	Moore, William	Mooney	Uttman, John	Dudleytown
Elkins, Francis	Houston	Mulholland, Daniel	Medora	Victory, Abraham	Reddington
Elkins, Joseph	Houston	Myers, Christopher	Courtland	Wade, Charles	Seymour
Estep, Francis	Brownstown	Myers, Franklin	Courtland	Walker, Matthew	Vallonia
Finney, John	Medora	Myers, George	Reddington	Watson, Omer	Vallonia
Flothaman	Sparksville	Noblitt, William	Rockford	Weller, Thomas	Rockford
Fredenburg, George	Dudleytown	Olds, George	Retreat	White, Jacob	Medora
Galliman, Isaiah	Tampico	Oliver, James	Seymour	Williamson, John	Crothersville
Galliman, William	Tampico	Owen, Thomas	Medora	Wilson, Aesop	Tampico
Garrel, George	Crothersville	Owens, William	Mooney	Woodall, James	Brownstone
Garrel, William	Crothersville	Paris, Clayborne	Freetown	Woodmansee, Gabriel	Seymour

Jackson County Soldiers
The Civil War

Deserters

6th Regiment

Robert Adams	Houston
Powell Banks	Vallonia
James Flinn	Leesvile
James Miller	Freetown
Frank Reno	Rockford
George Anshoot	Medora
John Reno	Rockford

22nd Regiment

Thomas Banks	Goss Mill
H.B. Baugh	Weddleville
David Crouch	Brownstown
James Cook	Seymour
Tom Gillespie	Vallonia
Henry Henderson	Houston
Dan Loudermilk	Spraytown
Francis Lucas	Medora
Peter West	Shieldstown

67th Regiment

James Hines	Reddington
James Robinson	Peter Switch
Henry Williams	Medora
David Wallace	Vallonia

140th Regiment

Benjamin James	Houston
John Metcalf	Freetown
George Patten	Reddington
Samuel Reid	Crothersville

8th Regiment

George Anshoot	Medora
Benjamin Moore	Kurtz
George Applegate	Tampico
Ike Elliott	Ch. Ridge

25th Regiment

James Combs	Tampico
Thomas Clark	Vallonia
William Foster	Ch. Ridge
James Morrison	Peter Switch

50th Regiment

James Acton	Vallonia
William Allen	Brownstone
John Allen	Brownstone
Elisha Burge	Vallonia
Hiram Collier	Seymour
K.C. Clark	Rockford
James Clark	Courtland
Aaron Boyle,	Bobtown
James Kiethly	Brownstown

145th Regiment

Thomas Gray	Bobtown
Abraham Graham	Vallonia
William Wolters	Seymour
Issac Weddle	Carr Township
David Weddle	Medora
Caleb Shelton	Courtland
Elijah Jewell	Tampico
John Shelton	Courtland
Patrick Sweeney	Spraytown

Pvt. Walter B. Marling
32nd Regiment – Co. G
Indiana Volunteer Infantry
Killed in Action – Dec. 31, 1862
Battle of Perryville

Both bodies were returned in canvas bags by train from Perryville to Louisville. From the train depot their father, Hiram W. Marling, brought the bodies of his sons by horse and wagon only to find his three daughters had died. There were three caskets on the Marling front porch at the one time. Hiram W. Marling also enlisted and served in the 82nd Indiana Infantry Regiment.

Pvt. Spencer B. Marling
82nd Regiment – Co. B
Indiana Volunteer Infantry
Killed in Action – Dec. 24, 1862
Battle of Perryville

MANSFIELD ALLEN, Civil War, Company "F" - 8th Indiana Volunteer Cavalry, was born in Kentucky in 1839, a son of William and Delila Allen. He served in the Grand Army of the Republic and later, after his discharge, he married Louisa Lucas in 1879. Mansfield Allen died in 1883 and was buried in the Wayman Cemetery.

He was the father of one daughter named Felila Jane Allen Soladine. Later, he was the ancestor of two grandchildren who lived in Jackson County and who produced a great-great-granddaughter named Patricia Stout.

ANDREW J. BANKS, Civil War, Company "B" - 22nd Infantry Regiment, Indiana Volunteers, was married to Mary E. Marsh and they became parents of several children. The family lived in Brownstown, and the Banks family lineage may be traced to pre-Revolutionary War origins in the colony of Virginia.

CHARLES OLIVER BAUGHMAN, Civil War, Grand Army of the Republic, born in Carrolo County, Illinois in 1844 to Isaiah and Mary Jane Steipleford Baughman. After his wife died, the family moved to an 80 acre farm located near Albion, Illinois. They settled there in 1852 and ten years later Oliver enlisted in the Union army.

He was assigned as a recruit to the 155th Regiment of Illinois Volunteers. He was inducted at Camp Butler, IL in February of 1865 at Olney. His enlistment was for one year of service. Records verify he was present for the muster of Company "E" on June 30, 1865.

One of his citations indicated he was detailed to assist General Robert E. Lee in changing uniforms at the command of General Grant. He returned his government-issued Springfield rifle and received $6.00 with his discharge.

He migrated to Jackson County and settled near a logging camp located near Medora. Shortly thereafter, he met and married Nancy Jane Scott, and to them eleven children were born.

Charles Oliver Baughman died June 15, 1937 and was buried in a family plot located near the old church.

DAVID LOUIS BECK, Civil War, Company "H" - 50th Regiment Indiana Infantry. Entire regiment taken prisoner at Munfordsville. Paroled to fight again. Killed during Battle of Spoonville. 1861-1863.

JOHN H. BERRY, Civil War, Company H - 82nd Regiment Indiana Volunteers, was born in 1819 in Westmoreland County, PA. He ran away from home and eventually settled in Cincinnati where he met and married Rachel Adams in 1845. In 1857 this couple settled in Brown County four miles north of Houston on a farm adjoining the Enes homestead. At the age of 43 years he and his neighbor left their families so they could enlist in the Grand Army of the Republic.

Their unit was involved in battle at Resaca, GA as part of Sherman's Army intent on capturing Atlanta. After advancing through Peach Tree Creek and Ezra Church they encamped where the Atlanta Stadium is now located. The Army began its march to the sea and from there it proceeded north through the Carolina's. After Appomattox, the unit was part of the grand parade through Washington.

He returned to Brown County to be with his family. When Rachel died in 1893 she was buried in the Christiansburg Cemetery. Soon after that, John moved to Houston to live with his daughter-in-law. When he died in 1910 he was laid to rest in the Christiansburg Cemetery beside his wife.

Among his descendants may be found two great-grandsons, John W. Lubker and Orville Lubker, Jr. They too served in the armed forces.

GOTTLEIB L. BRIETFIELD, Civil War, Company K - 10th Regiment Ohio Infantry Volunteers, Grand Army of the Republic, born March 18, 1835 in Prussia to Frederick and Minnie Baumfeldt Brietfield. He left the old country in 1846 and settled in Cincinnati, OH and volunteered to serve in the Civil War. He enlisted in the Northern Army and was assigned to Company K in the 10th Regiment of the Ohio Volunteers.

His unit was engaged in various battles, including that of Carnifex, Perryville, Stone River, Chicamauga and Chattanooga. He was wounded, had part of his ear shot off but survived to be discharged on June 3, 1864.

Official military records spelled his name as Gotlieb Brightfield, and he was married to Henrietta Holtmann and they became parents of 10 children. The family moved to Jackson County in 1866 and he purchased 134 acres in Washington Township where they lived until 1919 when they moved to Seymour. He died June 14, 1921 and his wife died in 1925. One of his daughters, Wilhelmina, later married William Toborg.

WILLIAM REED CALHOUN, Civil War, Company C - 52nd Regiment Indiana Volunteers, born in Pennsylvania to Noble Calhoun and Nancy Reed. He left Beaver County, PA, sometime between 1856-1861 with his parents and siblings settling in northern Jackson County. The Calhoun farm was located two miles north of Spraytown.

During the Civil War, Reed Calhoun volunteered. He joined the 52nd Regiment, Company C, of the Indiana Infantry. It was organized at Rushville and Indianapolis on February 1, 1862. A partial description of duty: Fort Donelson, siege of Corinth, Vicksburg, battle of Nashville, siege of Fort Blakely, occupation of Mobile, March to Montgomery. The 52nd was mustered out September 10, 1865.

This Regiment lost two officers and 26 enlisted men were killed and two officers and 175 enlisted men died from disease. Total lives lost were 205.

Source: A Compendium of the War of the Rebellion by Frederick H. Dyer. Copyright 1908.

Reed Calhoun never married. Family legend tells that he made an excellent living as a riverboat gambler. He never married, but enjoyed spoiling his many nieces and nephews. He was a very personable and generous man. His sister was Martha Calhoun Ault, wife of Valentine Felty Ault of Spraytown. Widow Ault later married Widower Wes Weekly.

On June 1, 1882, Reed's father and stepmother deeded a small piece of land on the farm to the county as White Creek Burying Grounds. It had been used as a graveyard for years. Reed Calhoun's place of death in 1928 is unknown, however, he came home one last time to be buried in the Calhoun Sutherland Cemetery. The cemetery is located on the Jackson County side of the Bartholomew County line, 2-1/2 miles north of Spraytown on State Road 58.

GEORGE WHITFIELD CARR SR., Civil War, born in Clark County October 7, 1807, a son of Thomas and Mary Buchanan Carr. Early in 1811 the family moved to an area which later became Jackson County. His father assisted with the construction of Fort Alexander at Vallonia and the family resides close by until 1817. A family homestead was then established just west of Medora.

George W. Carr was self-educated having only 6 months of school. He married Elizabeth Brown in 1828 and two years later he relocated to near Leesville in Lawrence County. George and his brother John Carr soon became active in Indiana politics. George represented Lawrence County while John spoke for Jackson County. The former served in the House six terms and in the Senate three terms, and was elected to preside over the Indiana Constitutional Convention of 1850-51.

After moving back home, he personally recruited six companies of men who were organized into the 93rd Regiment of Indiana Infantry Volunteers, and he was appointed to Lt. Colonel. He and his regiment reported to General Sherman and saw action in several battles and the siege of Vicksburg. He was compelled to resign his commission in 1863 because of ill health as a man of past 55 years of age.

His wife Elizabeth died soon after George returned home, and later he married Fannie Nighsonges of Vevay, and they remained on the Carr homestead. They maintained an orchard until Fannie died in 1886. George then sold the place and moved to Crawfordsville where he lived with his youngest son, William, who was the mayor. George died May 27, 1892 and was buried in the Carr Family Cemetery located near Medora. Indeed, he joined his parents and both wives and all lie at peace.

GEORGE W. CARR JR., Civil War, Grand Army of the Republic, 93rd Regiment - Indiana Volunteer Infantry, born near Leesville January 15, 1844, a son of George W. and Elizabeth Brown Carr. Prior to the outbreak of the Civil War, the family moved to Jackson County and resided on the family homestead, located west of Medora. Young George lived at home until 1862 when he enlisted as a private in Captain Burrell's Company, 50th Regiment, Indiana Volunteer Infantry for 90 days of service.

His company was assigned to guard Confederate prisoners at Camp Morgan in Indianapolis. Later they were ordered to Kentucky and on into Tennessee, and mustered out of service until August 1862 when George re-enlisted as a private in Company I, 93rd Regiment. His unit was one recruited by his father, Lt. Colonel Carr. The son remained in the 93rd Regiment and was later promoted to sergeant-major. He was discharged August 12, 1865 after participating in major battles, including the siege of Vicksburg. He returned to the family homestead and was enrolled in the nearby Weddleville School and later, in 1869, he became a teacher.

In December he married a former student named Gertrude Woody, and afterward they moved to Ashland, Kansas. In 1881 he was appointed to the Civil War Veterans Pensions Department in Washington, D.C. He remained with the Department until his death on March 16, 1893. He was buried in the Arlington National Cemetery.

George W. and Gertrude Woody Carr never had children, and after his death, she moved to California. She lived in San Diego until she died February 22, 1949, aged 95 years.

DAVID CLAMPITT, Civil War, Grand Army of the Republic, born March 8, 1825 in North Carolina to Richard and Jerimina Matthews. The family moved north and settled in Jackson County when he was a child.

Married Mary Kindred Clampitt, bore 7 children. Charter member of Liberty Christian Church.

Joined the army at Columbus on February 24, 1864, Company H, 120th Regiment of Indiana Volunteers. Received a furlough at Nashville, Tennessee. Was disabled and rode the train. Fell beneath the wheels and was killed October 18, 1864. Buried in nearby cemetery

FRANCIS M. CROCKET, Civil War, Company "E" - 53rd Regiment Indiana Volunteers. Wounded in Battle near Vicksburg. Discharged at Louisville. 1862-1865.

ELIAS P. EASTIN, Civil War, Grand Army of the Republic, a private in Captain Thomas Boyatt's 30th Indiana Infantry Regiment of Volunteers. He enlisted September 1, 1861 and was bound for 3 years service or for the duration of the war.

He was discharged from service on January 5, 1865. Later he received his bounty pension. He was born in Jackson County and was listed as being 5 feet 10 inches tall with hazel eyes and auburn hair. He was enrolled as a farmer.

He was the great-grandfather of Pat Eastin Scott of Medora.

DANIEL EMPSON, Civil War, Company "A" - 50th Indiana Volunteer Infantry Regiment, 1861-1865, son of Azariah and Martha Holmes Empson, was born October 28, 1839. Later he volunteered for the military service and was assigned to the 50th Indiana Regiment. As a corporal, he was involved in the battle for the Green River Bridge, where the entire regiment was captured, taken prisoners and later paroled to fight again.

His regiment advanced to Memphis and then proceeded into Arkansas where it took part in the Red River Campaign. He led his platoon at the battle of Parker's Crossroads and the Salene River. At the close of the war, he returned home along the Muscatatuck River in Grassy Fork Township.

He married Sarah Jane Waskom, the daughter of Jacob and Mary Downing Waskom. They became parents of 9 children including a son named Marion who remained on the family farm. He married Cora Mounts and they became the parents of five children including Francis, Howard, Harold, Josephine and Dorothy Empson.

WILLIAM EMPSON, Private, Company "K" - 137th Infantry Regiment, Indiana Volunteers, 1864-1865, a brother to Daniel, matured around Vallonia as a farmer while continuing his education to become a teacher. He entered military service and was commanded briefly by Noah Weddle.

Upon his discharge William Empson moved to Missouri, but returned to Vallonia. He later was married to Elizabeth Studsman. One child was born to them before she died. William Empson was married again to Mary Copeland. They also became parents of six children.

FREDERICK ENES, Civil War, 82nd Regiment of Indiana Volunteers, July 21, 1862 - June 9, 1865, born in 1828 near the city of Manheim, located in what later became Germany, to parents who were fish mongers along the Rhine River. The entire family of Adam Enes emigrated from England after a one-month trip to Rotterdam from which they crossed the channel. Some weeks later they reached the battery at New York City in 1846. The family headed directly to Dearborn County, and

all but Frederick Enes made their home in the village of Sunman. The young man migrated to Brown County where he had purchased governmental land just released for sale.

Many years later in 1927 the compiler accompanied his parents to visit his maternal grandmother, Lucy Enes Walls. He learned she was a daughter of Frederick and Saloma Bergdoll Enes. But the young boy also learned that his great-grandfather was a veteran of the "Grand Army of the Republic" during the Civil War.

Many years later the military records of Frederick Enes were unraveled in a way which proved that soldier was really larger than life itself,. He survived battle after battle in his effort to defend his adopted country. Never once did he enjoy a furlough during his three years of service. There were no letters sent and none received, but his entire paycheck was all she had for substance.

Frederick Enes was a private in Company "H" of the 82nd Regiment of Indiana Volunteers and who became the grandfather of the compiler's mother. She married Loren S. Noblitt and they bore a son named after his father. The son retired, became an historian who produced many historical works on Jackson County and finally was able to appreciate the Civil War experiences of his great-grandfather, Frederick Enes.

ISAAC EVERHART, Civil War, 290684, Private, Company "F" - 18th Regiment, Ohio Infantry Volunteers, born on February 25, 1821 to Barnett and Rachel Everhart. By the time he was nearly 37 years old, he had enlisted in the military service of the Grand Army of the Republic. He was answering the call of President Abraham Lincoln.

His unit saw action at the Battle of Nashville, Tennessee which raged for two days on December 15th and 16th in 1864. The Ohio unit saw continuous action during the remainder of the Civil War. Private Isaac Everhart was mustered out of the service with the rest of his comrades on October 9, 1865.

JOHN FORDICE, Civil War, Grand Army of the Republic, born in Washington County January 1, 1834 and was raised in the local area around Salem. He mustered into the Union forces when visiting Iowa. He was assigned to Company "H" 46th Infantry Regiment of Iowa Volunteers.

He survived the war and, after he was mustered out of service, he moved back to Salem and married Harriet Huckleberry on April 28, 1868, Eventually, they moved to Jackson County and raised four children.

John Fordice died January 12, 1905 in Brownstown but was buried in Seymour.

SQUIRE WHITNEY GILBERT, Civil War, Company "G" - 24th Regiment Indiana Volunteers, 1862-1865. Resident of Medora who married Cali Day. Became parents of four children.

BENJAMIN FRANKLIN HARBAUGH, Civil War, Company A - 24th Regiment Indiana Volunteers, 1861-1864, born May 19, 1845 in Lawrence County as the son of Harrison and Eliza Oldham Harbaugh.

At the age of 15 years he volunteered for military service with the Grand Army of the Republic. He was assigned to Company "A" of the 24th Indiana Regiment of Volunteers and after three years of service, Private Harbaugh was discharged in 1864 at Baton Rouge, LA. Military records confirm he was then 18 years old, 5 feet 4 inches tall, was of fair complexion, had hazel eyes and dark hair. Those who knew him believed he lied about his age, but reportedly said he would have lied a thousand times to get out.

On July 5, 1866 he married Nancy Jane Hand and they moved to a 50-acre farm located just west of Freetown. They lived in a log cabin until 1890 when they moved into a two-story frame house. Their great-grandson, Steve Loper and his wife, Phyllis, currently live in that house. Benjamin and Nancy became parents of 12 children: Ida Tinch, Andy, Charles, Elmer, Walter and Ralph. Daughters included Lydia, Hettie, Pearly Bell, Daisy, Myrtle and Gaynell Lutes.

His rheumatism affected him when later and when he was older, he could walk only with two canes. He was drawing a military pension by then. Benjamin Franklin Harbaugh died July 8, 1927 and Nancy followed him on March 28, 1932. Both are buried in the Freetown Cemetery East. They are survived by 2 grandchildren. Nonna Harbaugh Rudolph of Freetown and Betty Lutes Empson of Greensburg, Indiana.

JOHN HOLLAND HAZZARD, Civil War, Grand Army of the Republic. He can trace his lineage from Orange, Orange County where his parents settled after leaving the central area of Delaware. They settled near Paoli and he left home when he was a teenager and came to Jackson County.

He enlisted in Company C of the 137th Regiment, Indiana Volunteers. It is not known which battles his unit was involved in, but military records confirm his discharge was dated December 15, 1864.

JOHN WESLEY HELLER, Civil War, Company H - 7th Battery Indiana Volunteers, born August 27, 1843 in Brownstown Township as the son of Frederick and Sophia Loux Heller who emigrated from one of the Germanic Provinces and settled in Jackson County. They were among the first German-speaking immigrants to settle in America. John Wesley Heller lived in the local area all of his life except for a few years when his father served as a German-Methodist minister in New Albany.

At the outbreak of the Civil War, he enlisted in the "Grand Army of the Republic" and served more

than three years. He was involved in many battles including Stone River, Chickamauga, the Atlanta campaign and others. He survived and was discharged at the end of the war.

He returned home and resumed farming, and in 1879 he began manufacturing brick and tile. He was married to Phoebe Doerr in October of 1865. Ten children were born to them. Six of them survived and lived into adulthood: Fred, Thornton, Victor, John W., Bertha and James. Later two of them became partners in the brick business. Several buildings in Brownstown were constructed with Heller bricks.

In 1903 John and Phoebe Heller moved into a new brick home located on Spring Street. He lived there until his death on April 3, 1907.

ITHAMER HENDERSHOT, Civil War, Company "F" - 1st Regiment Indiana Volunteers. Wounded and received pension. 1862-1864. Died in Brown County 1910.

CHARLES HODDING, Civil War, Company "D" - 81st Regiment Indiana Volunteers. Discharged as an old soldier, 1862-1865. Two sons enlisted - Alonzo: Company "D" - 33rd Regiment and David: Company "B" - 49th Regiment.

EDMOND HUBBARD, Civil War, Company B - 50th Regiment Indiana Volunteers, born in 1812 at Hawkins County, Tennessee, volunteered for bounty September 12, 1864 at Indianapolis, IN and was trained for several days at Camp Morton.

He was assigned to Company B of the 50th Regiment of Indiana Volunteers. He acknowledged he was a resident of Medora, IN. Records show he was not quite six feet tall, had blue eyes and was of dark complexion.

He was transferred to Company "A" as a private under Thomas Boyatt, Captain. He died in a field hospital located in Little Rock, AR on the 20th day of December 1864 of cholera. His father was John Hubbard who had settled at Little York. By 1849 he and his family were living in Owen Township with his wife, Nancy Lynch Hubbard. She was later buried in the cemetery at Wray's Church.

WILLIAM KING, Civil War, Grand Army of the Republic, 1837-1911, was a volunteer of the Indiana Infantry Regiment. He served as a Captain, was wounded and discharged. He re-enlisted again and served to the end of fighting at the surrender at Appomattox.

He was a great uncle of children born to the Marling family of Vernon Township in Jackson County, including Sara Marling Lucas who serves as a director of the historical society.

William King was a member of the George Thomas Post #17 comprised of veterans of the GAR. He died in 1911 at the age of 74 years.

LEVI KINWORTHY, Civil War, 1861-1865, Company "B" - 22nd Regiment Indiana Volunteers, Pea Ridge, Perryville, Stone River, Chattanooga. Wounded in action and discharged.

WILHELM LAMPERT, Civil War, Accepted Bounty to Substitute as Private, Grand Army of the Republic, born February 16, 1835, in Mutterstadt, Bavaria, Germany. He was the only son of Martin and Alberdina Weigerter Lampert (Lambert). Family research would indicate lineage to the noble family Lampert von Gerolzhofen from the Middle Ages. In April 1848, prior to departing for America, he was baptized at St. Paul Evangelical Church in Mutterstadt. He emigrated with his parents and three sisters, settling first in Lawrenceburg, Indiana. After a flood destroyed their home, they moved to higher ground in Milan in Ripley County. On June 18, 1855, in Lawrenceburg, Wilhelm Lampert married Kathrina Gardnerer, born in Forstfeld near Strassbourg, France, the daughter of Anton Gardnerer. Widower Anton Gardnerer, a riverboat captain on the Ohio River, married Wilhelm's sister, Margaret Lampert.

Martin and Wilhelm Lampert owned three farms in Spraytown. Sometime between 1863 and 1865, Wilhelm brought his family, along with his parents to the farm situated directly in Spraytown. They lived in a small log cabin, which still exists in 2004, At the age of 30, a rich man paid Lampert to substitute for his son who had been drafted into the Union Army. He left behind aging parents, a wife and five small children. The war ended before he was assigned a regiment. His grandchildren told that this was how he became independently wealthy. Although he never became a soldier, he received a veterans pension for symptoms of old age, and was on the Veterans Disability list in Jackson County.

Wilhelm and Kathrina Lampert had eleven children, with only six surviving to adulthood. Two daughters remained in Spraytown. Tena married George Daab, and Kate married Charlie Huber. On July 16, 1917, Wilhelm died at the home of his second wife, Caroline Mundt, in Waymansville. He is buried in the Spraytown Cemetery next to his first wife and his family. He was not given a Civil War tombstone.

DAVID CASS LEWIS, Civil War, Company "C" - 137th Regiment Indiana Volunteers, born in 1848 at Cortland in Hamilton Township of Jackson County. He was a son of James and Phoebe Wheeler Lewis. He enlisted in the Grand Army of the Republic and was assigned to Company C, 137th Regiment Indiana Volunteers. He was discharged August 7, 1864 after serving in campaigns through Tennessee and Alabama.

He returned home to his farm located one mile west of Acme where the railroad crossed Highway #258. He died at his home and was buried in a nearby cemetery. His grave is marked by a flat governmental stone.

BYFORD E. LONG, Civil War, Company E - 67th Regiment of Indiana Volunteers, Grand Army of the Republic

Brownstown, Indiana
September 12, 1865

I remember many patriotic deeds performed by my comrades-in-arms and there was no way I could ever forget the sufferings I and others endured. For their sake I am interested the records of 67th Regiment of Indiana Volunteers be compiled to verify the heroic episodes performed in our efforts to uphold the Union of the United States in the late epic struggle during the battles of the Rebellion!

Who could forget that our Regiment was captured twice by those misguided brothers-in-arms, and in both instances, our papers were destroyed. As a result, the records of our wartime experiences will forever be based on incomplete and inaccurate memories!

Those memories are all that we have left, but they remain in historical fact and they are worthy of understanding by those who answered the call to defend their home lands against the Rebel attack on their/our beloved government.

Respectfully dedicated to those who follow in our footsteps, and may they be able to face their future boldly!

Byford E. Long, Captain
Company E: 67th Regiment
Loyal Indiana Volunteers

67th Regiment – Indiana Volunteers reassigned to the 24th Regiment – Indiana Volunteers.

FREDRICH LONG, Civil War, Company H – 42nd Regiment Ohio Volunteers, German immigrant Fred Long first settled in Loudonville, Ashland County, Ohio. He joined the Union Army while living in Ohio. The organization of the 42nd Regiment in Columbus, Ohio, was completed in November of 1861, led by the Major General James A. Garfield, later to become the 20th President of the United States. In the fall of 1862 the Regiment served in Western Virginia. Throughout the war, the 42nd was attached to many different Brigades. In December 1862 it found part of Sherman's army in the unsuccessful attack on the Bluffs at Vicksburg. It followed with the capture of Arkansas Post. It fought in battles leading to the surrender of Vicksburg. The last campaign was in Louisiana Company "H" mustered out December 2, 1864

Sometime between 1864 and 1867, Fred moved west to Jackson County, Indiana. Several settlers of Spraytown had migrated from Loudonville, such as the Huber families. Fred Long married Mary Louisa Spray. They bought a 160 farm in Section 34 of Salt Creek Township, in the Spraytown community. The Longs had eight children, some of whom moved to Carmi, Illinois, with many families from Salt Greek Township *(see Salt Creek Colony of Little Egypt by James Smith).* Fred and Louise Long were listed as members of the Methodist faith by the circuit rider from Bedford who visited Spraytown and White Creek.

Fred Long applied for Civil War Pension on November 19, 1881. Application Number 67912.3, Certificate 504.322. Mary L. Long applied for Widows pension on December 5, 1924, Application 126.377, Certificate 956,827.

Fred Long died in the autumn of 1924, and is buried in the Spraytown Cemetery. Mary Louise Long died in 1927 and is buried by her husband. Their granddaughter, Mary Denny Jackson, and her grandson, Leeland Huff, lived in Spraytown at the time of the publication of this book.

HIRAM W. MARLING, Civil War, 82nd Infantry Regiment of Indiana Volunteers, Grand Army of the Republic, Hiram and his two sons, Walter and Spencer Marling, enlisted together and were assigned to the 82nd Infantry Regiment of Indiana Volunteers. One went into Company "G" and the other was in Company "B" of the same regiment.

Privates Walter Marling and Spencer Marling were both killed in action during the Battle of Perryville in Kentucky. Their bodies later shipped home and placed on the porch until burial could be arranged.

URIAH MASSENA, Civil War, Grand Army of the Republic, born to Samuel and Barbara Kramer Massena December 8, 1842 in Pennsylvania. His father was a soldier who fought under Garibaldi in France. Records show he enlisted in Company "K" of the Pennsylvania Regiment of Volunteer Infantrymen.

His unit was assigned to General Sherman's army which moved through Georgia. He was among those troops which served more than three years and present at the end of fighting. He moved to Scott County, Indiana and married Nancy Jane Madden on September 8, 1866. Most of their children were born in Scott County, but later the family moved into Lawrence County.

Several years later they settled in Jackson County on a farm located near Medora where records indicate he was the father of ten children. One of the children became a teacher and married Ralph Goss, also a teacher.

FREDERICK MENGLER, Civil War, Company B - 82nd Regiment Indiana Volunteers. At the age of 21, Fred Mengler enlisted in the Union Army. In the official records, he is listed as Frederick Mauler. In the early years after his immigration, he spoke only Platte Deutsche and wrote in the old German script. Perhaps this is the reason his records are under the name Mauler. Records indicate that he was a resident of Jonesville in Bartholomew County when he enlisted. After the war, he settled in Jackson County, marrying a girl from the Borchers area.

Fred Mengler was mustered in on August 30, 1862, with men from Brownstown, Seymour, Crothersville, Dudleytown, and Scipio. This group of men, with only Mengler being from Jonesville, formed Company B of the 82nd Regiment. Their first assignment was in Perryville, Tennessee. Then came the battles of Murfeesboro, and Stones's River. But it was the battle of Chickamauga at Chattanooga that disabled him with a chest wound on September 20, 1863. It was not until June 9, 1865 that Mengler mustered out.

On March 20, 1878, Fred Mengler applied for Civil War Pension. Service: Company B, 82nd Indiana Infantry, Application No 251.299, Certificate 229.140. His widow Sophia applied for widow benefits on March 21, 1917, Application 1096.779, Certificate No. 840.247, State of Indiana.

After his time in the Civil War, German immigrant Mengler returned to the Borchers/White Creek area. In 1867 Mengler married Sophia Vorderhacke. When the 1870 Census was taken, Fred Mengler and family owned a tiny piece of property 1/2 mile north of Spraytown, which is now Pershing Township, Jackson County. In 1871 Mengler became a charter member of the Waymansville German Lutheran Church. In 1877, they buried an infant son at Borchers, During their married life, they moved between Borchers, Spraytown, Waymansville, White Creek, finally purchasing a farm one mile west of Jonesville. At the time of his death he was a member of the St. Paul's Lutheran Church at Jonesville, His great-granddaughter is Mildred Price Daab of Spraytown.

PVT. WILLIAM NOBLITT, Civil War Military Roll of Honor, 1861-1862, Eighth Cavalry – 39th Regiment Indiana Volunteers. The 39th Regiment of Indiana Volunteers was organized as an infantry unit at Indianapolis on August 29, 1861. On September 23, 1862 the men left the capital and headed south toward Louisville. After encamping at Muldraugh's Hill near Elizabethtown, they drew equipment at Camp Hefren, located just across White River near Shields Dam.

Marching on to the top of Crane Hill, they ate their evening meal in Brownstown. The next stops were at Nolin Creek and Camp Wood on the Green River. It was there where they were assigned to Buell's army in Nashville.

Following the Battle of Shiloh on April 7, 1862, where he was wounded, he became ill with influenza and was placed on medical leave and ordered to go home to Jonesville. He reached Evansville, IN where he died on May 16, 1862. William Noblitt was buried there in the military section of Oak Hill Cemetery.

JAMES PHILIPPS, Civil War, Company "E" – 93rd Regiment, Indiana Volunteers, enlisted into the Federal Army January 2, 1864 at Columbus, Indiana by Button Cody. He was mustered into the service a few days later in Indianapolis. This 19 year-old lad from Brown County was the son of George and Joann Berry Phillips.

He was in combat from January 1864 through April before he became ill and was ordered to go home on sick leave. By October of 1864 he was back on duty with his unit. Two months later he was captured at East Fork, Tennessee and confined in Andersonville Prison in Georgia. He was finally paroled April 28, 1865 and reported to Camp Chase May 20, 1865. He was mustered out of the service with his unit on June 16, 1865.

He married Sarah Jane Beabout, a daughter of Israel and Lucinda Jordan Beabout in 1877 while living in Brown County. The family moved to Medora in 1899 where they became parents of six children: Wiley Richard, Matilda Alice, James Bluford, Marinda Margaret (Rena), Benjamin H. and Henry Herschell. Death hit two children who were buried in Beem Cemetery.

JESSE MERLIN RYAN, Civil War, 1861-1865, born in Brown County March 25, 1846. He was the son of Alexander and Martha Shipley Ryan. Much later Jesse was first married to Sarah Newton and later in life he was married to Margaret Goble on February 12, 1874 in Jackson County. He was the father of four children, including one son, and he was also the stepfather of two daughters. Jesse Ryan lived in and around Houston and Maumee in Jackson County during most of his life.

He enlisted in the Indiana Volunteers during the Civil War and left for duty August 26, 1864. Promoted to the rank of Corporal in Company "H" of the 50th Regiment, he was among those captured January 20, 1865 while stationed near Clarksville, Arkansas. He and that group of prisoners were forced to march during freezing weather all the way to Camp Ford in Tyler, Texas.

During that forced march he became ill and developed an infection in his eyes which would bother him during the remainder of his life. Finally, on May 27, 1865 he was paroled at the mouth of the Red River in Louisiana. He was later discharged late in the afternoon on September 10, 1865.

He was later granted a pension of $8.00 per month in 1877 for the damage to his eyes. Jesse Ryan died at the age of 79 years and is buried at the Gorbetts Chapel Cemetery located in the Houston area.

JOAB SCOTT, Civil War, Grand Army of the Republic, enlisted in the Indiana Volunteers and records show he reported for duty in Indianapolis October 20, 1864 for one year of service. He was assigned to Company "K" of the 140th Regiment of Indiana Infantry Volunteers. One of the other recruits serving with him was none other than William Reno, later to become one of the gang members hung in the New Albany Jail.

Joab was born in Washington County in 1829; he was 35 years when he went into the army. He was also married to Isabel Gray and they became parents of eleven children, one of whom later married Charles Oliver Baughman.

Joab Scott was discharged October 22, 1865.

HENRY J. SMITH, Civil War, Grand Army of the Republic, born June 6, 1842 in Clark County to William and Sarah Wiseman Smith. He followed in his father's footsteps working in a sawmill located not far from Clarksville during most of 1858. He enlisted in Company "D" of Indiana Regiment of Infantrymen. He reported for duty October 22, 1861.

He was wounded and discharged in 1864 but re-enlisted the following day and assigned to Company "D" of Indiana Regiment of Infantrymen. He was with his unit throughout the war and was discharged as 1st Sergeant on September 13, 1865.

He returned to the Clarksville area and to his sawmill. Two years later he moved his family to Austin but remained only a short time. Then he settled in Jackson County on a farm located near Chestnut Ridge in Vernon Township. In 1880 the family moved to Seymour. Just one year later, on September 1, 1881, he exclaimed that President Garfield had died. It seems that was some kind of premonition and it became part of the folklore passed down through his father and to his grandson, Howard Smith of Medora, Indiana.

He was the father of eight children.

ISAAC STALKER SMITH, Civil War, Grand Army of the Republic, born in Freetown to Saluel and Mary Ann Hilda Wheeler Smith. He was raised in and around the rural area in the northwest region of Jackson County, Indiana.

When the war between the states broke out, Isaac Staulker Smith enlisted in the Grand Army of the Republic. He was assigned to Company H of the Indiana Volunteers. He was wounded with a bullet imbedded in his shoulder, and it could not be extracted so he remained in the hospital for many weeks.

After the war was over, he returned to Freetown and was married to Cordelia Laughum and they became parents of one son. Cordelia died in 1870 and he returned to marry Hannah Spurgeon. He was also a teacher and an assessor. He owned a lumber mill and flour mill and became the president of Freetown State Bank.

While serving as a trustee of his church, he died in 1924. Several of his descendants have survived and are living in Jackson County.

COLONEL GORDON TANNER, Commander, 22nd Regiment, Indiana Volunteers, Company "B", an attorney practicing law in Jackson County with his nephew, Thomas Tanner, left Brownstown charged with recruiting men to form Company B of the 22nd Regiment of Indiana Volunteers. His company completed its organization July 8, 1861. Tanner then led his men to Camp Noble at Madison to draw uniforms and supplies. One month later on August 16, 1861 his men were mustered into federal service at Camp Morton in Indianapolis.

The military command of the 22nd Regiment was assigned to Colonel Jeff C. Davis. Company B was headed by relatives, Gordon, Thomas and John Tanner. Their cousin George Tanner rode south and became a scout for General John Hunt Morgan. On August 17, 1861 the Regiment of 1,041 Jackson County volunteers boarded a train bound for St. Louis where they were assigned to General John C. Fremont. After crossing the river they headed west toward Glasgow, Missouri.

By August 26, 1861 the 22nd Regiment had a new commander, John Hendricks. They were charged to repulse the expected attack at Boonville. Major Gordon Tanner did attack the supply depot. Five companies advanced along the river, halted to close ranks and were met by a Rebel volley. Gordon Tanner was hit but did not die right away. He was later carried from the field by litter and taken to the boat, transferred to a wagon and hauled overland to the hospital at Jefferson City.

Gordon Tanner died October 4, 1861 and his remains were shipped back to Indianapolis where he was buried with full military fanfare. To honor his memory, the blue-coated men later organized the Brownstown Post of the Grand Army of the Republic. The cornerstone is on display at the museum building of the Jackson County Historical Society

JOSHUA WEEKLY, Civil War, Company "H" – 50th Regiment, Indiana Volunteers, born February 28, 1842 in Monroe County, Ohio as the oldest child of Thomas and Nancy Morris Weekly. When he was 10 years old his family moved to the Salt Creek area in Jackson County.

On August 19, 1862 he volunteered for service with Company "H" – 50th Regiment of Indiana Volunteers. Most of the men were from Houston. Mustered into service September 4, 1862 at Louisville, he was taken prisoner during the Battle of Munfordsville, KY. He was returned to Indianapolis, then home where he contracted measles. His illness was so strong that he was later stricken with lung disease and disability.

Joshua Weekly was discharged as a private June 4, 1865 and He returned home where he married Margaret Williams. They became parents to 10 children and all of them were products of Jackson County.

Joshua Weekly died January 18, 1916 at the home of his daughter, Hattie Hamilton. He was laid to rest at Taylor's Chapel located in Jackson and was buried with members of her family.

ELIHU MARION WELLS, 27th Regiment, Indiana Volunteers, a life-long resident of Jackson County, was born and reared in Jackson County. He was the son of Benjamin and Fannie Wells of Brownstown Township.

Elihu Wells enlisted in the "Grand Army of the Republic" in July 1861 He was assigned to the 27th Regiment of Indiana Volunteers and served four years defending the federal government. He was mustered out on April 12, 1865.

He returned to the Brownstown area and became a financial investor in stocks, bonds and real estate. Upon his death in 1928 Elihu Wells left more than $10,000 to the Indiana Baptist Convention in Indianapolis.

He was one of four Civil War veterans of the Union Army still living in Brownstown at the time. Included among his comrades-in-arms were Larken Kennedy, Alan Vanover, Marion Hatton and George Carter. But unknown to them and most other county residents was one Confederate veteran also living, Sgt. Walter Prather had fought as a scout for Capt. Hines and General John Hunt Morgan during the infamous raid through Jackson County in 1863. He outlived Wells by more than a dozen years and died December 7, 1941 at the Soldiers Home in Indianapolis.

ALFRED D. WILLIAMS, Civil War, Company H – 120th Regiment, Indiana Volunteers, born in Belmont County, OH in 1845 and later enlisted in the "Grand Army of the Republic" at Columbus, IN. He was assigned to drive supply wagons between military regiments on the move. Records show he donned his uniform in Indianapolis and was mustered out January 8, 1866 at Raleigh, NC.

After the war he returned home to the Spraytown area of Jackson County and continued farming the family land. He died July 26, 1917 and was buried in the White Cemetery. He has a large monument marking his gravesite.

GEORGE WILLIAMS, Civil War, Company H - 50th Regiment, Indiana Volunteers, born in 1817 to George and Sarah Williams then living in Belmont County, OH. They moved to the Spraytown area with their six children. Two more children were born in Indiana. George was 44 years old when he enlisted in Company H, 50th Regiment of Indiana Volunteers on December 1, 1961. He was discharged about one year later on November 25, 1862 after being wounded while on duty at the Green River Bridge in Kentucky

Years later on a hot sunny day while sitting on his front porch in Spraytown, someone told a story about George's military service. His unit had advanced to the Green River Bridge in Kentucky and was ordered to build a pontoon crossing. Before it was completed a scout brought word the Confederates were coming. The bridge was dismantled but George Williams was injured when they blew the bridge up but he was also shot. He couldn't be moved so was left hidden in the wreckage.

Several days later he saw a black lady come to wash her clothes in the river so George called out for help. Of course, she hid him in the loft of her cabin on a pallet of straw but he was always lying down. When he was well and able to rejoin his unit, he was never quite able to stand erect. Nor was he able to farm his land once the war was over.

George Williams died December 15, 1895 and was buried at the Taylor Chapel Cemetery.

WILLIAM ZIKE, Civil War, Grand Army of the Republic, born in Jessemine County, KY in 1840. Moved with his family into Jackson County. Enlisted in the army May 1, 1864 at Medora. Assigned to Company C, 137th Regiment, Indiana Volunteers and served faithfully until discharged September 21, 1864.

Captain Fielder A. Jones Commander

Lt. Stephen Storey

Frank Johnson
Gabriel Woodmansee
John Stockdell

Lt. Calvin Trumbo

Simeon Smith
Charles Lewis
Jacob Mitchell

with other enlisted men - August 21, 1861.
Alexander Gardner, Photographer

The
SPAINISH - AMERICAN WAR
APRIL 21, 1898 - DECEMBER 10, 1898

The Spanish-American War, which broke out toward the close of the 19th century, marked the emergence of the United States as a world military power. The conflict between the United States and Spain erupted over the issue of human rights supporting Cuban liberation from the despotic control exercised by the mother country. In 1895 revolution broke out during the depression in Cuba and the Spanish forces were unable to control the rebelling Cubans. Insurrection threatened to go on endlessly until the American newspapers printed sensational and exaggerated accounts of Spanish oppression.

It was then that President McKinley pressured Spain to grant the Cubans some form of limited self-government. Since neither the rebelling Cubans nor the Spanish overlords could end the unrest, the idea of colonial self-government seemed the best way of resolving the strife so close to the United States.

To protect Americans from the Cuban havoc, the battleship *Maine* dispatched to the Havana harbor on January 15, 1898. Two weeks later an explosion sunk the ship right there in the harbor and killed 250 American citizens on board.

Immediately *Remember the Maine* became the only slogan of the times and actually brought on the conflict. War was declared April 21, 1898.

Governor James A. Mount called for volunteers to form four regiments from the state militia to meet the Indiana quota of 7,420 men. Not one Hoosier was killed in action!

Battles were fought in several places, and finally the terms of the Treaty of Paris were signed on December 10, 1898.

William M. Tuell
Spanish -American War
February 12, 1897 - July 10, 1898
Date of photo: March 23, 1897

REMEMBER THE MAINE

JACKSON COUNTY COURT HOUSE
BROWNSTOWN

**6TH REGIMENT BAND
MARCHING TO FAIRVIEW CEMETERY
MAY 29, 1898**

JESSE "POP" JACKSON

Spanish-American War
46th Regiment – 28th Infantry Division
Philippines and Guam
1899 - 1906

MAY DAY GATHERING TO HONOR
THE
VETERANS OF THE SPANISH-AMERICAN WAR

COURTHOUSE YARD IN BROWNSTOWN
May 29, 1898

Front Row, L-R: Ollie Burrell, James Clements, John Laughlin, Peter Heller, Chas. F. Robertson, Chas. T. Benton, Ray Vermilya, O.R. Emerson, Wm. Gossman, Chas. Clark, Frank Falk, John Stotz. Middle Row, L-R: James Kent, Dr. Cummings Sr., Asa Reinhardt, Elmer Shepard, Wm. Wacker, Wm. Schwein, Frank Kerner, Oscar Allen, Andy Brodhecker, Thornt Heller. Top Row, L-R: John Branaman, D.A. Kochenour, Chas. Schwartz, Arthur Benton, Shannon Gray, Major Long, Jackie Waskom, J. Hamilton, James Henderson, John B. Burrell, Dr. S.W Shields, Henry Scott

JACKSON COUNTY VOLUNTEERS

IN THE
SPANISH-AMERICAN WAR
1898-1899

Jackson County organized the first volunteer company in Indiana at Brownstown on December 31, 1897. Company G was mustered into active duty April 26, 1898, and assigned to the 159th Regiment. Company G was mustered out on November 23, 1898.

Note: The list of Jackson County men who served in the Spanish-American War was compiled by the author from: Record of Indiana Volunteers in the Spanish-American War 1898-1899; issued by authority of the Sixty-First General Assembly of Indiana; 1900.

Company G

Captain
Applewhite, Ralph B.　　Brownstown

First Lieutenant
Branaman, John　　Brownstown

Second Lieutenant
Heller, Thornton　　Brownstown

First Sergeant
Hall, William A.　　Brownstown

Sergeants
Russell, William B.　　Seymour
Boyatt, Edward　　Brownstown
Gossman, John L.　　Brownstown
Hackendorf, Frank　　Brownstown

Corporals
Thomas, William　　Crothersville
Sewell, Sylvester　　Brownstown
Lubker, Percy　　Brownstown
Converse, George　　Brownstown
Richards, Polk　　Vallonia

Musicians
Easum, Claude L.　　Crothersville
Nelson, Ira A.　　Crothersville

Artificer
Murray, Edward B.　　Brownstown

Wagoner
Miller, David J.　　Brownstown

Privates
Adams, Ernest　　Crothersville
Agan, John R.　　Crothersville
Bantz, Asbury　　Crothersville
Bedel, John A.　　Crothersville
Bevers, John　　Mooney
Bond, Charles A.　　Columbus
Boyatt, Everette E.　　Brownstown
Briner, Edmond P.　　Brownstown
Brown, Morton　　Mooney
Browning, Earl　　Brownstown
Chappell, Arthur　　Crothersville
Chappell, Ennis　　Crothersville
Coombs, Edward　　Brownstown
Cochrum, Mathias　　Brownstown
Burkhalter, Abe　　Brownstown

Collins, David F.　　Crothersville
Easum, Clyde　　Haughville
Erwin, Ralph　　Brownstown
Goss, Bruce　　Brownstown
Goss, Everett　　Brownstown
Hegwood, Carl　　Clear Springs
Ireland, William　　Brownstown
Jenkins, Alfred　　Brownstown
Lewis, Shelby　　Crothersville
Mahurin, George W.　　Brownstown
Mellencamp, Charles　　Tampico
Moreland, Moses　　Brownstown
Moore, Arthur O.　　Crothersville
Nelson, Albert J.　　Crothersville
Payne, William　　Brownstown
Robbins, George　　Brownstown
Robinson, Clarence　　Tampico
Sanders, Gilbert　　Brownstown
Thompson, Hugh　　Crothersville
Weir, Robert M.　　Crothersville
Wray, Samuel　　Eclipse
Young, Claude　　Seymour
Young, Leslie　　Crothersville

Recruits
Adam, Charles　　Crothersville
Bevers, Isaac J.　　Medora
Benton, James H.　　Brownstown
Beavers, Elmer　　Goss Mill
Borden, Charles R.　　Vallonia
Brown, Rutherford B.　　Goss Mill
Cartwright, Louis A.　　Brownstown
Downing, Ralph V.　　Tampico
Durham, Charles B.　　Brownstown
Emmons, Cyrus　　Goss Mill
Gossman, George　　Brownstown
Gossman, Wacker　　Vallonia
Hegwood, Olin L.　　Mooney
Kindred, Thomas　　Kurtz
Martin, George W.　　Mooney
McCaslin, Murray　　Crothersville
Pruett, Thomas V.　　Houston
Ratcliff, James B.　　Ewing
Ryker, Herbert V.　　Vallonia
Scifres, George M.　　Tampico
Scott, Thomas L.　　Goss Mill
Stotz, Frank E.　　Brownstown
Trowbridge, Leonard　　Vallonia
Tabor, Jesse　　Ewing
Wilson, Willard　　Ewing
Wilson, John A.　　Brownstown

Note: No man from Jackson County was killed in the Spanish-American War. This fact was verified by the Office of Adjutant General of Indiana and by the author's research of Indiana Volunteers in the Spanish-American War, 1898-1899; Indiana Archives, Indianapolis.

161st Regiment, Indiana Volunteers

This regiment was a volunteer regiment organized for the Spanish-American War from Indiana. One Jackson County soldier served as an assistant surgeon with the staff officers and several Jackson County men served in Companies D and K of the Regiment. Most of this Regiment was mustered in on June 28, 1898.

Assistant Surgeon

Gerrish, Millard F.	Seymour

Company D
Sergeants

Carter, Everett	Seymour

Corporals

Groub, John C.	Seymour

Privates
Blue, Arthur	Seymour
Henderson, Charles C.	Seymour
Henderson, Arthur	Seymour
Hill, William	Seymour
Jackson, Matthew	Seymour
Prather, John K.	Seymour
Riley, David	Reddington
Robinson, Riley	Seymour
Scanlan, Charles J.	Seymour
Welch, Homer M.	Seymour
Wray, Millard	Clearspring

Company K
Privates
Skinner, Elihu M.	Brownstown
Turner, Joseph	Medora

(Most of the men in the 161st Regiment were mustered out April 30, 1899.)

EARL BROWNING, Spanish-American War, United States Army, born April 4, 1880 to Frank and Emma Cummings Browsning of Brownstown. His home was located across the street from Dr. Jack Shields. When he was just 18 years old he joined his father and they both enlisted in the army. He was assigned as a private to Company "G" of the 159th Indiana Regiment.

He was discharged November 23, 1898, but he re-enlisted six months later on July 19, 1899 and was assigned to Company "F" of the 21st Indiana Regiment. He was among those who reached the Philippines and was engaged in the fighting.

He was discharged June 18, 1901. He returned home and was married to Mary Sage Burrell and they became parents of two children, Jessie and Malcolm.

FRANK BROWNING, Spanish-American War, United States Army, born March 18, 1857 near Ratcliff Grove to Jesse and Caroline Richards Browning. He was inducted into the army on April 26, 1898 along with his 18 year-old son, Earl Browning. Both were sent to Camp Alger and then to Manassis Junction where they existed in pup tents.

After two months in camp he was ordered to Camp Meade, PA and just two months later he was discharged. He re-enlisted and was assigned to the 3rd Infantry on January 6, 1899 ready to set sail.

Weathering a severe storm in the Atlantic everyone was ordered below and there were 2,000 scared men. The storm passed and the ship continued through the strait of Gibraltar and into the Mediterranean Sea on to Port Said, Egypt. Someone fell overboard and all attempts to save him failed. Many days later the ship stopped at Colombo for several hours before proceeding on the Manila Bay.

Twelve of his comrades were killed and 40 others wounded on the first battle, but they captured a host of little towns with little resistance. He became sick for several months before being returned to the states.

Back in Brownstown after discharge, he was soon married to Emma Cummings and they became parents of four children. He became one of the ministers and a mail carrier in Jackson County.

ROBERT (BUD) EMPSON, Spanish-American and World War I, United States Navy, 1900-1918, born November 12, 1879 as one of several sons of Daniel and Sarah Jane Waskom Empson. Some thirty-five years after his father was discharged from his military service during the Civil War, Robert followed in the family footsteps and enlisted in the United States Navy in 1900. He served two months in the Spanish-American War.

The records are incomplete, but they seem to show he remained in the Navy throughout World War I. He was granted his honorable discharge at Fort Sheridan in Wyoming in December 1918. He reached Vallonia just before his birthday in 1919. He was present and stood at respectful attention during the Armistice Day ceremony held at the Fairview Cemetery in Brownstown on November 12, 1919.

Robert (Bud) Empson married Ella Mae Miller and they became the parents of twin sons, Robert and Roger. Their daughter, Edith Jane Empson, later married Howard D. Nichols. Robert (Bud) Empson died August 23, 1968.

THORTON POSEY HELLER, Spanish-American War, Company G – 159th Regiment, Indiana Volunteers, was named after his father's Civil War buddy and was born in Brownstown on January 7, 1874, the son of John Wesley and Phoebe Doerr Heller. When John returned home from the Civil War, he farmed and started making bricks on his farm. Thornton and his brother Victor, became partners in the firm which became known as "John W. Heller and Sons."

The Spanish-American War was declared on April 25, 1898 and was of short duration. Thornton Heller volunteered and served as a Lieutenant along with fellow officers, Captain Applewhite and Lt. John Branaman. All were from Brownstown and each awaited the end of hostilities which was announced in December 1898. Thornton Heller came home and married Ethel May Perry July 10, 1902. They became parents of five children: Vivian, John, George, Bernice and Lena.

In 1906 the Jackson Brick and Hollow Ware Company was organized under the ownership of Thornton P. Heller, Jonathon Robertson, Joe Robertson and Thorton's brother, John W. Heller, Jr. The factory was built close to the B/O Railroad tracks and active operations commenced in 1907. Thornton Heller built his home close by and the family lived there for fifteen years. He later purchased the home of his father located on Spring Street in Brownstown and that is where he died August 9, 1950.

CORPORAL JESSE A. JACKSON, Spanish-American War, Company E - Indiana Infantry, Jesse Jackson was born March 15, 1882 in Franklin County, six miles east of Brookville. His parents were Joseph W. and Nancy Jane Aston Jackson. On September 28, 1908 in Connersville, he married Lessie Pearl Brewer. At the time of Lessie's death in 1981, they had been married 74 years.

At the age of 16, he had a "falling-out" with his father and stepmother. He forged his father's name and joined the Army. He took his basic training in Minneapolis. When the Spanish were accused of destroying the battleship *Maine,* he received orders for Cuba. However, Teddy Roosevelt settled that conflict, and he was sent to Laredo, Texas, on border patrol. The reason was because the Mexicans were stealing goats. It was there that he marched 225 miles across desert and where he shot a 9-foot rattlesnake. He told that in 1905, Laredo was the toughest town he had ever seen; everyone carried a gun. Jesse also served in the Philippines. It was here that he fired at a running enemy, but missed. None the less, Jesse proudly displayed his marksman Medal.

After Jackson left the Army, he had many different jobs throughout his long life. He ran a threshing machine, worked as a farmer, mechanic, bar keeper, storekeeper, policeman, barber, wallpaper hanger, and lathe operator, to name a few.

Jesse and Lessie moved to Spraytown in 1922. They had three children: Ralph, Helen, and Jesslee. Jesslee was a veteran of WWII, and was wounded in the Battle of the Bulge.

When Jesse died on June 2, 1987, at the age of 105, he was Indiana's last veteran of the Spanish-American War. He is buried beside Lessie and his children in the Spraytown Cemetery.

PERCY D. LUBKER, United States Army, Spanish-American War, Company G - 159th Regiment Indiana Volunteers, son of David H. and Liyyie Lubker, was born near Brownstown in 1776. At the outbreak of the Spanish-American War he enlisted to help fill the ranks of new units being raised to meet the call issued by the Governor. His was the first such unit to be formed in the state of Indiana.

He served as a corporal in the original of volunteers who were mostly from the Brownstown area. He received his honorable discharge at the time of his mustering out of service in 1898.

He was married to Laura B. Robison in Brownstown April 2, 1905 and for several years he owned and operated a hotel in Brownstown. It was sold just before his death in 1911.

WORLD WAR I
1917-1918
IN MEMORIAM
JACKSON COUNTY VETERANS

RALPH TIDWELL
MAY 29, 1994

WORLD WAR I
JACKSON COUNTY MILITARY RECORDS
1914-1918

GOLD STAR HONOR ROLL

AKERS, STANLEY GARLAND, Private, son of George and Pearl Akers, born September 17, 1897, Freetown, Jackson County, IN. Farmer. Entered service September 6, 1918, Brownstown, Indiana. Sent to Camp Taylor, KY; assigned to Battery C, 70th Field Artillery. While home on furlough, he died from gun shot wounds, received from his own gun while hunting, October 17, 1918. Buried in Wegan Cemetery near Brownstown, IN.

ALLMAN, FRED, Private, son of Phillip and Sarah Allman; born May 16, 1891, Hamilton Township, Jackson County, IN. Farmer. Entered service June 26, 1918, Brownstown, IN. Sent to Camp Sherman, OH; assigned to 17th Company, 5th Training Battalion, 158th Depot Brigade. Transferred to Company E, 334th Infantry. Overseas in August, 1918. Died of pneumonia October 16, 1918, "in France." Survived by widow, Flossi Allman, and one son, Clarence Allman, Surprise, Jackson County, IN.

ARBUCKLE, WALTER, Private, son of Joseph E. and Carrie E. Arbuckle; born September 22, 1898, Scott County, IN. Moved to Jackson County in 1901. Contractor. Enlisted in Company K, 2nd Infantry, Indiana National Guard (152nd Infantry) July 20, 1917, Seymour, IN. Sent to Camp Shelby, MS. Overseas in June, 1918; assigned to Company K, 4th Infantry, 3rd Division. Killed in action July 25, 1918, battle of Chateau-Thierry. Buried in American Cemetery No. 608, Seringes-et-Nesles, France.

BREWER, FRANCIS MARVIN, Private, Son of C.W. (deceased) and Martha Brewer (Johnson); born February 28, 1897, Vallonia, Jackson County, IN. Farmer. Entered service January 30, 1918, Brownstown IN. Sent to Ft. Harrison, IN; then to Columbus Barracks, Ohio, and later to Ft. Oglethorpe, GA. Assigned to the 20th Company Engineers. Died in Walter Reed Hospital, Washington, D.C., July 17, 1918, following an operation for tumor. Buried in Vallonia Cemetery, Jackson County, IN.

BURBRINK, FRANK W., Private, son of Henry and Elizabeth Burbrink, born January 23, 1893, Seymour, IN. Farmer. Entered service August 26, 1918, Brownstown, IN. Sent to Camp Custer, MI; assigned to 3rd Company, 1st Training Battalion, 160th Depot Brigade. Transferred to Company G, 14th Ammunition Train. Died of pneumonia October 5, 1918, Camp Custer, MI. Buried at Jonesville, Jackson County, IN. Survived by widow, Alvina Burbrink, Seymour, IN.

CASEBOLDT, ROBERT SANFORD, Private, son of Sanford (deceased) and Mary Caseboldt (Hankins), born June 3, 1892, Medora, Jackson County, IN. Farmer. Enlisted in Company K, 2nd Infantry, Indiana National Guard (152nd Infantry), July 12, 1917, Seymour, IN. Sent to Camp Shelby, MS; assigned to Company M, 168th Infantry. Overseas in June, 1918. Killed in action September 12, 1918, St. Mihiel, France. Buried in St. Mihiel-American Cemetery, No. 1233, France.

COBB, HENRY ELKANAH, Cadet Aviator, son of John J. and Ella O. Cobb, born June 29, 1889, Seymour, IN. Educated in Purdue University, and at the time of his enlistment, he was supervisor of Manual Training in the Public Schools of Elgin, IL. Entered Military School for Aeronautics, Cornell University, November 8, 1917. Graduated February 16, 1918. Sent to Ellington Field, TX, where he died of pneumonia, April 23, 1918. Buried in Riverview Cemetery, Seymour, IN.

FOUNTAIN, VIRGIL, Private, son of William and Mary Fountain, born June 28, 1889, Jackson County, IN. Mail carrier. Entered service May 26, 1918, Brownstown, IN. Sent to Camp Taylor, KY; assigned to 28th Company, 7th Training Battalion, 159th Depot Brigade. Transferred to Camp Forrest, GA; assigned to Headquarters Detachment, 605th Engineers. Died of pneumonia October 10, 1918, on board the *George Washington*. Buried in Commune of Finistere, France.

GOSSMAN, VANCE HAROLD, Private, son of Charles W. and Carrie N. Gossman, born December 2, 1892, Vallonia, Jackson County, IN. Insurance agent. Entered service June 23, 1918, Indianapolis. Sent to Camp Sherman, Ohio; assigned to 5th Company, 2nd Training Battalion, 158th Depot Brigade. Embarked for overseas September 29, 1918; assigned to Company A, 309th Supply Train. Returned to U.S. in June, 1919; assigned to Base Hospital No. 25, Ft. Benjamin Harrison, IN, where he died August 28, 1919. Buried at Vallonia, IN.

GRAVES, MICHAEL CHARLES, Fireman, USN, son of Orlando C. and Elizabeth Farrell Graves (deceased); born January 19, 1898, Seymour, IN. Employee of Public Service Company, Seymour, IN. Enlisted in U.S. Navy, Louisville, KY in June 1917; assigned to fireman on the battleship *Iowa.* Died of pneumonia on board hospital ship *Solace,* October 10, 1918. Buried in Catholic Cemetery, Seymour, IN.

HACKMAN, HUBERT, Private, son of William F. and Emma Hackman, born February 23, 1895, near Tampico, Jackson County, IN. Farmer. Entered service August 8, 1918, Brownstown, IN. Sent to Camp Sheridan, AL for training; assigned to Machine Gun Company, 26th Infantry. Died of pneumonia October 28, 1918, Camp Sheridan. Buried in Sauers Cemetery, Jackson County, IN.

HAGAN, MARTIN A., Private, son of Charles and Minnie Otte Hagan, born October 18, 1891, Grassy Fork Township, Jackson County, IN. Farmer. Entered service July 22, 1918, Brownstown, IN. Sent to Camp Taylor, KY; assigned to 26th Company, 7th Training Battalion, 159th Depot Brigade. Transferred to Camp McClellan, AL; assigned to Headquarters Company, 35th Field Artillery. Died of pneumonia October 25, 1918, Camp McClellan. Buried in Wegan Lutheran Cemetery, near Brownstown, IN.

HARTWELL, CHESTER A., Private, son of James A. and Sarah E. Hartwell, born June 27, 1893, Seymour, IN. Farmer. Entered service October 13, 1917, Brownstown, IN. Sent to Camp Funston, KS; then to Ft. Sill, OK; assigned to Company L, 138th Infantry, 35th Division. Embarked for overseas June 19, 1918, from Camp Mills, L.I. Killed in action July 11, 1918. (Battle not known).

HUCKLEBERRY, LEBERT, Private, son of Anderson and Martha Huckleberry, born March 2, 1893, Washington County, IN. Moved to Jackson County in March 1903. Farmer. Entered service July 22, 1918, Brownstown, IN. Sent to Camp Taylor, KY, assigned to 2nd Company, 1st Development Battalion. Died of pneumonia October 9, 1918, Base Hospital, Camp Taylor. Buried in Monteden, Grave No. 8, Post Cemetery, Camp Taylor, KY.

MYERS, WILLIAM JOSEPH, Private, son of John E. and Katherine M. Myers, born June 1, 1897, Seymour, Jackson County, IN. Employed in Baltimore and Ohio Railway Office, Seymour. Entered service September 5, 1918, Indianapolis, IN. Sent to Arsenal Technical School, Indianapolis; assigned to Signal Corps. Died of pneumonia October 12, 1918, Indianapolis. Buried in Riverview Cemetery, Seymour. Jackson County, IN.

PRUDEN, JAMES HAROLD, Private, son of George and Minnie Broadaker Pruden, born November 5, 1890, Cortland, Jackson County, IN. Farmer. Entered service June 8, 1918, Brownstown, IN. Sent to Camp Taylor, KY; assigned to 28th Company, 7th Training Battalion, 159th Depot Brigade. Transferred to 2nd Company, 1st Development Battalion. Died from heart failure August 30, 1918, Camp Taylor. Buried in Cortland, Jackson County, IN.

SCHILL, JOSEPH E., Private, son of John and Lenora D. Schill, born August 16, 1887, Crothersville, Jackson County, IN. Laborer. Sent to Camp Taylor, KY, then to Camp Logan, TX; assigned to Company C, 33rd Infantry. Transferred to Camp Upton, NY; assigned to Company D, 131st Infantry, 33rd Division, Overseas in May, 1918. Killed in action August 9, 1918, Chipilly Ridge, France. (Burial place unknown).

STEWART, JAMES B., Private, son of James and Anna Stewart, born March 19, 1895, Jackson County, IN. Laborer. Enlisted in U.S. Regular Army, February 14, 1917, and sent to Columbus Barracks, OH, then to Ft. Sam Houston, TX; assigned to Company H, 3rd Infantry. Overseas in June, 1917; attached to Machine Gun Company, 26th Infantry. Died of pneumonia March 16, 1918, (place unknown). Buried, Menilla Tour; Meurthe et Moselle, Grave No. 812.

THOMPSON, CHARLES W., Corporal, son of John F. and Rose Thompson (Wolfe), born May 29, 1887, Sparksville, Jackson County, IN. Farmer. Enlisted in U.S. Regular Army March 9, 1915, Brownstown, IN. Sent to El Paso, TX; assigned to Company H, 16th Infantry. Overseas in June 1917, with Company B, 2nd Machine Gun Battalion. Took part in battles of Lorraine Sector, Toul Sector, Picardy, Cantigny. Killed in action July 19, 1918, battle of Soissons.

WILSON, ARVIE R., Private, son of Mr. and Mrs. Isaiah Wilson (mother deceased); born September 27, 1894, Brownstown, IN. Farmer. Entered service March 29, 1918, Brownstown. Sent to Camp Taylor, KY. Transferred to Camp Gordon, GA. Overseas in July 1918; assigned to Company L, 26th Infantry, 1st Division. Killed in action October 6, 1918 in battle of Argonne Forest.

Cited by Division Commander for bravery in action and meritorious services.

ZIMMERMAN, EDWARD PETER, Private, son of Peter and Emma Amelia Zimmerman; born February 18, 1892, Seymour, IN. Machinist. Entered service May 27, 1918, Brownstown, IN. Sent to Camp Taylor, KY; assigned to 28th Company, 7th Training Battalion, 159th Depot Brigade. Transferred to Camp Beauregard, LA; assigned to Company H, 153rd Infantry. Overseas in August 1918 with Company H, 127th Infantry. Killed in action October 26, 1918, in Argonne Forest. Buried in Argonne American Cemetery No. 1232. Romagne, France.

The Indiana Historical Commission was authorized by an act, introduced by Senator Oscar Ratts of Paoli, Indiana, and passed during the Seventy-Second session of the General Assembly, to present this copy of the Gold Star volume to you in memory of one of the heroes who gave his life for his country's cause.

Three thousand three hundred and fifty-four sons and fifteen daughters from Indiana paid the supreme sacrifice while serving with the American and allied forces during the World War. The story of their heroism and their devotion to duty which led them on to death comprises one of the most sacred chapters in all Indiana history.

In future years the records of these heroes, linked with those of the defenders of our Union, will be the great fountain source of inspiration for the children of Indiana.

On behalf of the Indiana Historical Commission, acting as the agent of the state, I take pleasure in presenting this volume to you.

Warren T. McCray
Governor of Indiana
June 14, 1921

World War I
Service Decorations And Commendations
Awarded To Jackson County Soldiers
1917-1918

ALLEN, DAVID C., (Freetown): Pvt., Machine Gun Company, 26th Infantry, 1st Division. Silver Star, General Order Number 6, July 12, 1919, for gallantry October 4-12, 1918 in the Meuse-Argonne operation. Silver Star, General Order Number 1, January 1, 1920, gallantry in action.

BECK, CHARLES LEROY, (Brownstown): Pvt., Company M, 126th Infantry, 32nd Division, Croix de Guerre with Palm (France), Order Number 16.044 "D", April 13, 1919; crossed enemy lines, captured 10 machine guns, killed or made prisoner 15 of the enemy. Military Medal (France), May 5, 1919; Distinguished Service Cross, General Order Number 21, War Department, 1919; award for gallantry October 14, 1918 near Romagne, France.

BOWMAN, NOAH FRANKLIN, (Seymour, born Crothersville), Sgt., Battery E, 10th Field Artillery, 3rd Division. Silver Star, General Orders Number 22, July 8, 1919, for gallantry July 15, 1918, on the south side bank of Marne River near Courboin, France.

BOYATT, CHARLES ROBERT (Brownstown), CPL, Company L, 131st Infantry, 33rd Division. Distinguished Service Cross, General Orders Number 17, War Department, 1924; destroyed machine gun nest and captured prisoners on November 10, 1918, near Bois d' Harville, France.

CALLAHAN, JACOB E., (Freetown), Mechanic A, 2nd Machine Gun Battalion, 1st Division. Silver Star, General Orders Number 5, June 1, 1919 for gallantry in four major French campaigns.

COX, JAMES COLLINS, (Brownstown), Pvt. (1st), Company K, 28th Infantry, 1st Division. Silver Star, General Orders Number 1, January 1, 1920, for meritorious service at Cantigny, wounded there on May 28, 1918, died from wounds on June 20, 1918. Buried at Aisne-Marne American Cemetery at Belleau Aisne, France, Grave 69, Row 9, Block A. Son of Thomas and Nora Cox, born May 19, 1901. Posthumous presentation.

FORD, JOHN W., (Seymour), Pvt. 1st Class, Supply Company, 18th Infantry, 1st Division. Silver Star, General Orders Number 5, June 1, 1919; wounded October 8, 1918, at Meuse Argonne, France.

GREENLEE, ORVIL EDGAR, (Kurtz), Pvt. 1st Class, Company M, 26th Infantry, 1st Division. Silver Star, General Order Number 1, January 1, 1920; Posthumous presentation for meritorious service, killed in action July 18, 1918, at Chateau-Thierry, buried at Chateau-Thierry, France. Son of George and Sarah (Utterback) Greenlee, born November 25, 1894, at Kurtz.

HODAPP, JOHN DALE PYE, (Seymour), Lt. Comdr., Supply Corps, U.S. Navy. Navy Cross, November 11, 1920, distinguished service on trip from Manila, P.I. to Gibraltar, summer, 1917.

KLEMME, JOSEPH EDWARD, (Seymour), Pvt. 1st Class, Company C. 1st Field Signal Battery, 2nd Division. Silver Star, General Orders Number 44, France, July 12, 1918; for gallantry in major battles in France, wounded November 8, 1918 at Meuse-Argonne, France.

LUBKER, FRED R., (Brownstown), Pvt. 1st Class, Company G, 61st Infantry, 5th Division. Silver Star, General Orders Number 11, Headquarters 9th Infantry Brigade, December 31, 1918; for distinguished work in liaison under enemy fire. Served in four major battles: Anould, St. Die, St. Mihiel, Meuse-Argonne, and Army of Occupation. Died January 18, 1918, at Brownstown from disease contacted from wet trenches in France. Buried in Fairview Cemetery, Brownstown. Son of William and Carrie (Vehslage) Lubker, widow Edna (Shelton) Lubker, daughter Rosemary (Lehman) and son James Frederick.

Minch, Edward Lawrence (Rockford), Pvt., Battery F, 42nd Artillery, Coast Artillery Corps. Croix de Guerre with Bronze Star, Order Number 11.510 "D" (French), November 14, 1918, for bravery under fire on July 15 and 16, 1918.

MITCHELL, CARL, (Seymour), CPL, Company I, 28th Infantry, 1st Division. Silver Star, General Order Number 46, for bravery carrying messages under fire during the Battle of Soissons on July 18-22, 1918. Died January 4, 1919, from wounds received in action. Buried near Kerhuon, France (near Brest). Son of Harrison and Mary E. (Weedman) Mitchell at Seymour on October 5, 1883.

MIZE, JAMES T., (Seymour), Sgt., Company D, 16th Infantry, 1st Division. Croix de Guerre with Palm, order number 11.220 "D", (French) November 6, 1918; wounded in destroying enemy machine gun on July 18, 1918 at Soissons.

MONTGOMERY, HOLLIS, (Crothersville), Sgt, Company K, 18th Infantry, 1st Division. Silver Star, General Orders Number 5, June 1, 1919, for gallant conduct in four major French battles, gassed May 4, 1918, at Montdidier-Noyon (recuperated).

NICHOLSON, DAVID, (Crothersville), Sgt., Company C, 2nd Machine Gun Battalion, 1st Division. Silver Star, General Order Number 26, July 23, 1920, for gallantry in Battle at Soissons on July 18-23, 1918.

RUDDER, LEROY F., (Medora), Cook, 16th Infantry, 1st Division. Silver Star, General Orders Number 5, June 1, 1919; for gallantry in three major missions in France. Wounded May 4, 1918.

TABOR, LOUIS JACKSON, (Brownstown), Pvt., 1st Class, 28th Infantry, 1st Division. Silver Star, General Orders Number 1, January 1, 1920, Posthumous; meritorious service killed in action July 18, 1918, at the Battle of Soissons, France. Buried at Fairview Cemetery, Brownstown. Son of Erasmus and Susan (Elkins) Tabor, born August 4, 1900.

THOMPSON, CHARLES W., (Brownstown), Cpl, 2nd Machine Gun Battalion, 1st Division. Silver Star, General Orders Number 1, Headquarters 1st Division, January 1, 1920, Posthumous; killed in action July 19, 1918, at the Battle of Soissons, buried at Fairview Cemetery at Brownstown. Son of John F. and Rose (Morgan) Thompson, born May 29, 1887.

WILSON, ARVIE R., (Brownstown), Pvt., Company L, 26th Infantry, 1st Division. Silver Star, General Orders Number 1, January 1, 1920, Posthumous; killed in action October 6, 1918, at Meuse-Argonne France. Buried at Meuse-Argonne American Cemetery at Meuse, France. Born son of Isaih and Sophie (Drappenstadt) Wilson on September 24, 1894.

Indiana Book of Merit, Indiana World War Records, *Vol. IV, compiled H.A. Rider, Indiana Historical collections, Vol. XVIII, Indiana Historical Bureau, 1932, Indianapolis.*

CHELSIE JACK BEBOUT, World War I, United States Army, born in Houston in 1893 to Lum and Eva Bebout. The family moved to Freetown soon thereafter.

He was drafted into the army in 1917 and sent to France where he served with the American Expeditionary Forces. He received his honorable discharge in 1919. When he reached home he married Alice Denny Bebout and they became parents of three children.

Chelsie Bebout retired from the Freetown Post Office in 1962 after 20 years of service as the postmaster. He is the grandfather of several children and enjoys three great-grandchildren.

He passed away and was buried in the Freetown Cemetery.

EARL R. BELDON, World War I, United States Army, Fort Taylor, Kentucky, 1918, was the youngest of eight children born to William and Mary Tatlock Beldon on November 17, 1893. After graduating from Brownstown High School, he attended Normal School and received his teaching certificate. He was assigned to teach at the School near Mt. Sidney, but eventually he moved west and lived in North Dakota. Then the time came when he returned to Brownstown.

On March 2, 1918 Earl Beldon married Cora May Waskom and during the last week in March, he was called to serve in the United States Army. Following the signing of the Armistice on November 11, 1918, Earl Beldon received a letter from a good friend, Pvt. Vance Gossman suggesting the formation of some kind of Memorial Day Service at Fairview Cemetery in Brownstown.

Before he could respond to the letter, he learned that Gossman had died at Fort Harrison and could not be present for the ceremonies - except as a dead veteran! But the idea of a Memorial Service had been born in the hearts of those two Jackson County military veterans.

During the "roaring twenties" Earl and Cora May Beldon lived in Cincinnati while he earned his law degree. Eventually, this loving couple settled down and enjoyed a growing family which included seven daughters. Each of them earned college degrees and made a mark on the society in which they lived.

ROY A. BELDON, World War I, United States Army, born in 1887 to Riley and Sarah Ellen Crabb of Grassy Fork Township. When he was just 18 years old he enlisted in the army on the very day war was declared. With very little basic training, he was shipped to France with the AEF and went directly to the front lines.

He was involved in the attack on Aunse Marne, Meuse Argonne and the Saizauruas under Theodore Roosevelt, Jr. Both were wounded and landed in the same field hospital at Vichy, France. It was there where the two men discussed the formation of The American Legion.

Back at his home in Jackson County, he was a rural mail carrier. In 1924 he married Maude Foster and they became parents of two children, Miriam Ruth and Robb Roy.

CLARENCE A. "BUCK" CARR, World War I, United States Army Medical Corps, born in Medora in 1895, the son of Alexander and Florence Wiggins Carr. He enlisted in the army April 30, 1918, leaving his Job on the B&O Railroad as a brakeman. He completed his basic training at Camp Taylor, KY. His company was shipped overseas to France on August 14, 1918 as a medic dedicated to helping the wounded.

He was assigned duty in an Ambulance Company #34, charged with carrying the wounded soldiers on stretchers passing through a cemetery while artillery fire was falling everywhere. The medics sheltered themselves behind some of the larger headstones but many of them were splattered to bits when hit by shrapnel. One time the medics were pinned down by a German sniper who was hidden behind the carcass of a horse killed in battle. He was firing through a hole cut in the body of that horse.

Clarence arrived back in the states June 30, 1919, was honorably discharged a few days later, but he had been exposed to mustard gas which, as the years passed by, caused him great difficulty. He married Hilda Davis Carr and they made their home in Seymour and he returned to his work on the railroad. To them were born two sons, Marion and Marvin Carr.

He refused to seek medical attention and died June 11, 1948. He was buried in the Zollman Cemetery located not far north of Medora.

ORVILLE COCKERHAM, World War I, ASN #2375596, Battery "E" - 1st US Field Artillery, June 14, 1917 - March 31, 1919, enlisted in the US Army at Jefferson Barracks, Missouri where he took his basic training. He was later assigned to Company "H" and Battery "E" of the Field Artillery. Discharged at Camp Taylor, Kentucky.

JAMES ELMER CUMMINGS, World War I, United States Army, born near Houston June 3, 1893 to Thomas and Eliza Waggoner Cummings. He attended the local school before migrating westward into Nebraska as a farm hand. He entered the army at Blair October 3, 1917 and, after basic training, was shipped overseas to France among the troops of AEF. He was assigned to Company "C" of the Headquarter Battalion of the General's Command as the officer's chef.

While stationed in France, he met Elise Marie Gremaud; they courted and were married in NYC after they returned April 20, 1920. Eventually they moved to Jackson County. He worked at the Shale Hill Operations near Brownstown before attending Purdue University. The couple settled in Hamilton Township where they became farmers and operated a poultry business. They became parents of two sons and three daughters.

He was active in community affairs and served as Commander of the American Legion Post 112. He was past Master of the Masonic Lodge and he belonged to the VFW, Elks, Knights of Pythias and the Order of the Eastern Star. He was the County Auditor and a member of the Fair Board for 20 years.

James E. Cummings died July 21, 1961 following the death of his wife.

EDWARD DAAB, World War I, United States Army, a Spraytown resident, Ed Daab was the grandson of the French immigrants from Alsace who helped settle Spraytown. Fluent in the Alsatian dialect, he was destined to return to their villages to fight for the freedom of his aunts, uncles and cousins.

At the age of 19, Ed went to South Dakota to drive cattle. He returned to Spraytown, working on bridge crews in Lawrence and Jackson Counties. He bought timber for Sherman Berry, was a carpenter at Camp Atterbury during WWII, and worked on production at Arvins. He was an excellent vocalist, played the guitar, and carried his harmonica with him to France. Even though Ed had only a 6th grade education from the Spraytown School, he was very intelligent. He spoke 3 languages, loved to read and write, He left behind a detailed account of his life during WWI.

On April 25, 1918, at the age of 28, Ed received his draft notice. Five days later, at Camp Taylor, Kentucky. he became a soldier. He was in Battery A, Field Artillery, 37th Division. He left from Camp Upton, Long Island, NY, arriving in France on July 16th. By September 26th, he was in Laimont near the city of Nance. He was on the front line until the Armistice was signed on November 11th. He wrote: "It is pretty quiet here now. Seems awfully queer not to hear all the guns rolling. They stopped yesterday, November 11th, the 11th month, the 11th hour. Could not hear a sound last night, except once in a while some fellow would pull out his automatic and empty it into the air just to celebrate a little. The Hun's have failed to get me so far."

On April 2, 1919, Ed Daab arrived in Newport News aboard the ship *President Grant.* From there he was sent to Camp Taylor, Kentucky, where he

mustered out around April 17, 1919. In his final letter to his sweetheart: "Maybe I'll see you next Sunday."

On May 19th, in Brownstown. Ed Daab married Myrtle Williams. They worked the family farm with his parents, George and Tena Daab. They had one child. Warren Daab. Ed died of a heart attack in 1964 and is buried with his family in the Spraytown Cemetery.

ADAM THEODORE DENNY, World War I, United States Navy, better known as just Theo, was born February 13, 1897 at Freetown to Adam and Jane Spurgeon Denny. He was the youngest of seven children, all of whom remained in the Freetown area.

During World War I he joined the navy and served nine months as one of the crew members on the Leviathan, one of the troop transport ships. He was aboard all sixteen cross-Atlantic trips, each carrying 10,000 soldiers.

In 1924 he married a schoolteacher named Mary England of Brownstown and they became parents of two children. Their son lives in California. Following the marriage they moved to Newcastle were he started to work in a plant which later became Chrysler Corporation.

He was 92 years old when he died and he was buried at New Castle.

FRANK DENNY, World War I, United States Navy, was a son of Adam and Jane Spurgeon Denny and was born in 1889. He was drafted into the Navy and completed his boot camp training at Great Lakes Naval Yard in Chicago. Records of his military service are unavailable.

He was married to Staussie Fleetwood of Kurtz and they became parents of three children: June, James and Bill. Frank was a Standard Oil Agent for more than 30 years delivering oil products to the western parts of Jackson County.

He was 80 years old when he died. He was buried in Fairview Cemetery in Brownstown.

GLENN R. EMPSON, Private ASN 4568637, 9th Regiment 21st Infantry Company, United States Army, born near Vallonia and matured in and throughout Jackson County, Indiana. By occupation he was a salesman of farm implements. He was 27 years old when he was drafted into the military service of his country. He was sent to Camp Gordon, Georgia for his basic training which commenced March 13, 1917.

Records show this young man from Grassy Fork Township was 5 feet, 8 inches tall, had brown eyes and brown hair. His complexion was described as being fair. A letter from the Adjutant General's Office noted Glenn R. Empson was discharged from the service November 16, 1918 to accept a commission as 2nd Lieutenant in the United States Army.

Lt. Glenn R. Empson served as an officer faithfully in the Expeditionary Forces in France until after the armistice was declared effective at 11:00 o'clock in the morning on November 11, 1918. He was returned to the United States and separated at Camp Gordon, Georgia. His release was signed by Colonel Edgar A. Frye on January 29, 1919.

WILLARD N. EVERHART, SR., World War I, Private - ASN 982388, United States Army,

born near Hayden in Jennings County, Indiana. He was a son of William H. and Abbie Everhart. He spent his youth maturing in and around Seymour. He was graduated from Shields High School. Sometime after World War I broke out, he enlisted on April 27, 1918 at the Jackson County seat in Brownstown. He was assigned duty in the 15th Service Company of the Army Signal Corps. He received his honorable discharge while stationed at Fort Leavenworth, Kansas on September 17, 1918.

CLARENCE R. FERGUSON, World War I, United States Army, grew up in the Honeytown region of Jackson County. He answered the call to arms when the country went to war in 1917. He served in France with the American Expeditionary Forces. He was assigned to the 135th Field Artillery Regiment which was part of the 37th Division.

He married Ruby Eller and to them were born four children: Evelyn, Clarice, David and Bob. David served in WWII and Bob saw action in Korea.

CARL JOHN HENRY FOSBRINK, World War I, United States Army, Company "H" of the 130th Infantry Division, served with the AEF in France October 4, 1917 to May 22, 1919. He and his wife, Florence Garris Fosbrink, lived in Brownstown and to them were born three children. He served as a janitor in the Jackson County Courthouse for several years.

DONALD M. FREDERICKSON, United States Army, Fort Slocum, NY - Panama Canal Zone, Company "B" - 2nd Field Artillery, 1931-1938. Married Myrtle Ballard and became parents of 8 children. Three sons served in the Marine Corps. Donald Frederickson died of a heart attack in 1974. One daughter was killed in an auto accident. Donald Frederickson is buried in the Smallwood Cemetery.

JOHN HARLAN GILLASPY, World War I, United States Army, 29th Company - 8th Battalion, born April 28, 1893 on the family farm located not far from Crothersville. He was the son of Alex and Minnie Gorell Gillaspy. Later he graduated from Indiana University with a degree in chemistry.

He was inducted into the army in 1918 at Camp Taylor in Kentucky. He was soon promoted to Corporal in his unit and assigned to train the army recruits entering Camp Taylor. Later he was transferred to the Chemical Corps where he spent most of his time in the laboratory located along the east coast. He was

working on explosives and when the war ended, he was stationed at Nitro, West Virginia.

After he was discharged in Ohio he returned home to the family farm so he could take over the farming since his father had died. He was soon married to Etta Baringer and to them were born four children, including Ruth, Dale, Harlan and John. John Haskell Gillaspy died in 1975.

CLARENCE ALLEN HALL, World War I, United States Army, born July 17, 1893 to Lock and Nancy Hall of Brownstown. He was 24 years old when he enlisted in the army. He was inducted September 5, 1917 and was assigned as a cook, Company "C" of the 107th Artillery in the 28th Infantry Division.

He served until May 23, 1919 when he was discharged at Fort Dix in New Jersey. He returned home to Jackson County and married Gertrude Smallwood and they became parents of a son named Harry. Gertrude died in 1917 and Clarence was later married to Ella Rucker and they had one daughter, Doris.

His first son was a soldier in World War I. Clarence Hall died February 26, 1956

WALTER HALL, World War I, United States Army, born July 29, 1894 to Oliver and Emma Hubbard Hall of Weddleville, Indiana. He was inducted into the army on September 19, 1917 at Brownstown and left for Indianapolis.

Following basic training he was shipped overseas on September 3, 1918. Although he was wounded he survived the war and was returned to the states to receive his discharge July 16, 1919 at Camp Sherman, Ohio.

Once back home he married Nellie Devers and they gave birth to a son, named Kenneth Hall. He later married Jerry Phillips and they provided two grandsons. Walter Hall died October 5, 1991.

WILLIS L. HAWN, World War I, United States Army, was born on August 25, 1891 to Charles Willard and Donie Casey Hawn. They lived in Mt. Sidney, Indiana, a community that was once south of the Russell Chapel Church. Willis' father died suddenly from a heart attack leaving a family of eight children and his wife. Life quickly changed for Willis, trading school for a job as a farm-hand. When America entered The Great War, Willis was among the first group of men to leave Jackson County for Camp Taylor, Kentucky.

In May of 1918 Willis traveled overseas via ship, part of the 335th infantry. Most of his time was spent in France where he fought battles against

German advances. After the war was won Willis was able to tour the area before returning home. He often spoke fondly of Calais and Nice. While in France he had befriended an American photo journalist for the army who gave him many small photographs that were extras,

Willis was released from duty April 25, 1919. He returned to Jackson County and farming to help his mother. In 1924 he married Nona Rucker and settled down near Tampico. Together Nona and Willis had two children, Marjorie June born June 18, 1926, and Roscoe Lloyd born November 3, 1929. He would often share his treasured photos and stories with visitors. Many long hours were spent reminiscing. He was proud of his service to his country, and recalled conflicts he participated in as well as the sights of Europe. Although there was much suffering, he had been indoctrinated with the idea that this had been the war to end all wars. Willis was a member of the American Legion.

When WWII began to take other men into conflict, Willis stopped sharing the stories and photos. It was hard to realize his and others call to duty had been in vain. It was most difficult for Willis when his only son was sent to the Korean Conflict from which he never returned.

CLAUDE HURLEY, World War I, United States Army, born January 15, 1897 to George and Louisa Hurley in Jackson County. He was raised at Brownstown and graduated from local high school in 1915. Three years later he entered the army along with Ralph Tidwell and others from Brownstown. They were sent as a group to Camp Taylor, KY, located near Cincinnati for basic training.

They were then assigned to Company "B" in the Student Army Center at the University of Vermont. He had not completed the training when the war was over. He was discharged at Burlington December 6, 1918.

Ralph Tidwell boarded the ship bound for France, but the ship was turned around at sea. He was discharged shortly after he landed stateside. Claude Hurley returned home and served as the first Adjutant of the American Legion Post 112 at Brownstown. Ralph Tidwell was the last World I veteran in Jackson County.

Claude Hurley became an educator and served Jackson County schools for 51 years. He was married to Lorene Wattles and they became the parents of three sons who grew up near Brownstown.

Claude Hurley died October 30, 1987.

CLARENCE LAMPERT, World War I, United States Army, born in Spraytown on November 7, 1889. He was the son of Johannes Lampert and Emma Magdalena Daab. All of his grandparents were from the northern part of Alsace. France and all lived in Spraytown.

Clarence lived his childhood in Spraytown and attended the Spraytown School. On June 5, 1917, Clarence registered for the draft. He was working on the Ben I. Perry farm and living at R.R. 4, Columbus. On July 22, 1918 he was mustered in at Camp Taylor, Kentucky. By September 17th, he was at Camp McClellan, Anniston, Alabama, a soldier in Battery D, 36th Regiment,

About 1921 Clarence went with his parents and brothers, Ed, Charles, and John, to Orange County, California. He worked as a crate handler for 25 years at Villa Park Lemon Association. a wholesale packing firm. Each Christmas he sent boxes of California fruit to his cousin, Ed Daab, in Spraytown.

Clarence never married. He died at Chapman Hospital in Orange, California on September 16, 1977, of kidney failure. He is entombed at Melrose Abbey Mausoleum in Anaheim, California.

EDWARD HOWARD LAMPERT, World War I, United States Army, born in Spraytown, Jackson County, Indiana. He was the son of Johannes Lampert and Emma Magdalena Daab, All of his grandparents were from the northern part of Alsace, France. This made the situation in Alsace very near and dear to his heart.

Ed Lampert's cousin kept a list of his assignments and addresses during his military career. On January 5, 1918, Lampert arrived in Battle Creek, Michigan, becoming a soldier in the 31st Company, 8th Battalion, 160th Depot Brigade. From there he went to 266 Aero Squadron, Selfridge Field, Mt. Clemens, Michigan. The last address listed was Park Field, 160th Squadron E, Memphis, Tennessee. On December 5th, 1918. his cousin wrote home from the front line in France: "I wonder what Ed Lampert says now … he was raising thunder because he did not get to come over."

After the war, in 1922, he went West to settle in Orange County, California. He was a supervisor for 27 years at the Santa Fe Oil Company, which was an oil field. In 1928, he married Clara Aulwes in Santa Ana, California. They had no children. He died on May 14, 1987 at the Anaheim Hospital of heart failure. He is entombed at Melrose Abbey Memorial Park in Anaheim. California.

FRED LUBKER, World War I, United States Army, son of William and Carrie Fislar Lubker, was born in 1899 at Mooneytown one mile north of Brownstown. His mother died when he was only a few days old, and from that time on he lived with his aunt, Dora Fislar Waskom, near Vallonia.

He enlisted in the army September 7, 1917 at Fort Dodge, Iowa and was shipped overseas April 16, 1918. He landed in France and saw active duty at St. Sie, St. Miehl and the Meuse sector. During that time he was cited for bravery for remaining under continual artillery and mortar fire.

Following the Armistice signed November 11, 1918, he spent some months with the occupation forces in Germany. Upon return to the States, he was discharged at Camp Sherman, OH in 1919. He then entered Oakland City College and received his degree in horticulture.

On December 23, 1922 he married Edna Shelton and for a time they lived in Little Blue, MO. When his health broke, they moved to Brownstown. He died on June 30, 1930 from the effects of gas and shrapnel wounds.

BERT M. LYON, World War I, United States Army, born October 2, 1922 at Cortland, Indiana. Completed high school, drafted and inducted on December 9, 1946. Assigned Headquarters, 454th Bomb Group. Trained as RASAR Mechanic, Rifleman. Shipped overseas to European Theater. Saw action at Rome-Arno, Southern France, Rhineland.

Returned to states July 19, 1945 and discharged October 16, 1945 at Indianapolis.

Earned academic credit and promoted to Staff Sergeant. Returned to Brownstown.

BURRELL LYON AND UNIDENTIFIED FRIEND, World War I, United States Army, born July 17, 1893 at Hillsboro, Indiana and reared as a farmer. Enlisted and inducted July 22, 1918 at Brownstown. Assigned Number 3887081, Headquarters Company, 35th Field Artillery. Discharged February 6, 1919 at Camp Zachary Taylor, KY. Unmarried with excellent character. Returned home to Jackson County February 8, 1919.

HARRY MARCOTT, World War I, United States Army, born May 19, 1898 in Watseka, Illinois to William and Elizabeth Platt Marcott. There is no information regarding his childhood days or schooling. Records indicate he enlisted in the army and was assigned to the 129th Infantry in Company B. His enlistment was dated July 29, 1917 at Hoopestown, Illinois for a term of six years.

He was gassed during his service in France and had to be discharged June 6, 1919. Records verify his character was beyond reproach. After he was released from the service, he married Genevieve Sharland Marcott and they were blessed with five children, including two sons who were also in the military service.

CYRUS L. MILLER, World War I, American Expeditionary Forces, a descendant of Abraham Miller, was born in 1900 on a farm located between Brownstown and Vallonia. He enlisted in the army April 24, 1918 in Indianapolis. After his basic training, he was shipped overseas to France. He was one of the soldiers standing at attention when General Pershing uttered the famous words, "Lafayette, we are here."

He was among those who fought in the Meuse-Argonne Offensive as a member of Company "C" of the 6th Engineers from Jackson County. He returned home to receive his discharge on August 23, 1919 at Camp Sherman, Ohio.

HENRY SIMON MILLER, World War I, American Expeditionary Forces, a descendant of Adam Miller, was born near Vallonia in 1894 to Elijah

and Mary Elizabeth Fordice Miller. He was raised on a farm located not far south of town.

He enlisted in the army when he was 21 years old, and assigned to Company "B" of the 7th Field Artillery Regiment. He was among those shipped overseas to France. He survived the war and returned to the states and granted his furlough June 27, 1919 at Camp Sherman in Ohio.

He was married to Mattie Geneva Shelton.

ALLEN S. MONTGOMERY, World War I, United States Army. One of four brothers serving in World War I, he was born to H.C. Montgomery of Hanover, Indiana. Graduated from Hanover College in 1880. Appointed Principal of Hanover Academy. Henry C. Montgomery died in 1937.

Allen S. Montgomery served as Lieutenant. Assigned to Artillery Battery and discharged December 14, 1918. Allen S. Montgomery was born August 15, 1898. Enlisted and received commission as Lieutenant. Assigned to Artillery Battery. Discharged December 14, 1918.

Returned home to Seymour, graduated from Hanover College and Michigan State University. Teacher and Coach at Owasso High School. Married Tekla R. Wrobleski August 18, 1922. Became parents of two daughters. Allen S. Montgomery died September 14, 1984.

COULTER M. MONTGOMERY, World War I, United States Army, born October 13, 1892 to Henry and Jane Swope Montgomery. Spent his entire life in Seymour. Graduated from Hanover College and Indiana Law School. Admitted to the bar in 1916.

Entered army and was trained at Fort Harrison. Commissioned and promoted to Captain. Assigned to Company B, 10th Infantry Battalion. Transferred to Fort Custer, Michigan. Served as Court-martial and Judge Advocate. Discharged Member of American Legion Post 89 in Seymour.

Married Hildegarde Destinon of Sauers January 14, 1934. Became parents of three children: John, Jane and Kenneth Coulter. Prosecuting attorney for Jackson County and active in community affairs. He died suddenly September 12, 1956.

FRANK MONTGOMERY, World War I, United States Army, was one of four brothers serving during WWI. Born to H.C. Montgomery of Hanover, Indiana. Graduated from Hanover College in 1880. Appointed Principal of Hanover Academy. Henry C. Montgomery died in 1937.

Frank Montgomery served as 1st Lt. in France. His unit saw action during the final attack on the Germans. After the Armistice was signed he was appointed Assistant Adjutant-General. Returned to Seymour and appointed Professor at Hanover College. Relocated to Pompano Beach, Florida

COULTER & FRANK MONTGOMERY, World War I, United States Army. Two of four

brothers serving as officers during WWI. Captain Coulter Montgomery and Lieutenant Frank Montgomery. Born to H.C. Montgomery of Hanover, Indiana. Graduated from Hanover College in 1880. Appointed Principal of Hanover Academy. Four sons graduated from Hanover College. All served in WWI as officers. Henry C. Montgomery died in 1937

T. HARLAN MONTGOMERY, World War I, American Expeditionary Forces, 1st Lieutenant, became an attorney in the law firm of Montgomery and Montgomery in Seymour

CHARLES W. PATRICK, World War I, United States Army, born to William and Blanche Murphy Patrick. Played Guitar and sang during youth at Surprise, Indiana. Entered the service and assigned to Field Artillery. Sent to Battery D for his tour of duty. Discharged at Camp Custer, MI January 27, 1919. Returned to Jackson County and lived near Surprise. He died and was buried in Riverview Cemetery.

JOHN OTTO PATRICK, World War I, United States Army, born to William and Blanche Murphy. Musically inclined, he played guitar and sang favorite songs. Hometown was Surprize. Entered military service in 1918 and shipped overseas to European Theater of Operations. Gassed during battle in France. Returned to Jackson County. Marriage resulted in divorce after becoming father of one child.

CLYDE H. PETERS, World War I, United States Army, born February 12, 1888 to William and Anna Fislar Peters of Vallonia. He was raised with a sister and brother and attended the local school.

He enlisted in the navy August 26, 1918 and was assigned to the Ambulance Corps. He was discharged more than one year later on January 23, 1919 at Camp Custer in Michigan.

He married Arie B. Hert, a teacher from Springville, on September 10, 1925. They lived in Driftwood Township and he served as Postmaster for a time. Both were on-going members of the American Legion and Auxiliary. Clyde Peters died September 5, 1950.

WILLIAM R. PETERS, World War I, United States Navy, born November 15, 1891 in Jackson County near the Vallonia depot. His parents were

William and Anna Fislar Peters. He enlisted in the navy March 29, 1918 and took his boot training at Great Lakes Naval Base.

He was sent to Newport, RI for deployment. He was assigned to the USS *St. Louis* which crossed the Atlantic Ocean six different times transporting troops to France.

He received his discharge as a Carpenter's Mate, 2nd Class at the Pittsburgh base August 11, 1919.

He returned home to farm his land and he opened a butcher shop in Bedford during the depression. He died at the Veterans Hospital in Indianapolis April 3, 1958.

DAYTON PORCH, World War I, United States Army, born near Maumee to George and Ann Lutes Porch. He registered for the draft June 5, 1917 and was unable to get married. He was drafted March 4, 1918 into the army.

Records indicate he was stationed for a time at Camp War Horse in Georgia before his unit was shipped overseas to France. He served in Company "A" the 605th Engineers.

He was in the trenches for almost three months and believed to have suffered with trenchfoot. He was on a pass receiving treatment when the Armistice was signed November 11, 1918.

When he returned home he was married to Myrtle Butler of Heltonville, Indiana. They became parents of three children

ALFRED POTTSCHMIDT, World War I, United States Army, born November 2, 1893 and was raised on a farm located near Wegan. He was inducted into the army late in August 1918. After completing basic training he was shipped overseas to France. He was among those who fought in the offensive of October 28, 1918.

He was captured and held prisoner of war for a time but he was then repatriated to the American command. He returned to the states and was discharged June 10, 1919.

He arrived back home to Jackson County and he and his wife, Lillian Melloncamp Pottschmidt, farmed in the Pleasant Grove community in Brownstown Township. They were parents of three children.

Alfred Pottschmidt died December 15, 1977 and his wife followed in April of 1982.

ROSCOE RATLILFF, World War I, United States Army – 308th Field Artillery, 1918-1919, born in 1895 in Taylorsville, IN the son of William and May Kelly Ratliff. His father was a farm hand and, as a boy Roscoe learned to be an automobile mechanic. He spent most of his younger days in Bartholomew County around Edinburg in the area which later was formed into Camp Atterbury. Roscoe was inducted into the Army June 29, 1918 at Franklin, IN.

He was assigned to Headquarters Company of the 308th Field Artillery as a private. On October 26, 1918 his unit departed for France and he served for about six months. It was May 1919 when he was returned to the States for demobilization. He was discharged at Camp Sherman, Ohio, May 29, 1919.

Roscoe married Gladys Pedicord in Medora in 1937. He was the owner, and operator of an auto repair shop in Brownstown. He died April 14, 1960.

JAMES RAY, World War I and World War II, United States Army and United States Navy, born at Huron in Lawrence County July 3, 1899 to Joe and Ida Ray. As a teen-age boy he moved with his family when they settled in Jackson County on the Hinckle farm near Medora. He was a student at Brownstown High School and, during his senior year he enlisted in the army. During the war he served in England, France and Russia before he received his discharge August 22, 1919.

He was married to Celia Devers of Ratcliff Grove in 1921, and to them were born seven children. In 1924 he felt called to the Holy ministry and eventually founded the Shady Springs Campground after successfully inaugurating the Trinity Pentecostal Chapel in Seymour. Both were part of the Pentecostal Holiness Church movement.

In 1942 Rev. Ray left his work in the powder plant at Charleston to enlist in the navy. He served in Hawaii during World War II, and received his discharge July 4, 1945 as a machinist mate 2nd class. After returning to Seymour and, in 1946 he began holding services in the old schoolhouse located on Lynn Street. In 1947 the congregation was able to purchase one of the chapels from Freeman Field. The first service was held in their new chapel on Easter Sunday in 1949.

Rev. Ray was killed in an automobile accident in 1961 but he should be remembered as having served his country in both wars and his Lord for 37 years.

CLARENCE RICHARDS, World War I, United States Army, born in Jackson County to Louis and Narra Smallwood Richards, made his home not far from Brownstown.

He was inducted into the service of his nation August 27, 1918. After completing his basic training, he was assigned to the army Medical Corps and stationed at the base hospital unit. He was discharged from Camp Sherman in Ohio. He returned to his home and married Effie Reedy.

They were parents of four sons; two of them were later destined to serve in the navy, while the other two joined the National Guard.

Harry married Barbara Rhodes. They became parents of six children: Jerrie, Harry, Stacey, Michelle, Natalie and Jonathan. They were able to enjoy their 14 grandchildren.

Charles married Dorothy Jane Empson. They had three children: Charles, Joy and Jan, who blessed them with 8 grandchildren.

Howard married Dorothy Grein. They became parents of two children, Michael and Tammy. They also have grandchildren.

Paul was married to Patty Hinton. They had a daughter, named Linda who presented them with a grandson.

EDWARD H. ROTHERT, World War I, United States Army, born April 19, 1891 in Jackson County. Parents were Henry William and Anna Meyer Rothert. Married Elsie Lawell in 1918 before service.

Inducted April 30, 1918. Served stateside faithfully as Company Clerk. Assigned to Railway Trainman. Discharged March 15, 1919, Camp Zachary Taylor, KY.

GEORGE HENRY ROTHERT, World War I, United States Army, born November 9, 1894 to parents, Henry and Anna Meyer Rothert. Inducted into army August 18, 1918 and served as a Private. Assigned to Company E, 1st Battalion, 77th Infantry Division. Returned to the states, discharged at Cincinnati May 12, 1919. Married Hattie Koester in 1920. Became parents of five children

JOHN T. RUDE, World War I, United States Army, born June 24, 1891 to Bert and Jessie McCord Rude of Crothersville. He attended the local school and migrated westward to Iowa as a farm hand.

He enlisted July 25, 1918 at Newton, Iowa and was a model recruit. During his tour of duty he was commended for his faithful service. He was discharged as a Private at Camp Dodge on February 22, 1919. He returned to Newton.

He married and became father of one son. Later he returned to Vallonia where he worked for August Pollert, Bill Peters and other farmers of the area. He closed out his career from the Vallonia Nursery. He died August 12, 1957 and is buried in the Vallonia Cemetery.

OSCAR G. SCHNEIDER, World War I, United States Army, born and raised on a farm in Driftwood Township in Jackson County. He was employed in the dry goods store in Vallonia before entering the service.

He was inducted into the army April 30, 1918 at Louisville and sent on to Camp Taylor for basic training. That became his home base as a cook until he was discharged on November 26, 1918.

He married Freeda Shoemaker and they made their home near the village of Vallonia. He was

employed for many years at Bundy Brothers Mill. He later worked for the Farm Bureau mill located in Brownstown. They became parents of three children.

He died in 1968 following the death of his wife in 1953.

LAWRENCE HAUER SHIELDS, World War I, United States Army, Company "M" 11th Infantry Division, son of Seth and Isabelle Brown Shields, was born October 7, 1893 in Ewing, IN. He was later inducted into the army August 11, 1917 at Jefferson Barracks, MO was immediately assigned to Company M of the 11th Infantry Division.

Pvt. Shields (737115) was sent to Chickamauga Park, GA for his basic training. Shortly thereafter he was shipped overseas to France. He was engaged in the battles of St. Mihiel and Meuse Argonne. Extraordinary heroism was demonstrated by Pvt. Shields in battle raging on September 12, 1918 when he rushed forward to silence a machine gun. His act of bravery saved the lives of his comrades and opened the way for advancement of his division.

Pvt. Shields was awarded the Silver Star for gallantry in action. He was discharged August 26, 1919 but re-enlisted two years later and served in Manila, the Philippine Islands. He was discharged in 1924 at Fort MacArthur, California.

Lawrence H. Shields died April 26, 1962 and was buried in the Fairview Cemetery in Brownstown, IN.

CHARLES PETER SILENCE, World War I, United States Army, born March 9, 1894 in Washington County. Raised in Jackson County near Brownstown. Inducted into the army May 4, 1918 when war broke out.

Shipped to France after completing basic training. Assigned to the infantry, he was sent to the front lines.

While in action against the Germans he was gassed. Shipped back to the states, he was discharged June 20, 1919. Returned to his home and was called to the ministry. Of the Free Will Baptist Faith he visited the sick. Ordained by the Church of the Nazarene.

Married and the father of two sons. Both served in the military during WWII and Vietnam. Died in August 1964.

VIRGIL HUDSON SMALLWOOD, World War I, United States Army, born July 12, 1891 to Beverly and Mary Lewis Smallwood. He was raised with a large family of brothers and sisters. Virgil grew up in Jackson County and attended the local school.

He joined the army in August 1917 and served in the states until he was discharged at 103 Spruce Square in Philadelphia.

After he returned to Brownstown he married Frona Schrader, but they had no children. He owned and operated a creamery located near the corner of Walnut and Sugar Streets. It later became the Ball Museum purchased by the Jackson County Historical Society.

Virgil returned from Cummins in Columbus. He died March 6, 1959.

GEORGE FREDERICK SNIDER, World War I, United States Army, born March 14, 1876 in Shelby County to Jacob and Mary Huffman Snider. He was raised in the local area and, when he was 18 years old he enlisted in the army and was assigned to the Bancock Campaign which began July 27, 1895. He was discharged at Fort Russell in Wyoming in May.

He re-enlisted two years later in 1899 and was made a Sgt. in Company "L" in the 19th Infantry Regiment during the Spanish-American War. After just one year of service he was discharged July 25, 1900.

Years later, on February 15, 1918 he enlisted once again and served until August 21, 1918 and was discharged to receive a commission as a 2nd Lt. assigned to the official guard unit. On March 18, 1919 he was discharged while he was stationed at West Baden. During WWII he served on the Jackson County draft board and as the veterans officer. He was commander of the American Legion, Post 112 in Brownstown.

On May 27, 1916 he married Maye Barkman Snider and they resided in the county seat. They became parents of two daughters.

George Snider died January 6, 1973 and his wife followed about a year later.

ALFRED L. SPURLOCK, World War I, United States Army, born January 9, 1897 in Kentucky and much later he enlisted August 11, 1918 in Manchester, KY. He was inducted four days later and was assigned as a private to Battery "A" in the 13th Regiment at Camp Jackson, SC. He was discharged December 20, 1918.

He re-enlisted and was assigned to the Quartermaster's Corps and was at several camps in the states. He received his discharge August 20, 1920. An affidavit indicating his faithful service was signed by the Secretary of War August 19, 1944.

The reason why he didn't remain in service very long during each hitch, was that he contacted TB and had to be hospitalized periodically for long periods at a time. He met and married Mary Baker Spurlock and to them were born four sons. After they returned to the county seat, records show he was appointed the Veterans Service Officer

GLENN STILLWELL, World War I, United States Army, born January 13, 1894 at Clearspring in Owen Township to parents, Joseph and Nettie Alcy Lockman Stillwell. Graduated from Clearspring High School in 1915

Enlisted in the army May 23, 1918. Completed basic training, shipped overseas to France, and was in battle the night of arrival. Served in the occupational forces in Germany. Assigned to 1st Artillery Brigade of the First Division. Meuse-Argonne Medal, Victory Medal. Discharged September 25, 1919 from Camp Taylor in Kentucky.

Married Goldie Mae Hanner September 25, 1920. Became parents of two daughters. He was American Legion member and Jackson County Assessor for 12 years.

RALPH LESTER STILWELL, World War I, United States Navy, born July 7, 1898 to Smith T. and Lydia Ann Acton Stilwel. Attended schools in Brownstown Township. Enlisted February 8, 1917 at Indianapolis for four years. Assigned to the USS *Missouri*. Served as Storekeeper 3rd Class. Discharged September 9, 1919.

Returned to Freetown home of grandfather William Acton, Civil War, Company H, 50th Regiment of Indiana Volunteers.

Ralph Lester Stilwell married Clarice Braden November 26, 1924. Became parents of two daughters, Laura Ann and Mary Sue. Ralph died December 11, 1973 and Clarice died February 14, 1991

ALBERT ELMER THOELE, World War I, United States Medical Corps, was a rural Jackson County native who was married and raised three daughters on a farm located south of Seymour after he returned from his military service for the United States. He entered the Army March 29, 1918 and was assigned to the field hospital wards in France. He was discharged June 29, 1919.

After the war, Mr. Thoele became a leading member of the Lutheran Church and the surrounding farming community. He died in 1953.

RALPH A. TIDWELL, World War I, United States Army, born November 2, 1896 in Jackson County on a farm located not far from Brownstown. As a young man he found work as a paper laborer.

On August 28, 1918 he enlisted in the army and was sent to Camp Taylor, KY to complete his basic training. He was assigned to Company "F" 158th Brigade as a Private in the regular army. His military services were in the states, but he boarded a ship bound for France. Out in the ocean his ship turned back due to the end of the war in November. He received his discharge on Christmas Eve in 1918.

Records verify his faithful service, and an affidavit signed by his commanding officer indicated he returned home to Brownstown.

He was confined to a wheel chair at Hoosier Christian Village. His final appearance in public was as the last veteran of WWI in Jackson County. He was honored during the Veteran's Day Ceremony held in 1993. Just over one year later he died March 22, 1995 and was buried at Fairview.

WRIGHT VERMILYA, World War I, American Expeditionary Forces, born in Jackson County and raised in the Tampico area of Grassy Fork Township. When he was just 19 years old he enlisted in the army April 12, 1917 at Lafayette, Indiana. He was among those shipped overseas to France and fought under General Pershing.

He survived the war and returned to the states. He received his discharge April 10, 1919 and records show he was a 1st Sergeant.

HERSCHEL VERMILYA, World War I, American Expeditionary Forces, born in Jackson County and raised in the Tampico area of grassy Fork Township. When he was barely 18 years old, he enlisted in the army April 12, 1917 at Lafayette, Indiana. He was among those shipped overseas to France and fought under General Pershing.

He survived the war and was returned to the states. He received his discharge July 17, 1919 at Camp Zachary Taylor, KY. The records show he was listed as a Sergeant.

RALPH S. WEDDELL, World War I, United States Navy. At age 17 years he joined the navy during WWI. Sent to Great Lakes Naval Station for boot camp training. Assigned to destroyer USS *Jarvis*. Assigned ocean patrol duty in the North Atlantic. Was granted liberty to visit London and historical sites. Spent much time with airmen and sailors of all nations. Avid reader of the Brownstown Banner.

Discharged at Great Lakes and returned home to Medora to the family farm. Raised sheep and cattle. Member of the local Legion and VFW Posts.

Married Mabel Brown Weddell and became parents of 3 children. Blessed with seven grandchildren.

FRED WESSEL, World War I, United States Army, born September 23, 1892 on a farm located in Grassy Fork Township. He was drafted into the army during World War I and served as a medical corpsman in France. His son, Lowell, followed in his father's footsteps and served his country during the Korean Conflict. Fred Wessel returned to Jackson County and retired from farming in 1957. He died in 1960.

JOSEPH LESTER WILLIAMS, World War I, United States Navy, Gunnery Instructor, born in a

two-room log cabin at Spraytown on July 5, 1892, to Luther Williams and Samaria Elizabeth "Lizzie" Ault. During WWI, he enlisted in the United States Navy. He was a gunnery instructor. During the epidemic of 1918, he contracted influenza. He received an honorable discharge after the war. He was a member of the Elks and Eagles. He was a member of the American Legion, and played in their drum and bugle corps.

On July 26, 1924, he married Edith Leach. They had one child, Margaret. He lived 15 years in New Albany. He was a mechanic in Seymour, and was a member of the Seymour Fire Department for several years. He was a congenial man and well liked by all that knew him.

After suffering a stroke, Joseph Williams died at the U.S. Marine Hospital in Louisville on January 31, 1943. His funeral was at the Spraytown Free Methodist Church. He was buried near family in the Spraytown Cemetery.

LOUIS NOBLE WILLIAMS, Pre-World War I, United States Navy, born January 22, 1890 in a log cabin not far from Spraytown to Luther and Samaria Elizabeth Ault Williams. Louis joined the Navy and was assigned to the battleship USS *Minnesota* where he was trained to be the coxwain petty officer in charge of deck hands. He used bells to call out the various details, and they remain with his family as a memorial to his service.

He enjoyed his travels while in the Navy, and he was named the Expert Sharpshooter of the Fleet in 1912 and 1913. He was married to Mae McKain and to them were born 9 children, and all four sons from Jackson County later served in the military forces of their country.

Louis Williams died March 11, 1945 and was buried at Garland Brook in Columbus, IN.

SIMEON WOLKA, World War I, United States Army, 1918, born November 11, 1892, lived and died in the Wegan area of Jackson County July 20, 1961. He was a son of William and Emma F. Wolka.

EMIL F. ZABEL, World War I, United States Army, born in Brownstown March 19, 1895 to Philip and Emilie Myers Zabel. He was raised locally and graduated from high school in 1915 at the county seat. He entered Purdue University and continued his studies until called to service.

He entered the army September 19, 1917, completed his basic training and was assigned to the AEF. He was one of those bound for France on September 9, 1918. Records verify he served in Company A of the 309th Engineers. He was returned home to the states July 1, 1919.

He received his degree in civil engineering from Purdue in 1921 and was employed by the Illinois Highway Department until 1929. He then returned to Indiana and was city engineer for Seymour for one year. He became a surveyor for Jackson County and served in that capacity for 8 years. He finished his working days as a civil engineer for the Indiana State Highway Department on bridges until his retirement in 1965.

Emil was married to Malinda Horstman and they were to become parents of two daughters, Mary Jane Peck and Phylis Zabel. Emil Zabel died March 23, 1967 and Malinda passed away April 27, 1983.

DAYTON H. ZIKE, World War I, United States Army, born October 25, 1894 in Freetown to Jacob and Frances Zike. He was married to Bertha Fields Zike. Dayton joined the army October 3, 1917, completed basic training and was shipped overseas to France September 16, 1918.

Assigned to the 335th Infantry Division, he saw action on the western front. After the Armistice was signed he returned home to the states and was discharged May 15, 1919.

He farmed and worked as a logger in the sawmill business until he died July 9, 1953.

WORLD WAR II
DECEMBER 7, 1941-SEPTEMBER 2, 1945

The years between 1918 and the present time are now ancient history for many comrade friends, just as they are for most people around the world. There are a few people not yet old enough to remember the tragic events of the depression, World War II the post-war struggles and the collapse of the Soviet Union. All history buffs are encouraged to consider the memories recorded herein as a tribute to the veterans of any time period of the American republic.

They may learn from these actual records in their own way and at their own pace. It is hoped they might understand the events of the 20th century in a way which will help them not repeat the mistakes of yesteryear!

Within those people now living may be found veterans who became of age during the brief period of peace won by their older kinfolk. Even before some of them could exhaust their G.I., another generation of young men was called to military service. They were to fight a *police action* in Korea to curb the growth of communism world-wide.

Then came Vietnam, the unwanted war. For those who stood tall and answered the call to duty. Their service became a badge of honor. Time has vindicated their deeds of valor, and it is heartwarming to learn that most are glad they served their fellow man.

The memories recorded on these pages run parallel with the lives of successive generations of veterans. All comrades who believed in and fought for our historic freedoms from the very spirit of the American people.

Time marches on for each of us. Before we depart this life, let it be understood that some of our memorable military records have been recorded for others to *recall*. Those memories may now live on in the hearts of our loved ones yet to follow!

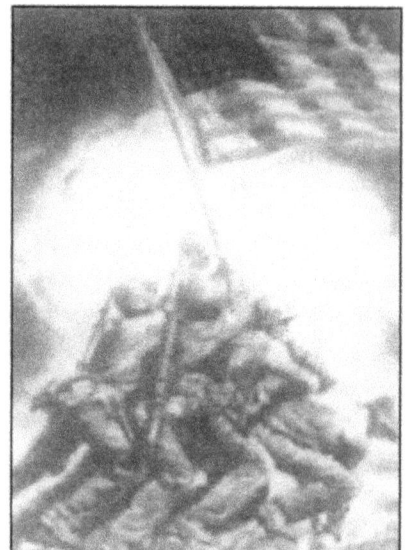

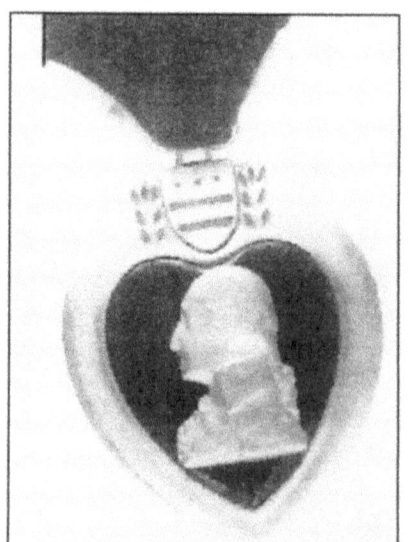

WORLD WAR II
JACKSON COUNTY ROLL OF HONOR
1941-1945

The Adjutant General's Verification of those Army service men killed in action or as a result of the war are included on the list signed on September 2, 1946 by John N. Owens for the record.

KIA	Killed in Action
DNB	Died non-battle
DOW	Died of Injuries
NDF	No Death Finding

Name	Number	Rank	Status
Baker, Carl R.	35689946	PVT	KIA
Blair, William A.	35699681	SGT	DNB
Barksdale, Leon			
Bechtel, Newton H.	35832670	PVT	DNB
Beldon, James F., Jr.	01320922	1 LT	DOW
Blackwell, Marion F.	7041881	TEC 5	KIA
Blair, William A.	35699681	SGT	DNB
Bobb, Virgil F.	02000594	2 LT	KIA
Brown, Melvin M.	15341585	PFC	DNB
Brown, Oren C.	35101917	PFC	KIA
Chastain, Edwin W.	35479650	PVT	DNB
Cline, Gilbert			
Cole, Morris A.	35244830	PFC	DOW
Cook, Keith E.	37447666	PFC	KIA
Cottingham, Robert H	35688528	PVT	FOD
Crawford, Fred			
Davers, Clyde	35253480	PFC	DOW
Davis, Roy J.	6799091	PFC	DNB
Eisele, Luther D.	36794803	PVT	KIA
Findley, Curtis E.	35835116	PFC	KIA
Fleetwood, Donald	35868001	PFC	KIA
Fleetwood, Robert			
Fleetwood, Verlas M.	35498677	PFC	DOW
Frost, C. Owen			
Gumm, Wesley M.	36768146	SGT	KIA
Hancock, Loren W.	38698603	PVT	KIA
Harrington, Max			
Hattabaugh, Paul E.	35704748	PFC	KIA
Hoevener, Lawrence L.	35040826	PFC	KIA
Heckman, Omer H.	35101271	PFC	KIA
Henderson, Warren N.	35685773	SSG	KIA
Hubbard, Billie E.	0-446921	1 LT	DNB
Hunnicutt, William 0.	36813549	PVT	FOD
Kriete, Howard W.	35707168	PVT	KIA
Kriete, James F.	35699707	CPL	DNB
Landau, William A.	35040827	PFC	KIA
Lewis, Albert M.	35687416	PFC	DNB
Lewis, Frank W.	15095499	AV C	DNB
Loper, Glenn E.	35689930	PFC	KIA
Mackey, Willard A.	35687405	CPL	KIA
McKain, William K.	01703133	1 LT	DNB
McKinney, Robert D.	35109919	SSG	KIA
McMilian, James W.	35692922	SGT	KIA
Mikeles, Donald	35108681	PFC	
Mitchell, Richard L-			
Moore, Donald L.	35700386	SGT	KIA
Morgan, Franklin L.	35103473	PFC	KIA
Morgan, Kenneth B.	35496558	PFC	KIA
Nowling, James E.	15083423	PVT	DOW
Oberring, Albert J.	35685775	PFC	KIA
Pafenberg, Forrest	15102933	CPL	KIA

Peek, Howard H.	35894002	PVT	KIA
Poore, Kelso M.	35100870	SSG	KIA
Putnam, John C.	35242751	PVT	FOD
Ranabauer, Howard B.	35101915	PVT	KIA
Reynolds, Clinton O.	35698649	PFC	FOD
Reynolds, Wilford	35697959	PFC	KIA
Richardson, Billy	35697968	PFC	KIA
Rigel, Raymond L.	35243845	PFC	KIA
Rose, Herschel A.	35709455	PVT	KIA
Schwalbach, James E.	42015202	PFC	KIA
Smith, George O.	35702063	PVT	KIA
Speer, Robert E.			DOW
Spray, Dallas C., Jr.	35100873	SSG	KIA
Stahl, Robert E.	0-720596	2 LT	DNB
Steinkamp, Ralph F.	35694339	PVT	DOW
Steltenpohl, Melvin W .	35702909	PVT	DNB
Thomas, Max V.	35809178	PFC	KIA
Tidd, Winfred A.	35699680	PVT	KIA
Trapp, Ermil R.	35694453	TEC5	KIA
Waldkoetter, Walter J.	35252583	TEC4	KIA
Weddel, Clayton C.	35243823	PFC	KIA
Wells, Charles R., Sr.	15333419	PFC	KIA
Whitsett, Archie Jr.	35839548	PFC	KIA
Wieneke, Harold M.	35697973	PFC	KIA
Williams, Harlen N.	35838288	PVT	DOW
Wonning, Earl H.	0-688490	2 LT	FOD
Woodson, George M.	35109924	SGT	KIA
Wright, Albert J.	35694334	PFC	KIA

EARL ACTON, World War II, United States Army, born April 11, 1926 to Walter and Mary Baker Acton. Enlisted December 21, 1945 just after World War II and completed basic training at Camp Crowder, MO.

Dispatched to the European Theater of Operations and served during the occupation of Germany. Discharged at Camp Kilmer October 18, 1948.

Married Dorothy Motsinger and became parents of three children.

HUBERT ACTON, World War II, United States Army, 3rd Armored Division in North Africa and European Theater.

LESTER E. ACTON, World War II, United States Army, born at Cortland in 1923 to Walter and Mary Baker Acton.

Inducted into the army April 3, 1943 at Louisville, KY. Was trained as a cook and completed Bakers school. Was shipped overseas to the Pacific Theater of Operations.

Returned to the states February 20, 1945. Was awarded medals and ribbons reflecting his service. Discharged and returned to work at Arvin Industries.

Married Clara Griffin and they were parents of three children.

MELVIN ACTON, World War II, United State Army, born in 1929 in Ewing to Howard and Tweetie Allman Acton. Melvin lived in Jackson County most all of his life until his death in 1996. He joined the Army in 1946. His basic training was done at Fort Knox, Kentucky, and his AIT for infantry was at Fort Polk, Louisiana. He was deployed directly from AIT to the South Pacific where he assisted in removing Japanese soldiers from numerous islands, experiencing considerable combat. He was out of the army for one year, re-enlisted and was sent to Korea. He spent 1950-1952 in combat in Korea where he was wounded, and received a medical discharge. His brother, Floyd Neal Acton, also from Jackson County, was killed in the Korean conflict.

Melvin married Priscilla Smith in 1954, and had four sons, Steve, Robert, Gary, and Doug, all of which reside in Jackson County. Robert served in the Marine Corps from 1974-1982. Doug also served in the Army. Steve's son, Luke, is participating in Operation Enduring Freedom in Kuwait at the time of printing.

PAUL ADAMS, United States Army, Private, 8th Armored Infantry Battalion. Paul Adams enlisted at Indianapolis, Indiana, on the 19th day of March 1945 to serve in the United States Army. Paul "Ted" Adams was born February 14, 1920 at Norman, Indiana to James Monroe and Rosalie Cordell Adams.

He married Elizabeth Williams on December 31, 1939. They were the parents of five children: Martha Adams Killey, Mary Gail Adams Hanner, Edith Adams Hall, Harriet Jane Adams Starks, and Dennis Gene Adams.

Paul was a Marksman with the M-1 Rifle and received the WWII Victory Medal at time of his honorable discharge on December 13, 1945. He received his discharge while stationed in California.

CLARENCE B. ALLEN, World War II, United States Navy 1942-1945, born in 1913 and later was graduated from Brownstown High School. He continued his education and received his degree in chemical engineering from Purdue. He decided to enlist in the Navy, and was promoted to 2nd Lt. almost immediately.

He was ordered to the European Theater where he was in charge of landing craft maintenance, and witnessed his unit taking Prime Minister Churchill across the Rhine River.

He returned to Brownstown, was employed as an engineer for Kimberly-Clark Corporation and died on February 10, 1988. He was a brother to Eudora Horstman of Brownstown.

ARNOLD EUGENE ALLMAN, World War II, United States Army, born September 8, 1916 as a grandson of Sampson and Estella Stilwell Allman. He was raised on a farm located west of Medora.

Inducted into the army April 27, 1944. Completed basic training and shipped overseas. Served in the European Theater of Operations. Assigned to Company W, 1256th Combat Engineer Battalion. Carried out duty as a truck driver. Received EAME Theater Ribbon w/2 Campaign Stars, Good Conduct Medal and European Victory Medal.

Married to Mary Reynolds and they were parents of three sons. Divorced and later married Elizabeth Bell.

ARTHUR A. ALLMAN, World War II, United States Army, born December 29, 1919 in Jackson County and raised by Simpson and Estella Stilwell Allman.

Inducted into the army September 14, 1942, completed basic training and appointed machine shop foreman. Shipped overseas to the European Theater

of Operations. Assigned to Company B, 819th Aviation Engineer Battalion. He was able to visit brother during service.

Returned to the states, discharged at Camp Atterbury December 14, 1945. Returned home to his wife, Sylvia Collier, and they became parents of two sons.

RUSSELL W. ALTEMEYER, World War II, United States Army, born May 26, 1913 at Brownstown, Indiana. Induction at Camp Atterbury, Indiana, assigned to Company 4 – 51st Military Police Battalion. Shipped to Asiatic Theater of Operations.

Authorized to wear appropriate medals and ribbons: A/Pacific Ribbon with one Campaign Star, American Defense Medal and Good Conduct Ribbon. Discharged October 12, 1945 at Camp Atterbury.

DONALD "HAMMIE" ANDERSON, World War II, United States Army, was 32 years old when he was called to serve his country during WWII. He entered the Army October 25, 1943 and after Basic Training was sent to the Asiatic Pacific Theater. Although Hammie never talked much about his military experience, his military separation papers show that he was involved in some way at the Battle of Luzon in the Southern Philippines, where he received a Bronze Star. It is also known that he was part of the Occupying Force that entered Japan following their surrender.

Hammie was a Tech Sergeant in the 862nd Quartermaster Fumigation and Bath Company. He served eleven months and twenty days overseas and was discharged January 13, 1946. His discharge being Honorable and at the "Convenience of the Government Over 35 years of age."

Donald Anderson was born December 13, 1910 in Cortland, Indiana. It is known that he attended Indiana University for at least one year. Most of his civilian working years were spent at the Gerwin Shoe Factory. On December 16, 1949, he married the former Flossie Bernice Myers. They had no children but were much loved by all of their nieces and nephews and the children of their many friends.

Hammie was a very happy and positive person to be around. He and Flossie loved to attend the local High School basketball games and were active in the community. Hammie passed away in May 1978 at the age of 67. Flossie passed away in September 1985 at the age of 66.

GEORGE J. ARMSTRONG, was born October 13, 1919 in Linton, Indiana to Elmer and Kate

Armstrong. He received his elementary education and was graduated from Linton-Stockton High School in 1937. Three years later he enlisted in the Army and served in the Pacific Theater during World War II. He received his honorable discharge November 21, 1945, but re-enlisted in the Air Force March 20, 1947 and was assigned further training at Keesler Field, Mississippi before being transferred to San Marcos, Texas. From there Sgt. Armstrong was enrolled in the Military School of Service Principles at Stewart Air Base in Tennessee. He was selected to attend the NCO Academy at the Strategic Air Command Headquarters at Barksdale, Louisiana.

In 1957 George Armstrong was awarded a commendation for meritorious service, and later in 1964 he received the Air Force Commendation Ribbon for service as the NCO in charge of the recovery branch of the 307th Bombardment Wing stationed at Lincoln, Nebraska. His medal is accompanied with a written citation which reads: …The distinctive accomplishments of Chief Master Sergeant Armstrong culminate a distinguished career in the service of his country and reflect credit upon himself and the United States Air Force…!"

While awaiting retirement from the military service, he was married in 1951 to Bernice Snyder. That union was blessed with the birth of Jerry W. Armstrong, now deceased, and Carolyn Sue Beck. The family moved to Brownstown and George Armstrong was appointed the County Probation Officer. In 1967 he was employed by Arvin Automotive Tech Center until declining health terminated his work life.

George was an active member of the Brownstown VFW Post 10807 until he suffered a massive stoke while enjoying his retirement in Bradenton, Florida. George J. Armstrong was buried in 1994 at Immanuel Lutheran Cemetery in Seymour.

BILLY R. AULT, World War II, United States Army, a son of Jesse Ault of Seymour and a graduate of the local high school. He first saw action in Germany. He returned home to Jackson County.

DALE K. AULT, World War II, United States Army, son of Jesse Ault of Seymour who graduated from Tampico High School. He served overseas and saw action in France and the Ardennes.

After the war had ended he was employed by the Hamilton-Cosco Company until he died.

GERALD KEITH AULT, World War II and Korea, United States Army, born in 1919 to Frank and Maida Mize Ault in Spraytown and later graduated from Freetown High School in 1939. He was then employed as a truck driver and mechanic at Carpenter's Garage in Freetown.

In April 1941 Gerald Keith Ault was drafted into the Army and assigned serial number 35102460. He completed his basic training at Camp Shelby, Mississippi and assigned to the motor pool. He transferred to Camp Edwards in Massachusetts for amphibian training. He was then stationed at Camp Gordon Johnson, and on October 3, 1944, he traveled to Washington, D.C. and married Helen Spurgeon who was working for the War Production Board.

In January 1945 Keith was shipped overseas to the Philippines and began delivering mail and supplies throughout the islands of the South Pacific. He was returned to the States in 1945 and re-enlisted in the Reserve Program following his discharge at Camp Atterbury. He was called to active duty in 1950 and was sent to Fort Hood, Texas. By November he was wounded in battle for "Chosen Reservoir" in Korea.

Corporal Ault was awarded the Purple Heart and returned to the States to recuperate. Eventually he returned to duty in Virginia and was later discharged with permanent disability in 1951. He was employed as a bus driver for the Brownstown Schools where his two children were students. Gerald Keith Ault passed away August 9, 2001.

HARLAN R. AULT, World War II, United States Army Air Corps, born to Jesse Ault of Seymour and graduated from Tampico High School. He was inducted on October 17, 1942 and after basic training, he was stationed at Scott and Chanute Field, Illinois. He was a cook during the entire time of his military endeavors.

Returned home to Jackson County and returned to Bakers Dozens operational dozen. Completed tour of duty and was discharged. Married to Virginia Rosmeyer and they became the parents of a daughter named Sharon.

Harlan died in November 1988.

JESSE AULT, JR., World War II, Company D, 290th Infantry Division, was killed in action during the Battle of the Bulge, 1943-45.

FELTNER BAKER, World War II, United States Navy, born December 2, 1916 to B.P. and Addie Baker. Was raised with a family of five sisters and three brothers. Joined the navy early in World War II and assigned to the USS *John Penn* which was sunk near Guadalcanal by torpedo hit and plane crash into the ship. Feltner died along with others.

A hero by any description because he gave his life for his country and sacred flag of the United States.

CARL R. BAKER, World War II, 101st Airborne Infantry, was killed June 9, 1944 in Normandy.

HOBERT H. BAKER, World War II, United States Army, was born January 2, 1922 in Manchester, KY to B.P. and Addie Baker but the family moved to Brownstown when he was only a child. He grew up around the county seat, attended the Slygo school and graduated from Brownstown High School.

He was drafted into the army December 7, 1942 and reported to Fort Harrison with 28 other recruits from Jackson County. He was assigned 94th Infantry Division and sent to Kansas for basic training. He was then placed in Company K, 302nd Infantry Regiment.

Following further training, his unit was shipped overseas to England on August 6, 1944. One month later he arrived in France and was in combat with Patton's 3rd Army fighting in the Battle of the Bulge at Saar-Mosselle triangle of the Siegfried Line. Shortly thereafter Sgt. lost his entire squad, including his assistant, Ernest Burnside of Freetown who died as a result of shrapnel wounds.

On February 19, 1945 while attacking a pillbox with a new squad, he was wounded in his right foot from German artillery, only after a near miss when his helmet was hit by shrapnel. He was sent to Scotland and then returned to Fort Custer for convalescence.

He returned to Brownstown, found work as a mechanic and started his own dealership. He married Geneva Hobbs of Salem and they now reside a few miles southeast of Brownstown. He had two daughters.

JOHNNY ROY BAKER, World War II, United States Army, was born in Lawrence County January 27, 1920 to Shirley and Edith Baker of Leesville. He was one of three children in the family. Upon reaching maturity he was drafted into the army on May 9, 1944. He completed basic training at Barkley, TX.

He was sent to Camp Crowder, MO to receive special training for the medical corps. He was shipped overseas to the Philippines and stationed at Leyte and Mindoro where he was assigned to the 8th Malaria Control Unit. He was dispatched to Manila to wait for his return to the states. He was ordered to Indianapolis to receive his discharge, after which time he returned to Brownstown and was re-united with his wife, Annamary Henderson Baker and family on January 26, 1946.

He retired from General Motors in Bedford after 30 years of service and now resides near Norman, Indiana.

TED BAKER, World War II, United States Navy, born on June 6, 1926 in Kentucky. Served in the navy during WWII. Married Florence Meeks in 1945 and they became parents of three daughters. Resided near Brownstown and operated Baker's Body Shop.

EMMETT E. BANE, World War II, United States Army, entered the army in 1943 and was assigned to Battery B of the 282nd Field Artillery Battalion. He was shipped overseas to the European Theater of Operations and made part of the 3rd Army under General Patton who was bound to reach Berlin first.

Emmett was a projectionist motion picture specialist who served thru France, the Rhineland and Central Europe. Upon discharge he was authorized to wear the American Theater, EAME Ribbon with three Campaign Stars, Good Conduct Ribbon and Victory Medal for WWII.

Emmett married Lucille Goss and they became parents of two children, Sharon Smith and David Bane. Emmett is co-owner of a trailer park in Brownstown.

IVAN E. BANE, World War II, United States Army, entered the army in 1942 and served with the Transportation Command Unit #1902. He was trained as a truck driver and Expert Rifleman. He was shipped

overseas to the South Pacific Theater of Operations and stationed in central Burma.

His assignments were special; he delivered vital military supplies via the Burma Road, His citations included the Good Conduct Medal and the Asiatic-Pacific Medal.

He married Rosa Cockerham and they became parents of seven children: Glen, Richard, Gloria Baughman, Edith Gambrel, Vickie Hawn, Linda Hounshel and Bill Bane.

Ivan owned and operated a sawmill and logging business at Freetown. He is now retired.

FRANK B. BARD, World War II, 306th Medical Battalion, 81st Division, Philippine Islands. Eventually promoted to the rank of Major, he was the recipient of several commendations for the exceptional medical care of the troops during actual combat. After "VJ" Day Dr. Bard returned home from the service in 1946 and took up his practice in Crothersville. He was a member of the County Board of Health, served on staff of the Memorial Hospital in Seymour for some 20 years before expiring September 9, 1988.

ADRIAN "ANDY" BARKSDALE, United States Army Air Force, 1944-1945, PVT, 15 404 204, was born May 27, 1926 and lived on 235 S. Park Drive across from home plate of the Geyser Park baseball diamond in Seymour, Indiana. He is the son of Andrew Arthur and Emma "Dimp" Tiemeier; his brother was Thomas Leon Barksdale, FC3, United States Navy.

After graduating from Shields High School in 1944 he entered the Army Air Force August 22, 1944 and was honorably discharged October 30, 1945. His basic training was at Sheppard Field at Wichita Falls, Texas. He then had a stop over at Good Fellow Field at St. Angelo, Texas continuing to Keesler Field at Biloxi, Mississippi where he attended Aircraft Mechanic School. He hoped to be a pilot and did qualify for Cadet training but when World War II ended all of the service men in his unit were discharged. He originally, was classified as an AAF

Pvt. Supply Technician and his job was listed as a driver of a 2-1/2 ton truck hauling supplies, equipment, and tools from incoming aircraft, and to assist in taking inventory.

On July 3, 1949 he married Lucille Kruse and they had six children and had four grandchildren. The children are Daniel Leon, Janice Carol (died 1953), Teresa Ann (died 1955), Sheila Ann, Sharon Carol, and Cheryl Diane. His grandchildren are Jeffrey Noel, Laura Melissa, and Kyle Daniel from his son Dan and Christopher Mark Gullion from his daughter Sharon. He became a self employed Building Contractor and still resides in Brownsburg, Indiana.

THOMAS LEON BARKSDALE, World War II, United States Navy, born October 8, 1924 to Andrew and Emma Tiemeier Barksdale. Graduated from Seymour High School in 1942. Enlisted in the navy January 14, 1943 and completed basic training at Great Lakes Naval Station. Assigned advanced weapons control at Norfolk, VA. Sent to California and assigned to USS *Indianapolis*.

Saw action at Marshall Islands, Asiatic Raids, Marianas, Caroline Islands, Iwo Jima Operation, Okinawa. Delivered components for the Atomic Bomb. Sailed to Guam and Leyte; hit by Japanese torpedoes. Leon T. Barksdale was buried at sea. Awarded Purple Heart. Memorial Burial Service at Immanuel March 31, 1946.

JACOB FRANK BAUGHMAN, World War II, United States Army, was born May 26, 1917 to Thomas and Neva Callahan Baughman. He was raised on the family farm located a few miles west of Brownstown. He was drafted and inducted into the army January 15, 1944 and stationed first at Fort Thomas, KY.

He was assigned to Company "B" of the 806th Tank Destroyer Battalion and stationed at Fort Hood, TX. He was ordered to Mississippi prior to being shipped overseas to Japan in the Pacific Theater. He was qualified as a gun expert and was listed as a 1st class gunner with the antitank gun crews.

Frank Baughman married Opal Ray May 23, 1937 and to them were born three surviving children, including Herschel Lee, Bonnie Jean and Connie June born in 1944. After a divorce, Frank Baughman died of cancer in 1993.

MORRIS BAUGHMAN, World War II, United States Army, Drafted into the army March 1, 1946. Basic training at Camp Robinson, AR. Joined the paratroopers, completed Jump School at Fort Benning, GA and completed eight jumps, washed out. After further training assigned to the Military

Police at Camp Gordon, GA. Discharged September 7, 1947.

RUSSELL BAUGHMAN, JR.,

RUSSELL BAUGHMAN, JR., World War II, United States Army, was born in 1927 to Russell and Gladys Barkman Baughman. He joined the army in 1944 and was assigned as a cook. Records verify he never was shipped overseas. He was discharged in 1946 and returned home to Columbus.

In 1950 he married Chrystal Freeze but they had no children and years later he married Juanita Morgan. He died in 1994 in Brownstown.

STANLEY LEROY BAUGHMAN, World War II, United States Army, was born May 19, 1924 to Thomas and Neva Callahan Baughman of Jackson County. He was raised on the family homestead and attended the Clearspring School.

He was drafted and inducted into the army May 8, 1943 at Indianapolis and assigned to the medical division. He was stationed in Texas and Louisiana before reporting to the east coast. His unit was shipped overseas to the European Theater of Operations. He went into action in Normandy and advanced through Belgium, the Rhineland and on into Germany. After VE Day he was returned to the states and discharged December 27, 1945.

He was authorized to wear various medals and ribbons reflecting his service engagements. Stanley married Anna Jane Dalton in 1955 and they became parents of four children, including Stanley Leroy, Barbara Jean, Rachel Ann and Sherry Lynn Baughman. The family lived near Medora. Stanley died January 27, 2000 and his wife followed him less than one year later on October 29, 2000.

HAROLD BECKMAN, World War II, United States Army, was born August 26, 1915 in Seymour, Indiana to Henry and Rosa Alwes Beckman. In November 1941 he was drafted into the army. He took his basic training at Camp Wheeler in Macon, Georgia. After basic training, he went to Fort Lewis, Washington to join the 41st Infantry Division. After spending several weeks at Fort Lewis, he went to San Francisco, traveled under the Golden Gate Bridge and boarded the *Queen Elizabeth,* the world's largest ship at that time. There were over 10,000 troops on the ship headed for Melbourne, Australia.

The trip to Australia took around 21 days. There were two battle ships, at all times that went ahead of them for protection from the Japanese. When the *Queen Elizabeth* arrived in Australia they camped north of Melbourne and received more training. Next he went to Rock Hampton for still more training.

From Rock Hampton he went to Papua, New Guinea for combat with the Japanese. They landed at Port Moresby and then flew to Buna on the east coast. As they walked to the front line, the United States Band played for them. While in combat with the Japanese in New Guinea, he had to wade in waist deep water to get to the front line. After being in combat for some time, he contracted Malaria and was sent to Port Moresby to be treated. While he was at the hospital, he was administered medicine by a soldier named Henry Schulte, who was also from Seymour.

After he recovered from malaria he was sent back to join his infantry. Several weeks later he went with his infantry back to Australia for replacement because they had lost so many men. Later he was chosen to go back to the United States on rotation. While he was still overseas he saw General MacArthur as he drove by him in a jeep and also saw Eleanor Roosevelt as she addressed the troops in Australia.

After he returned to the United States he received a furlough for several weeks, then was sent to Fort Benning, Georgia. Next he was sent to the United States Air Force Base in Barstow, California and worked in the motor pool until the fall of 1945. He was discharged from the United States Air Force on October 20, 1945 from the, Army Air Force Separation Base at Bauer Field in Fort Wayne, Indiana.

In 1947 he married Edith Bedel and have been married to her for almost 57 years. They have two children, Roger Beckman and Joyce Vehslage.

HOWARD L. BELDON, World War II, United States Navy, was stationed in Cuba during his service tour of duty. Currently resides in Tampico, Indiana. Married to Dorothy Cunningham.

RUSSELL R. "RUSTY" BELL, World War II, United States Army, ASN #35813547, was born November 22, 1925 in Freetown as the sixth child of Henry and Delilah Lucas Bell. As a young man he was drafted into the United States Army January 15, 1944. Along with Earl Goecker the two men were sent to Camp Kohler, California as part of the 276th Pole Line Construction Company of the Signal Corps. Their task was to erect telephone poles and string lines.

His outfit was sent to the Pacific but he was transferred to the 3139th Motor Messengers which was sent to Europe. The men arrived in France on the eve of the Battle of the Bulge. While involved Russell Bell met Doyl Engle, Doyl Hatton, Russell Phegley and his own brother, Leo Bell. All were Jackson County men.

While crossing the Rhine River, orders were issued asking for two men from each unit to volunteer for the infantry. He and his buddy, Harry Peterson were transferred into the 75th Division and sent to Belgium and on to Holland. They were in Germany when the war ended. Those two men remained friends and in touch with each other until Howard died.

Following a 90-day furlough, Russell Bell re-enlisted for another year and was deployed to Japan. While on leave he returned to Jackson County and married Wanda Cockerham February 23, 1946. When "VJ" came he was sent to Camp Stoneman, California and discharged January 15, 1947.

JOHN FRANKLIN BERGDOLL, World War II, United States Army Air Corps, son of John and Orpha E. Bergdoll of Medora. Graduated as a star in athletics from the local high school in 1942. Matriculated at Indiana University.

Enlisted November 10, 1942 and shipped overseas to the Pacific Theater. Served in the China-Burma-India as a meteorologist. Given a dagger as a present by George Speer, he carried that gift around the world and back home. Discharged January 9, 1946 at Camp Kilmer, NJ.

Returned to Jackson County, but moved to Greenwood. He is the 5th generation of Bergdoll lineage. Currently retired but serves as a TV weather watcher.

CHARLES W. BLACKWOOD, World War II, United States Army, son of Berky and Hallie Blackwood, was born November 27, 1914, Vallonia, Indiana. He married Myrtle Compton and has one daughter Rosa Charlett Blackwood.

As a civilian he worked for Bundy Brothers of Vallonia Indiana, from November 1937 to 1944. Drove a 1-1/2 ton truck for feed company. Entered active service on April 27, 1944 at Fort Harrison, Indiana.

Military assignments: 2-1/4 months basic training engineers (521), 13 months, tech 5 truck driver heavy 931, 5 months tech 4 automotive mechanic (014).

Severed with the 1281st Engineers Combat Battalion, Company B in the European and Asiatic and Pacific Theater of Operations for 17 months, drove 4 ton diamond (t) dump truck, hauled gravel for building and road construction, maintained and serviced truck, drove day and night over all kinds of roads.

Decorations and Citations: Occupation Medal (Germany), EAME Theater Ribbon, Asiatic-Pacific Theater Ribbon, Philippine Liberation Ribbon, Good Conduct Medal, WWII Victory Medal. Honorable Discharge was signed by Harry S. Truman, President of the United States.

EARL O. BLAIR, World War II, United States Army, the military memoirs of Earl O. Blair, a Sergeant in the Army of The United States of America,

during WWII in the European Theater of Operation. He was assigned a Serial Number of 35090068 and was in the 3013 Quarter Master Bakery that produced a ton of bread per hour, 24 hours daily.

Earl was born December 20, 1922, in Tampico, a small town in Jackson County, Indiana, to Loyal and Lilly Hawn Blair. He was a graduate of Tampico High School. He entered the service on February 8, 1943, completing Basic Training at Vancouver Barracks, Washington and Camp Sutton, NC. In August 1913, Earl left to go to England. A few days after D-Day, he was transferred to Normandy Beach, France, and then to Belgium, Holland, and Germany. After spending two years, two months, and 11 days overseas, he left Germany on December 5, 1945, to return to the United States. He was discharged on December 23, 1945, at Camp Atterbury, Indiana.

Earl married Mary Meeks May 10, 1942, at Russell Chapel Church, near Tampico. After the completion of his military duty, they moved to Muncie, Indiana, and had two children, Dennis and Diana, who also reside in Muncie. Earl has eight grandchildren and eight great-grandchildren.

WALLACE BLAIR, World War II, United States Navy, was born January 30, 1927 in Jackson County to Loyal and Lillie Hawn Blair. He attended Tampico High School before he went in service to defend his country.

He enlisted in the navy when he was 17 years old in 1944. He completed boot camp training in New York and was granted liberty to come home to visit his parents. He returned to New York and his unit was shipped overseas where he was stationed in England and Germany.

He received his discharge at an unknown location in 1946.

He married Georgia Maxie on October 11, 1947 as soon as he found work at Cummins in Columbus. Along with his farming he was able to care for his family of five children for more than 30 years

He died and was buried at Russell Chapel Cemetery with military honors.

WILLARD ALLEN BOLING, World War and following United States Navy, was born in Sparksville on February 13, 1921 and was the son of Albert Boling and Grace Henderson Boling Lane. His stepfather was Clausel "Pard" lane. His half-brothers were Jim Lane, Dick Lane, and half sisters are Evon Martin and Bonnie Norton. He grew up in Sparksville and loved to fish and hunt every chance he got. He went to school at Medora where he was on the basketball team. After graduating

in 1939, he married Eldora Ruth Shoults about a year later. They were living in Texarkana, Texas when Pearl Harbor was bombed. They moved back to Jackson County and he joined the Navy.

He went to boot camp at Great Lakes, Illinois. During his time in the service, he was stationed in Connecticut (twice), Panama Canal, Pearl Harbor and Detroit.

He received a commendation front Rear Admiral Nunn for saying a boy's life, using a decompression chamber on the USS *Cero*. Another commendation for developing an emergency method of operating the distiller units aboard USS *Tang* while deployed on a mission. Failure of units would have meant a serious problem and aborting a special operation. A commendation for leading Naval Reserve Submarine Division 9-228 to be the number one Reserve Submarine Division in the United States; this was his last assigned duty, where he retired as Leading Engineman, Instructor and chief of the Boat.

He received six Bronze Stars, six Good Conduct, WWII Victory, American Campaign, Asiatic-Pacific Campaign and National Defense Service. He completed numerous service courses, graduating number 1 in S/M Damage Control "A" School.

While in his travels, he took his family with him wherever he was stationed. Eldora and Willard Boling had three children: Peggy Lynn (July 14, 1948), Jerry Allan (May 18, 1951), and Tim Drew (January 1, 1953).

He retired in Medora, Indiana and was employed with the State Highway Dept. at Unit 2 where he was the Foreman. Every chance he got he would go fishing and hunting while getting better acquainted with his family.

CARL C. BONEBRIGHT, Sergeant, enlisted in the United States Army while residing in Chicago, Illinois. sometime in mid-1944. After he had completed basic training he was sent overseas and stationed in France. Housed in tent city for nearly two weeks, he was finally ordered to Nuremberg, Germany where he joined the 3rd Armored Division Headquarters Unit.

He replaced a former driver who had been killed during his line of duty, and became the chauffeur to Lt. Colonel Sweat, an ex-prisoner of war. Shortly thereafter, he was transferred to the Intelligence Duty for the War Criminal Trials. Being present and on duty each day, he was to witness the trials of Karl Donitz and Albert Speer. Both were eventually sentenced to prison terms of 20 years.

Carl Bonebright was on hand when Martin Bormann was condemned to death in absentia. He stood by when Hermann Goring committed suicide before he could be executed. Thus ended the Nuremberg Trials which had been conducted by an International Military Tribunal through numerous sessions.

Leaving the trial scene, he was on hand just minutes after the death of General George Patton who died as a result of injuries suffered during a jeep accident. Bonebright was ordered to be one of three flag bearers at the ceremony when President Truman reviewed the troops then stationed in Europe. He was discharged June 26, 1946 and returned to Vallonia.

IRVIN E. BOZARTH, ASN 15209891, Company A, 82nd Chemical Warfare Battalion, United States Army, Irvin E. Bozarth (standing in picture) with one of his military buddies in 1944 while serving in the Army during World War II. He was stationed in Panama, Japan and several of the islands located around Japan. He served his country for nearly six years before he received his honorable discharge. He returned to his home located on SR 235 near Medora. His friend has been identified as William Meridith from Kentucky.

GEORGE W. BRACKEMYRE, World War II, United States Army, born in Seymour November 3, 1921 and resided there his entire life. Graduated from Seymour High School in 1939. Entered the army and completed basic training at Fort Benning.

Was shipped overseas to the European Theater and assigned to the 10th Armored Division of Patton's 3rd Army. He saw action during the Battle of the Bulge. Was Gunner on a half track vehicle. Received the Good Conduct Medal, WWII Victory Medal, EAME Theater Ribbon, Purple Heart and Distinguished Service Cross. He was discharged in 1945.

Returned to Seymour and resides with his wife, Imogene.

WILFORD M. BRACKEMYRE, World War II, United States Army, was inducted into the U.S. Army May 9, 1944, and received his basic training at Ft. Benjamin Harrison in Indiana. He was born at Acme, IN, Jan. 5, 1919, and has lived most of his adult life in Jackson County, Indiana.

Private First Class Wilford Brackemyre served with Company B, 324th Infantry. His Military Occupational Specialty was Rifleman 745 and he received his Combat Infantryman Badge December 26, 1944. He served in the European Theater in the Central European Campaigns, receiving the EAME Campaign Medal with one Bronze Star, Good Conduct Medal, WWII Victory Medal, and the Bronze Star Medal. He served in Europe from November 2, 1944 to July 15, 1945 and volunteered for the Invasion of Japan in the Pacific Theater. He served one year, six months and 11 days and was separated with an Honorable Discharge at the Separation Center, Camp Fannin, Texas, November 19, 1945.

Wilford returned to Seymour, and his wife Bernice and son to resume his civilian life and work.

SAMUEL WALTER BRASHER, World War II, United States Army, born in 1924 to Harvey and Audrey Brasher, he was the oldest of 10 children.

Mr. Brasher entered the service on March 3, 1943 at Ft. McPherson, Georgia. After further training at Fort Jackson, South Carolina and Camp Atterbury, Indiana, he was shipped to Eastern Belgium as a medic in the newly formed 106 Infantry Division, "Golden Lions."

During the "Battle of the Bulge" on December 16, 1944, he was taken Prisoner of War along with 7,000 others. In its entirety, the Battle of the Bulge was one of the worse battles in terms of losses to the American forces in World War II. They soon discovered that they had arrived before their ammunition had, leaving his division defenseless. Mr. Brasher along with the other POWs were marched by the Germans for seven days and seven nights without a bite to eat or drink. They were packed into waiting train cars where they were bombed by Allied planes, who thought they were destroying Nazi supplies. Those surviving were unloaded and forced to march to the camp. The POW camp was so crowded that the new prisoners had to stay outdoors in sub-zero conditions, again being bombed by Allied fire. Brasher survived being a POW for six months, until Russian forces entered the camp to free the prisoners. He once said, although it would have been easy to succumb to the hunger or the cold while in the POW camps, he kept the thoughts of his bride awaiting his return in Jackson County. The Nazi's had confiscated the only picture he had of her, but that could not destroy the one he had in his mind.

Upon his return to the state's he came home to his wife, Hazel Hall Brasher, and also to a new son, which was followed by eight other children. He lived most of his life in Crothersville, Indiana, as a carpenter. Among the medals he received are the Bronze Star, Purple Heart, POW Medal, European, National Defense and Good Conduct Metals. He was given an Honorable Discharge on October 21, 1945.

WALTER EDGAR BROOKS, World War II, United States Navy, Jack, as he was called by all who knew him, was the son of Charles and Annice Galyen Brooks. He was born in Butlerville, IN on July 14, 1908. He entered the military on June 15, 1943 and was discharged as a Chief Machinist's Mate, V-6, on October 6, 1945. Jack enlisted in Flagler Beach, Florida where he was living and working on construction at the time. Upon entering the service, he was assigned to the Construction Battalion (better known as the C.B.'s). He was moved from place to place during his years in the C.B.'s building temporary sites to be used by the military. His assignments were mostly in the warmer climates of the War Zones. After being discharged, Jack moved back to Brownstown, IN where he had lived with his parents before his marriage. He operated heavy equipment for himself and others. He was a partner in Mitchell and Stark Construction Company when he died in November 1959. He left behind a widow Jewell Brooks who continued to reside in Brownstown. He was proud of what he had accomplished while serving his country and continued to participate in civic activities, especially through his involvement in the local Masonic Lodges, until his death.

JAMES THOMAS BROWN, World War II, United States Army, was born December 18, 1926 and moved from Terre Haute to Jackson County. He graduated from Brownstown High School in 1945. Two weeks later he was inducted into the army and reported for duty at Camp Atterbury. He was sent to Fort Sill, OK for basic training in the field artillery.

Once completed, he was directed to New York in November 1945 and shipped overseas to the European Theater of Operations. His unit was stationed in Germany with Battery "A" of the 91st Field Artillery, 1st Armored Division. A year later he was returned to the states and stationed at Fort Meade, Maryland awaiting to be discharged November 18, 1946.

When he was settled back in Brownstown he was married to Gleda Weddle and they went into dairy farming. Later he became vice president of Brown Beverage Company. He was later appointed County Veterans Officer and he served eight years until his death on March 23, 1991. He was the father of four surviving sons, including Steve, Jim, Tom and Jerry.

JUDGE ROBERT R. BROWN, ASN 55503973, 6th Armored Division U.S. Army, Germany, was drafted into the United States Army, upon his graduation and was assigned to the 6th Armored Division. He served in the post WWII era from October 1954 to August 1956 when he received his discharge. Upon his return home he continued his education. He later received the Doctor of Jurisprudence Degree, with honors, from Indiana University School of Law.

He practiced law under the firm name of Whitcomb & Brown in Seymour with the former Governor of Indiana, Edgar D. Whitcomb. Later, after serving as prosecuting attorney of Jackson County for six years, he was seated as Judge of the Jackson County Court, 40th Judicial Circuit of Indiana, and served for more than 28 years in Brownstown.

Judge Brown served two years as president of the Indiana Judges Association, State of Indiana Representative to the National Conference of State Trial Judges, Board of Directors Member of the Indiana Judicial Center, Hearing Officer for the Indiana Supreme Court Disciplinary Commission, member of the Indiana Supreme Court's Committee on Rules of Practice and Procedure, and served 15 years as a member of the Board of Directors of the Indiana Law Enforcement Training Board for the Police Academy of Indiana, as well as being active in community affairs in Jackson County. He has been honored as a "Sagamore of the Wabash" on four separate occasions by different governors of the state of Indiana.

Upon retirement from the bench, he joined the law firm of Montgomery, Elsner & Pardieck in an "of counsel" position. As such, he served two years as the Jackson County Attorney and continues to serve as counsel for the renovation of the Jackson County Courthouse and its annex. He serves as a mediator throughout southern Indiana and also fills in for Judges around the state who are ill or on vacation, as a Senior Judge. He is admitted to practice law before all state and federal courts as well as the Supreme Court of the United States.

Judge Brown and his wife, Donna, will celebrate their 50th wedding anniversary in August of 2004. They have three grown children and five grandsons.

OTIS F. BRYAN, United States Air Force 1927-1973, was born January 3, 1908 on a small farm in Grassy Fork Township of Jackson County, Indiana. He spent his teen-age years roaming the country around Seymour. He attended Indiana University and was active in the Reserve Officer Training Corps. In 1927 he received an appointment as a flying cadet, and graduated in 1929 as a pursuit pilot. He was assigned to the 2nd Bombardment Group stationed at Langley Field in Virginia. His military career had begun.

In June 1929 he left the Air Corps and became a co-pilot with TWA to fly the mail under governmental contract. He was later promoted and served as chief pilot, and by 1941 was Vice President of TWA. A short time later he was recalled to active duty. Subsequently, he was selected to organize the Eagle Nest Flight Center at Albuquerque, New Mexico. He was in charge of training Air Corps pilots and navigators.

During WWII Otis F. Bryan was assigned as the pilot to fly the President of the United States to Casablanca, Cairo and Yalta. Throughout the war years he flew many leading personalities, including Eisenhower, Marshall and Admiral Leahy.

Otis F. Bryan left the service in 1948 to become the Vice President of the Soriana Company in the Philippines. Later he was elected Vice President of the General Precision Company in New York. He retired in 1973 and settled-down as a rancher in Greeley, Kansas.

MALCOLM W. BUCKNER, World War II, 93rd Bomb Group, 8th U.S. Air Force, European Theater, D-Day Invasion of Normandy, married Lt. Mary Blackmore, a nurse from Indiana, after the war ended. This transplanted Texan and his wife established their home in Indianapolis where he ran his own roofing business. In time, Malcolm learned his ancestors were Hoosiers living in the area at Paoli and Martinsville. From that time Malcolm Buckner made himself at home near Houston in Jackson County.

DELMER W. BUESCHER, World War II, United States Army, entered the Army in January 1944, two months after marrying a Jackson County girl, the former Frances Roberta Richardson, in Indianapolis, Indiana. Delmer took his basic training at Fort Hood, Texas and advanced training at Camp Carson, Colorado.

Following his training Delmer became a member of the "Tank Destroyer Force" which was assigned to the 9th Armored Division. He arrived in Le Havre, France on. Thanksgiving Day 1944 and remembers the harbor being full of sunken ships at the time of his arrival. Delmer and his unit didn't receive their Thanksgiving Dinner until the following day, and it was raining so hard that he had to empty his mess kit of rain water three times, before he completed his meal.

It is known that Delmer was involved in the Battle of The Bulge, which started December 16, 1944 and also that he and his unit took part in the taking of the Remagen Bridgehead on March 7, 1945.

PFC Buescher functioned as a cook during that period of time he was in Europe. On rare occasions he would tell the story of having a flashlight shot out of his hand while performing his duties. That incident took place on the very day his unit received word that the war had ended.

His Military Service ended in February 1946 and he returned to Indiana. Delmer and Frances moved to Redding Township in Jackson County in early 1947. Delmer worked at Farm Bureau in Columbus as a short haul truck-driver for most of his working years.

While living in Redding Township they raised two daughters, Linda and Nancy Frances passed away June 11, 1992 at the age of 68. Delmer passed away May 10, 1996 at the age of 73.

BERNARD LEE BURNSIDE, World War II, United States Army, was born May 28, 1924, a son of William and Bernice Lyon Burnside of Freetown. He was inducted into the army March 18, 1943 at Louisville, KY. He reported for duty at Ft. Harrison in Indianapolis.

He completed basic training at Fort Leonard Wood, MO and was assigned to the newly-activated 75th Infantry Division. He was in Company F of the 291st Regiment. He completed training at various army schools. On a furlough he went home and married Betty Jane Persinger.

He was shipped overseas to the European Theater of Operations as part of the 9th Infantry and he saw action in North Africa, Sicily and took part of the invasion of France. His unit linked up with the Russians May 10, 1945, just two days after VE Day was declared. He was one of a few men from Jackson County present to hear Gen. Patton deliver his victory speech at Nuremburg.

He was authorized to wear several ribbons and was awarded the Bronze Star for bravery under fire. He was discharged at Camp Atterbury April 13, 1946.

ERNEST RALPH BURNSIDE, World War II, United States Army, was born April 20, 1922 a son of William and Bernice Lyon Burnside in Freetown. He was inducted into the army in December 1942 and reported for duty at Ft. Harrison, IN. After being issued clothing and supplies, he was sent to Camp Phillips, KS. He was assigned to Camp Phillips where he joined Company K, 302nd Infantry Regiment of the 94th Division,

After completing his basic training, he was shipped overseas on August 6, 1944 as a rifleman. He fought in northern France and the Rhineland campaigns as a Sergeant before going to the hospital. When he returned to his unit he was promoted and served as the supply Sgt.

He was authorized to wear various ribbons and medals and each was noted on his discharge received December 20, 1945.

RAY WILLIAM BURNSIDE, World War II, United States Army, was born December 31, 1919 a son of William and Bernice Lyon Burnside at Freetown. He was inducted into the army at Louisville, KY and then reported to Ft. Benjamin Harrison, IN. He was issued his serial number, clothes and equipment.

He was directed to Florida for his basic training before being assigned as a military policeman to serve in the Panama Canal Zone. When a position opened he was promoted to S/Sgt of the supply depot. When he was sent home and authorized to wear various ribbons and medals, he was discharged at Camp Atterbury.

THOMAS BYARLAY, World War II, United States Army, PFC, was born in Owen Township, Jackson County on September 1, 1922 to Otis and Maybelle Byarlay and lived all his life near Medora.

He was inducted into the Army at Louisville, KY on December 26, 1942 and entered service on January 2, 1943 at Fort Benjamin Harrison. After a week, he was sent to Camp Maxey, Texas, where he received shots and some basic training. He was assigned to 623rd Ordinance Ammo Co. and remained for the duration.

He left there for Yuma, Arizona, then Needles, California on desert maneuvers until August 23, 1943. He left there for Townsville, Australia, arriving September 16, 1943. After some training there, he left for New Guinea then on to Dutch, New Guinea. From there it was island hopping - Hollandia, Bink, Wadke, Morotia, then Philippines, Mindora, Palawan, Mindanao and Leyte.

He worked in ammunition delivering from boats to troops in frontline, handling bombs, dynamite, TNT and poisonous gas. He also defused unexploded bombs and shells, dumping them at sea.

Most of his time was spent by being separated from the main company by going to different battalions with just a few men in each detachment.

He went to Palawan, Philippine Island. A large number of U.S., British, Australians and other Allies were burned to death there. They were put in tunnels and burned with gasoline by the Japanese. He left there and went to Mindanao, then to Leyte. He left here for U.S. arriving home on July 27, 1945.

On November 12, 1945 he was discharged at Ft. Meade, Maryland.

The rest of the unit went on to Japan and were in the harbor when the treaty was signed.

The 623rd has held 54 annual reunions and plans for the 55th to be held in 2004 at Scottsburg, IN. Out of 200 men, only a few are left.

LOUIS A. CARR, World War II, United States Marine Corps, was born near Medora on November 20, 1921, a son of Lewis and Goldie Darr Carr. He graduated from the local high school in 1941 and enlisted in the marines. He completed his boot training at Camp Elliott near San Diego a few days before the Japanese on Pearl Harbor. He held dual military qualifications as a mortar Crewman and BAR man. He was assigned to the 2nd Marine Division in 1942 and shipped overseas to the South Pacific. Through the remainder of 1942 he was in combat on the Solomon Islands of Tulagi and Guadalcanal. In January 1943 his division moved on to Wellington, NZ for rest and recuperation.

Beginning in November 1943 he was part of the amphibious assault and capture of Japanese-held atoll of Tarawa. They went on to take the Marianna Islands, Saipan and Tinian. On August 1, 1944 he was evacuated from combat due to a back injury and sickness from malaria. After months in a military hospital located in Klamath Falls, OR, he was assigned duty at the naval shipyards in Philadelphia. He received his discharge early in August 1945. His memories of the battle horrors never left him. Andy Rooney wrote a report on the battle for Tarara and stated " during the fight for one square mile of coral, 4,690 soldiers were killed." During the three day battle 1,026 Marines were killed and 1,196 wounded.

Louis died of lung cancer in 1999 and full military honors were accorded him at his burial in Custer National Military Cemetery at Battle Creek, MI.

GAIL REX CARTER, World War II, United States Army Air Corps, enlisted in the U.S. Army as a private in 1942. He reported to Ft. Harrison December 8, 1942 and was assigned to Armament School. While at school he applied for pilot training and was accepted. He proceeded to the University of North Dakota for pre-cadet training in the Western Flying Training Command. He graduated from flight training June 27, 1945. Upon completion of B-24 flight training he was assigned to the 15th Air Force in Italy. He flew bombing missions in northern Italy and southern Europe.

After WWII he returned to the U.S. and was relieved from active duty in 1946.

He was recalled to active duty at Randolph Field, Texas in October 1950 where he was trained to fly the B-29 bomber. He was then sent to the 307th Bomb Wing in Okinawa. He flew bombing missions over North Korea.

Upon return to the States he was assigned to the 301st Bomb Wing where they transitioned into the B-47 bomber. He elected to stay on active duty until retirement. He retired in December 1966 with the rank of Lt. Colonel.

After retirement Col. Carter flew business jets for Executive Jet Aviation, Columbus, Ohio for twenty years. He then retired the second time and lives northwest of Cortland, IN with his wife, Mildred Kleffman Carter. They have two children, Lance Marc Carter and Sharon Matthews Millard.

ROBERT N. CARTWRIGHT, World War II, United States Navy, born August 22, 1924 in Madison County, IN and graduated from Alexandria High School in 1942. He was called to defend his country in 1943 and drafted into the navy. He completed his boot camp training at Great Lakes in Chicago. Shortly after that he was assigned to the USS *Winged Arrow,* on which he served as Pharmacist Mate 1st class.

His ship was sent to the Pacific for most of the war. He was brought home to the states and discharged in March 1946. Under the GI Bill he attended Butler University and graduated with his degree in 1950. He then found employment in Indianapolis and later in Anderson, IN.

In 1954 he purchased the Taulman Drug Store in Crothersville which he operated until he closed it in 2001. From that time he has been retired and involved in volunteer projects all over the county. He was a member of the Seymour Library Board of Directors for 16 years. He now serves as a trustee of the VFW Post 1083.

OLIVER E. CHASTAIN, World War II, United States Army, born July 22, 1920 to Grover and Ina Martin Chastain. Graduated from Trinity Springs High School in 1938. Inducted August 1942 and trained as an infantryman. Shipped overseas to European Theater of Operations. Saw action at

Omaha Beach in Normandy 240th Field Artillery Medical Detachment. Wounded during the Battle of the Bulge Discharged December 1, 1945 Restored military medals and ribbons lost in a fire - Purple Heart, EAME Ribbon with 4 Campaign Stars and American Victory Medal. Returned home and married Bealah Pipher in 1949. Parents of three children. Retired from governmental service after 30 years.

CHARLES D. CLAMPITT, World War II, United States Army, born September 3, 1919 to Mack Henry and Elesta Terrill Clampitt at Arno, IN. He moved to Jackson County in 1934 and married LaVerne Freeman in 1945.

He entered the U.S. Army as a private at Ft. Benjamin Harrison on Dec. 13, 1940. He was a truck driver, rifle expert and carbine marksman.

He served in Trinidad during 1941 and 1942 and went to the European Theater in 1943. He served in battles in Northern France, Rhineland and Ardennes.

He received the EAME Theater Ribbon with three Bronze Stars, American Theater Ribbon, American Defense Service Medal with Bronze Star and Good Conduct Ribbon.

He received his Honorable Discharge as PFC from 26th Quartermaster Co. at Camp Atterbury, IN on July 21, 1945.

He became a semi-truck driver and later a security guard at Indianapolis, IN.

He died January 17, 1983 at Indianapolis and is buried at Liberty Cemetery, Norman, IN.

JAMES M. CLAYCAMP, World War II, United States Army, born February 20, 1920 in Jackson County to Fred and Matilda Mellenbruch Claycamp. He was raised on a farm in the north sections of the county. After completing one year of high school, he was married to Verna Schroer on October 4, 1942.

He was inducted into the army at Fort Harrison and sent to Camp White in Oregon for his basic training. After being assigned to Company C, 355th Regiment of Engineers, his unit was sent to Needles, California for desert training and building bridges across the Colorado River near Yuma. When deployed to Blythe, California he was promoted just before they were alerted to go overseas duty.

Leaving Virginia for New York, his ship sailed for England and docked at Liverpool. He was then sent to the advanced section of the communications and stationed near the Swindon area in England. One month after D-Day he landed on Omaha Beach July 4, 1944; his unit went against the Germans at St. Lo. From there on, the bridges of several regions were repaired while maintaining the Red Ball Expressway. Following the 9th Army in France, Holland, he was assigned to the clean-up detail for removing the battle debris.

The war ended May 8, 1945 and it was a special day in Europe. He was returned to the states and received his discharge at Camp Atterbury October 16, 1945. He was authorized various medals and ribbons to reflect his service.

WALTER L. COCKERRAM, World War II, United States Marine Corps, enlisted at Louisville, Kentucky December 3, 1943 Completed boot camp training at San Diego, CA and was assigned to be a

tank crewman and saw action at Tinian, Marianas, Okinawa and took part in the occupation of Japan after the Atomic Bombs were dropped.

He received his honorable discharge March 29, 1946.

ROBERT DEAN COFFMAN, World War II, United States Navy, served in the United States Navy near the end of World War II. He went on active duty on January 27, 1945. He enlisted at Brownstown, IN and was discharged at Great Lakes, IL on July 18, 1946.

Born to Oren and Jean Brooks Coffman on July 11, 1929, in Brownstown, IN. He graduated from Brownstown High School.

He served on the USNABPD San Bruno out of California and then served at the US Naval Supply Depot Navy #3149. He served as a Ship's Cook and discharged as a Seaman First Class. He was awarded the Victory Medal, American Area Campaign Medal, Philippine Liberation Ribbon, and the Asiatic-Pacific Area Campaign Medal.

Bob worked as a brick mason for most of his life. He lived in Plainfield and had worked for Bailey Construction for many years. After retiring, he moved to Jackson County where he spent a great deal of his time volunteering for several organizations. He received his 50-year membership pin from the Masonic Lodge in Brownstown. He was active in the Brownstown Christian Church and the Hospital Guild of Seymour. He was President-Elect for the Jackson County Fair Board at the time of his death. He, not only was a member of these groups, but also a key figure in construction projects needed by these organizations. He was instrumental in the construction of the gate and sign now leading to the Jackson County Fairgrounds.

Robert Dean Coffman died on October 29, 1999. He was survived by his wife Rebekah, his son James Allen Coffman and a grandson Sander.

PAUL R. COLE, World War II, United States Army, born September 25, 1925 at Acme in Hamilton Township. Parents were Ralph and Stella Summons Cole.

Drafted from Cortland High School March 8, 1944. Completed basic training at Camp Blanding. Shipped overseas to the European Theater of Operations. Assigned to Company A, 411th Infantry Regiment, 103rd Division. Saw action the Rhineland as an infantryman. Wounded January 7, 1945 in France; March 21, 1945 in Germany. Combat duties ended on the battlefield. Recuperated in the Chicago General Hospital. Discharged December 15, 1945.

Returned home and became Postmaster at Cortland. Married Fern Murphy of Seymour. Parents of one son. Residents of Acme, Indiana.

CHARLES COMBS, Army Of The United States, Private First Class, 688th Ammunition Ordinance

Depot, Schofield Barracks, Oahu, Hawaiian Islands, November 1943-July 1947.

To you who answered the call of your country and served in its Armed Forces to bring about the total defeat of the enemy. I extend the heartfelt thanks of a grateful Nation. As one of the Nation's finest, you undertook the most severe task one can be called upon to perform. Because you demonstrated the fortitude, resourcefulness and calm judgment necessary to carry out that task, we now look to you for leadership and example in further exalting our country in peace.

LOGAN H. COOPER, World War II, United States Navy, born April 10, 1926 in Harlan County, Kentucky. In 1939 he moved to the Honeytown (Indiana) area, where he lived and worked on the Allie Hess Farm. He attended Brownstown High School.

Being too young for the service when the war started, he got a job helping clear the land that was to become Freeman Field in Seymour. He used an axe to trim trees after they had been cut down with a crosscut saw. After the land had been cleared, Logan and two other boys picked up sticks and roots until the concrete runways were poured.

He was inducted into the Navy, November 9, 1944 and completed his basic training at USNTC at Great Lakes Illinois. From there to Treasure Island, California. After Treasure Island he was shipped to the South Pacific Island of Saipan, where he was assigned to a support unit. Fireman 1st class Logan H. Cooper was mustered out April 2, 1946. His total payment upon discharge was $46.36 with an additional travel allowance of 14.65. He returned to R#1 Brownstown and went to work at Noblitt & Sparks.

Logan spent the rest of his life in Jackson County working at Noblitt & Sparks, then starting his own business, Logan Cooper Sales & Service, which ran for over 40 years. He passed away September 30, 1996 and is buried at Clearspring, Indiana. He never forgot what he saw during WWII and what people had to sacrifice for our freedom.

WINFRED L. "BUD" CORNETT, World War II, United States Army, born February 4, 1920 at Freetown to Bill and Alma Cornett. He graduated from Freetown High School in 1938. The next year he married Maxine Phillips and to them were born a son and a daughter. He moved his family to Indianapolis in 1941 and was employed by Allison Engineering before entering the army in 1944.

He was sent to Camp Blanding in Florida for basic infantry training. He was given a leave before being sent to Fort Meade in Maryland for processing

for overseas duty in Europe. He served in England, France and on into Germany. He was last stationed in Berlin as in infantryman before leaving Bremerhaven March 10, 1946 on the way back to the states. He was discharged from Camp Atterbury, Indiana March 26, 1946.

In 1984 he married Kathleen Scott and she died in 2001. Two years later, he married Norma Harbaugh and she had two daughters. He now is able to enjoy grandchildren and great-grandchildren. He has been a member of the Church of Christ where he has served as an Elder for more than 30 years. He lives with his wife, Norma in Seymour, Indiana.

EVERETT R. COTTINGHAM, World War II, United States Army, born September 8, 1925 to Adrian and Ethel Ransome Cottingham. He graduated from Paris Crossing High School in 1943. He was raised with three brothers, all of whom were in the service of their country.

He went into the army in 1943, was shipped to the European Theater of Operations. He saw action in the Rhineland and Central European Campaigns. He was wounded in Austria May 2, 1945 and was placed in several different hospitals. He was released in Martinsburg, WV and discharged June 5, 1946.

He was authorized to wear the EAME Ribbon with 2 Campaign Stars, a Purple Heart and the Good Conduct Medal.

ROBERT H. COTTINGHAM, World War II, United States Army, born in 1920 to Adrian and Ethel Ramson Cottingham. He was raised with three brothers who also served in the military ranks.

Robert saw action in the Battle of the Bulge and was reported missing in January 1945, but records show he died in battle. It is believed his grave is in France.

NEAL CRAVENS, World War II, United States Air Corps, 1942-1945, ASN 15104858, born on the family homestead located east of Crothersville in the farm house built in 1904. Indeed, he dug a full basement almost entirely by hand, with the help of a scoop and a trusted mule. In mid-1942 Neal enlisted in the US Air Corps, received his basic training at Fort Harrison.

He was then trained as a ball turret gunner assigned to a B-24 Liberator Bomber. His group and

squadron of planes was shipped to a base in Italy. It was from there where Staff Sergeant Neal Cravens completed more than 30 missions over the Axis-controlled areas of Hitler's Germany.

Upon receiving his honorable discharge in 1945. Neal returned home to Vernon Township. One year later he purchased the Gorrell farm located not far from the Copperbottom Schoolhouse which he had attended as a young lad.

Neal Cravens and his wife, Marianna, became parents of four daughters who represent the 6th generation of family members to be connected with the farm.

CHARLES CRECELIUS, World War II, United States Army Air Corps, born May 23, 1921 in French Lick, Indiana. He entered the Army Air Corps (now U.S. Air Force) in October 1942 as an aviation cadet to train as a pilot. By October 1943 he was selected to be among the first pilots to fly the newest bomber in the Air Force, the B-29. At first he was deployed in India and flew over the Hump to deliver fuel and bombs to an airfield in China and then, from there, flew on the first B-29 raids on Japan. Later his unit moved to an island in the Pacific and he completed 50 combat missions against Japan, including the last air raid against Japan.

After WWII he remained in the Air Force and flew the B-29, B-50 and then the 10 engine B-36. He was one of the very first pilots of the B-36 and was the leader of the first B-36s to fly direct from Texas to England non-stop. On April 27, 1951, while flying over Oklahoma his B-36 was struck by a P-51 fighter plane and he and most of the crew were killed in the collision. His medals include the Distinguished Flying Cross and Air Medals.

Charles Crecelius moved to Seymour from Knox, Indiana in 1934 when his father, Philip Crecelius, served as a Conservation Officer there. He graduated from Shields High School in 1939.

FRED L. CRECELIUS, World War II, United States Army Air Corps. In March 1944 Fred entered the Army Air Corps (now U.S. Air Force) and was trained as a ball turret gunner on the B-17. In late 1944 he was sent to England to fly on raids over Germany. Family history reports that on his crew's first mission they were shot down over Belgium and crash-landed in an area between the German and American forces. Fortunately they were able to make it to the American lines and eventually back to England.

He stayed in the Air Force after WWII and served as an aircraft mechanic and flight engineer.

In 1949 he started pilot training as an aviation cadet and trained to be a jet fighter pilot. He served in Europe, Africa, Middle East and Southeast Asia and flew many different types of aircraft. Medals received were Bronze Star and Air Medals.

Fred was born Feb. 25, 1926 in French Lick, Indiana. He moved to Seymour from Knox, Indiana

in 1934 when his father, Philip Crecelius, served as a Conservation Officer there. He attended grade school and Jr. High in Seymour.

Lt. Col. Crecelius retired in 1972 and now lives in Arizona.

JESSE CRECELIUS, World War II, United States Army Air Corps, born February 22, 1915 in French Lick, Indiana and joined the Army Air Corps (now U.S. Air Force) in March 1942. He went into pilot training and received training at several locations including: Thunderbird Field, Phoenix, Arizona; Minter Field, California; Victorville, California; Ephrata, Washington; and Lewistown, Montana. Ultimately, he was trained as a pilot on B-17 bombers.

In 1943 Lt. Crecelius flew via South America to North Africa for bomber operation against the enemy in Italy. On the 10th of November 1943, while on a bombing mission of railroad targets at Balzano, Italy, their B-17 received battle damage and crashed into the sea about 20 miles from Corsica. Despite rescue efforts, Lt. Crecelius and his crew members were never found. His medals include Air Medals and the Purple Heart.

Jesse Crecelius moved to Seymour from Knox, Indiana in 1934 when his father, Philip Crecelius, served as a Conservation Officer there

CHARLES TOM CUMMINGS, World War II, United Sates Navy, served in the United States Navy during World War II. Tom was born September 25, 1925 near Houston, Indiana. He was the son of James W. Cummings II and Helena B. Lutes Cummings.

At the age of 18, his trip to Louisville, Kentucky for the physical examination was the first time he had traveled outside the state of Indiana. Tom was drafted into the military service November 13, 1943, in the middle of his senior year at Clearspring High School. His mother was given his diploma during the graduation ceremony in May.

He was sent to Great Lakes for boot camp. He also attended Signalman's School and was one of only 9 out of 320 who graduated with test scores of 90% and better. This earned him the rank of 3rd class Petty Officer.

Tom was stationed at Treasure Island in California, with other Navy signalmen and radio operators. His first ship was the *John G. Brady.* It was a Liberty ship and they carried supplies to the front lines. Tom's job as signalman was to send and receive messages from the other ships by means of lights, using Morris code and flags representing letters or code.

During his tour of duty, Tom was at Midway, the invasion of the Philippines and was waiting at Okinawa for the invasion of Japan when the war ended.

January 10, 1946, while on a 30 day leave, Tom came home and married Ruth Sutton. He was discharged from the Navy as a signalman second class on April 13, 1946. Tom has lived and worked in Jackson County his entire life. He and Ruth raised three children, Sandy (Howe), Tom Jr. and Karen (Terrell). Tom was a farmer, County Commissioner, first president of the Jackson County Rural Water Utility, active in the Brownstown Christian Church and continues to serve on the Jackson County Fair Board. Tom retired as a rural mail carrier from the postal service in 1987.

GEORGE AUGUST CUMMINGS, World War II, United States Navy, born December 17, 1937 in Cortland to James and Elise Marie Cummings. He graduated from the local high school in 1945 and joined the navy immediately. He reported to Great Lakes Naval Station for his boot camp training.

He was sent to San Diego, CA for training in the Radar School and was assigned to be a radar specialist aboard the USS *Eldorado* for almost a year. In the Pacific area, he served on the Amphibian Flag Ship. Later, he served on the Destroyer, USS *Chandler* 717 and received additional training at Pearl Harbor.

He was discharged December 21, 1948, returned home to attend Purdue for his degree in agriculture in 1951. He began teaching as an instructor to Korean Veteran Agriculture class at Brownstown High School. Later, he earned his doctoral degree and served at North Caroline State University as a professor and doing research.

He married Ruth Sumwalt August 8, 1961 and they became parents of three children, Mike, Mark and Cynthia.

JAMES T. CUMMINGS, World War II, United States Navy, born at Cortland November 9, 1925 to James E. and Elise Marie Cummings. He was raised in the local area and later graduated from Cortland High School in 1943. He enlisted in the navy on May 8, 1943 at Indianapolis, Indiana.

He reported to Great Lakes Naval Station to complete his boot training. He was transferred to Alameda, CA and spent two months in Commando training at Hollister and Monterey, California. He was assigned to one of the Dutch ships, the *Bloemfontein,* along with 4,000 other troops but he was eventually stationed at the CASU (Aircraft Service Unit #15). He was assigned as a storekeeper supplying parts for airplane repair.

He was stationed in Guadalcanal and New Hebrides until June 1, 1944. Returned to Alameda Naval Base, received leave and then reported to New Orleans, LA where he was discharged on May 2, 1945.

He returned home, enrolled at Purdue and received his degree in agriculture in 1949. He became a teacher and, on June 15, 1951 he married Lois Heath in Cowan. They were blessed with the birth of a son, Donald, who became a dentist in Seymour.

James Cummings is retired and a member of the Brownstown Christian Church along with a host of other organizations and honors.

NORVILLE CUMMINGS, World War II, United States Army, drafted into army October 25, 1943 from Jackson County. Reported to Fort Knox, KY for training. Assigned to combat engineers at Fort Leonard Wood, MO. Joined 35th Engineers at Camp White in Oregon. Sent overseas to European Theater of Operations. Saw action in France, Belgium, Luxembourg with VIII Corps. Constructed bridge across Rhine River. After Bastogne, he returned stateside and was discharged February 6, 1945.

RONALD GLEN CUNNINGHAM, World War II, United States Navy, South Pacific Theater of Operations, 1941-1945, born October 21, 1920 in Jackson County, and later he joined the navy in 1942. As a Quartermaster 1st Class, he served in the Pacific Theater of Operations

Upon receiving his honorable discharge from the service, Glen Cunningham returned to Tampico in Grassy Fork Township of Jackson County. It was there in 1946 where he was married to Earline Alma Beldon. Sometime later they became parents of three sons. Eventually he returned to Guam to teach school.

During the war, Glen was commander of a PT boat which was sunk in a typhoon. Glen received a minor head cut when his PT boat overturned on top of him. It is not known just when his family was informed of the accident. All of the crew members were rescued with only minor injuries. He was given a second command on which he served until the end of the war.

FREDDIE G. DAILY, World War II, United States Army, born April 23, 1920 to Charles and Nellie Bedel Daily. He attended the Seymour schools and was graduated from the Shields High School.

He enlisted in the army and reported to Fort Harrison in Indianapolis on February 4, 1942. He was assigned to the 819th Company of the Engineers Battalion. He was shipped overseas to the European Theater of Operations. He saw action

in Normandy, Northern France, the Rhineland and Central Europe. He was authorized to wear several medals and ribbons.

After returning to the states he was discharged October 9, 1945 and was employed at Fort Harrison. He was forced to retire due to some heart problems. He was married to Evelyn Brewer and they became parents of two children. Following a divorce he married Bonnie Bowman. He died of cancer October 2, 1983.

SHIRLEY H. DAILY, World War II, United States Army, born June 13, 1923 to Charles and Nellie Bedel Daily. He attended the Seymour schools and was graduated from the local high school before being drafted into the army.

He reported to Louisville January 25, 1943 and after basic training, he was assigned to Company C of the 735th Battalion of Patton's 3rd Armored Division. He saw action in Normandy, France, the Ardennes, Rhineland and Central Europe.

He was authorized to wear various medals and ribbons depicting his service. Returning to the states he was discharged October 29, 1945. When he reached home he was employed by several different concerns.

He was married to Lois Walker and to them were born four children. He died of cancer September 16, 1983.

TAYLOR M. DAILY, World War II, United States Army, born June 3, 1917 to Charles and Nellie Bedel Daily. He attended schools in Seymour and was graduated from the local high school. He was then employed by the Seymour Woolen Mills until the 2nd world war broke out.

He enlisted in the army February 23, 1942 and reported to Fort Harrison in Indianapolis. He was assigned to the 436th AAA Battalion of the Infantry before being shipped overseas to the European Theater of Operations. He was in action in North Africa, Sicily, Naples, Rome-Arno, the Rhineland, Central Europe and Southern France. He was on the line for 362 consecutive days and was wounded in Italy in 1944.

He was authorized to wear various medals and ribbons, including the Purple Heart. He returned to the states and was discharged in October 1945. After he reached Jackson County he was again employed by Arvin Industries in Seymour. He was married to Betty Ledbetter and to them were born four children.

He died of cancer January 5, 1976.

MELVIN DARLAGE, Company "B" – 301st Battalion, 94th Infantry Division, 3rd U.S. Army. Along with seven army buddies in his unit, Melvin Darlage was ready to move forward with the 94th Infantry Division in the attack on the village of Orsholz. Their objective was to destroy the pillboxes and German bunkers forming the Siegfried Line.

Even though the January 18, 1944 weather showed temperatures well below zero and with 15 inches of snow on the ground, the assault was ordered. By daybreak the following morning his unit was surrounded and directed to find its way back to the American lines. Finally, the orders came to surrender!

Melvin Darlage and the other soldiers of the 94th Division found themselves prisoners of war from January 19th until March 30th, that was the day when they were liberated!

After the war had ended and the men were returned home, several of those ex-POWs in his unit met in a reunion at the Darlage home on U.S. Highway 50 in Jackson County.

JAMES LEON DARLING, World War II and Korea, United States Marine Corps, born in Mississippi September 16, 1919 to parents, John and Lula Caldwell Darling.

Married to Blanche A. Brooks in Brownstown. Enlisted in Marine Corps and served in World War II European Theater of Operations and was stationed in Japan. Remained in the service and assigned to Germany during the Berlin Crisis. Served in Vietnam until hospitalized. Promoted to Drill Instructor at Camp Lejeune

Awards include Bronze Star, Silver Star and Purple Heart. Retired to Indianapolis. Died December 7, 1982 and was buried at Fairview Cemetery.

CLYDE DAVERS, World War II, United States Army, born August 27, 1913 to Tom and Nancy Pearl Matlock Davers in Terre Haute. He was raised mostly around Medora and later was employed as a driver for Fisher Brothers Circus who always wintered near his home.

Records show he entered the army January 19, 1942 and was soon promoted after his training as an infantryman. His unit was shipped overseas in August 1942 and he served in Company "G" of the 39th Division. They saw action in North Africa and Sicily before being stationed in England.

He took part in the D-Day invasion of Normandy on June 6, 1944. He was awarded the Purple Heart for wounds received in Algiers. His wounds in action in Germany October 1, 1944 during the Battle of the Bulge were too much. Clyde Davers died October 2, 1944.

HORACE LEROY DAVERS, World War II, United States Coast Guard, born November 26, 1922 to parents, Rassie and Bertie Cockerham Davers. After his father died, he was raised in Jackson County by Raymond Weddell.

Enlisted in the Coast Guard September 21, 1942. Reported to Louisville Station. Stationed at Alameda, California and assigned to fuel tanker. Served in Pacific Theater from Philippines to Japan. Discharged at St. Louis April 1, 1946.

Married Lola May Blackwell February 23, 1946. Retired from Fisher Body Works at Marion. He died October 27, 2003.

DONALD WAYNE DAVIS, World War II, United States Army, born December 27, 1926 at Medora to Roy and Edith Goss Davis. He attended the elementary grades and graduated from Medora High School in 1944.

He was inducted March 16, 1945 into the army, completed basic training and was shipped overseas to the Pacific area. He landed at Manila in the Philippines. In January 1946 he was transferred to Tokyo where he was assigned as a clerk.

He returned to the states October 7, 1946 and received his discharged December 10, 1946. When he arrived home he bought a truck and hauled brick for the Medora Brick Company. In September he married Aileen Stegner and they became parents of two children. He died February 13, 1988.

W. DURBIN DAY, World War II, United States Navy, born October 7, 1902 in Seymour. As a boy he worked at several jobs, such as candling eggs, carrying bobbins at the Seymour Woolen Mill, and cleaning the business college. His last job was at the Maxon Drugstore, where he attained his apprentice license in pharmacy.

Using his apprentice license, he worked at the Haag, I.U., and Riley pharmacies in Indianapolis while attending college. He graduated from Butler in 1923 and in 1926 from the I.U. School of Medicine. Receiving a commission in the Navy as a Lt.(jg), he interned first at the San Diego Naval Hospital. Then he served with the Asiatic Fleet in the Philippines where he was attached to the submarine division, and in China attached to the Chinese Navy Yard. Following his internship in the Navy, he did a residency in surgery at Hines Veterans Hospital, Chicago. Returning to Seymour he maintained both a general and surgical practice.

In March 1941, he was called to active service in the Navy, serving as a medical officer in the Fleet Marine Force in California. After Pearl Harbor, he served a year in the South Pacific. Then he served as chief medical officer at Camp Pendleton, California, where he helped train the 3rd and 5th Marine Divisions in medical amphibious warfare. From there he was assigned as the chief medical officer on a transport that took troops into combat and returned as a hospital ship. He was in many major battles in the Pacific, including Okinawa. His last assignment was rendering aid to Nagasaki. When he received his discharge from the Navy in December 1945, he held the rank of Captain. He served 32 years in the Navy, including both his active and reserve duty.

Dr. Day returned to Seymour, where he practiced medicine until 1989. His family included his wife, Julia Holt Day, three children, nine grandchildren, and twenty-eight great-grandchildren. He passed away at the age of 101 on October 26, 2003.

SIMON DEHART, World War II, United States Army, born February 11, 1919 in Avawam, Kentucky to Charles and Millie Brown DeHart. He entered the U.S. Army in early 1943 at Fort Knox and was assigned as supply clerk. He was in Company K, 3rd Battalion 5307 Composite Unit Infantry.

He battled throughout India with "Merrill's Marauders" and was wounded in Burma on June 12, 1944. He spent sixty-seven days recovering from his wounds.

He was awarded the American Theater Ribbon, Asiatic/Pacific Ribbon with Bronze Service Star, Purple Heart, World War II History Medal, Good Conduct Medal and the Distinguished Unit Award. He was discharged in December 1945.

He is the father of five children: Bige DeHart, Ruby Brasher, Linda Glover, Warren DeHart and Jerry DeHart. He is retired and now lives near Crothersville.

JAMES T. DENNY, World War II, United States Coast Guard, born in 1920, a son of Frank and Straussie Fleetwood Denny at Freetown. He graduated from Freetown High School in 1938.

He was drafted into the Coast Guard in 1944 and served during the remainder of World War II. After his discharge, he returned home to his wife, Helen Davis Denny of Medora. He is now deceased,

ERNEST GLEN DISMORE, World War II, United States Navy, 1944-1945, born February 28, 1913 on a small farm located in Washington County near New Salem, Indiana. He was a son of Lewis and Rena May Nixon Dismore, and attended the Chestnut Grove #1 school through the 8th grade. He was employed by Morgan Packing Company in Austin as a young man, did odd jobs and worked on the WPA for $21 per month

He married Edna Mae Woods in 1934 and they became parents of Raymond, Fairie, Richard and Glenda. In 1940 the family moved to Vallonia where he worked for the Bundy Brothers Garage.

He completed his boot training at Great Lakes Naval Station and was assigned to the U.S. Submarine Base in Pearl Harbor as a Machinist Mate 3rd Class (T) SV-6 USNR. Following his military service he returned to Vallonia. He operated a shop from his home and later worked at the Arvin plant in Seymour.

He passed away in 1980 and was buried in the Beech Grove Cemetery located at New Salem, Indiana.

JOHN ROBERT DORSEY, World War II, United States Army, born March 8, 1919 in Jackson County to John Horace and Clara Krause Dorsey living on a farm located in Vernon Township. He grew up with a sister helping his parents with the farm chores and trapping fur-bearing animals for spending money. He graduated from Crothersville High School in 1937.

He was employed by the American Can Company in Austin before he found work at Freeman Field in Seymour as a mechanic in the early 1940s prior to his entrance into the military service.

He entered the Army Air Corps at Fort Harrison in November 1943 and was sent to Keesler Field in Mississippi for basic training. He was then ordered to Sheppard Field in Texas before being stationed in Victorville, California. His assignment never changed - he was a mechanic working planes. He was discharged at Camp Atterbury and was authorized to wear various ribbons reflecting his career.

He was married to Dora Chandler May 8, 1948 and to them were born five children. He operated an automotive and farm repair shop and was retired as a rural mail carrier at Crothersville. Robert died June 2, 1975.

JAMES MEREDITH DURHAM, World War II, United States Army, was drafted and inducted into the army in September 1942. He was assigned to several camps during his first two years in service, including being stationed in Wyoming and California. After he shipped overseas to England, he awaited the time for movement across the channel into France and on to Germany.

Following V-E Day he returned home and was sent on to the Pacific area and stationed on Okinawa, but the Japanese had surrendered. He returned to the states and was discharged December 2, 1945. He was authorized to wear appropriate medals and ribbons reflecting his service time.

When he died December 8, 1976 he was survived by his wife, Edna, and six children. He lived at 18 East Laurel Street in Seymour, Indiana.

MORRIS W. DURHAM, World War II, United States Army Air Corps, born in Seymour August 18, 1916 to parents who owned a farm located near Vallonia. He graduated from Vallonia High School and Indiana Business College. He enlisted in the Army Air Corps before Pearl Harbor and was sworn in at Bowman Field in Louisville, KY.

He was assigned to the 54th Bomb Squadron of the 46th Bomb Group then stationed at Barksdale Field, OK. The group was shipped out to Blythe, California for final maneuvers before moving overseas. He was promoted to Sergeant in charge of the supply and maintenance of planes. Given the title of crew chief, he continued his service as crew chief.

Morris W. Durham met his future wife, Avenelle Lane at Lake Charles in Louisiana while he was assigned to the 416th Bomb Group. Shortly he was transferred to Florence, SC where he attended the Douglas Aircraft School in Santa Monica, California. Sent back to Florence, he was in an auto accident and spent time in a hospital. When released he was married Christmas Eve at the base chapel.

He was assigned to a plane named *"Dirty Gertie"* and finally reached the rank of Master Sergeant before being discharged. He returned home to his family of three sons, Samuel, Don and Glenn.

Morris W. Durham passed away in August 2003.

JOSEPH L. EGLEN, JR., World War II, United States Army, born in 1906 in Washington County, the son of Joseph and Ethel Bell Hendershot Eglen. His family moved to Medora when he was a child. He graduated from the local high school in 1924 and attended Hanover College. A short time later he was employed by the B&O Railroad.

He was 35 years old in 1941 but was forced to enter the draft due to Pearl Harbor. One draft board member told him he would not be called because of his age. And if called he wouldn't be given an assignment to duty.

Two years later he and his unit were shipped overseas to England and in 1944, he was in combat along the French coast. He was a Sergeant in Company A, 81st Engineer Battalion which moved across Normandy, the Rhineland and into the Ardennes. He was wounded September 10, 1944 and evacuated back to England, but he was back in duty later and fought to the end of the war which was announced May 8, 1945.

He was authorized several ribbons and medals, including the Purple Heart and the Victory Medal. He was discharged at Camp Atterbury September 24, 1945. Both of his brothers also fought in WWII. He returned to Medora and continued to work on the railroad. He was married to Nora Mae Weddell. He died in 1983 and was buried at Fairview Cemetery in Brownstown.

WILLIAM E. EMLAY, World War II, United States Army, born November 16, 1920 in Jackson County, Indiana and lived there most of his adult life. He attended Shields High School.

William entered into the U.S. Army September 6, 1944, at Indianapolis, IN. He was attached to Battery C, 499th Armored Field Artillery, and attended the service school for Cooks and Bakers at Fort Knox, KY. His military occupational specialty was Cook. He served in the European Theater and received the European-African-Middle Eastern Theater Ribbon, American Theater Ribbon, Good Conduct Ribbon and Victory Medal. He was separated from the U.S. Army March 30, 1946 at Fort Custer, Michigan.

William returned to Seymour and his wife Lucille and children to resume his civilian life.

DANIEL B. EMPSON, World War II, United States Army, born in 1910 at Dudleytown in Jackson County to parents, Dr. Blaine and Mattie Empson. He is grandson of Daniel Empson, a Civil War Veteran.

Inducted into the army, he completed basic training at Camp Swift, Texas. Stationed at various army installations 1941-1946.

Resides with his wife, Marie, in Louisville

FRANCIS MARION EMPSON, World War II, United States Army, born on April 13, 1924 on the Empson family farm near Tampico, Indiana and was the son of Marion and Cora Mounts Empson. He graduated from Tampico High School in 1942. He served in the U.S. Army during World War II for two years and seven months.

A member of ROTC at Purdue University, he enlisted in the Army on Oct. 29, 1942 and reported for active duty on May 8, 1943.

Following basic training and his first assignment at Fort Eustis, Virginia from May 1943 to February 1944, he was transferred to Camp Stewart, Georgia and Camp Gordan, Georgia. He was then transferred to Camp Swift, Texas in January 1945 and was a supply sergeant with Headquarters Company 91st Chemical Mortar Battalion when the war ended. He was honorably discharged from the Army on December 14, 1945 holding the rank of Tech Sergeant.

Taking advantage of the newly legislated GI Bill of Rights, Francis returned to Purdue and graduated with a BS in Agriculture in 1949.

He was married to Betty Lutes, also from Jackson County, for 37 years and they had two daughters, Beverly Moore of Greensburg, Indiana and Vivian Burbank of Panama City, Florida. He is deceased and survived by them as well as four grandchildren: Becky Hedge Nightingale of Ann Arbor, Michigan; Bill Hedge of Anderson, Indiana; Steven Mattingley of Melbourne, Florida; and Lisa Mattingley Turturro of Lakeland, Florida.

HAROLD EMPSON, World War II, United States Navy, born February 1, 1926, a son of Marion and Cora Mounts Empson. He remained at home on the family farm until he graduated from Tampico High School May 1, 1944. The next day he entered the U.S. Navy. He completed his boot training at Great Lakes Naval Station and was assigned to the heavy cruiser, the USS *Boston* as one member of its crew of 1,800 men.

His ship was part of Admiral Halsey's 3rd Fleet operating in the Pacific Theater. Harold was a Quartermaster, 3rd Class Petty Officer in the navigation division. He was selected to steer the ship during General Quarters and Battle Stations. After the fighting was ended the USS *Boston* was engaged in disarming the Japanese coastal weapons and armament. He was transferred to the USS *Leary* OD 879 in December 1946 and remained on board in Japanese waters until discharged.

His vivid memories include the bombardment of Iwo Jima and the heavy casualties of the Okinawa Campaign. He was awarded the Asiatic-Pacific Medal with 6 Battle Stars, Philippine Liberation Medal with 2 Battle Stars, Philippine Occupation, Japan Occupation, EAME, American Area and Victory Medals.

Harold attended Purdue University but received his business administration degree from Hanover College. He was employed by Cummins Engine Company for four years before becoming an insurance claims adjuster. He lives in Louisville and is the father of 3 children. Jayne married Kenneth Williams and they became parents of 4 children; Union Michael, Jennifer Lynn, Jessie Warren and Daniel Wayne. John Harold is married to Susan and they have 3 children: Danielle Irene, Rachel Nicole and Justin Matthew. Douglas Eric is married to Pattie and they are parents of 2 sons, Eric Robert and Ryan Douglas.

WILLARD N. EVERHART, JR., ASN 35709449, United States Army, born in Seymour, Indiana to Willard and Adda Belle Everhart. He matured in and around the rail cross roads of southern Indiana and was graduated from Shields High School with the class of 1937.

Some time after World War II broke out following the disaster at Pearl Harbor, he was drafted into the military service of his country in October 1943. He completed his basic training at Fort McClellan in Alabama.

He was shipped overseas to the European Theater of Operations and served in Company G of the 330th Infantry Regiment. As a rifleman, with his combat badge, he was wounded in action twice and awarded the Purple Heart each time. He survived major campaigns in Normandy, Southern and Central Europe and received his discharge at Camp Atterbury on January 2, 1946.

JAMES EARL FARLEY, World War II, United States Army Air Corps, born December 12, 1929 to Willie Carl and Millie Campbell Farley. He has one sister named Mary Kate.

He enlisted in the Air Corps in 1947 at the age of 17 years. After basic training he was assigned to 367th Bomb Squadron in the 306th Bomb Group. He was listed as a sheet metal worker and qualified as a tail gunner when transferred to MacDill AFB at Tampa, Florida.

Misfortune struck him and he was diagnosed with a rare disease later known as Hodgkins. There was no known cure. He died at Camp Atterbury in Columbus, Indiana.

FRANK F. FEE, SR. World War II, United States Navy, 1945-1946, served on USS *Moore* Destroyer Escort.

DAVID EDGAR FERGUSON, World War II, United States Army, son of Clarence and Ruby Ferguson, graduated from Freetown High School in 1940. He served in the Army Infantry for three years and was considered one of the best soldiers in the 84th Division.

His tour of duty included Louisiana and Texas before he was shipped overseas to England, Omaha Beach and on across France, Holland before taking part in the Battle of the Bulge. He was wounded and eventually returned to the States.

In 1945 he married Betty Jane Shipley and they became parents of four girls. By 1950 they owned a bakery but elected to sell it. He then became an employee of Texas Eastern Gas Corporation. He retired with 40 years of service and now resides in Kentucky.

His father served in World War I and his brother saw action in Korea.

OTIS MERLE FERGUSON, World War II, United States Army, born December 1, 1917 near Pleasant Grove. Parents were Alex and Artie Cockerham Ferguson. Attended the Hays Elementary School.

Entered active service in the army September 8, 1942. Reported to Indianapolis but sent to Great Lakes. Shipped overseas to the European Theater of Operations. Received as an infantryman October 4, 1944. Saw action in the Ardennes and the Rhineland. Wounded March 12, 1945 in Germany. Discharged October 13, 1945. Medals include EAME Ribbon with 3 Campaign Stars, Good Conduct Medal, Purple Heart and Combat Infantry Badge.

Returned to Brownstown and married Frona Weaver. Became parents of one son. Both employed by Kieffer Paper Mill.

ARTHUR E. FIELDS, World War II, United States Army, born March 3, 1920, in Freetown, Indiana, the son of Cecil and Wilma Fields. He attended school there and was employed by Arvin Industries in Columbus at the time he was drafted into the service.

He was assigned at Fort Benjamin Harrison, then sent to training in October 1942 at Fort Blanding, Florida, with the 30th Infantry Division known as Old Hickory. In May of 1943 he was transferred to Forrest, Tennessee. In November of 1943, he was transferred to Camp Atterbury, leaving there in January 1944 to fight in the battle of Normandy. He embarked from New York on the USS *Argentina* arriving at Port Glasglow, Scotland, on February 10, 1944,

Fields was classified as a Heavy Motor Crewman. He supervised the operation of an 81mm motor crew, which set up, aimed, and fired weapons from carrier and ground mount to place explosive shells or smoke on enemy position.

He received the EAME Theater Ribbon, Bronze Star, and Good Conduct Medal. He spent one year, seven months, and 28 days of foreign service.

He returned back to Camp Atterbury on October 13, 1945, where he received an Honorable Discharge, having served three years for his country.

DOYLE L. FISH, World War II, United States Army, born June 25, 1922 to Leslie and Cleophis Clampitt Fish. He graduated from Clearspring High School in 1940 and went into the Army the following year. He was inducted June 11, 1941 and was trained as an automobile mechanic.

He was stationed at Fort Knox Kentucky and Fort Hood, Texas before his unit was ready to be shipped overseas to the European Theater of Operations. He saw action in Normandy, northern France and the Rhineland. He was discharged October 24, 1945 and was authorized to wear appropriate medals and ribbons representing his service.

One month after returning home he married Dorothy Kunkel of Heltonville and they became parents of four children. He died in July 1993.

EITHEL FISH, World War II, Infantry, Pacific Theater. Killed May 18, 1944.

WILLIAM CLIFFORD FISH, World War II, United States Army, born in Seymour, IN to James and Betty Moore Fish in 1962. He attended Brownstown Central High School before enlisting in the army in 1980. He served two years in Germany during the post-war era.

He is married and the father of a son, Michael, and lives in Muncie, IN.

CHARLES ROBERT FITCH, World War II, United States Army, 35 702 083, Private First Class, 3573rd Quartermaster Trucking Company, Army of the United States.

He was born in Hanover, IN, June 2, 1914 and lived most of his adult life in Seymour, where he worked and had property.

He entered the U.S. Army at Fort Benjamin Harrison and after his basic training was assigned to Truck Driver Light 345 and was qualified as such,

along with a Mechanics Badge and MM Rifle Training.

He served his country 2 years 11 months and 4 days of which 1 year 9 months and 4 days were served in Northern France, European Theater, June 27, 1944 to March 10, 1946. He was awarded the American Theater Ribbon, European-African-Middle-Eastern Ribbon w/1 Bronze Star, Good Conduct Medal, and World War II Victory Medal.

He was separated out of the U.S. Army at Camp Atterbury, IN, March 23, 1946.

He returned to Seymour and his wife Fredith Gorbett, Fitch and resumed his civilian life, he worked at the shoe factory, Arvins, and Seymour Mfg., from which he retired.

JOHN FITCH, World War II, United States Army, born at Paris Crossing, IN, March 11, 1920. He lived and worked in Jackson County most of his adult life.

Private First Class John Fitch 35481122 entered the U.S. Army June 6, 1942, at Louisville, KY. He received his basic training at Ft. Knox, with Battery B, 897th Field Artillery Battalion. He was qualified with MM Rifle, and his military occupational specialty was Truck Driver Light 345.

John Fitch served 3 years 5 months and 20 days of which 1 year 7 months and 19 days were in the European Theater in Battles and Campaigns at Normandy, Northern France, Rhineland and Central Europe from April 16, 1944 to November 13, 1945. He was wounded at Laval, France August 5, 1944 when a mortar round hit the jeep he was driving mortally wounding his Colonel and Lieutenant. Decorations he received were the American Theater Ribbon, EAME Theater Ribbon w/4 Bronze Stars, Good Conduct Medal, Purple Heart, and WWII Victory Medal. He was separated from the U.S. Army at Camp Atterbury, IN, November 29. 1945.

John Fitch returned to Seymour, and his wife Madline June Amos, Fitch and his step-son Danny, to resume his civilian life. They had six more children, 4 boys and 2 girls.

HAROLD FLEENOR, World War II, United States Army, was raised by his grandparents, Charles and Alice Fleenor of Tampico, after his mother died. He was an honor student and graduated from the local high school in 1934. He later became an accountant for Citizens Gas Company.

After completing basic training, he was shipped overseas to the European Theater of Operations. He served as a radio dispatcher. He was wounded November 5, 1943 and later died at Naples in Italy.

DONALD FLEETWOOD, World War II, U.S. Army, 135th Battalion, 34th Infantry, European Theater.

CHARLES RAY FORGEY, World War II, United States Army, born in Freetown August 4, 1923, a son of Cecil and Lucy Brock Forgey. He was raised there and graduated from the local high school in 1941. Two years later he was drafted into the army and reported for duty at Louisville, KY January 23, 1943. He was sent to Fort Lewis, WA for basic armored tank training and assigned to the 735th Tank Battalion as a medium tank crewman.

His unit arrived in Scotland February 6, 1944 and was then sent to the coast of France and campaigned through Normandy, the Ardennes and the Rhineland area. He served as a tank commander; on October 3, 1944 his tank was destroyed and he was returned to England to recuperate, before being sent back to his unit.

He was discharged October 19, 1945 at Camp Atterbury and he then returned home to Freetown and resumed his work at Cummins in Columbus. He was also in the cream and egg producing business with his father. He then became postmaster. He and his wife, Anna Mae Manuel retired to Brownstown where he served on the Town Board until December 2003.

He became the father of two sons, Stephen and Jerry.

FLOYD ERNEST FORGEY, World War II, United States Navy, born December 7, 1925 to James and Edith McNiece Forgey and raised on the family farm near Pleasant Grove community near Brownstown. He attended the Hays school and graduated from Brownstown High School.

During his senior year he was drafted into the navy April 4, 1944 and reported to Great Lakes Naval Station. Following boot camp training he was sent overseas and stationed at Pearl Harbor. He became a permanent attachment there until he returned to the states for discharge at Great Lakes.

He had served more than two years in the navy and was discharged May 4, 1946 and then he came home to Jackson County and entered Indiana Central College. Later he retired as superintendent of the Farm Bureau Elevator at Beech Grove.

HARRY LEROY FORGEY, World War II, United States Navy, born January 24, 1922 in the Pleasant Grove area of Jackson County to James and Edith McNiece Forgey. He was raised on the family farm and attended Hays school before graduating from Brownstown High School in 1940.

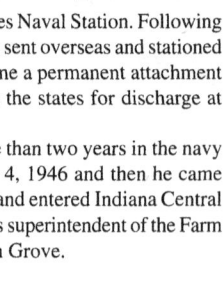

He was employed at Noblitt-Sparks Industries in Franklin until 1942 when he was inducted into the navy. He reported for

duty at Great Lakes on November 24, 1942 and, following boot camp training, he attended service schools in Detroit and at Treasure Island near San Francisco.

He was assigned to the USS *Devastator*, a mine sweeper and participated in three major invasions, including Iwo Jima. Their ship returned to Hawaii in 1945, and he was later discharged from Great Lakes on January 28, 1946, after which he returned to Brownstown.

He attended Purdue and settled in Michigan where he became an electrical engineer for Consumers Power Company in Jackson until he retired.

Harry Forgey died in 1992.

ALVIN L. FOSBRINK, World War II, United States Army, born November 21, 1924 to Carl and Floence Garris Fosbrink of Brownstown. He was raised in the local area and graduated from high school in the county seat in 1942. Less than one year later he was drafted into the army.

He reported for duty March 25, 1943 and was eventually assigned to the infantry in Company "A" of the 526th Armored Battalion. His unit was destined to be sent to the European Theater of Operations. He served across France, Belgium, Germany and Luxembourg.

He returned to the states and was discharged December 28, 1945 and was authorized to wear the appropriate medals and ribbons reflecting his battle experiences.

After settling at home, he was married to Ruby Fee March 16, 1946. To them were born two sons, Carl Lee and Jerry Fosbrink. After he received his, degree in electronics, he was employed by Cummins for more than 40 years. He earned a pilot's license and enjoyed his flying over Jackson County.

Alvin Fosbrink died January 12, 1993.

LOUIS NOEL FOSBRINK, World War II, United States Army, born to Andrew and Carrie Persinger Fosbrink of Jackson County, Indiana. Drafted in early 1942 but records are incomplete. He married Katherine Owens and they became the parents of four children. Louis Noel retired from Cummins Engine Company.

RODNEY M. FOSBRINK, World War II, United States Army, born to Andrew and Carrie Persinger Fosbrink of Brownstown. He graduated from the local high school.

He was inducted into the army January 12, 1942 and completed his basic training in Texas. He was then shipped overseas to the European Theater of Operations.

He returned home to Jackson County and married Fairy Ault and they became parents of two daughters. He retired from Seymour Manufacturing Company.

WAYNE EARL FOSBRINK, World War II, United States Army Air Corps, born April 18, 1921 to Carl and Florence Garris Fosbrink of Brownstown. He grew up in the local area and was employed by Kieffer Paper Mill before being drafted into the army. He married Carrie Imogene Scott January 31, 1942.

Less than one year later he reported for duty on October 17, 1942 at Camp Atterbury. He was sent to Georgia for basic training and assigned to the 496th Air Service Squadron. After completing training at several bases, his unit was shipped overseas to the European Theater of Operations. He saw duty in North Africa and Italy.

When the war was declared over on V-E Day, he returned to the states and was discharged. He was authorized to wear various medals and ribbons reflecting his services. Although work was scarce when he became a civilian, he was employed at Freeman Field in Seymour until it closed. He was then employed by Cummins where he worked until retirement in 1983.

He became the father of three daughters and the family made their home in Redding Township. He died of a heart attack while on vacation in Vermont in September 2000.

PERRY WILLIAM FOSTER, WWII and Korea, United States Navy, born November 15, 1922 in Jackson County. Trained as RADAR Specialist. Served in World War II, February 2, 1942-November 6, 1945. Served Korean Conflict, December 3, 1951-November 25, 1952. Assigned to USS *New Mexico*. Operated in South Pacific area, Aleutian Islands, Guam. Ship was hit by Japanese Suicide planes. Returned to Pearl Harbor for repairs in 1945 Korean Conflict action on USS *Kirkpatrick* in Mediterranean Sea. Discharged. Retired. as Postmaster at Vallonia August 12, 1980.

PASCAL FRAZIER, World War II, United States Army Air Corps, 401st Squadron, 36th Fighter Group, 9th Air Force. Pascal (Pat) Frazier was born July 1, 1921, at Oscaloosa (Letcher County) Kentucky. He was inducted into the United States Army on October 6, 1942 in Huntington, West Virginia. Assigned the serial number 35448132, he served his country in World War II from October 6, 1942, through September 28, 1945.

From December 1942 to the summer of 1943, he was assigned to duty on the island of Trinidad. On

March 23, 1944, he was sent to England with the 401st Fighter Squadron. He served with the 9th Air Force, 36th Fighter Group, as an airplane armorer.

Battles and campaigns: Normandy, Northern France, Rhineland, Central Europe, Ardennes (Battle of the Bulge), Air Offensive Europe.

Decorations and citations: EAME Theater Ribbon w/6 Bronze Stars, American Theater Ribbon, Good Conduct Ribbon per 36th Fighter Group, Distinguished Unit Citation w/1 Oak Leaf Cluster per 9th Air Force, Belgian Fourragere per 9th Air Force.

Pascal was in Germany when the war came to an end. He held the rank of Corporal when he was rotated back to the separation center at Camp Atterbury in Indiana where he received an honorable discharge on September 28, 1945.

Pascal and his wife, Alva Ison Frazier, moved to Jackson County in 1950 where they raised a family of six children. He did some farming and retired from Golden Operations in Columbus, Indiana in 1984. Living in Freetown, Indiana, he passed from this life on February 12, 1987.

LEWIS H. GALATI, World War II, United States Army, was a Seymour boy who graduated from Shields High School in 1944. He was inducted into the army at Camp Atterbury, Indiana shortly thereafter.

He was sent to Camp Wheeler at Macon, Georgia for basic training of some fifteen weeks. Before being shipped overseas to the European Theater of Operations, he was assigned to the 3rd Army of Infantrymen.

His unit landed at Glasgow, Scotland and from there they were sent to France, Liege in Belgium and on to Strasbourg, Germany. Following V-E Day on May 8, 1945, he served in the occupational forces until he received his discharge at Fort Sheridan, Illinois on August 23, 1946.

EMIL J. GERKENSMEYER, World War II, United States Army, born in Jackson County August 13, 1910 to Rev. Fredrick and Louisa Rust-Gerkensmeyer. The father was the pastor of the St. Paul - Borcher's Lutheran Church located in the far northeast corner of the county.

Emil was a veteran of World War II who served in the 28th Division holding the nickname of "Bloody Basket." Records show he was authorized to wear the Good Conduct Medal, European Theater of Operations ribbon with five campaign stars and the Combat Infantryman's Badge.

Upon receiving his discharge, he returned home to Seymour and was employed by the Woolen Mills

until they closed. He became an employee of the Excell Shirt Factory until retirement.

He was a member of St. Paul and Redeemer Lutheran Church. He died in January 2000.

FRED R. GILL, World War II, United States Army. Fred of Oberlin, LA was inducted into the Armed Forces November 23, 1942. He entered into active service December 1, 1942 at Lafayette, LA. He left Allen Parish and was sent to Camp Howze near Gainesville, TX. He was assigned to the 84th Infantry Division, to the 309th Medical Battalion after basic training. Then they were ordered to Louisiana Maneuvers, near Merryville, LA for eight weeks of maneuver training.

After maneuvers on November 15, 1943, he was sent to a permanent home at Camp Claiborne, LA for further training. This was near his home at Oberlin, LA and he got to be at home with his wife, Marjorie, and baby son, Ronald, most every weekend. In April 1944, the 84th Infantry was placed in a more intensive training program. Late in August 1944, the 84th received its orders for overseas movement by way of Camp Kilmer, NJ. They moved into the European Theater of war and landed in England, then through the English Channel into France. From there to the Belgium Bulge. Back to Holland and across northern Germany. Fred was active there until the war in Europe was over. He spent 15 months in combat before going back to France and across the Atlantic to the United States and Camp Kilmer, NJ.

Fred was discharged December 10, 1945 at Camp Shelby, MS and arrived home December 11, 1945.

Fred and his wife, Marjorie, reside in Medora, where they are both active in the Medora Pentecostal Church. Fred is Director of Prayer Services for the church.

HARLAN L. GILLASPY, World War II, United States Army, Company C, 253rd Division, 7th Army, 35903939. Harlan Gillaspy was born May 24, 1923 in the Copperbottom neighborhood near Crothersville. He was the son of John and Etta Baringer Gillaspy. Leaving the family farm to answer his notice, he served in the army as an expert rifleman. His infantry unit took part in northern France, the Rhineland and Central Europe.

He was wounded April 6, 1945 in Germany. He was authorized to wear the World War Victory Medal, Purple Heart and the EAME Ribbon with three Campaign Stars. He was discharged November 2, 1945.

He returned home to the family farm where he spent the remainder of his life as a farmer. He never married. Harlan passed away January 8, 2003.

ROBERT DALE GILLASPY, SR., World War II, United States Army Air Corps, born December 18, 1921 in Vernon Township to John and Etta Baringer Gillaspy. He was raised in the local area and graduated from Crothersville High School and later received his degree from Purdue University.

He was inducted into the army January 16, 1943 and after basic training he was shipped overseas to the Pacific Theater of Operations in August 1944. A year later he was returned home to the states as a sergeant in the Air Corps after serving in the 547th Night Fighter Squadron. His unit was in action in New Guinea, the Philippines and the Western Pacific.

He received his discharge December 26, 1945 and was authorized to wear various medals and campaign ribbons reflecting his service.

He was married to Elizabeth Stahl February 3, 1952 and to them were born two children, Robert Dale, Jr. and Carol Ann. He was married November 19, 1982 to Mary Virginia Keller Gillaspy. He operated his own trucking company. He died January 21, 1997 and is buried in the Crothersville Cemetery.

WILLIAM A. GOBLE, World War II, United States Army, 1942-1945, mustered into the service October 5, 1942 and later assigned to the 30th Infantry Division which saw action in Normandy and the Rhineland; he was wounded July 9, 1944.

He earned the Combat Infantryman's Badge, EAME Ribbon with 3 Bronze Campaign Stars, WWII Victory Medal and a Purple Heart.

Married Nora Simpson and became father of four children. Retired from Cummins August 1977 and he died in December 1995.

RALPH E. GOEBEL, World War II, United States Army Air Corps, born May 14, 1916 at Granite City, Illinois to Albert and Rebecca Steinhauer Goebel. When his father died the family moved back to Ohio and the young lad grew up there in the home of his step-father, David Myers.

The teen-age boy worked in the local railroad shops. He elected to join the army October 23, 1941 at Patterson Field, Ohio where he was trained in food services. He attended school in Fort Harrison and was charged with feeding as many as 5,000 men in the field.

He saw action in Normandy, Rhineland and Central Europe and was awarded the appropriate medals and ribbons reflect his service. He was discharged October 3O, l945.

He returned home and moved to Crothersville where he found work in the shoe factory. He and his wife, Jean, became the parents of a son, Dennis.

EARL A. GOECKER, World War II, United States Army, was drafted into the army from Jackson County and reported for duty at Louisville, KY. He was born in 1919 on a farm located not far from Seymour. His call to duty was received February 5, 1944 and he was assigned as a telephone lineman for the 276th Signal Hospital Construction Company.

His unit was shipped overseas to the Pacific Theater of Operations where he saw action in New Guinea, the Philippines and Luzon. He was authorized to wear various medals and ribbons representing his service. He received his discharge on December 29, 1945 at Camp Atterbury, IN.

GERALD F. GOECKER, World War II, United States Navy, born to Henry and Ida Klinge Goecker. He enlisted in the navy and was inducted in May 1945 and completed basic training at Great Lakes Naval Station in IL.

He served aboard the aircraft carrier, the USS *Hornet* in the Hawaiian water throughout the war. He was discharged in January 1946.

He married Edna Pfenning Goecker and they are the parents of three children, Alice Hutchinson, Sarah Benter and Rita Stahl. Each of those daughters produced grandchildren.

HAROLD W. GORBETT, World War II, United States Marine Corps, born at Westport, IN in 1927 to Chester and Lois Phegley Gorbett. He graduated from Cortland High School in 1945 and, in September he was drafted into the Marines. He completed his boot camp training at Paris Island, SC.

He was sent to Norfolk, VA where he was shipped out through the Panama Canal and on the Honolulu. From there he went to China for almost a year. He was later sent home to Oakland, CA. and then he flew to Kansas and from there on to Chicago where he received his honorable discharge in September 1946.

In 1948 he married Leona B. Bebout and they became parents of one son, Jerry. He became a grandfather at a later date. Harold retired from Cummins in 1983 after 32 years

LEON GOSSMAN, World War II, United States Navy, 867 25 57, born May 20, 1921 in Brownstown as one of five children which graced the family of Charles and Viola Gossman. Later he graduated from Brownstown High School in 1940. He started working for the

Allison Division of General Motors in 1940 and left for the Navy in 1943. He completed his boot training at Great Lakes Naval Station.

He was assigned to the USS *Baldwin* YY 624 which took part in the D-Day invasion of Normandy and Southern France. He made three Trans-Atlantic convoy escort crossings to Casablanca and Morocco. His ship escorted the cruiser carrying President Roosevelt to the Yalta Conference.

Later his ship served as the flagship for minesweeping operations off both the Korean and Chinese coastal waters. His ship was placed out of commission June 20, 1946, and later it was towed out to sea and sunk because of extensive wartime damage.

He returned home and resumed his old job at Allisons, and on June 5, 1948, he was married to Ruth Gillaspy. To them were born two sons, Edward and James. Leon Gossman retired in 1980 and four years later they moved to Brownstown.

BOBBY HARRIS GRAY, 7656955, Seaman 1st Class, Great Lakes Boot Camp, Illinois.

HUGH L. GRAY JR., United States Navy. Hughl L. Jr., 6273254, 2nd Class Mate, Great Lakes Boot Camp, USS *Beale* DD 47.

HERSCHEL RAY GRESHAM, World War II, United States Army Air Corps, born to Samuel and Carrie Garis Gresham July 23, 1920. He graduated from Brownstown High School in 1938. Much later he was inducted into the Air Corps in Indianapolis.

He was assigned to the 334th Bomb Squadron of the 95th Bomb Group and flew 17 missions over Germany. He was shot down on the last bombing raid November 30, 1944 on the Foggia Air Field in Italy.

EDGAR HACKMAN, 310th Regiment, 78th Infantry Division, United States Army, European Theater of Operations, born on a farm in Grassy Fork Township to Martin and Edna Nierman Hackman, and much later he was graduated from Tampico High School in the class of 1942. During his 2nd year of college at Purdue University, he enlisted in the service at Fort Harrison but completed his basic training at Camp Robinson in Arkansas. He was trained in a specialized program at Rhode Island University.

After transfer to Camp Pickett in Virginia, Edgar was assigned to the 78th Infantry Division before departing for Europe in October 1944, His combat duty was maintaining communications between regimental and battalion headquarters. He was in the "Battle of the Bulge," through the Ruhr Valley and on to the Ludendorf Bridge at Remagen, where his unit crossed the Rhine River before it was blown up.

In April 1945, Edgar was awarded the Bronze Star for meritorious duty while in combat against the enemy. As crew chief in the regimental wire section, he and men installed 500 miles of communications lines while under constant small arms fire.

Edgar Hackman received his honorable discharge at Camp Atterbury and returned to Purdue University and graduated in 1947. He taught school for 40 years, and served as a County Fair Director for 50 years. In addition he has received other honors, including becoming a member of the Indiana County and Fairs "Hall of Fame." He was appointed a director of the Indiana State Fair Board in 2001, Edgar is married to the former Pauline Krumme and they have two sons and four grandchildren.

EUGENE HACKMAN, United States Army Air Corps, #45038248, was inducted at Fort Lewis, WA, 1945-1947. He was discharged at Camp Atterbury as a sergeant. A maintenance sergeant while at Headquarters in Naples, Italy.

EVERETT H.J. HACKMAN, World War II, United States Army, born May 12, 1927 in Jackson County. Parents were Walter and Emma Hageman Hackman. Raised on the family farm near Tampico.

Inducted February 8, 1946 into the army at Indianapolis. Completed basic training at Camp Crowder. Received medical training in Colorado and Washington. Assigned as a Medic in the 754th Tank Battalion.

Shipped overseas to the South Pacific Theater. Service in Guam, Saipan, Okinawa and Korea. Discharged July 11, 1947.

Returned to the home farm. Worked for Dixon's at Freeman Field for 43 years. Grassy Fork Township Trustee.

HERMAN HACKMAN, World War II, United States Army Air Corps, 2nd Lieutenant, entered the Enlisted Reserve Corps while he was a student at Purdue University in 1942. He was sworn into active duty May 8, 1943 while stationed at Fort Eustis, Virginia. He decided to apply for Cadet Training in the Air Corps and once he was accepted he received further training at Oshkosh, WI and later to Long Beach, California. He received training in navigation and later in gunnery while stationed in Kingman, Arizona.

Upon completing his training as a Navigator, he received his Wings and was promoted to Flight Officer with the class of 44-44-N. He passed the test for Radar Observer at Langley Field, Virginia before he was transferred in 1945 to the 15th Air Force then stationed at Foggia, Italy. He returned to the United States October 3, 1945 and was released from active duty. He completed his course work at Purdue and graduated on the G.I. Bill of Rights on June 15, 1947.

Herman Hackman was recalled to active duty as 2nd Lt. in mid-May 1951 to train Navigation at Ellington Field, Texas. He served in that capacity for 18 months. His wife, Edith, and their two sons lived together in a trailer park located on the base in Texas.

MARTIN HACKMAN, JR., World War II, son of Martin and Edna Nierman Hackman, was born September 25, 1921 in Grassy Fork Township of Jackson County, Indiana. He graduated from Tampico High School with the class of 1940.

Martin had two brothers who were in the military service: Edgar Hackman served in the U.S. Army and Donald Hackman was in the U.S. Air Force. He also had two sisters and another brother.

While Martin Hackman, Jr. was in the U.S. Air Force, he was married to Verna Eggesman Hackman in Albuquerque, N.M. He served as a mechanic during WWII.

After being discharged from the service, he lived and farmed in the Wegan area. From 1955 to 1998 he worked in the auto service area of Renner Motors in Columbus. While there, they were blessed with three children.

Martin Hackmann died at the Columbus Regional Hospital on October 1, 1999.

BILLY HALL, World War II, United States Army, born near Crothersville, the son of Charles and Gertrude Russell Hall in 1925. There were two brothers and five sisters in the family.

He played harmonica with the "Little Rascals" after his brother was drafted into the army in 1942. Billy continued his work at Camp Atterbury and, after he graduated he worked at Freeman Field and American Can until he turned 18.

In November 1943 he left Seymour with several others for Fort Thomas, KY. He completed his basic training at Camp Croft, SC and was assigned to the Infantry Replacement Center. His unit was shipped overseas on the *Queen Mary* on June 6, 1944 when they heard the news about D-Day landings. After disembarking in Scotland, they landed on Omaha

Beach before the end of June, and was eventually assigned to the 2nd Infantry Regiment of the 5th Division which became part of the 3rd Army.

He saw action across France and into Luxembourg during the Battle of the Bulge. By the middle of March they were ready to cross the Rhine River near Frankfurt, Germany. By the time V-E Day arrived they were in Czechoslovakia and he was shipped home to the States, ready for a furlough and redeployment to the Pacific Theater. After the two Atomic bombs were dropped, he was discharged at Camp Atterbury in 1945.

He was later married to Mary Hinderlider in 1946 and they became parents of three children. He retired from Arvin Industries after 42 years of employment. He passed away September 27, 1995.

HARRY KENNETH HALL, World War II, United States Army, born July 21, 1912 to Clarence "Red" and Gertrude Smallwood Hall. Harry was raised near Brownstown and later graduated from Brownstown High School.

He was inducted into the army November 6, 1943 and assigned an artillery mechanic and he qualified as a rifle sharpshooter. He was into the 5th Signal Company which served in the Ardennes, Rhineland and Central Europe for eight months when V-E Day was announced. He was discharged on Nov. 25, 1945 at Camp Atterbury so he could return home. He was authorized to wear appropriate medals and ribbons reflecting his campaigns.

He married Lucille Hansome and they became parents of a son. He was named Charles Allen Hall and later married Patty Gilbert.

Harry Hall died July 23, 1981.

JAMES E. HALL, World War II, United States Merchant Marines, United States Navy, enlisted in the Merchant Marines in August 1943 and in November he entered the navy. He was trained at Great Lakes Naval Station. He received further training in radio operations in Pennsylvania and graduated as radioman then waited for orders.

He volunteered for foreign duty and was assigned to a secret naval group known as SACO, ie Sino-American Cooperative Organization. It was the forerunner of the modern SEALS. He was sent to California and shipped overseas to Pearl Harbor, Melbourne and Calcutta.

He operated as radioman and worked for the Chinese secret service for a year behind enemy lines, reporting weather conditions, troop movements and shipping. At one time he wore an army uniform all through the Gobi Desert to Chungking.

He was awarded the Chinese Victory Ribbon, Asiatic-Pacific Ribbon with a Bronze Campaign Star. He was discharged December 18, 1945 and almost 50 years later, he received the War Resistance Memorial Medal from the Chinese government.

JAY F. HALL, World War II, United States Navy, born October 14, 1923 at Crothersville, Indiana. Completed elementary grade school. Married. Employed at Cordes Hardware Store.

Inducted October 4, 1943 at Louisville, Kentucky. Completed boot camp training at Great Lakes. Assigned to USS *Persepcen.* Served on USS YMS-89 and USS *Wm H. Butner.*

Discharged as Seaman 1st Class at Great Lakes Naval Depot on October 23, 1945. He died May 14, 1977.

RALPH HAMBLIN, World War II and Vietnam, United States Army, was born in Clay County, KY and died April 16, 2003 at Colorado Springs of cancer at age 74 years. He attended Flarwoods Elementary School, Leslie High School and the Oneida Baptist Institute. In 1945 he misrepresented his age and registered for the draft in Manchester, KY.

Unknown to him at the time, his military career was destined to span almost three decades and would take him all over war-torn Germany and Vietnam for two tours of duty 25 years later. During the latter part of his career, he led an adventuresome life serving his country.

He was being trained for service in Japan when the atomic age opened. He was then assigned to the European Theater of Operations serving in the occupation forces who participated in the Berlin Airlift. Ralph returned to the states and Tampico in 1948, but he was a changed man, so he, re-enlisted in the army and remained a soldier.

He was authorized to wear various medals and ribbons reflecting his service achievements. He retired April 1, 1974 at Fort Carson, CO.

EDWARD M. HAMILTON, United States Army, #36806862, Private 1st Class, 94th Infantry Division. Awarded Purple Heart, Oct. 4, 1943–Oct. 31, 1945, enlisted in the Army during the first week in October 1943. Refusing a deferment because of farm work, he answered the call of his country when his number came up by the Selective Service system. He was sent to Ft. Thomas, KY. and three days later was shipped to Virginia where he completed his basic training at Ft. Eustis in anti-aircraft detection.

He was selected for training as a radar operator; was selected for promotion but the need for radar operators had vanished by the time he had finished his training. Everyone then boarded the train and were sent to camp near Fort Benning, GA.

Along with others, Edward Hamilton lived in a tent, four men crowded together among the pine trees. The men soon found out Phenix City was off limits and they began basic training all over but it was geared for the infantry. Most were sent to Meridan, MS where they received basic training once again. Many of the men were assigned to the 4th Army.

Edward Hamilton received communications training, and was separated from the others for good.

He was presented a furlough which permitted him to go home. He reported to Fort Dix, NJ. where he boarded the *Queen Mary* and set sail overseas. Landing near Glasgow, England his group was moved in just a few hours to Southampton on the coast. They all knew what was coming, and he was assigned to the 94th Division in the 376th Regiment and Albert Lawson was the platoon sergeant

Lawson was wounded and sent back to England, but Hamilton served the Siegfried Line of defense. He was hit while still in France and received the Purple Heart. Ernest Burnside of Freetown was wounded in the snow before the unit dropped back to rest before relieving the men caught in the Battle of the Bulge.

While resting later Hamilton's feet were frozen, and because he was hard of hearing, he joined his unit and was shipped home to New York City. Three days later he headed for Camp Atterbury where he received his discharge.

JAMES H. HAMILTON, JR., World War II, United State Air Force, Major, Retired.

GLEN L. HAND, World War II, United States Air Corps, enlisted in the military services of his country March 13, 1943 and completed his basic training in Alexandria, Louisiana. He received his silver gunners wings while stationed at Harlingen, Texas in August of 1943. He was promoted to T/Sgt. and his unit was shipped overseas to the European Theater of Operations.

Glen L. Hand was a turret gunner on a B-17 fortress assigned to the 8th Air Force Bomb Squadron. On March 7, 1944 Sgt. Hand was reported missing on a bombing mission over Germany. The Red Cross confirmed he was a prisoner of war confined at Stalag #6 but he was moved several times during the next 14 months.

While a prisoner at Stalag #357, he escaped the guards through an area of black mud. In company with some Russian prisoners, he hid in the woods where he could watch the Germans in full retreat. The ex-prisoners attached themselves to the advancing Russians and he made his way to safety behind the Allied lines.

He returned to the states and was stationed in Florida before being discharged.

CHARLES ERVIN HANNER, World War II, United States Army, born September 22, 1920 at Sparksville to Walter and Lillie Cockerham Hanner. After he became an adult, he was a farmer.

He was drafted late in 1943 and was inducted into Company B of the 62nd Infantry Battalion at Camp Wolters, Texas. He saw active duty from December 23, 1943 to November 6, 1944.

After he returned to the states and was discharged, he was employed by Cummins until he retired. He was married to Mabel Burrell and they became parents of three daughters.

JOSEPH W. HANSOME, World War II, United States Army, born January 31, 1919 to Charles and Mary Baughman Hansome. He was raised near Brownstown but graduated from Clearspring High School. He married Dorothy Sherrill early in May 1941 and they became parents of one child while they lived in Crothersville, Indiana.

He entered the army September 4, 1942 at Fort Harrison, Indianapolis and was assigned as clerk-typist. After two months of training he was shipped overseas to the European Theater of Operations. After V-E was declared, he returned to the states and received his discharge at Camp Atterbury.

He was authorized to wear appropriate medals and ribbons reflecting his service of more than three years.

He died October 20, 1975.

PERRY EUGENE HANSOME, World War II, United States Army, born April 17, 1924 to Charles and May Baughman Hansome on a farm located near Brownstown. He graduated from Clearspring High School. He was drafted and inducted into the army March 6, 1943 in Louisville, KY and placed into the Air Corps.

He completed basic training and qualified as a carbine expert marksman and was assigned to the 78th Lightning Division. Shortly there afterward he was involved in a vehicle accident and placed in a body cast for 13 months. He recovered and was released from the hospital in Florida. He was transferred to a convalescent hospital at Bowman Field, KY early in June 1945.

Once at home, he married Bonnie Emphress on June 2, 1951 and they became parents of two children, named Cherrie and Bryan. Both are married and they have children to be enjoyed by their grandparents.

Perry Hansome died July 20, 1969.

RAYMOND W. HANSOME, World War II, United States Army Air Corps, born January 28, 1917

to Charles and May Baughman Hansome of Jackson County. He graduated later from high school at Clearspring. He was drafted and inducted into the army at Fort Harrison in Indianapolis January 12, 1942.

After completing basic training he was assigned as an airplane mechanic in the 4th Engine Overhaul Squadron. He was stationed at several stateside bases before being shipped overseas to Australia. He received his discharge January 17, 1946 at Camp Atterbury. He was authorized to wear appropriate medals and ribbons reflecting his campaigns.

He married Crystal Stewart November 16, 1946 and they settled near Vallonia, but they eventually moved to Beech Grove. They became parents of a daughter, Brenda, who blessed them with three grandchildren.

Raymond died October 7, 1997.

BILLY HARBAUGH, World War II, United States Army, born October 26, 1921 in Freetown to Frank and Jesse McLean Harbaugh. He had one brother Allen Bain Harbaugh. He graduated from the local high school in 1939.

He joined the army October 17, 1942 and completed basic training. His unit was shipped overseas to the European Theater of Operations where he served in Northern France, Rhineland and the Ardennes known as the Battle of the Bulge.

He was a truck driver and held the rank of T/Sgt. in the 3600th Company. He was discharged at Camp Atterbury January 4, 1946. The following year he married Norma Jean Stogdell and they became the parents of two daughters, Brenda and Nancy. They now enjoy three grandchildren.

Billy was an auto mechanic and operated Harbaugh's Garage in Freetown for many years. He retired in 1987 as a member of the Church of Christ where he had served as an Elder. He died on Christmas Day in 2001. He was buried in the Freetown Cemetery.

MARION D. HARVEY, Army of the United States, #35104021, Private 1st Class, induction at Fort Harrison. Service Time: 4/23/1941 - 4/21/1945. Wounded in Normandy, Purple Heart. Hospital at Fort Custer, MI. Heavy Machine Gunner, Combat Infantryman. European Campaigns, Normandy, Northern France and Central Germany.

LLOYD E. HAWN, World War II, United States Navy, born March 23, 1926 at Mt. Eden in Jackson County. His parents were Edward and Kissie Bryant

Hawn. Attended Gaiter Elementary School and Little York High School.

He entered the navy September 5, 1944 at Indianapolis. Completed boot camp training at Great Lakes Naval Station and placed in the casual draft Register in California. Assigned to the 5th Special Navy Construction Battalion and shipped overseas to the Philippine Islands. Discharged June 6, 1946 at Great Lakes.

Returned to Little York and employed at the county REMC. Married Lois Otte February 6, 1949 and became parents of two children. They are residents of Brownstown.

HUBERT W. HAZARD, World War II, United States Army, born 4/4/1924, in Jackson County, Indiana. Graduated high school in 1942.

Drafted 3/6/43 with active duty 3/13/43 at Fort Benjamin Harrison. Assigned to 78th Infantry Division, Company K, 310th Regiment. Basic Infantry and Advanced Training at Camp Butner, North Carolina. Two-month maneuvers in Tennessee January, February and March of 1944.

Camp Picket, Virginia, March 1944 and left the United States to go overseas 10/14/1944 and arrived 10/25/1944. Fought from 12/13/1944 until the end of the war as an infantryman. Three Battle Stars for Rhineland, Ardennes and Central Europe. He fought in the Battle of the Bulge and received two Bronze Stars (V and Oak Leaf Cluster), Good Conduct Medal, Presidential Unit Citation, American Campaign Medal, European, Africa, Middle Eastern Campaign Medal, WWII Victory Medal, Army Occupation Medal, and Combat Infantryman Badge.

Went to Berlin November of 1945. Left Bremmerhaven 12/25/1945 and arrived in the US on 1/9/1946. Was discharged 1/9/1946 at Camp Afterbury.

OMER HECKMAN, World War II, United States Army, was born on a farm in Jackson County on February 7, 1913, to George and Mary Tiemeyer Heckman. He was one of ten children. Omer Heckman joined the Army in April 1940, and was assigned to the 3rd Infantry Division.

He was killed during battle in Italy on May 8, 1944. PFC Omer Heckman is buried in the US Military Cemetery in Nettuno, Italy.

Omer Heckman and his brother, Ray H. Heckman, who was also serving in the Army, had the good fortune to meet with each other in Europe in early 1944, when Omer was on his way to Italy.

RAY H. HECKMAN, World War II, United States Army, born on a farm in Jackson County on October 16, 1915, to George and Mary Tiemeyer Heckman. He was one of ten children.

He joined the Army at Fort Benjamin Harrison on April 27, 1942, and was assigned to the 301st Ordnance Regiment, 602nd Battalion, Company F. He served as a vehicle inspector in Tunisia, Rhineland,

Southern France, and Central Europe. He returned to the USA on October 8, and left the Army on October 13, 1945, at Camp Atterbury, Indiana.

Early in 1944, Ray had the good luck to meet with his brother, Omer, who was also serving in the Army. Omer was on his way to Italy, where he was killed in battle on May 8, 1944.

Ray Heckman married his sweetheart, Rosemary Taylor Heckman, on November 3, 1945. They bought the farm where Ray had grown up, and built a new house where they raised two children. Ray continued to farm until his retirement. He died of complications from cancer on December 18, 1998.

Ray Heckman never talked much about the war, but everyone who knew him understood that he was very proud of his service in the US Army.

CARL F. HEHMAN, World War II, United States Army, born September 10, 1918 in Kansas to Martin and Sophia Trimpe Hehman. He moved with his family when they relocated to Jackson County and settled south of Seymour. He attended the Lutheran School and became a farmer until he entered the army.

He was inducted November 9, 1944 and completed basic training at Camp Wheeler, GA. He was sent to France and saw action in Central Europe in the 82nd Airborne Division which made it all the way into Berlin. He was authorized to wear various medals and ribbons reflecting his service.

He returned to the states and was sent to Fort Bragg, NC as a light truck driver and discharged June 29, 1946. He came home to the Sauers area where he and his wife, Dorothy Claycamp Hehman, farmed until his retirement. He was also a carpenter and mechanic at Browning Brothers Garage. They raised three daughters.

CHARLES E. HEHMAN, World War II, United States Army, was inducted into the army April 2, 1941 at Fort Harrison in Indianapolis. He was a son of George Heyman and Elizabeth White Heyman in 1919. He was trained in the military to serve as a rifleman assigned to the Headquarters Unit guarding some German prisoners.

He was shipped out to the Panama Canal Zone as a guard and served until May 16, 1944. He was discharged soon thereafter and married Edna Pottschmidt and they became parents of two sons.

DONALD L. HEIWIG, World War II, United States Signal Corps, 2nd Lt. and Captain, Allied Military Communications Systems, 1942-1947. Mayor of Seymour, 1949-1957.

JAMES PERSINGER HELLER, World War II, 3rd Ordinance Regiment, Camp Atterbury, 1943-1945, son of John and Margaret Brown Heller, was born in 1919 on the Heller Family farm located one mile southwest of Brownstown in Jackson County, IN. He was later graduated from the local high school in 1929 and then he attended Butler University. He was employed at the Jackson Brick and Holloware Company in his hometown. Later he became president and general manager of the Medora Brick Company.

He was inducted into the army September 4, 1943 at Fort Harrison in Indianapolis. Pvt. Heller (35707803) was stationed at the Aberdeen Proving Grounds and assigned to Company B-1st Ordinance Regiment as the supply clerk. In June 1944 he was transferred to Camp Atterbury as supply clerk until the end of the war.

He was discharged August 30, 1945 and returned home to Brownstown and continued with the manufacturing of brick and clay products until 1994. James P. Heller died December 13, 1999 and was buried in the Fairview Cemetery in Brownstown, IN

JOSEPH E. HENDERSON, World War II, United States Army, entered service March 6, 1943 and discharged January 13, 1946. Assigned to the 231st Port Company of the 492nd Battalion. Served as a carpenter in the Pacific Theater of Operations. Awarded various medals and ribbons representing his service

Re-enlisted December 13, 1950 but due to failing health was discharged March 31, 1951. He died in January of 1984.

World War II Veterans. Six Hilderbrand Sons Who Served Their Country

Arthur Hilderbrand, at left is shown with his eight children in this photo taken in Houston at the annual family reunion held sometime in May 1947. From left is Harold, Choral, Robert, George, Paul, Kenneth, William and the only daughter, Alice Marie Hilderbrand.

The patriot sons of Arthur and Nannie Rose Hilderbrand all served their country during World War II representing several branches of the American military services. The six sons all returned home safely, and four of them are still alive in 2004. Harold was a marine; Robert was in the Air Corps; William served in the navy, while the other three sons completed their tours of duty in the army. The entire family of Hilderbrands were residents of the Houston area of Jackson County.

Arthur Hilderbrand, the father of those six sons and one daughter, died in 1949 and is buried in the Hickory Grove Cemetery. Harold and Chloral Hilderbrand are both dead, but the annual family picnic and reunion continues to be celebrated at Otis Park located near Bedford, Indiana. All deserve to be saluted with honor.

GEORGE HILDERBRAND, World War II, the oldest of six brothers to serve in the military forces of the United States, was drafted into the army in 1942. He was inducted at Camp Atterbury but received training in Kansas, Mississippi and Tennessee. He was then assigned to the 94th Infantry Division and shipped overseas to England. His unit went into action when they crossed the channel into France and advanced on into Germany and finally reached Czechoslovakia when V-E Day was proclaimed.

He is married and resides near Hope with his wife, Martha. They became parents of five children.

HAROLD HILDERBRAND, World War II, United States Marine Corps, enlisted in the Marines in 1931 and served a single hitch as a private until he was discharged in 1935. He re-enlisted later in 1942 after Pearl Harbor.

He died in 1974 and his wife, Bessie passed away in 1989. Of their three children, one son is dead but the 2 daughters still live in Indiana.

KENNETH HILDERBRAND, World War II, United States Army, was drafted into the army and was inducted in 1943. After completing basic training, he was assigned to the 65th Infantry Division as a medical technician. His duties were to assist in the surgery wing of the army hospital.

After he was discharged in 1946, he returned home and operated an auto sales in Columbus. He and his wife, Virginia still reside there and he is retired. They were parents of two children.

PAUL W. HILDERBRAND, World War II, United States Army, 35694472, entered the army from Houston, IN on January 3, 1943. He completed his basic training at Fort Lewis, WA and was shipped overseas to the European Theater of Operations. He served under General Patton in the 735th Tank

Battalion after the D-Day invasion of Normandy. His unit was in combat during the Battle of Metz and again in the Battle of the Bulge.

He was authorized to wear 5 Campaign Stars and Victory Medal when he received his honorable discharge in 1945. He returned home and settled for a time in Chrisman, IL.

ROBERT HILDERBRAND, World War II,

United States Army Air Corps, enlisted in the Army Air Corps in 1941 and completed basic training in Texas. He was selected for special training in Chicago, Illinois. He was then assigned to the 8th Air Service Group attached to the 423rd stationed in England.

He returned to the states in 1945 and discharged in August. He was married, and he and his wife, Alice, lived in Bedford. They became parents of four children. He died in 1992.

WILLIAM HILDERBRAND, World War II,

United States Navy, the youngest of the six brothers, enlisted in the navy in 1944. After completing his boot camp training, he was aboard ship in the Pacific Theater of Operations. At the time of his discharge in 1946, he was listed as a Seaman 1st Class.

He returned home to Jackson County and was employed by Arvin Industries Incorporated in Columbus. Several years later he began work in maintenance for the Seymour School Corporation where he retired.

He and his wife, Helen became the parents of five children, and now reside in Easyville.

JOHN I. HILL, World War II, United States Army,

born March 26, 1917 at Leesville to Styles and Fannie Gillen Hill. When he was just two weeks old, his family moved to Jackson County, Indiana. Much later he drafted into the army on April 15, 1944. He completed his basic training at Camp Wheeler, Georgia.

He was assigned to "L" Company, 47th Regiment, 9th Infantry Division and shipped overseas to England in September 1944. His unit saw action first in November 1944 along the German border when they set out to capture the Siegfried Line. Other campaigns included the "Battle of the Bulge" during the winter months of 1944. He survived by living in a fox hole providing his only shelter.

He was involved in the battles for the Ruhr and the Hürtgen Forest. He was with the first infantrymen to walk across the Rhine River Bridge at Remagen. Three days later the Germans arrived to counter attack and retake the bridge. By noon they were driven back but the toll left only 27 survivors of "L" Company.

During the campaigns in Europe he never missed a day of combat. After V-E Day he was assigned to the office of "Stars and Stripes" and a few months later he was shipped back to the states ready to be deployed to the Pacific. He was discharged May 16, 1946.

ORVILLE F. HOENE, World War II, United

States Army. The military Memoirs of Orville F. Hoene, a technician in the Army of the United States during World War II. Assigned a serial number of 35965585 T45. Orville served from December 1944 to April 1946.

He was born June 5, 1925 on a farm in northern Jackson County in Hamilton Township, Indiana, son of Fred and Elizabeth Vornholt Hoene. He was reared as a farmboy on his mother's homestead, with three other brothers, Ivan, Herbert and Paul. He graduated from Cortland High School in 1943.

He was drafted into the Army in December 1944 and received his basic training in Camp Phillips, Little Rock, Arkansas. He was shipped to England and then onto Europe. Peace was declared as the ship was going overseas. He knew his older brother Ivan was missing in action; months later when he was in France, he was informed that his brother was released from concentration camp and sent home (no e-mail back then!).

He spent most of his time working at an Army Post Office in France. Christmas of 1945 was spent with two buddies with a family in Switzerland on a furlough.

In April of 1946 he was sent home on a cargo plane, which also made a stop in Iceland.

Upon returning home he and a friend, Burrl Schleuser decided to go to Coyne Electric in Chicago, the Army paid tuition under the GI Bill. He graduated with a certificate for electronics.

In December of 1949 he started working as an apprentice lineman for Public Service Electric Company in Seymour, IN. He worked there until his retirement in April 1988, as line working foreman.

He married Marilyn Hackman in September 1951. They have three daughters, Judy Wonning, Kathy Humphrey and Carla Cockerham; and five grandchildren; Seth and Louis Wonning, Nicolas and Nathan Humphrey and Whitney Cockerham.

In his retirement, he developed Parkinson's disease and died of a heart attack on May 26, 1996.

LAWRENCE L. HOEVENER, World War II,

United States Army, born December 3, 1915 to Henry and Minnie Kriete Hoevener in Jackson County. He was inducted into the army March 5, 1942 and assigned to Company F of the 109th Combat Regiment, 28th Division.

Lawrence Hoevener was killed in action in Luxembourg December 16, 1944 during the Battle of the Bulge. His body was interred temporarily in a governmental cemetery in Belgium. Later his parents requested his remains be sent home for burial in the Sauers Cemetery following the Memorial Service held December 16, 1945.

He was married to Eunice Hunt Hoevener and they became the parents of a daughter born December 18, 1943, whom he never got to see. He had kept her picture in his billfold where it was found when he

was killed. That daughter later married James Bradley Patrick who serves in the military.

ROY H. HOEVENER, World War II, United

States Army, 35965545, born July 29, 1926, a son of Henry and Minnie Kriete Hoevener of Jackson County. He was raised on the family farm. Military records indicate he attended county schools because he lived near Brownstown.

He was called to duty on December 5, 1944 and reported to Fort Harrison in Indianapolis.

He was assigned to the field artillery and completed basic training after which he attended several service schools. When certified, he became a field lineman in HQ Battery, 19th Field Artillery Battalion charged to maintain the phone wires for communications. He served directing the 155 howitzer guns during the Luzon campaign. He was awarded various medals and ribbons reflecting his service during his tour of duty in the Pacific Theater of Operations centered on the Iowas in Kansis.

He was discharged at Fort Sheridan on August 1, 1946 and went home almost immediately where he married Joyce Garrison. To them were born two sons and two daughters.

VIRGIL HOLLE, World War II, United States

Army Air Corps, born January 31, 1923 near Brownstown, IN in Jackson County. He was drafted at Louisville, KY and assigned to the air corps and served as a supply technician and trained as a rifleman. He was shipped overseas October 8, 1943 to the European Theater of Operations. He saw action in Normandy, France, Battle of the Bulge and central Europe.

He was authorized to wear various medals and ribbons for his service time. He was discharged on December 11, 1945 at Camp Atterbury, IN.

EMORY T. HOPPER, World War II, United

States Army, born in 1917, one of 9 children born to Perry and Adeline Henry Hopper of Lexington, IN, before they moved to Crothersville, from where he entered the army January 12, 1942 at Fort Harrison. He was sent to Fort Meade, MD where he met his wife.

He was assigned as a radio operator on a medium tank. It was later when he became a driver of a tank dozer before joining Company A, 741st Tank Battalion. He served with this unit through Normandy and northern France. He was the only survivor of his crew and was burned badly on August 1, 1944 and his survival was due to the action of Ed Lucas of Brownstown. He was identified three days later because his dog tags were burned.

After spending time in a field hospital in France he was returned to the states for more treatment at Wakeman Hospital at Camp Atterbury before being discharged March 23, 1946. He was the composer of these few verses:

My life has been enriched by this soldier lying here,

His life has not been ended
Though his body lies still.
You ask me how I know
this soldier so well,
See that man lying here
Is the only one I had
That soldier I love is my dad.

LLOYD F. HOWARD, WWII and Korea, United States Navy, graduated from Shields High School and began his tour of duty on 29 July, 1946. After boot camp at Great Lakes Naval Training Center, he was sent to school at the Ward Island Naval Training station at Corpus Christi, TX. A year later he graduated as an Aviation Electronics Technician Third Class.

His assignment was with a new patrol bomber squadron, VPML-4, being formed at NAAS, Miramar, San Diego, CA. His planes were the new P2V2 Neptune made by Lockheed with two 2400 HP Pratt & Whitney engines. The planes were hot and would do a slow roll into a dead engine! They were the FIRST naval aircraft with all flush antennae.

His squadron was assigned to go to Alaska and photograph it from 20,000 feet. To do this, they had their eight 20mm nose cannon replaced with cameras. Alaska had never been photographed and his squadron was the FIRST to do so. Cameras were also mounted on their radar scopes to photograph the screens in conjunction with the aerial photographs. It was his job to keep the radar (the newest military radar available) in perfect condition. His squadron lived on a seaplane tender, the USS *Floyds Bay,* which was anchored at a bay of Annette Island, Alaska. While there he became an Aviation Technician Second Class.

At the end of his tour of duty, if he shipped over, he was told he would be sent to Cape Canaveral, FL. Who knows, if he'd re-enlisted he may have eventually become an astronaut! Instead, upon his discharge, 27 July 1948, he elected to return to Purdue where he graduated as an electrical engineer in 1951. (While in school, he was a Staff Sgt. in the Air Force Reserve at Atterbury.) He married Harriett Barnett of Indianapolis and they have four children. After 17 years with GE, he enrolled at Brite Divinity School, Texas Christian University, where he became a minister with the Christian Church (Disciples of Christ). He is now retired living in Sun City West, AZ.

WALTER L. HUNT, World War II, Vietnam, United States Army Air Corps and Air Force, was a resident of Jackson County and graduated from Tampico High School in 1937. He was employed by REMC where he started his career as a surveyor. He also worked for the Missouri rural electric service out of Branson. He also played a part in the surveying of Freeman Field.

He married Ruth E. Johnson Hunt and they became parents of two daughters. He joined the Army Air Corps in 1943 and was sent to the Cadet School at the University of Florida. He graduated as a bombardier and he and his crew flew many missions in the Pacific Theater of Operations utilizing the newly developed Norden Bomb Sight.

He was listed on the ready reserve status and, during the Cold War, he was called to active duty with the rank of S/MSG. He attained his engineering degree and was stationed in Iwo Jima, Guam, Japan, France and Germany. Indeed, he was transferred 33 times during his 21 years military career.

After the war he returned home and was employed as an engineer for the State Highway Commission of Indiana until he retired. He and his wife, Ruth spent half a year in Jackson County and the other half in Florida.

CHARLES WENDELL HURLEY, World War II, United States Navy, born March 12, 1927 at Brownstown to Claude and Lorene Wattles Hurley. He was raised in Jackson County and was later graduated from Brownstown High School in 1945.

He entered the navy from high school on April 12, 1945 and was inducted at Indianapolis. He reported for duty at Great Lakes Naval Station to complete his boot camp training. He was assigned to the Hospital Corps and was sent to Idaho. He completed his tour of duty at Sampson NB in New York and was discharged in Brooklyn November 9, 1946.

He returned to the county and attended Indiana University, Butler and Purdue and graduated with his teaching degree. He taught at several local schools before being appointed the Principal of North Vernon High High School in 1960.

He married Mildred Nan Shelton in 1953 and they became parents of 5 children. He died November 17, 2002 and his wife followed him just about one year later on August 23, 2003.

RUSSELL L. HURLEY, World War II, United States Navy, born March 26, 1922 to Claude and Lorine Wattles Hurley of Brownstown. He graduated from the local high school in 1940 and enlisted in the navy September 24, 1940. He completed his boot camp training at the Great Lakes Naval Station. Shortly thereafter, he was assigned to the USS *Colorado* which was sent to the Pacific Theater of Operations.

Russell (Bud) was stationed at Pearl Harbor before and after the December attack on December 7, 1941. He saw action in the Philippines and, while in action at New Guinea he contracted dingue fever, but was able to continue his service. He was promoted through the ranks to gunner's mate 1st class by the time of his discharge on November 25, 1946.

He was authorized to wear various medals and ribbons representing his service after returning to Brownstown, he was married to Alice Josephine Empson and they became parents of four children, including Carol, Michael, Barbara and Bradley. Bud Hurley worked for the postal service and he was active in the Brownstown Christian Church, Masons, Scottish Rite and the American Legion, Post 112. He died June 3, 1998.

ARNOLD HUTCHINSON, World War II and Lifetime, United States Army. Arnold (Frank) Hutchinson was the son of Frances Hehman of Brownstown born February 2, 1940. After enlisting in the army he served in Germany between 1959 and 1962 and was on duty when the Berlin Wall was erected. After returning to the states, he was assigned to the 82nd Airborne Division stationed at Fort Bragg, NC.

From there he went into combat in the Dominican Republic uprising. He then entered Special Forces training school and joined the 5th Group back at Fort Bragg. In December 1970 he was shipped overseas to Vietnam where he was a member of Special Operations. He also served as a convoy rider. He returned to the states in December 1971 and was assigned as an instructor at Fort Bragg, NC.

He received his discharge in December 1978 as Sgt. 1st Class. He was married to Alice Goecker Hutchinson and they became parents of three children, Greg, Lori and Mark.

HARLESS L. IMLAY, World War II, United States Army, born in Jackson County, Indiana February 16, 1924, and graduated from Shields High School.

Cadet Harless L. Imlay entered the U.S. Army August 4, 1944. He attended AAC Pilot Schools and received his Lapel Button. His Military Occupational Specialty was Pilot SE Fighter 1055, his service was in the Pacific Theater with the 8th Fighter Group Army Air Corps in Campaigns in Ryukyus Islands, China, Air Offensives, Japan from August 1945 to July 1946. He received the American Theater Ribbon, 1 Overseas Service Bar, American Pacific Theater Ribbon w/3 Bronze Stars, Victory Medal, Army of Occupation Medal (Japan). 1st Lieutenant Imlay was separated from the U.S. Army Air Corps at Ft. Sheridan Separation Center, Ft. Sheridan, IL July 12, 1946.

He returned to Seymour to live and work for a short time and after he married he sought out the type of work he was destined for, "Flying."

MARSHALL E. ISAACS, World War II, United States Army, inducted February 27, 1943 at Camp Atterbury from Cortland.

Assigned to Company G, 17th Infantry Division, shipped overseas to the Pacific Theater of Operations. Rifleman. Philippines and Aleutian

Islands. Appropriate medals and ribbons reflecting his service. Discharged November 27, 1945.

MARVIN H. ISAACS,
World War II, United States Army, inducted into the army October 17, 1942. Trained as Technician 4th Grade.

Hq. Battalion, 490th Field Artillery. European Theater of Operations. Rhineland, Ardennes and Central Europe. Disability Discharge November 20, 1945.

WILLIAM WAYNE ISAACS,
World War II, United States Army, born in Hamilton Township April 18, 1921. Parents, William and Hazel Ritz Isaacs. Graduated from Cortland High School in 1938. Married Mary Maxine Hiten October 28, 1942.

Drafted October 21, 1942. Reported for duty November 4, 1942. Completed basic training at Fort Benning. Assigned to be surgical technician with 71st Infantry Division. Overseas service in European Theater. Rhineland, Central Europe and Germany.

EAME Ribbon with 2 Campaign Stars, American Theater Ribbon, Good Conduct Medal. Discharged to Army Reserves August 16, 1951.

JESS LEE JACKSON,
World War II, United States Army, was a son of Jesse A. and Lessie Pearl Jackson. He was married to Mary Denny Jackson and to them were born a daughter named Barbara Joan. Jess passed away October 17, 1989.

He was inducted into the army in March 1942 and assigned to the 109th Infantry Regiment of the 28th Division. That National Guard unit was called to duty from Camp Pickett, VA where he received advanced training. They were shipped overseas from Boston October 8, 1943 and landed in Wales. Training in amphibious operations followed and after D-Day, they arrived in France. During battle he was wounded near Luxembourg evacuated to a field hospital. Further treatment followed in one hospital after another until he was sent back to the States.

He was eventually granted a medical discharge November 19, 1945. In addition to the Purple Heart, he was authorized to wear various ribbons and medals for his service.

ORVILLE JACKSON JR.,
World War II, United States Army Air Corps. Brownstown, born October 1, 1924. He left school to enlist in the service at Louisville, Kentucky in March 1943. He served until March 1946 with the 4th Army Air Forces Base

Unit as an airplane and engine mechanic. While in service he reached the rank of corporal, but separated out as Private First Class, serial number 35699713, at Camp Atterbury, Indiana.

During WWII, Orville Jackson Jr. received the American Theater Ribbon, Good Conduct Medal and Victory Medal World War II. He completed the airplane mechanic course at Keesler Field in Mississippi and the B-24 course at Ypsilanti, Michigan.

One of the places he was stationed was Topeka Army Air Field at Topeka, Kansas. This is where he met his future wife, Ora Maxine Meyers, of Burlingame, Kansas. They married at Lyndon, Kansas after his discharge from service in March 1946. Later, they returned to Brownstown, where they raised two sons, Garland and Terry.

Orville worked for Cummins Engine Company, Columbus, Indiana for 32 years, from 1951 to 1983. He married Lorene Keller Jones after his wife died in 1983. Orville Jackson Jr. was known by many as "Junior." He died December 1, 1993.

RAYMOND CARL JACKSON,
Post World War II, United States Army Air Corps, born May 7, 1928 to Thornt and Flossie Booker Jackson. Raised in Jackson County, graduated from Brownstown High School in 1947.

Entered the Air Corps July 8, 1946 at Indianapolis, trained at various fields across the nation. Assigned to 2nd Maintenance Squadron as RTC Repairman, stationed at Lowry Field, Colorado, discharged July 7, 1949

Married Thelma June Snyder; parents of two children. Became college professor at Texas Tech University. Residents of Lubbock.

ROSCOE M. JACKSON,
World War II, United States Army, born August 2, 1925. Parents. Thornt and Flossie Booker Jackson. Graduated from Clearspring High School in 1944.

Drafted into the army April 15, 1944 at Fort Harrison. Completed basic training at Camp Robinson, Arkansas, assigned to the 86th Infantry Division, shipped overseas to European Theater. Awarded the EAME Ribbon with one Campaign Star, Good Conduct Medal, Purple Heart, WWII Victory Medal. Discharged May 26, 1946 at Camp Atterbury.

Married Joanne Persinger December 31, 1946 in Seymour. Parents of three children. Retired from Cummins in Columbus, residents of Mt. Zion area of Jackson County.

HAROLD WAYNE JAMES,
World War II, United States Air Corps, born January 29, 1921 in Jackson County to Ernest and Grace Fisher James. He was raised with five sisters and one brother. After he finished school in 1939 he was employed by Indiana Bell Telephone Company.

He was drafted and inducted into the Army Air Corps that same year to serve his country during World War II.

Records fail to denote his service overseas. But, it is verified he received his discharge sometime in 1946.

He returned to his job with Bell later that year and was married to Leona Persinger. To them was born a daughter named Brenda. In 1983 he retired from Indiana Bell after 43 years of service to the company.

Jesse James died October 17, 1998 and was buried in Crown Hill Cemetery in Salem with Pat Garriett serving as one of the pall-bearers.

LEROY KENDALL,
World War II, United States Army, born February 20, 1924 in Seymour, Indiana. He spent the early years of his younger life living in Jeffersonville, but later graduated from Lebanon High School. Shortly afterwards he joined the Army and was sent to Fort Leonard Wood, Missouri for his basic training.

Completing further training in both Louisiana and Kentucky, he was shipped overseas to the European Theater of Operations. Just a few days after D-Day he landed in France, and his unit was in continual combat for more than seven months. Wounded in the Battle of the Bulge at Bastogne, he was returned to England for recuperation following release from the hospital.

He was assigned to the First Airborne Battalion and while training for his next campaign, he was sent well behind the enemy lines to open a Prisoner of War Camp. During the advance, he was one of the first American troops to enter Berlin. Taking over command of one of Hitler's buildings, he had his photo taken while standing on the balcony facing his army friends.

During the time Leroy Kendall was stationed in England, he met and later married a pretty little English girl named Emily Lloyd. That union lasted nearly fifty-five years.

JOSEPH H. KENNY,
United States Army, 400th Armored Field Artillery Battalion, 3rd Army, born March 27, 1908 in Peru, IN the son of Kendrick and Eleaner Underwood Kenny. He graduated from Peru High School in 1927 and received his degree from Franklin College in 1931. Four years later he was married to Bernice Heller on June 7, 1935.

He was drafted into the US Army in 1943, two days before his thirty-fifth birthday. He completed his basic training at Fort Knox and departed with the 400th Armored Field Artillery Battalion when they were shipped overseas. Serving as S/Sgt., he led his men from Liverpool to Omaha Beach on D-Day July 19, 1944. His unit was placed under the command of General Patton and his 3rd Army.

The 400th Battalion was in the campaigns of Normandy, Northern France and Central Europe. He found the Battle of the Bulge was the most severe of all his experiences. He was awarded his ribbon and authorized to wear five Campaign Stars, Good Conduct Medal and the Bronze Star Medal.

After arriving back into the States, he received his honorable discharge on October 17, 1945. He was in constant combat 299 days and nights! After the war was over, Joseph and Bernice Heller Kenny traveled back to Europe in commemoration of his wartime route across France and into the 3rd Reich. Joseph Kenny lived in Brownstown until his death on December 2, 1988. His wife Bernice is still living in Columbus.

CLARENCE KIDD, United States Navy, #948-85-49, Gunner's Mate, 1944-1946, Great Lakes Naval Training Center. Enlisted from Norwood, Ohio. Boot Camp Training at Norfolk. Gunner's Mate aboard LST #882, Guam, Saipan, Iwo Jima, Pearl Harbor, Japan, Naval Reserves 1951.

OREN MARTIN KILLEY, World War II, United States Marine Corps, enlisted at Indianapolis, Indiana, on the 12th day of May 1944 to serve in the United States Marine Corps. Oren was born February 18, 1926 at Vallonia, Indiana, to Frank and Iva Hattabaugh Killey. He married Vernon Louise Nowling on May 18, 1946. They were the parents of five children: Arthur Killey, Connie Killey Lovins, Alvin Killey, Reta Killey Schneider, and Alan Killey. Oren passed away on June 25, 2000 and is buried in Vallonia Cemetery.

Oren participated in action against the enemy at Okinawa, Ryukyu Island May 3, 1945 through June 21, 1945. He participated in the occupation of China from October 1, 1945 through April 5, 1946.

He received his discharge from the United States Marine Corps on May 5, 1946 from the Marine Separation Center, NavTraCen, Great Lakes, Illinois.

RALPH KINDRED, World War II, United States Air Corps, European Theater of Operations, Africa, Italy, Sicily, Corsica, France, 1942-1945.

Married Mary Stahl and became parents of two sons, Terry L. and C. Barry.

WILLIAM L. KINWORTHY, World War II, United States Army, European Theater of Operations, 3rd Army under General Patton, re-deployed to Philippines, 1942-1946.

PAUL L. KIRKHOF, World War II, United States Army, 1942-1946, basic training at Fort Lewis, Washington, assigned to 736th Tank Battalion. ASTP Program, Illinois State College. 742nd Ordinance (LM) Company, 42nd Infantry Division, shipped overseas on USS *General Gordon* to Europe.

Went in to Southern France, discharged and employed by Noblitt-Sparks, Ind. Operated his own firm and retired in 2002.

MOSIER KIRTS, World War II, United States Navy, 1945-1945.

ALBERT F. KLINGE, World War II, United States Army, 87th Infantry Division, was drafted into the army three years after he graduated from high school. He was eighteen years old when his number was called. He refused deferment and was inducted July 2, 1944. He reported to Camp Atterbury but completed his basic training at Fort McClellan. His Christmas was spent on the high seas being shipped to Scotland.

His unit was taken to Southampton by train and they were ordered on to a boat taking them across the channel into France. They were ordered to board some boxcars which took them to the front lines. Within minutes, he was in a foxhole. His company was suddenly surrounded by German SS Troops amidst the "Battle of the Bulge."

Everyone was fighting for their lives, and he always professed faith in God to bring him safely back home when the war was over. But the complete account of the following weeks must wait until he reaches home. If anyone follows the records, they will understand that he made it home but only after he had matured quickly and suddenly in battle.

His records were preserved by Kathryn L. Macaslan of Columbus, Indiana.

WILLIAM I. KOVENER, World War II, United States Army Air Corps, a lifelong resident of Jackson County, was inducted August 7, 1942 at Fort

Benjamin Harrison, Indiana, as an Airplane Maintenance Technician in the 132nd AAF BU.

Kovener received training at Lincoln, Nebraska; Allison Airplane Mechanical School, Indianapolis, Indiana; Westover Field, Holyoke, Massachusetts; and at Bedford, Massachusetts where he received his corporal rating.

In November, 1943, he was stationed at Hillsgrove Airfield, Providence, Rhode Island, where he received his staff sergeant rating as crew chief. He was later stationed at Suffolk Field, Long Island, New York.

Kovener was honorably discharged at Fort Dix, New Jersey, as a staff sergeant, on September 28, 1945.

His wife, Lena Faye Shannon Kovener, made a home and worked at each city on his tour of duty. Many lifelong friendships were formed during this time. Following the war, they had two sons, Gary Shannon, born September 13, 1946, and Richard Wayne born March 22, 1952.

William L. Kovener passed away October 18, 2002, at the age of 92.

ARTHUR R. KOZIK, World War II, United States Army, born Mansfield, Ohio, July 16, 1920. Drafted February 16, 1920. Reported to Fort Harrison, Indianapolis. Assigned 78th Infantry Division, 309th Company. Shipped overseas to European Theater and served through campaigns during the Battle of the Bulge, the Ardennes, Rhineland and Central Europe.

Awarded Good Conduct Medal, EAME Ribbon w/3 Bronze Campaign Stars, Combat Infantryman's Badge and the WWII Victory Medal. Discharged October 23, 1945 in Pennsylvania.

Returned to Indianapolis and was employed by RCA and later by Dage Electric in Beech Grove. Married Mary Foster of Vallonia. Associated with several electronics firms and retired in 1985. He died February 16, 2002 and was buried in Vallonia.

HUGH K. LAWSON, World War II, United States Army Air Corps. After he graduated from Clearspring High School, he helped on the family farm at Norman until he enlisted in the service. He was inducted July 10, 1940 and sent to Chanute Field, Illinois to enroll at Park Air College where he was trained as a mechanic.

After Pearl Harbor was bombed he was assigned as a crew chief for the offensive against Japan. Later, while serving on Iwo Jima, he helped service the *Enola Gay* and slept in a fox hole during the first atomic explosion. He was promoted to T/Sgt. and after he received his discharge November 25, 1945, he returned home to Norman, IN and purchased a small farm.

During the first years following service he worked at the air base near Columbus until 1969 to complete his career.

On August 5, 1949 he married Eva June Mullen of Brownstown and they became parents of three children. He died December 2, 2001.

OTIS LEE, World War II, United States Navy, born May 10, 1913 in Morgan County, Tennessee to William and Sarah Hawn Lee. After his father died, he moved to Indianapolis and lived with his sister. He worked in the Taystee Baker. In 1938 he married Doris Tatlock of Tampico who had moved to Indianapolis after she graduated.

He enlisted in the Navy at Indianapolis September 21, 1942. He completed his boot camp training at Great Lakes Naval Station. His pay was $78.00 per month, but later he was given a medical discharged due to broken foot when he was a child. When he was released he returned to Indianapolis and returned to his old job at the bakery.

He and his wife moved to their present farm located near the village of Tampico. He was a farmer, bee-keeper, tended his own orchard and drove school bus. He also worked at Arvin for several years.

He is the father of two daughters, Norma Neukam and Linda.

JOHN M. LEWIS, World War II, United States Army, Pacific Theater of Operations, born in 1913 at Seymour to John M. Lewis and Emma Ann Crabb Lewis. After receiving his law degree in 1938, he joined his father's law practice. In 1939 he was married to Josephine Deputy and, upon her death in 1975, he married Myra Hill in 1978.

John M. Lewis III organized the 138th Heavy Tank Battalion of the Indiana National Guard before he joined the United States Army in 1943. During his 3-year service time, he was awarded the Bronze Star, Army Commendation Medal and the Pacific Theater Service Ribbon. He was granted Military Rites at his funeral and burial was at Riverview Cemetery in Seymour.

LEONARD L. LEWIS, World War II, United States Army, 1942-1943, enlisted from Surprise, IN at Louisville, KY and served honorably until discharged at Camp Forrest, TN because of ill health. Returned home to Jackson County, IN.

RAY LEWIS, World War II, United States Army, born May 21, 1907 and grew to manhood as a farmer in Jackson County. He was inducted into the army

March 16, 1945 and separated August 17, 1945 for age and family concerns. He received his discharge at Camp Atterbury after being stationed at Fort Sill, OK.

He and Jessie Lewis were parents of four children, ranging in ages between a few months to 20 years.

CLIFTON B. LONG, World War II, United States Army Air Corps, born in Hunlock Creek, Pennsylvania, the Army actually brought him to Seymour. After basic training, he went into the Army Air Force and was assigned to a guard squadron. His first posting was in Dothan, Alabama, and he was there when Japan bombed Pearl Harbor. He was transferred to Freeman Field while it was under construction to provide security. This is when he met Sarah Bernadine Haas, a county native, at the First Baptist Church social. They were married in First Baptist, and were active members of the church. He was transferred to Alaska and was there until the end of the war.

He missed the birth of his son, Clifton Ray Long, in 1945 while in Alaska. He and Sarah lived in Jennings County for a short time, returning to Jackson County where Ray was graduated from Seymour High School. Sally Beth was born in 1956, and also graduated from Seymour High School. Ray joined the Air Force where he was a forward air controller in Vietnam. Sally Long Acton continues to live and work in Jackson County as a RN at Schneck Medical Center. Luke, son of Steve and Sally Acton, is in the Indiana National Guard, and is participating in Operation Enduring Freedom in Kuwait at the time of printing.

JOHN W. LUBKER, World War II, United States Navy, the third child of Orville and Lottie Lubker, was born in 1917 near Brownstown. He graduated from the local high school in 1935 and went on to Coyne Electrical School in Chicago and graduated in 1939. In September 1940 he was employed by the Allison plant manufacturing engines. Although deferred from military service, he enlisted in the Navy in 1942.

He was sent to Bunker Hill Naval Air Base where his commanding officer spent some time taking him flying in the training planes. Most of his service was in charge of the aircraft instrument shop.

In 1943 he was sent to Oceania Naval Base near Virginia Beach, VA. Further training was to lead him to an aircraft assignment, but he was stationed in New York City for gyroscope training. He was forced to undergo surgery and a hearing test which kept him from serving on an aircraft carrier or even overseas. He was placed in charge of the instrument shop back

in Oceania before being assigned to Manteo, NC, attached to a squadron of F4Us used to bomb German U-Boats.

The war came to an end on September 2, 1945 and he was discharged from Great Lakes Naval Base in November 1945.

ALBERT LUCAS, World War II, United States Army, was drafted and inducted into the army in April 1944 and, after basic training, was assigned to the 746th Railroad Battalion which was the initial unit to be created for military action. He served as conductor and was shipped overseas to the European Theater of Operations.

He and fellow soldiers were credited with the capture of a German Caboose used exclusively by the Storm Troopers of the 3rd Reich.

He returned to the states and received his discharge in May of 1946 and went to work on the B&O Railroad. He and his wife, Sara Marling Lucas, became parents of three children, Elizabeth, Daniel and Warren Lucas.

BERNARD LUCAS, World War II, United States Army, went into the service in 1942 and served in the last regiment of the Horse Cavalry stationed at Fort Riley, Kansas as an instructor until September 1946. His home was near Freetown, IN.

CECIL L. LUCAS, World War II, United States Army.

EDWARD R. LUCAS, World War II, United States Army, born October 26, 1919 in Jackson County and was a product of the local area. He was inducted into the army January 2, 1942 at Fort Harrison in Indianapolis, Indiana. After completing basic training, he was assigned serial number 35252566 and placed into 741st Tank Battalion.

Possessing the rank of Corporal, he saw action at Omaha Beach on June 6, 1944 and all the way across France into Bastogne. It was there where they were held back by the German Panzer tanks during the Battle of the Bulge. Later his unit crossed the Remagen Bridge into Germany. He was among the Allied troops who arrived in Pilsen, Czechoslovakia the night before V-E Day was proclaimed.

He was wounded and awarded the Purple Heart as he survived from D-Day to V-E Day, May 8, 1945. He was discharged on October 23, 1945.

He was married while stationed near Pilsen to Ann Kadleconda. She arrived in New York on July 4, 1946 and became known as the army wife born on Independence Day. Three days later they were at home near Brownstown and to them were born a son and daughter.

JOE LUCAS, World War II, United States Navy, went into service in October 1944 from Brownstown, IN and completed his boot camp training at Great Lakes Naval Station in Chicago. He served until February 1946.

KENNETH LUCAS, World War II, United States Army, 17th Airborne Divisions.

DALLES E. LYON, World War II, United States Army, born July 14, 1910 at Freetown, Indiana. Enlisted and inducted March 25, 1943 at Louisville, KY, qualified as sharpshooter. Carpenter Specialist, assigned to 50th Base Headquarters. Discharged at Hammer Field at Fresno, California, November 6, 1943, returned home to Indianapolis.

PAUL O. MACKEY, World War II, United States Army, born September 1, 1923, at Rural Route, Seymour (BobTown) in Indiana. He was the youngest of twelve children. He lived in the town of Seymour when he was inducted into the United States Army February 25, 1942, at Indianapolis, Indiana.

Assigned the serial number 35095104, he served his country in World War II from February 25, 1943, to January 21, 1946.

Paul was in the Pacific Theater where he served as a Medical Technician, 409, Grade 5, 35th General Hospital.

Battles and campaigns: New Guinea in the East Indies, Luzon in the Philippines.

Decorations and ribbons: American Theater Ribbon, Asiatic-Pacific Ribbon w/2 Bronze Stars, Philippine Liberation Theater Ribbon, Good Conduct Medal, Victory Medal World War II.

When the war ended, Paul was rotated back to the separation center at Camp Atterbury in Indiana where he received an honorable discharge on January 21, 1946

Paul came home to Seymour, Indiana and returned to his job at Arvin Industries in Seymour. On February 24, 1946, Paul married the sweetheart who had waited for him, Shirley B. Morris. They raised three children in Seymour, Indiana.

Paul retired from Arvin Industries in 1971. They moved to Jonesville, Indiana, in Bartholomew County in 1973, living there until 1999 when they moved back to Seymour. Paul passed from this life October 13, 2000.

MANION CHILDREN, who served their nation in the military forces. Seven sons and one daughter were born to the Harry Manion Family of Jackson County. Everyone of those children was inducted into the military forces of the United States during World War II and the period thereafter. The children were raised in the Durland community in Brownstown Township located east of the county seat of government. All attended Durland Elementary School and graduated from Brownstown High School.

John F. Manion, completed his high school studies in 1926 and went on to receive his degree from Purdue University. He was employed in Indianapolis and Dallas before entering the navy early in World War II. He was shipped overseas to the Pacific Theater of Operations and actually met his brother in the Philippine Islands.

Glenn Manion, finished high school in 1928 and went west to find employment in Dallas, Texas before joining the navy a few months later. He was also shipped overseas to the Pacific Theater of Operations. He also met one of his brothers in the Philippines.

Paul Manion, completed high school in 1931 and continued his studies at Purdue University. Upon receiving his degree he remained on the staff until he was inducted into the navy. He was assigned duty in communications and the news service.

Lyle Manion was employed by the REMC construction crews before he reported for his army duty on April 2, 1941. He was inducted into service at Louisville. He served as a clerk until he was discharged June 12, 1944 at Fort Bragg, North Carolina.

Fred M. Manion, left his hometown area after completing high school in 1934. He was employed by REMC construction crews until he entered the navy March 21, 1942. He reported for duty in Indianapolis and was assigned to the Naval CBs Construction Battalion station in the Asiatic-Pacific area, including the Philippine Islands. His unit was transferred to the European Theater where he served as an electrician until he was discharged December 25, 1945. He was authorized the EAME Ribbon.

Gerald D. Manion, was employed at REMC as a member of the construction crews before

entering the navy during World War II. He was assigned duty with the survey crews and was discharged October 20, 1945 as a Quartermaster 1st Class.

Norma Jean Manion, graduated from high School in 1939. Less that five years later, she was inducted into the navy March 7, 1944. She was assigned duty at the Naval Air Station in Seattle and was discharged March 20, 1946.

Donald E. Manion, a 1946 graduate of Brownstown High School, was employed by Noblitt-Sparks Industries before enlisting in the army. He was inducted August 4, 1948 at Bloomington. He served as a clerk-typist throughout the Korean War years and was discharged in Washington, DC August 3, 1951. He had served three years.

JAMES H. MANUEL, #626 06 98, Seaman 1st Class, Pacific Theater of War, 1941-1945, Great Lakes Naval Training Center, Destroyer Base at San Diego, AGC, Brooklyn, New York.

ELROY MERLE MARCOTT, World War II, United States Navy, born January 23, 1925 in Illinois to Harry and Genevieve Sharland Marcott. The family moved to Ratliff Grove in 1932 and he graduated from Brownstown High School in 1941. Two years later in 1943 he was inducted in the navy and completed his basic training at Great Lakes Naval Station in Chicago. He was trained to be a radioman 3rd class SV-6-USNR.

While still in training, he went home and married his hometown girlfriend, Mary Hanner and they were blessed with 2 daughters, Dianne and Derenda, and each was married and produced grandchildren, He was a heavy-equipment operator after the war. He retired in 1988 and he returned to Brownstown. Once home he became a heavy equipment operator. He retired.

He was proud to serve his country and offered to be under control at all times, commencing with 1988. He was proud of his service committed to freedom.

Elroy's father, Harry Marcott, served in the army with his father in the army, along with his brother, Victor Marcott.

SHIRLEY L. MARLING, World War II, United States Army Air Corps, born in 1922 in Jackson County and graduated from Shields High School in Seymour with the class of 1940. He enlisted in the army soon after he had finished school.

He completed basic training at Maxwell Field, AL and was assigned as an airplane engine mechanic until he was transferred to Knollwood Field in North Carolina. There he was ordered to report to General

Walter B. Weaver first as a crew chief and then as a personal aide.

His unit was shipped overseas to the European Theater of Operations for service in France, Belgium, Holland and Germany. As a member of the flying crews he was authorized to wear appropriate medals and ribbons reflecting his engagements.

He was returned to the states and discharged in September 1945 at Camp Atterbury. He was employed by Eli Lilly in Indianapolis. He and his wife Helen Eggersman were parents of a son, Dennis Marling.

JAMES ALBERT MARSHALL, World War II, United States Navy, born March 9, 1926 in Vernon Township to Jesse and Idessa Fogeling Marshall. He was raised in Hamilton Township and attended Cortland High School. He joined the navy and completed his instruction while in service.

He was inducted in Indianapolis in 1944 and completed basic training at Great Lakes Naval Station. He was assigned to the USS *YMS #5* as the ship's cook. His home base was at Atlantic City.

He was discharged from Great Lakes May 18, 1946. He returned to the Surprise area and married Rebecca Oathout. He was then employed by a body shop in Seymour. He later operated his own shop near his home. He retired as a bus driver after 40 years of service. He and Mrs. Marshall were parents of two children.

James A. Marshall died May 4, 1996.

RUSSELL L. MARTIN, World War II, United States Army, ASN #30498681, 1942-1945, was inducted into the United States Army in October 1942 at Fort Harrison in Indianapolis. He was sent to Camp Polk in Louisiana for his basic training. Upon completion he was ordered to Camp Shank in New York. It was there where he boarded the *Queen Mary* transporting troops to England, where he was assigned to Company B, 69Th Tank Battalion of the Sixth Armored Division of General Patton's 3rd US Army.

On D-Day of June 6, 1944 he crossed the English Channel and drove his Sherman Tank onto the Omaha Beach of Normandy. His unit advanced on through France, Belgium and then into the Battle of the Bulge at Bastogne. The tank units never wavered nor stopped; they kept advancing through the Axis strongholds of Germany until they reached the gates of Buchenwald Prison Camp. His tank pushed the gate and the forces went in so Russell could pull down the Swastika and hoist up the American Flag.

Advancing on to Berlin, the Americans met the Russians coming in from the East. By April 1945 the Germans were devastated and their troops surrendered on May 7, 1945. The next day on May 8, 1945 was declared to be the anticipated V-E Day.

Russell Martin earned the E.A.M.E. Theater Ribbon with 3 Bronze Campaign Stars, Good Conduct Ribbon, WWII Victory Medal and Unit Distinguished Award. He was discharged December 11, 1945 and returned to Brownstown where he served as Chief of Police for 25 years. In 1970 he was married to Josephine Empson Hurley. Russell Martin was born May 22, 1921 and died November 30, 1992. He is the father of three children by a former marriage. They are Roger, Steve (deceased) and Linda Kamman.

CYRUS CRESSON MCCORY, World War II, United States Army Airborne Command, enlisted January 10, 1941 at Columbus, IN and was sent to Camp Atterbury for his basic training as a parachute instructor. He was ordered to Fort Benning, GA where he remained on duty training others to jump from a plane.

He was sent overseas and stationed in the Philippines during the war. His service time was almost five years. He was authorized to wear various medals and ribbons. After he was discharged he returned home to Jackson County and resides with his wife, Dorothy.

He was killed on a work construction site in 1992.

CLAUDE RAYMOND MCCRARY, World War II, United States Army, was born in Brownstown May 8, 1919 to John and Lavesta, Hurley McCrary. He was raised in the local area and graduated from Brownstown High School in 1937.

He enlisted in the army November 20, 1940, long before the attack on Pearl Harbor. He served more than one year in the states and 3 years overseas in Hq. Company of the 1st Regiment in the 1st Division as message center clerk.

He was captured by the Germans on February 4, 1943 and held as a POW from 1943 until 1945. He received his release May 3, 1945 and returned to Camp Chaffee, Arkansas where he was granted his discharge August 27, 1945.

He returned home and attended Indiana University. He became the county assessor from 1959 until 1966 before teaching for 18 years in and around Brownstown.

On August 22, 1954 he married Dorothy Cripe and they became parents of four children.

CARL MCINTOSH, World War II, United States Navy, was born in Kentucky April 30, 1922 to William and Caudill McIntosh before they moved to Paris Crossing, Indiana in 1934. He attended school and helped on the family farm. He was drafted in 1942, passed his physical in Indianapolis before joining the navy November 5, 1942

After completing boot camp training at Great Lakes, he reported to the New York Receiving States on Long Island. He was assigned to the destroyer USS *Thorn;* later reassigned to the USS *Dashtell* in 1943. Eventually he went aboard the USS *Stevens.*

His ship departed New York for the Pacific and participated in the invasions of Marcus Island, Tarawa, Hollandia, Guam, Leyte, Mindanao, and the Lingayen Gulf. After V-J Day the USS *Stevens* was sent to Korea and China to assist in the surrender of Japanese troops.

His ship returned to Long Beach in December 1945 and he was ordered to Great Lakes to receive his discharge. He returned to Seymour where he was employed at Noblitt-Sparks Industries. In 1948 he married Mary Satterwhite of Austin and they became the parents of three children. He later worked for Cummins but he died July 12, 1981.

CHAUNCEY E. MCKINNEY, World War II, United States Army, born November 19, 1919 in Medora to Frank and Lula Belle Dixon McKinney and was one of four sons to be called to military duty. He was drafted and inducted into the army August 31, 1942.

He reported for duty at Camp Shelby, MS and completed basic training along with his brother, Harold. Both were assigned to Company A of the 759th Railway Battalion stationed at Camp Claiborne, LA. Both were later transferred to Camp Van Buren, in Arkansas.

His unit was shipped overseas and arrived in North Africa in the month of May 1943. On November 14, 1943 he was involved in the battle for Anzio beachhead. He saw action on through Italy and France and the Rhineland. Chauncey was sent back to the states and was discharged September 2, 1945. It was then he first saw his daughter, Beverly Jeanne born October 11, 1943.

He returned to civilian life and was employed by Marion-Kay in Brownstown. He died June 2, 1988.

EMIL M. MCKINNEY, World War II, United States Army, Company F, 168th Infantry, European Theater, 1941-1945, Morocco, Tunisia, Naples, Foggia/Rome. Son of Virgil McKinney.

HAROLD FRANK MCKINNEY, World War II, United States Army, was born in Medora to Frank and Lula Belle Dixon McKinney and was one of four sons to answer the call to military service. He graduated from the local high school in 1935.

He was drafted and inducted January 16, 1941 at Louisville, KY and sent on to Fort Thomas, KY, then to Fort Bliss, TX and assigned to the 7th Cavalry Division. While stationed there he received instruction in the Lutheran Faith and was confirmed October 12, 1941. He married Oguerita Burge October 9, 1941.

When the Railway Operating Divisions were created, Harold was transferred to Camp Shelby, MS and assigned to teach recruits close-order drill. He was surprised when he saw his younger brother, Chauncy, for a short time. His unit was sent to Arkansas in November 1942. Six months later he was shipped overseas and arrived in North Africa May 11, 1943. In November he was involved at Anzio where his unit started to rebuild the railroad which had been destroyed. Throughout Italy and on back to England into France, the Rhineland and across to Fulda, Germany. They worked German prisoners of war until the war over in Europe.

He returned to the states and was sent to Camp Atterbury July 8, 1945 and saw his daughter, Ellen Sue, for the first time. Harold and Oguerita had two other children, Judith Elaine and Dennis Keith. He was employed by Cummins in Columbus. He died October 20, 1986 while suffering from Lou Hehrig's disease and was buried Weddleville Cemetery.

NOBLE E. MCKINNEY, World War II, United, States Army, born January 27, 1916 in Medora to Frank and Lula Belle Dixon McKinney, the oldest of four sons to serve in World War II and each was in action in the European Theater of Operations

He was inducted June 4, 1942 at Louisville, and assigned as a section hand of Railroad Company 199. He was involved in campaigns fought in Tunisia, Naples/Foggia, Rome/Arno, Rhineland and Central Europe.

He was authorized to wear various medals and ribbons reflecting his service. He arrived back in the states August 16, 1945 and received his discharge a few days later at Camp Atterbury.

He died January 23, 1986.

WILBUR E. MCKINNEY, World War II, United States Army, born February 2, 1922 at Medora to Frank and Lula Belle Dixon McKinney. He was destined to become the 4th son to serve in the armed forces. He was drafted and inducted one year after Pearl Harbor Day at Louisville, KY.

He was assigned to Company "B" of the 319th Engineer Battalion and shipped overseas on August 6, 1944 for the European Theater as part of the Railroad hands participating in Normandy, and Central Europe. One of his buddies stepped on a mine and was killed, but Wilbur was injured and confined to a hospital in England.

He eventually returned to the states and was discharged Jan. 2, 1946. He died August 31, 1985.

MARVIN S. MCMAHON, World War II, United States Army Air Corps, born June 30, 1920 in Lake City, IL the son of Herman and Lona McMahon. It is not known just when his family moved to Jackson County.

He went into the service and was assigned to the air corps, and saw his action through World War II, from January 1941 to August 1945. He was assigned to the European Theater of Operations and held the rank of T/Sgt.

In 1945 he married Mildred Radcliff and they became parents of two sons, Ronnie and Jackie McMahon. After he was discharged he was employed by Arvin Industries at the Greenwood plant as a supervisor.

FRANCIS IRVIN MCPIKE, World War II, United States Army Air Corps, graduated from Shields High School in Seymour in 1935 and enrolled in a military course of instruction at Fort Harrison. He was then employed by Kieffer Paper Mill, but quit to enlist in the Air Corps March 11, 1941 long before Pearl Harbor was bombed.

He completed basic training at Randolph Field, Texas and was sent to Scott Field for radio operator training. While stationed there he was married to Helen Louise Fish, and that union was destined to endure for 60 years from Pearl Harbor Day.

He reported for duty at Foster Field, Texas at Christmas time in 1941. He was assigned to maintain radio equipment and was transferred to Connecticut with the 61st Fighter Squadron then ready to be shipped overseas to England.

After V-E Day was proclaimed he went to the 267th Bomb Group and returned to the states. He reported to Camp Atterbury and was discharged September 15, 1945. He entered the Indiana National Guard and was assigned to the 38th Signal Company as a M/Sgt. until 1951.

WALTER MELLONCAMP, World War II, United States Army Air Corps, born March 18, 1918 in Jackson County to Louis and Ida Melloncamp. He was raised on a farm and graduated from Tampico High School in 1937. He was employed in the area until he obtained a private pilot's license. With that ability he enlisted in the Army Air Corps January 7, 1942.

He completed basic training at Sheppard Field for training in aircraft maintenance. He was sent to Long Beach, CA for specialized training on C-47 planes. He was assigned to the 9th Troop Carrier Squadron which was stationed at various bases training paratroopers and glider pilots.

In 1943 he was shipped overseas to the European Theater as a member of a C-47 crew. He served in the Algiers area of North Africa. Early in 1944 he was made crew chief in military transport service bases at Naples. His TC planes flew missions throughout entire European Theater.

Following V-J Day he was returned to the states via a Liberty ship. He was discharged October 15, 1945. Utilizing the GI Bill, he graduated from Purdue in 1951. Subsequently, he was employed at Flight Headquarters at Wright-Patterson AFB in Ohio. He and his wife Myrt are currently retired and reside at Dayton.

RALPH E METZ, World War II, United States Army, born in 1914 to Henry and Iva Carpenter Metz in Vernon Township. He attended school in Uniontown but graduated high school in Crothersville. Much later he was inducted into the army in 1941 and left the county with one of the largest group of inductees. He completed his basic training at Camp Shelby, MS. After maneuvers he was assigned to the 113th Medical Battalion, Company A of the 38th Infantry Division bound for the Pacific Theater of Operations.

His primary duty was to assist the medical officers in the administration of medical attention to casualties brought in from the front lines. Overseas for 17 months, he saw service on Oahu, New Guinea, Leyte and Luzon, including the battles of Bataan and Fort Stotsenberg.

He was awarded several campaign ribbons with battle stars and the Philippine Liberation Ribbon with a star representing the "Avenger of Bataan."

He returned to the States November 14, 1945, and went to work for Central Pharmacy and sold life insurance. He later retired from Thompson Dairy. Ralph Metz died October 25, 1990 and is buried in the Uniontown Cemetery.

VIRGIL R. METZ, World War II, United States Army, born in 1921, the son of Henry and Iva Carpenter Metz, and was raised on a farm located near Uniontown. He later was graduated from Crothersville High School before entering the army in October of 1942.

He completed basic training at Camp Polk, LA for the 11th Armored Division. He was involved in field maneuvers in Texas and finished his range practice before moving to Needles, CA for desert training. His aviation cadet training was in Amarillo, TX, then he was assigned to a replacement depot in faraway Memphis, TN. Following several more movements, he was sent to Fairhope, Alabama for Merchant Marine Training.

He was ordered aboard a Victory ship, *USS Walter R. Weaver,* departing for the Philippines. At the time the war ended on September 2, 1945, he had been promoted to S/Sgt and was discharged January 6, 1946.

Virgil later met and married Ruth Wood from Hancock County, IN and resided in Whiteland, IN with their 3 children. After retiring from the post office service, they moved to Ocala, FL. He now lives in Tampa but still has a family living in Jackson County.

MAX MIDDENDORF, United States Air Force Reserve, Lt. Colonel, Medical Staff at Grissom Air Force Base. Married Eva Hoffman and located in Brownstown. Became parents of three children, Heather Marie, Heidi Marcia and William Jonathan. Dr. Max Middendorf is a Brownstown dentist.

RICHARD MITCHELL, World War II, United States Army, Camp Meade, Fort Benning, Italy, 735th Engineering Company deployed to the Pacific. Drowned November 17, 1945 on Luzon. Buried in the Houston Cemetery

HOWARD F. MONTGOMERY, World War II, United States Army, born September 22, 1924 in Redding Township and later graduated from Shields High School in Seymour, Indiana. Later in 1942 he was drafted into the army and was called to active duty in February of 1943.

He completed basic training at Fort Leonard Wood, Missouri and was assigned to Company B, 291st Regiment of the 75th Infantry Division stationed at Grinnel College, Iowa. During leave in October he transferred into the Air Corps at Freeman

Field and was sent to Sheppard Field, TX for pre-flight instruction and training as a nose gunner. Upon graduation, he was married to Ruthanna Uffman of Columbus on April 6, 1944.

His unit of B-24 Liberator Bombers was shipped overseas to Liverpool, England before flying to Casablanca, North Africa aboard Churchill's personal plane. He was assigned to the 762nd Squadron of the 460th Bomb Group in the 15th Air Force stationed in Italy. From there, bombing missions were carried out against various targets of the German 3rd Reich. When V-E Day was declared, he was sent back to the states for further training at the Tampa Air Base in preparation for re-deployment to Japan.

Upon declaration of V-J Day, he reported to Camp Atterbury and received his discharge. He completed 40 years of employment at Cummins because of his academic achievements at Purdue University in 1952 as the first person to complete the program at IUPUÇ in Columbus. His daughter, Judy, resides in Jackson County while sons, Robert and Lynn, remained in Bartholomew County.

NORVAL C. MONTGOMERY, World War II, United States Army, born November 19, 1927. Resident of Jackson County, Indiana when inducted into the army March 8, 1946 at Camp Atterbury. He was assigned as a truck driver.

He was attached to Hq. Company, 4th Army to drive army vehicles. Was responsible for all maintenance during hauling of materials and supplies. Received discharge September 14, 1947.

RICHARD H. MONTGOMERY, World War II, United States Army, was a lifelong resident of Jackson County. He was born January 9, 1923, graduated from the local high school and went on to earn his law degree at Princeton University. During the war he enlisted and was assigned to the 75th Division of the army. His unit was in action in the European Theater of Operations.

During the Battle of the Bulge he served with distinction and was awarded the Bronze Star for heroic action and the Purple Heart for wounds. His citation reads: S/Sgt. Richard H. Montgomery, Co. E, 290th Infantry for heroic action … against the enemy on 23 January 1945 in Belgium … crawled across open ground under withering fire to save a comrade by carrying him 200 yards back to safety where he could receive medical attention … this action bestows great credit to Sgt. Montgomery and his unit…. The Purple Heart was awarded for wounds he received.

After the war he was married to JoAnn Summers and they became the parents of three children. His sister, Polly Schneck submitted this data.

JOSEPH F. MOODY, World War II, United States Navy, was born in Greentown, Indiana on Feb. 3, 1910 in Warren County. He graduated high school in Greentown. He was working as a school bus driver in Little York when he enlisted. He enlisted in the Navy on 12/14/1942.

Among other places Joe Moody's tour of duty took him to Newfoundland, Saipan, Okinawa and Hawaii. In traveling from duty station to duty station

he was aboard numerous ships including the USS *Anteaus, Yarmouth,* and the *Sea Marlin.* He was discharged as an Electrician's Mate 1st Class on 10/28/45.

In 1953 Joe Moody made his home in Crothersville, IN where he currently resides with his wife Mary Moody. Many of Joe's children and grandchildren have served in the armed forces as well. Included in those are Michael J. White who served in Korea in 1991. Andrew B. Smith who served in the original Gulf War, and Jeffrey Anthony who also served in the original Gulf War. Michael now lives in Florida and Andy and Jeff live in Scott and Jackson County Indiana. Joe Moody has many fond memories of time serving this country. Included in them is a time when he and his buddies were singing to the 17th CB Battalion and the 2nd Marine Division on Saipan in 1944.

HARRELL L. MORRISON, World War II, United States Navy, was born August 30, 1918 to Hugh and Josie Baker Morrison in the western part of the county. He graduated from Heltonville High School in 1937. Three years later he was married to Inez Henderson and to them were born five children.

He joined the navy and completed his boot camp training at the Great Lakes Naval Base in Chicago and at Coronasa, California. He was assigned to the USS *Sibley* carrying troops to Iwo Jima and Okinawa. Following the war, he served in the occupational forces.

He was authorized to wear appropriate medals and ribbons reflecting to his service.

Harrell Morrison served in the navy from May 1944 until January 1946.

ARNOLD MYERS, World War II, United States Army, Company K, 60th Battalion, 5th Infantry Division, crossed the Rhine River into Germany with the 9th Infantry Division on his 20th birthday in September 1944. Although he was First Sergeant of his company, he was wounded during the Battle of Hürtgen Forest near Aachen, Germany. He was transported back to a field hospital for medical care. In early January 1945, he was transferred on to England. In March he returned to the States on a hospital ship and spent several months at Fort Custer, MI.

Sergeant Myers received his honorable discharge on August 13, 1945, two days before the Japanese surrender.

He went into service October 27, 1941, received his basic training at Camp Wheeler, GA and one year later was stationed at Fort Benning where he was promoted to First Sergeant. In August 1942, he returned to Jackson County to marry the former Helen Louise Crecelius in Columbus, IN. To them were born four children, including Richard, Jim, Linda and David.

Arnold Myers passed away January 19, 1983.

HAROLD MYERS, born in Alfordsville, IN on January 12, 1917 to Harry and Olive Myers. He graduated from Washington, IN, High School in 1935. Harold Myers was a F.W. Woolworth Co. store manager at the time of his enlistment on March 8, 1945. He was married to Mary B. Baker of Wheatland, IN on Dec. 25, 1937 and had a young son, Michael. Harold was in Company C, 20th Battalion of the Infantry. Upon discharge on October 27, 1946 he was ranked T Sergeant of the 731st Engineer Base. His military occupation was listed as an "administrative non-commissioned officer." His basic training was at Fort McClellan.

Harold served in the occupation of Japan. While in Japan, he supervised and directed 19 enlisted personnel and 12 Japanese interpreters, typists, and clerks. He was stationed in Japan for a year. For his service he received the Asiatic-Pacific Theater Ribbon, Philippine Liberation Ribbon, and the Army Occupation Medal-Japan. Harold rarely talked about his time spent in the, military service.

During his military service, Harold's wife and son lived in Seymour, IN. They wanted to be close to Harold's parents, Harry and Olive Myers, and other relatives living in Seymour. During Word War II, Harold and his two brothers, Arnold and Bill Myers all served in the military.

Upon his discharge from the Army, Harold resumed his employment at F.W. Woolworth Co. He was employed as a store manager for 25 years in the cites of Chicago, Gary, and Marion, IN. Harold purchased two stores in the early 1960s. He divided his time between the stores in Pendleton and Lapel, IN. He was a successful self-employed merchant for 17 years.

Harold and Mary raised four children (Michael, Rita, Phil, and Tom). He lived in Pendleton until he passed away Aug. 1, 1995 at the age of 78 years. He was a member of the American Legion for over 30 years. Harold was a patriotic American who strongly believed in the right to vote. Though a quiet man, he showed leadership throughout his adult life.

WILLIAM "BILL" MYERS, World War II, United States Marine Corps, South Pacific Theater of Operations, was born in Daviess County on January 31, 1926 to Harry T. and Olive Erma Jackman Myers. The family moved to Seymour in 1939. Eventually,

Bill Myers graduated from Seymour High School in 1945, but he was one of several boys who enlisted in the military service prior to receiving diplomas.

Bill Myers completed his boot training at Camp Pendleton, CA and was shipped out to the Pacific Theater of Operations where he spent nearly two years defending his nation. He finally returned home to Seymour and soon after his arrival, he moved to Moline, IL where he was employed by Sears. It was there where he married Raeona Cox and to them were born 2 boys, Steven and Kim, and one daughter, Sally.

There was a second marriage to Virginia Harold of Columbus, IN. Bill Myers passed away August 31, 1983 while residing with his daughter in Tyler, TX.

RAYMOND F. NEAL, World War II, United States Navy, 1943-1946. Entered the service June 5, 1943. Stationed at San Diego, California. NRS Louisville, KY. NTS Great Lakes Naval Station.

Served overseas in South Pacific Theater. Awarded appropriate medals and ribbons including the Philippine Liberation Medal w/2 stars. Discharged February 18, 1946.

Married Mildred Jenkins and was father to 2 children. Moved to Jackson County in 1956. After Mildred's death, he married Mary Denny. Died in July 1995.

ROY WALTER NEAWEDDE, World War II, United States Army, born in Seymour, December 24, 1918 to Theodore and Katherine (Otting) Neawedde. He was drafted on January 16, 1941, inducted in Louisville in the basement of the Post Office, and sent for basic and medical training to Fort Bliss, TX. On December 7, 1941 while visiting Carlsbad Caverns, NM, their guide informed them that Pearl Harbor had been bombed. That next day those still left in camp had to get rid of everything that wasn't government issue. At the Express Office he received a silver dollar as change, which he has carried in his pocket to this day.

In the spring of 1942, Roy was sent to Camp White, Oregon to train with the 91st Infantry Division. Trained as a medical technician, part of his job was to give immunizations. After the needles were put in hot water, he would sharpen them for the next day.

In 1943 Roy was made S/St and sent to Camp Adair, Oregon to train with the 70th Infantry Division, and in 1944 was sent to Fort Leonard Wood, Missouri to prepare for Europe. Roy married Dorothy Rothert of Dudleytown, July 8, 1944 while on leave.

He was deathly sick during the entire voyage of the *Mariposa* and landed at Marseilles, France. That first rainy night the soldiers had only a blanket to cover their heads. While heading for the front, they passed many trucks loaded to the top with body bags. During the Battle of the Bulge, Roy worked in the First-Aid Station for 20 to 22 hours a day. After the surrender of Germany, the soldiers were given a tour of one of the horrible prison camps.

While given a medical exam in preparation for the South Pacific, the doctor told him that he should have been classified a 4/F, as his eardrums had burst as a child. He asked his CO to leave him in 1/A, so he could stay with his men. This was never recorded in his record.

He was sent back to the U.S. and discharged at Camp Atterbury, IN, December 8. 1945.

JOHN L. NEHRT, World War II, United States Army, was born on January 27, 1926 in Crothersville, Indiana the son of Homer R. and Lillie E. (Kiewit) Nehrt. During his early years he was a carrier for the *Louisville Courier Journal*. He graduated from Crothersville High School with the class of 1944.

On November 9, 1944 John was inducted into the U.S. Army receiving his basic training at Ft. Sill, Oklahoma and assigned to a replacement group. In April 1945 this replacement group was at Camp Kilmer, New Jersey ready to go overseas when President Franklin D. Roosevelt died. Their group was retained expecting to be in the Honor Guard for the President, but April 16, 1945 they were sent on and the next group kept for the Honor Guard.

From New Jersey they went to Weymouth, England, crossed the English Channel thru the minefields and landed at LeHavre, France. From France they were motor-marched to Verviers, Belgium and on thru Germany to Regensburg. There he was assigned to the 288th Field Artillery Observation Battalion, Battery A and sent to Grafenwohr, Germany where they were billeted in a permanent German Base which had been somewhat damaged before they reached Grafenwohr. John's military occupation was a Flash Ranging Observer.

While stationed at Grafenwohr, John was able to visit Nüremberg, Garmish, Berchtesgaden and Switzerland.

On August 7, 1946 the Battalion left from Bremerhaven, Germany bound for the U.S.A. where they arrived on August 16, 1946. John received an Honorable Discharge from the Separation Center at Fort Sheridan, Illinois on August 21, 1946 with the rank of Sergeant. He had served five months and 12 days in continental service and one year, four months and one day in Foreign Service.

John married Clarice R. Kovener on June 21, 1947 and they are the parents of three children: Michael L. Nehrt, now residing in Rock Springs, Georgia, Cynthia K. Cozart of Crothersville and Holly N. Foster of Seymour. He retired July of 1988 from the American Can Co. at Austin, Indiana after working 44 years. He and his wife now reside at 310 West Main Street, Crothersville, Indiana.

LEONARD A. NEWKIRK, World War II, United States Army Air Corps, was raised in Jackson

County and graduated from Cortland High School. He was drafted and inducted into the Air Corps on October 31, 1942 at Louisville, Kentucky. He was assigned serial number 35498673 and given a specialty of an airplane wood worker.

His unit was sent overseas to the European Theater October 8, 1943. He was in the campaigns of Normandy, the Ardennes and Central Europe. He returned to the states October 27, 1945 and received his discharge at Camp Atterbury, Indiana on November 1, 1945.

He attained the rank of Sergeant and was authorized to wear various medals and campaign ribbons reflecting his service in the EAME with 5 Bronze Campaign Stars, Good Conduct and Presidential Unit Citation.

He was married to Leonia Conrad Newkirk in 1965 and they remained at the farm in Ogilville.

THOMAS W. NEWKIRK, World War II, United States Army, was born at Medora August 12, 1918 to Thomas and Jessie Zollman Newkirk. He later graduated from the local high school. He was drafted into the army at Louisville July 11, 1941 and completed his basic training at Camp Wheeler, then was transferred to Fort Benning. He was assigned to Hq. Company of the Special Troops of the 4th Infantry Division. His unit was shipped overseas to the European Theater of Operations and he saw action in Normandy, across France, the Rhineland and the Ardennes.

He was discharged at Camp Atterbury September 3, 1945 and was authorized to wear the EAME Ribbon with 5 Campaign Stars, Good Conduct and American Defense Medal.

He returned to Medora, moved to Indianapolis and was employed by Lilly but eventually he worked for Bundy in Seymour. He retired from the Indiana Telephone Company. He and his wife, Rose Schneider, became parents of two sons.

WOODROW W. NICHOLSON, World War II, United States Army, born July 26, 1919 to William and Stella Nicholson, residents of Washington County. Graduated from Tampico High School in 1939.

Served with 19th Infantry Division in the Philippines. Killed in Action April 19, 1945, and buried in the Little York Cemetery. Engraved marker reads:

Pfc. Woodrow Nicholson
19th Infantry
World War II
July 26, 1919-April 19, 1945

HARLAN H. NIERMAN, World War II, United States Marine Corps, was born near Wegan in Jackson County to Walter and Elnora Melloncamp Nierman. He grew up in Seymour but moved back to the farm for the remainder of his school years. He joined the Marine Corps January 4, 1943 just after he received his high school diploma.

He completed his boot camp training in San Diego at the naval base but never served overseas. He was assigned to several stateside bases, including Cherry Point, Quantico, Parris Island, Logan and El Centro. In each case, he trained pilots to land and take off by radar.

He was discharged as a T/Sgt on May 21, 1946 and enrolled at Purdue to graduate with a degree in electrical engineering. He was employed by several engineering firms. In January 1966, he accepted a position in Lakeland, Florida where he worked the rest of his life.

He was married to Jayne Beldon December 27, 1947 and they became parents of three children, David, Janice and Pamela.

ELMER L. NOBLITT, World War II, United States Naval Command, 1944-1946, was born March 26, 1923, the son of Lafayette and Ora Chasteen Noblitt of Seymour, Indiana. Married to Virginia Watson, he was the father of two sons, Daniel and John. Elmer L. Noblitt died on December 24, 2003.

LOREN W. NOBLITT, World War II, United States Army Airborne Command, was born May 8, 1922 in New Jersey to Loren S. and Minnie Walls Noblitt. He moved as a child with his family when they re-located to Columbus in 1927. He attended elementary school in the capital city. He attended Shortridge High School, Western Military Academy in Alton, Illinois, Morgan Prep School in Tennessee and was later graduated from Columbus High School in 1940. After completing one year of college, he withdrew to work at Arvin Industries producing bombs for the war effort.

He enlisted in the Army Airborne Command August 21, 1942 and completed basic training at Bowman Field, KY. Trained as a parachute rigger, he made his initial jump at Fort Benning, GA. He was assigned to the 44th Squadron, 316th Troop Carrier Group and shipped overseas to the Middle East where his unit supported the British 8th Army under General Montgomery advancing across North Africa against General Rommel. Survived 9 battle campaigns in the Middle East, North Africa and European Theater.

December 20, 1942, embarked on the USS *Mariposa;* February 23, 1943, attached to the British 8th Army; July 11, 1943, parachute drop - invasion of Sicily; August 1, 1943, Ploesti Oil Field Bombing Mission; September 12, 1943, assault on Salerno/Foggio in Italy; June 5, 1943, Anzio/Rome Campaign; June 6, 1944, D-Day parachute drop – Normandy; September 17, 1944, D-Day Parachute Assault on Nijmegen; January 5, 1945, Hospital Rest/Recuperation; May 23, 1945, redeployed to Camp Atterbury; September 2, 1945, V-J Day declared – discharged.

Aided by the GI Bill, he completed his education with the B.S., M.Sc., Litt.D., J.D. and Ph.D. degrees. Freedom Foundation Teachers Medal, 1964; National Educator of the Year, 1970; Retired Superintendent, Visalia Unified School District; Instructor of Adult Bible Classes 50 years. Married 55 years to Kathryn Kamman Noblitt.

WILLIS J. NOELKER, World War II, United States Army, was born in Jackson County to Louis and Louise Noelker. Records are brief but verify he was drafted into the army from his home at 312 West Brown Street in Seymour, IN.

He was assigned to the 78th Lightening Division and saw action in Europe. His unit returned home in August 1945. He was discharged October 14, 1945.

He was married to Katherine L. Noelker. The Records confirm he died March 22, 1997.

MORRIS L. NOLTING, World War II, United States Army, 79th Infantry Division, landed on Utah Beach – D-Day Assault on Normandy. Honorable Discharge in 1945.

WILLARD WALTER NOWLING, World War II, United States Navy, born April 24, 1914 at Brownstown in Jackson County. Enlisted May 13, 1942 at Indianapolis. Boot Camp completed at Great Lakes Naval Station. Stationed at various posts. Discharged at Portsmouth, NH on February 3, 1945.

ROBERT W. NUTTER, World War II, Korea and Vietnam, United States Navy and the United States Air Force 1943-1966. He was born January 11, 1925 in Seymour, Indiana, the son of Ed Nutter and Rose F. Barrows, and the grandson of Willy Scott of Freetown. Robert spent most of his life on a farm west of Freetown. He graduated from Freetown High School in May 1943.

After graduation, Robert entered the Navy. He completed boot camp at Great Lakes, Illinois. He was assigned to the U.S.S. CHICOPEE AO-34, a fleet oilier. Robert took many trips across the Atlantic. In October 1944 they passed through the Panama Canal on the way to the South Pacific. On arriving in the

South Pacific they participated in the invasion of Iwo Jima and Okinawa. In May 1945 Robert was transferred to Pearl Harbor. After a short stay, he returned to the states on 30 days leave. Robert was then assigned to Iowa State College as a staff member in the Navy V-6 and V-12 programs.

Robert spent 3 years in the Navy and was discharged on May 8, 1946 as a Petty Officer 2nd class at the Great Lakes Naval Training Center.

In February 1948 he enlisted in the United States Air Force at Seymour, Indiana with subsequent assignment to Headquarters 10th AF at Selfridge AFB, Michigan. Robert was married to Anna Lee Lutes, the daughter of Ford and Gaynell Lutes. They had two sons, Scott and Robert II. Anna Lee passed away on April 5, 1979. In January 1952 Robert was selected to set up the 2nd Air Reserve District at Indianapolis, Indiana, a training unit for reservists.

In May 1954 he received overseas orders for assignment to Headquarters FEAF at Tokyo, Japan. In May 1956 FEAF Headquarters was relocated to Hickman AFB, Hawaii and designated as PACAF. Robert was assigned as NCOIC of Officers' Personnel Records Section.

In May 1958 he rotated to the states with assignment to Patrick AFB in the Customs Office. In August 1959 Robert attended the AFSC NCO Academy at Kirtland AFB, New Mexico. Upon completion of the school, he was assigned to the school as Chief, Administration Section.

Robert remained at the school until he retired on January 1, 1966 with the rank of MSGT. He now resides in San Diego, California.

EARL M. OATHOUT, World War II, United States Army Air Corps, drafted unto the army July 16, 1941 at Camp Atterbury, 21st Air Services Command. Trained as a plumber and rifleman.

Shipped overseas to the Pacific Theater of Operations. Stationed at Luzon and New Guinea. Appropriate medals and ribbons authorized for his service. Discharged November 13, 1945.

RAYMOND OATHOUT, World War II, United States Army. Inducted into the army and assigned to be a tank gunner. He fired weapons to destroy enemy personnel and inspected engines. He was shipped overseas to the European Theater. He saw action in France, the Ardennes and the Rhineland before being discharged.

He was authorized to wear the World War II Victory Medal and 4 Campaign Stars. While serving in battle his ears were damaged and he was confined to a London hospital for surgery.

He remained hard of hearing all of his lifetime.

ROBERT RALPH OATHOUT, World War II, United States Navy, entered the navy April 20, 1945. Trained as a Painter 3rd Class. Shipped to the Asiatic Theater of Operations. Discharged July 31, 1946.

THOMAS ARTHUR O'CONNER, World War II, United States Navy, was born in Omaha, Nebraska on May 31, 1914 to Arthur Vincent and Wilma Pfeiffer O'Connor. When he was very young, the family relocated to Indiana and settled in Seymour. He attended St. Ambrose Catholic School and in 1932 graduated from Seymour High School.

While employed with the Brown and Williamson Tobacco Company, Thomas A. O'Connor enlisted into the United Stated Navy for active duty on April 27, 1943, leaving behind his wife, Frances Woodard O'Connor and an infant son. He completed his boot training at the Great Lakes Naval Training Station, and shortly thereafter was assigned to overseas duty in the Pacific Theater.

Thomas A. O'Connor served as Quartermaster 1st Class on an amphibious landing ship (LST) which transported tanks and troops to sites of invasion. His theater of wartime action included service in the Soloman Islands, New Guinea, the Philippine Islands, and Okinawa.

After thirty-one months of active service in the South Pacific, Quartermaster 1st Class/E6 Petty Officer Thomas A. O'Connor was discharged from the United States Navy on December 7, 1945. He returned to his family in Seymour and a management position with the Sears and Roebuck Company. After pursuing other business ventures over the years, he retired from Amoco Corporation in 1979.

Thomas Arthur O'Connor passed away on November 24, 1986, at the age of seventy-two, survived by his wife Frances and five children: Thomas, Patrick, Maureen, Daniel, and Margaret.

FORREST PAPHENBERG, World War II, Army Air Corps, European Theater, was killed June 6, 1944.

DON DENNY PATRICK, World War II, United States Army, born to George and Margaret Denny Patrick, volunteered for governmental program and guaranteed not being call unless United States entered war.

S/Sgt. Patrick went directly into army when war was declared. Assigned to Medical Evacuation Unit during Battle of the Bulge. Unit was pinned down by German mortars. Soldier from Tennessee stood and noted his buddy blown to bits. Announced that he should not have been there. Eased the tension of battle.

Returned to states and discharged December 17, 1945. Army records destroyed by fire in St. Louis.

GALE E. PATRICK, World War II, United States Army Air Corps, the Pacific Theater of Operations 1943-1946.

JACK HAROLD PATRICK, World War II, United States Army, born June 18, 1925 in Jackson County to parents, George and Margaret Denny Patrick. Graduated from Seymour High School in 1943.

Volunteered for service. Inducted at Louisville September 13, 1943. Assigned to 1st Battalion, 361st Engineer Special Services Regiment. Shipped overseas from New York. Landed in Scotland, sent to England and crossed channel to France. Saw action during Battle of the Bulge. Transferred to Marseille on V-E Day.

Shipped to New Guinea and Philippine Islands. After Atomic Bombs were dropped, he was stationed in Japan.

After V-J Day he returned to states. Medals include Good Conduct Medal, WWII Victory Medal, EAME Theater Ribbon, Asiatic-Pacific Theater Ribbon, Philippine Liberation Ribbon. Discharged at Camp Atterbury March 10, 1946.

JAMES W. PATRICK, World War II, United States Army, European Theater of Operations, was wounded near Siegfried Line.

ROY C. PAUL, World War II, United States Army Air Corps, 8th Air Force. When World War II broke out, after Pearl Harbor on December 7, 1941, Roy Paul enlisted in the Army Air Corps. Following his basic training, he shipped overseas to the European Theater of Operations. As a navigator on one of the B-17 Flying Fortress Bombers of the 8th Air Force, he completed 35 missions over Germany. He returned to the states in March 1944.

After he married Dorothy Hagemeier, Roy Paul became the plant manager of the Medora Plastic Factory. He died October 27, 1982.

LEROY CHALLENOR PEARSON, World War II, United States Army, Company F, 250th Regiment, 65th Infantry Division. Pfc. Pearson was born in Dillsboro, Indiana, July 18, 1914, and moved with his parents, Roy and Mabel Pearson, to Jackson County, where he spent the greater part of his life. To friends and family, he was simply known as Chat. He graduated from Houston High School in 1932. On August 14, 1936, he married Lottie Crider and together had one son, Gary.

Before entering the army October 21, 1943, he was employed at Nobblitt-Sparks Industries in Columbus for about five years. Serving in the United States Army, Company F, the 259th Regiment, and the 65th Infantry Division, he was killed in the liberation of France, October 26, 1944.

CECIL PERRY, SR.,

CECIL PERRY, SR., World War II, United States Army, born August 14, 1921 and spent his youthful years in Jackson County. He was drafted into the army in 1944 and sent to Camp Wheeler, Georgia for basic training.

His unit was shipped overseas to the European Theater of Operations. He saw action in Germany during the Battle of the Bulge and his feet were frostbitten. He was relieved of duty and sent to the hospital in North Carolina, then transferred to Wakeman General Hospital at Camp Atterbury. He received his discharge October 30, 1945.

Cecil married Generva Arnold Perry and they became parents of six children: Buck, Sue, Gene, Connie, Phil and Jane. He died April 26, 1994.

FREDERICK R. PETERS, World War II, United States Army, born in Jackson County July 28, 1922 to Fred and Clara Claycamp Peters.

Peters took basic training at Camp Carson, Colorado, with advanced training in bridge building there and in Louisiana. From there he went to Africa, England and Normandy for the D-Day landing on Utah Beach. He was assigned to the 237th Engineer Combat Battalion.

As a sergeant in the Combat Engineers, he was in the first wave unto Utah Beach. As a Sergeant it was his job to blow the sea wall, clear the barbed wire and clear the mine fields to make a path for the men, trucks and heavy equipment to pass through. After accomplishing this, he and his men headed toward France, clearing mine fields and building bridges. The ultimate goal for his battalion was Germany, where he was involved in building the famous "Beer Bridge" over the Rhine River.

He and his wife Norma enjoyed a return visit there on the 40th anniversary of the D-Day invasion.

After separation from the Army in 1945, he returned home and married Norma Oberman. They had four children: Dennis, Larry, Janet and John. After farming and carpentry for several years, he bought a grocery store in Vallonia, Indiana which he operated for about ten years.

He worked as a salesman for Sears until his retirement, and returned to the Brownstown, Vallonia area until his death in March 2001.

THE PFEIFFER FAMILY OF VETERANS

The Pfeiffer family of veterans enjoyed a family reunion when the boys reached home on a furlough at the same time.

One of five soldiers to escape when his Regiment was surrounded and bombarded by the heavy Japanese mortar fire, Pfc. Theodore Pfeiffer was wounded on Okinawa. Blinded and suffering from leg wounds, Ted lay in pain for eighty-two hours

before being rescued. He recovered his sight and was sent back to the United States.

Heading this Pfeiffer family of veterans, Howard Pfeiffer maintained the military records.

Pfeiffer Family, Howard Pfeiffer Jr., World War II, US Army; Ted Pfeiffer Sr. World War II, US Army; Ted Pfeiffer Jr., Vietnam, US Marines; James Pheiffer Sr., Vietnam, National Guard.

BRYCE DWIGHT PING, United States Army, #355 617 47, Private 1st Class. Service Time from October 1942-December 1945, New Guinea and the Philippine Islands. Current residence with his spouse Wilma, 5594 South State Road 39, Brownstown.

The life of Bryce Ping, a backwoods boy from Brown County, was changed suddenly on October 9, 1942. He was scheduled for his army induction exam, and was one of fifty men out of 100 pronounced fit for duty. Later he boarded a bus bound for Fort Harrison in Indianapolis. From there he was sent to Camp Lee in Virginia where he completed his basic training.

Sometime later he was ordered to Camp Gordon in Florida and became one of the amphibious engineers. About Easter time he was assigned to Fort Ord, California. Further training took place in the Mohave Desert. He received a furlough and decided to visit his relatives who lived in Washington.

His unit was ordered overseas and made the trip on one of the Liberty Ships, which was really a cargo ship. The men were onboard 28 days and received only 2 meals each day. When the crew spotted a periscope, everyone thought it might be an enemy submarine but it did not attack. It was while stationed in New Guinea that Bryce Ping contracted jungle rot, and was transferred to Milne Bay. Much later he was assigned to one of the Dutch-Australian bases.

Sometime after February in 1945, his unit of men heard about the dropping of the Atomic Bombs. Japan surrender almost immediately, and by November he was ordered back to the United States. He arrived in Camp Atterbury on Christmas Eve. He walked 17 miles to reach his home in Brown County.

CLARENCE RAY POGUE, World War II, United States Army, was born December 22, 1910 to James and Lydia Bell Trotter Pogue in Moorsville. The family lived in Jennings County but they settled in Jackson County in 1933. Being raised in the local area he became a carpenter and brick mason.

He was drafted and inducted into the army April 14, 1942. After completing his basic training, he was assigned to the

8th Infantry Regiment of the 1st Cavalry Division. His unit was shipped overseas to the Pacific Theater of Operations. He returned to the states and received his discharge February 7, 1946.

He was authorized to wear appropriate medals and ribbons reflecting his service assignments. Ray Pogue never married and died in Seymour March 6, 1988.

OMER L. POLLERT, Post World War II, United States Navy, was the son of Edward and Emma Pollert of Brownstown. He was inducted into the navy January 6, 1945 in Indianapolis and placed on a train for Sampson, New York to complete his boot camp training.

Not long afterward he was assigned to a gunnery school in Newport, RI. That training was for 12 weeks, then he boarded the USS *Los Angeles,* then docked at the Philadelphia naval yard. He was a crewman during a "shakedown" cruise in the Atlantic Ocean.

It sailed to Guantanamo Bay, Cuba it was overhauled at Terminal Island in California before it sailed out for China and on to Hong Kong. The war had ended and the crew was put aboard another ship and sent back to the states.

He was discharged at Great Lakes Naval Station in Chicago June 20, 1946.

PAUL T. PREUS, World War II, United States Army Air Corps, a son of a Lutheran school teacher and church organist, graduated from Seymour High School in 1934. Entering West Point Military Academy as an alternate selection for appointment, he became a pilot after he received his degree in acquisitions in 1938.

He was promoted from Captain to Lt. Colonel shortly after he selected Seymour to be the home base for Freeman Field. His foresight proved more than providential; the project aided the ailing economic fortunes of Jackson County. The new air base at Seymour was named to honor Richard Freeman of Winomac, Indiana who was killed in 1942. This special friend of Paul Preus had completed his early training at White River Flying Field located on the lower Rockford Road.

Once the site was approved on May 6, 1942, the military career of Col. Paul Preus advanced rapidly. He became a Brigadier General in 1956 when he was appointed Commander of Hickam Field in Honolulu. In 1962 he was named to the Aid Defense Command. General Preus retired from active duty in the service in 1966. He passed away in 1987 while living at his home located in San Antonio, Texas.

HOWARD WAYNE RATCLIFF, World War II, United States Army, was born May 21, 1905 in Jackson County to John and Mary McElfesh Ratcliff. Always known as "Buck" he grew up with two other children even after the death of his parents.

He joined the army June 4, 1942 at the age of 37 years and reported to Louisville, KY. He was sent to Aberdeen Proving Ground, MD and later to Fresno, CA. While there he developed a severe case of nose bleeding and ulcers. He was given a medical discharge early in May 1943.

December 31, 1949 he married Gladys Louise Baughman and adopted her two children. He lived near Freetown for the rest of his life until he died March 14, 1976.

He had always enjoyed his five grandchildren.

HAROLD T. REEDY, World War II, United States Army, born August 6, 1923 in Illinois to Bruce and Mayme Simpkins Reedy but moved with his family when they re-located to Freetown. He graduated from Freetown High School in 1941 and later married Neva Berry and they became parents of five children.

He was inducted into the army January 18, 1943 and reported to Fort Harrison, but completed his basic training at Fort Lewis, WA. He received armored tank training and was assigned to the 235th Tank Battalion. His unit was shipped overseas and arrived in Scotland on February 26, 1944, and from there they were sent to France and then on into Germany. They joined Patton's 3rd Army during the Battle of the Bulge. He was then sent back to the states for discharge.

He was a member of the Church of Christ in Freetown, Washington Lodge 13 F&AM in Brownstown. He was a farmer but later operated stores in Surprise and Freetown. Harold died September 8, 1989 and was buried at Pleasant Hill Cemetery at Acme.

BILLY RICHARDSON, World War II, US Army, European Theater, was killed April 12, 1945.

RAYMOND RIGSBY, World War II, United States Army, was inducted into army October 17, 1942. Assigned to Medical Detachment, 55th Armored Battalion, 11th Armored Division of the 3rd Army under Patton. Served in Ardennes, Rhineland, Central Europe.

Awarded EAME Ribbon w/3 Campaign Stars, Bronze Star, Good Conduct Medal and Victory Medal WWII.

In early January 1945 he was under attack near Longchamps, Belgium. Wounded with hundreds of others, he played dead. His feet were frozen. After release from hospital returned to states and discharged in December 1945.

Returned home to Scottsburg, married Glenna Taskey in 1948. Employed by Central Pharmacy and Seymour Hospital. Became father of 3 children. Raymond Rigsby died May 24, 1990

RONALD W. RITZ, World War II, United States Army Air Corps, was born October 4, 1917 in Kolen, Montana to Walter and Mabel Esares Ritz and raised in the Honeytown area of Hamilton Township. He graduated from Cortland High School in 1934.

He volunteered and was inducted into the Army Air Corps in January 1942 at Fort Harrison in Indianapolis. He was sent to Bauer Field for his basic training. He was assigned to the 1705th AF Base unit the military police and served for three years before being returned to his home near Honeytown. He was discharged before Thanksgiving Day in 1945.

He farmed, was employed by the Highway Garage and worked as a substitute rural mail carrier. He and his wife, Dorothy Oathout, reside between Brownstown and Seymour where they raised 3 children.

RALPH R. ROBBINS, World War II, United States Navy, was born to Dawson and Maude George Robbins on May 9, 1911. He was raised in Jackson County and later was to be married to Lora Hansome in September 1935. They became parents of two children while they lived near Crothersville. They later moved to Indianapolis where he was employed by the city.

Records show he joined the navy and became a Seaman 2nd Class. He was discharged Nov. 28, 1945 at Great Lakes Naval Station. When he returned home, he picked up life and his marriage endured for 57 years.

He died August 18, 1993 and Lora followed him to the grave three years later in 1996.

JOE ROBERTSON, World War II, United States Army Air Corps, enlisted in Army Air Corps as an Aviation Cadet in September 1942. Did cadet training at Boca Ratan, FL, and Yale University. Was commissioned in November 1943.

Served as Aerial Photo Intelligence Officer (MOS 8502-8503) in Heavy Bombardment Training Command (B-17s and B-24s) at Davis-Monthan Field, Tucson, Arizona, until 1945. Was promoted to 1st Lieutenant and transferred to Biggs Field, in El Paso to serve as Aerial Photo Combat Training Officer on General Newton Longfellow's Staff of the 16th Wing, 2nd Air Force.

Received a commendation/citation from General of the Air Force, General Henry "Hap" Arnold, for developing and implementing the use of a Camera/Bomb Combination System that was connected to the Norden Bomb Sight on the Super Heavy B-29 Bomber such as those that carried the atom bomb to Hiroshima.

Was honorably discharged from US Army Air Force on December 16, 1945, and remained in Reserve until 1950.

Current resident of Brownstown, IN. Married Virginia Baxter and they have son, Dr. Joe E. Robertson Jr., and grandchildren, Katie Faye Robertson and C.J. Robertson.

RAYMOND MURRELL ROBISON, World War II, United States Army. Most people knew him as Friday. He was a colorful character who knew countless numbers of people in his life. Friday was the first born to George and Myrtle McKinney Robison in Ewing, IN on October 28, 1922. He was the first of their four sons to serve his country. He graduated from Brownstown High School.

He was inducted into the US Army on January 4, 1943 and entered active duty in Louisville, Kentucky on January 11, 1943. Friday was discharged on December 27, 1945. He earned the rank of sergeant during this time. He was one of those who saw more than his share of action during his time in the service. His parents even received the dreaded telegram from the Army saying that Friday was missing in action. They were notified a few weeks later that he was all right. He was involved in several important campaigns in Northern France, Ardennes, Rhineland, and Central Europe. His unit was Battery C, 253rd Armored Field Artillery Battalion. Tanks were his specialty. He was put in charge of his own tank and 3 others. At the end of the war, he was part of the liberation of concentration camps in Germany. Friday was awarded the American Theater Ribbon, EAME Theater Ribbon with Bronze Stars, Good Conduct Medal, Soldier's Medal, Victory Medal, and the World War II Bronze Star.

After Friday was discharged, he married Mary Boaz. He and Mary had 3 children: Nancy, Gerda, and Stanley Ray. He farmed for a living most of his early years. He refereed basketball games all over the state of Indiana, but mostly in Southern Indiana. Friday was proud of this part of his life, especially when he was chosen to referee on the state level. He also was widely known for his involvement with Belgium horses and mules. He was active in showing, breeding, and participation in various parades in the Midwest. He was a member of the Fair Board on the Grounds Committee for many years. He also had worked for Hobbs Line Construction. At the time of his death on December 11, 1997, he was caretaker for the Lake and Forest Club in Brownstown, IN.

Friday took great pride in the fact that he had served his country.

ROBERT L. ROBISON (January 25, 1924-October 12, 2001), World War II, United States Army, was the son of George and Myrtle McKinney Robison, and a veteran of World War II, serving in the U.S. Army. Enlisting on March 6, 1943, he spent his early days as a private at Ft. McClellan, Alabama, in Company D, 7th Battalion.

Bob later became a Technical Sergeant in

Company B, 1st Battalion, 150th Infantry, 38th Division, and spent much of his military service in the Caribbean Defense Command, defending the easternmost lock of the Panama Canal. His last few months of military service were spent training for a possible ground invasion of Japan, in the Gilbert Island chain. His military occupation, as a Rifle Non-Commissioned Officer, included working with and supervising operation of enlisted men in supplying ammunition for loading, aiming, and firing M-1 rifles at enemy and enemy positions, as well as assisting in capturing enemy and enemy positions.

He received his honorable discharge from the service on January 28, 1946 at Camp Atterbury, Indiana, receiving an American Theater Ribbon, Good Conduct Medal, and a Victory Medal of World War II.

After his military service, he attended the University of Nebraska in 1946-47, and later attended Indiana Central College in Indianapolis. He completed his undergraduate work at ICC in 1951, where he was a member of the basketball and baseball teams.

After graduation, he taught and served as head basketball coach at Tampico High School from 1951 to 1963. In 1957 he received his Master of Science degree and principal license. He served as a teacher and grade school principal at Vallonia for one year before teaching and coaching at Medora from 1964-1967.

From 1967 to 1969 he served as high school principal at Clear Spring for two years, and then as assistant principal at Oolitic High School for five years from 1970-1974.

Bob retired from teaching in 1977, and worked as a general contractor until his retirement in 1986. Married on March 6, 1953 to Marjorie Stotz, he was the father of two sons, Steven K. Robison and Jon C. Robison, and grandfather to four: Jennifer, Mark, Lisa, and Stuart.

DON R. ROLLINS, United States Army, #35965546, Private 1st Class, was inducted at Indianapolis in 1944. He was born in Lawrence County near Bedford, and came to Jackson County as a baby when his family moved to a new home near Clearspring. Don graduated with the class of 1944. Two months later he registered for the military draft. He passed the physical exam in September of the same year. He was inducted in December and sent to Camp Atterbury before boarding a troop train headed for Camp Blanding, Florida.

He completed basic training as a rifleman, and in April 1945 was ordered to Fort Ord, CA. Upon arrival he went onboard a ship heading west under the Golden Gate Bridge. On May 8, 1945 V-E Day was declared and fighting ceased in Europe, but Don R. Rollins landed in the Philippine Islands.

His unit joined the old American Division, but his military assignment was confined to amphibious landing training. The invasion on Japan was scheduled for November 1, 1945, but the atomic bomb was dropped August 16, 1945. After a second bomb was dropped on Nagasaki, the invasion plan was canceled and V-J Day was declared September 2, 1945.

Later his unit was ordered home to the United States. He was soon on the way home to be discharged November 10, 1946.

GLENN R. ROSS, World War II, Navy, Pacific Theater, was killed while serving in the USS *Indianapolis.*

GLENN L. ROTHERT, World War II, United States Army, born 1923 in Jackson County to parents, George Henry and Hattie Koester Rothert. Inducted into the army March 4, 1943.

Completed basic training. Assigned as ambulance truck driver. Shipped overseas to the European Theater. Saw action in the Ardennes, Rhineland and Central Europe. Received EAME Ribbon w/3 Campaign Stars, Good Conduct Medal and WWII Victory Medal. Returned to the states and discharged January 24, 1946.

Married Madeline Hackman in 1949. Parents of one son.

PAUL DENEAL RUCKER, World War II, United States Navy, was born October 20, 1916 in Hamilton Township to Arthur and Laura Wheeler Rucker. He was raised near Acme and Surprise grade school. He graduated from Cortland High School in 1934. He became a teacher and remained in the classroom for his entire life.

He enlisted the service at Indianapolis August 24, 1942 and was sent to Great Lakes, Naval Training Base where he received surgery to qualify him to complete basic training. He received special training in aviation machinery at Norfolk. He was assigned to an aircraft carrier unit 32 repairing planes for duty.

He returned to the states and was stationed at Bunker Hill Naval Air Base located near Peru, Indiana in July 1945. He was discharged at Chicago October 11, 1945. He returned home to Jackson County to resume his teaching career of 42 years.

He and his wife, Gertrude Motsinger Rucker of Medora, reside on Redding Road near Rockford after have raised three children.

LYNN WILLKOM RUDDICK, World War II and Following, United States Army Air Corps, was born in Seymour, Indiana on July 19, 1917, and was from a farm family of seven brothers and sisters. His parents were Aaron A. and Flora (Willkom) Ruddick. Lynn graduated from Seymour HS in 1935, and

enlisted as an infantryman in the U.S. Army in 19??. He volunteered for the Army Air Corps and received his aviator Wings in 1943 at Pampa Army Air Field in Texas. He then made the transition to the Air Force as 1 of 3 men from his home state of Indiana to receive his regular commission from President Harry S. Truman. Colonel Ruddick logged over 6,000 flying hours during his 29 year career in the Air Force.

Lynn served overseas in Japan, Newfoundland, Greenland, Turkey, France, Germany, Vietnam, and did 2 tours of duty in the Philippines.

Colonel Ruddick was a decorated Air Force officer and aviator, and earned several commendations, including: WWII Victory Medal, Army of Occupation Medal, American Defense Service Medal, American Campaign Medal. Armed Forces Expeditionary Medal, Longevity Service Award with 3 Bronze Oak Leaves, Air Force Commendation Medal for Meritorious Service with two Oak Leaf Clusters.

After his many years of distinguished and honorable military service, Lynn and his wife Faye (Johnson) moved to the small town of Angelus Oaks In the mountains of southern California, where he devoted his energies to serving his community. Lynn was instrumental in forming the Angelus Oaks Volunteer Fire Department, and was in the first EMT class to graduate from Crafton Hills College. Lynn also served on the Glen Martin Mutual Water Company Board of Directors for many years.

Lt. Colonel Lynn Willkom Ruddick (USAF) passed away in Angelus Oaks on August 19, 2003. He was 86. Lynn and his wife Faye have lived in Angelus Oaks for 34 years since he retired from the Air Force in 1969. Let us remember, it is because of men like Colonel Lynn Ruddick that we enjoy our liberty and freedom every day.

CLARENCE CARVAN RUDOLPH, World War II, United States Army, was born on June 25, 1921, in Jonesville, Indiana. At an early age he moved to Freetown, Indiana, with his parents, Thomas and Lana Mobley Rudolph.

Carvan graduated from Freetown High School in 1940. He entered the United States Army on July 22, 1942. During World War II he served in the 40th Division, 160th Infantry Service Company. He was stationed in the South Philippines where he earned the American Theater Ribbon, Asiatic-Pacific Theater Ribbon with Bronze Star, Philippine Liberation Ribbon, Good Conduct Ribbon, and the Victory Medal of World War II. He was discharged on December 23, 1945, at Camp Atterbury, Indiana.

On February 15, 1946, he married Norma Harbaugh. One son, Michael Rudolph, lives in Freetown. Carvan died on June 3, 1973. His wife, son, and three grandsons, Clinton, Benjamin and Brian Rudolph, survive him.

CECIL BERNIE RYAN, World War II, 62nd Armored Division, Field Artillery, was born September 12, 1918 in Jackson County as the son of George A. and Sarah G. Ryan. He married Laticia Smith November 12, 1947 in Lawrence County. They became parents of Dennis Wayne, Wanda Sue and Kenneth Allen Ryan.

At the time of his induction he was living in Kurtz and was the oldest of eleven children. Because of the age difference, he acted as a surrogate father to the younger children since their father had died when they were very young. On January 2, 1941 Cecil was ordered to Louisville and while in service, he sent his paycheck home to his mother.

He was assigned as a truck driver and spent nearly three years overseas serving in Tunisia, Sicily, Normandy, Northern France, Central Europe and the Ardennes. He was wounded and received the Purple Heart, along with his other decorations which included seven Bronze Stars for the several campaigns.

Cecil attained the rank of Tech 5 and after V-E Day was declared, the small town boy was rotated back to the United States. He arrived July 31, 1945 and sometime later received his honorable discharge.

Cecil Ryan died April 23, 1984 and was buried in the Kurtz Cemetery beside his father and mother.

WOODROW OREN AND BURRLL DEAN SCHLEHUSER, World War II, United States Army and United States Navy. Woodrow Orren and his brother, Burrll Dean, were sons of Walter and Cora Dringenburg Schlehuser. Both were destined to serve military tours of duty in World War II.

Woodrow "Woody" was assigned to the Army Armored Division and sent overseas to the European Theater of Operations. He saw action in Normandy, northern France and Rhineland during his two-year tour of duty. He was authorized to wear the EAME ribbon with 3 Campaign Stars, European Victory Medal, Purple Heart and Good Conduct Medal.

In 1947 he married Helen Kuehn and was father to four children: Jalynn Whittymore, Donn Orren, Royce Ann and Glenn Allen Schlehuser.

Burrl Dean was a 1945 graduate of Cortland High School and elected to join the naval reserves during the war in the Pacific Theater of Operations through July 16, 1946.

He was authorized to wear the Asiatic-Pacific Area Campaign Medal and the American Victory Medal. After he returned to the states, he was married to JoAnn Mann and they raised three children, Michael and Alan Schlehuser and Leesa Olsen.

He retired from the Henry County REMC after 42 years of service.

JOHN CARL SCHLEIBAUM, World War II, United States Army Air Corps, was born September 1, 1922 and later enlisted in the air corps at Indianapolis. He reported for duty June 27, 1942 and after completing basic training was assigned as a tail gunner. He was sent to gunnery school at Buckley Field in Colorado.

He was in a plane crash while in training at Brownsville, Texas and spent nine months in the hospital receiving treatment for his burns. He was discharged May 1, 1944.

He was married to Mary Kate Farley Schleibaum and they were parents of three daughters, Kathy Sue, Brenda Carol, Barbara Jo and one son named John Richard Schleibaum.

He died March 16, 1987.

PAUL E. SCHNECK, Post World War II, United States Air Force, was a medical doctor stationed in Germany following World War II when he was assigned to the United States Medical Hospital in Wiesbaden, West German. The photo was taken from *"Stars and Stripes"* and shows Captain Schneck with his wife, Polly and one of their children

GEORGE H. SCHNEIDER, World War II, United States Navy, October 7, 1944-March 12, 1946, was born in Grassy Fork Township and was baptized on November 11, 1923 R Wegan Lutheran Church. He attended Waskom and Wegan schools for his elementary grades and graduated from Tampico High School with the class of 1942.

He enlisted in the navy in 1944 and completed boot camp training at Great Lakes Naval Station in Chicago. He was trained as a radio operator and shipped overseas to the Pacific Theater of Operations. A news clipping from the *Brownstown Banner* in the January 16, 1946 edition reported that "...Mr. and Mrs. Edward Schneider of Brownstown have received word their son, George, has been promoted to the rank of Radioman, 3rd Class, and is now stationed at the naval base on Sangley Point in the Philippines..."

It required 21 days to return to the states after the war was over. His ship the USS *McIntyre*, paused for a night at the Golden Gate Bridge before they boarded a troop train. When he reached the city of Chicago, he was issued his discharge authorizing him to wear various medals and service ribbons.

He reached Seymour on March 12, 1946 and from there rode one of the Greyhound Buses on to Brownstown.

ALFRED F. SCHUERMAN, World War II, United States Army, born August 26, 1918 in Washington Township to parents, Henry John and Anna Wischmeier Schuerman. He was raised on the family farm where he matured.

Inducted into the army April 7, 1942. Reported to Fort Benning, Georgia and was then sent to Biloxi, Mississippi. Stationed at Fort Hood, Texas and sent to Camp Stoneman, CA.

Shipped overseas to the Philippines in the Pacific Theater. Returned to the states January 20, 1946. Transferred to the 806th Tank Battalion. Discharged and hitchhiked home to Scottsburg via ride from Raymond Garriott.

Married Marlene Moenning and became parents of four children. Alfred Schuerman died May 8, 1996.

JASON EUGENE SCOTT, World War II, United States Navy, 1944-1946, born February 15, 1926 at Freetown. Inducted into navy April 4, 1944. Trained as Radioman 2nd Class. Served aboard various ships in Pacific Theater.

Discharged May 17, 1946. Married Charline Rhiner November 12, 1948. Became parents of three children, Connie, Gregory and Tammy. Charline died February 17, 2001. Eugene Scott enjoys his children and grandchildren.

RALPH SCOTT, World War II, United States Army Air Corps, entered the military service as an aviation cadet in 1943. Prior to taking action he was enrolled at the University of Missouri. In March 1945, he completed his training and was commissioned a 2nd Lieutenant when he was awarded his wing as a pilot.

Ralph Scott advanced through the commissioned ranks and was promoted to the rank of Major. He saw service in Greenland, Japan and Okinawa. He chose to retire after 22 years of service.

He was married to Carolyn L. Denny August 24, 1946 and they became parents of one daughter. Carolyn is now deceased. He had three grandchildren.

Major Ralph Scott was a native of Freetown. He died in November of 1978 and was buried in the Freetown cemetery.

RUSSELL A. SHERRILL, World War II, United States Army, born August 27, 1923 near Bedford to Willie and Ida Sherrill who moved to Medora. He later graduated from Clearspring High School in 1942 and in on January 18, 1943 entered active duty at Fort Harrison. He was sent to Fort Lewis, WA for basic armored tank training so he could become a medium tank crewman. He was then assigned to Company B, 735th Tank Battalion.

On February 24, 1944 his unit landed in Scotland, and then on to France where he served in

Normandy, through France and the Rhineland area. In their attack on Ft. Driant they were unaware that the supporting regiment had set up back of his unit. That left his tank at the head of the line. It was surrounded by Germans and the crew had to surrender as prisoners. On one of the moves from camp to camp, Russell Sherrill and Pail Otto escaped on January 31, 1945. This began their escape across Germany, Poland and the Ukraine to Odessa located on the Black Sea. They had gone 1,200 miles to reach safety on an English freighter bound for Port Said, Egypt which required further travel for another 1,300 miles to Naples on another freighter.

Finally they were returned to the United States on May 6, 1945 and arrived just two days before V-E Day was announced. Returning to Jackson County his primary occupation was that of a banker; first as a cashier at Citizen's State Bank in Ewing. In 1966 he became president and director of the State Bank in Medora.

He was married to Charlotte Lucas of Brownstown and they became parents of four children, including three daughters: Donna Penn, Debra Burcham, and Diane Coon. Their son, David Sherrill, is deceased. The parents reside on a farm near Medora Junction.

RAWLAND SHIRLEY, World War II, United States Army, was known by most people as Podney. He was born March 2, 1922 on a small farm in Grassy Fork Township of Jackson County. He was the son of William and Josie (Thomas) Shirley. He attended Waskom and Tampico Schools and was a box stitcher by trade, prior to entering the United States Army.

He began his military service with initial training at Fort Benjamin Harrison, in December of 1942, but not without incident. Military records support the story his family told of dropping him at the bus station and bidding him farewell, only to discover he was anxiously awaiting them as they arrived home. His parents never figured out how he beat them home that day. Nine days later he successfully began his military career.

He became a Platoon Sergeant at Camp McKain, Mississippi and a Staff Sergeant while stationed at Camp Phillips, Kansas. He served in World War II, landing on foreign soil July 17, 1944. Serving with Company M, 357th Infantry Battalion, his principal position was to lead fellow soldiers, after nightfall, on missions of searching out and destroying German tanks and other military equipment. He was involved with battles and campaigns in Northern France, South Belgium, the Rhineland area of Western Germany, and Central Europe. He returned to the United States on December 27, 1945, arriving at Fort Dix, New Jersey.

He was given honorable separation from the United States Army on January 20, 1946 at Camp Atterbury, Indiana, having earned the American Theater Ribbon, EAME Theater Ribbon, and Good Conduct Ribbon, along with Expert Infantry Badge, Combat Infantry Badge, and Victory Medal. He was honored as an Expert Rifle Marksman and received four Bronze Stars.

Shirley held tight a personal story connected to a memorable souvenir brought back from the war, a 1941 Model P. 08 German Luger ... now passed down to his oldest grandson.

Shortly after his military discharge, he was married to Ada (Maxie) Shirley. Shirley had two children: Jack L. Shirley of Lakeland, Florida, who served, with the U.S. Army during the Vietnam Conflict and Joetta Shirley-Fee of Bartholomew County. Grandchildren include: Jennifer Shirley-Mellencamp, Jason Fee, Heather Fee-McCormick, and Chasidy Fee-Hoffman, all of Jackson County and Blake Shirley of Florida. Great-grandchildren are Mikayla, Makenna, and Todd Fee, Dalton and Bradon Hoffman, and Marley and Mitchell McCormick, all of Jackson County. Working as a heavy-equipment and farm machinery mechanic, he spent many years with the Medora and Brownstown Brick Plants, later retiring from Cordes Implement in Seymour, Indiana. Shirley passed away on January 16, 1999.

ERMAN SHOEMAKER, Corporal 55419507, Company A, 76th Battalion, 11th Airborne Division, United States Army, born September 7, 1932 near Vallonia, Indiana. He graduated with the class of 1950 from the local high school. He helped his father on the farm until he was drafted into the army shortly after the Korean Conflict ended.

He Started his basic training with the Airborne Division at Fort Campbell, Kentucky, and upon completion, he received specialized training in the operation of an M-47 tank. He became skilled in the various operational positions of the tank. He remained with the unit and became part of the "combat-ready" 11th Airborne Division on call for deployment at any time to defend the national freedom.

Eventually he was assigned work in the orderly room as Company Clerk, and part of his duties included making out the morning report as part of the clerical functions. He reached the rank of corporal by the time of his discharge in June 1955. He returned home and resumed the farm work. He is married to the former Betty Jane Hansen and they became parents of four children, Kisa Lohmeyer, Carol Delph, Bruce Shoemaker and Julie Dietrickkh.

WALTER F. SIEFKER, World War II, United States Army, 268th Field Artillery Battalion, First Army. Walter Siefker was born near Seymour on September 25, 1911, a son of John and Rosena Dickmeyer Siefker. He graduated from Immanuel Lutheran School in 1927 and spent his youth helping his parents on the farm, harvesting and cooking sugar cane juice to make Siefker's Pure Steam Cooked

Sorghum. Walt later drove a tractor-trailer for the Silver Fleet Motor Express and worked for his brother at Siefker's Machine Shop.

After Pearl Harbor Day in 1941, he was classified as "1-A" and was required to wait for his call to service. He decided to marry Amy on January 11, 1942. He answered the call and was assigned number 35505954 on August 7, 1942 at Fort Harrison, IN. He was sent to various camps in Texas and on to Fort Bragg, NC. Finally his unit was shipped overseas to Scotland and on to Northern France, the Netherlands and into the Ardennes. He was in combat during the Battle of the Bulge and was awarded the Bronze Star for "meritorious and heroic achievements."

His rank was T/4 with specialty as a welder, and being fluent in German, Walt often served as the company interpreter. He was authorized to wear a host of ribbons and medals. He hoped and prayed the war would end quickly so he could be home for Christmas. He was discharged honorable from Camp Atterbury December 23, 1945.

Returning to civilian life, he was employed by the County Farm Co-op and later offered a position at Seymour Manufacturing Company. He retired in 1976. He was a member of Immanual Lutheran Church, the local service clubs and fire chief of the Jackson-Washington Townships Volunteer Fire Department.

FRANCIS SMALLWOOD, World War II, European Theater of Operations, landed on Omaha Beach in Normandy, France, Central Europe, Czechoslovakia, 1941-45.

ELMER W. SMITH, World War II, Korean Police Action, United States Navy, served in the navy from August 1944 to October 1945. Completed basic training at Great Lakes Naval Station. Stationed at San Diego, California.

Served in Korean era from February 1951 to June 1952 Assigned to USS *Ruff* AMS-54 from North Carolina.

Currently resides at Tampico, Indiana, Jackson County. Married to Faye Cunningham and the father of one child.

HOWARD E. SMITH, World War II, United States Navy, was often called "Howdy." He was born in Brownstown in 1925 to Mark and Jessie Browning Smith and was raised on a farm near Medora. He graduated from Medora High School in 1943 and later that year he was inducted into the Navy. He completed his boot camp training at Great Lakes, Illinois and was assigned

to the Medical Corps School for additional training.

He went on to Norman, OK and then to Camp Pendleton, CA and trained with the 5th Marine Division. In November 1944 he was assigned to the USS *Marathon* and boarded the ship at Astoria, OR. He was shipped overseas to Hawaii and then to Guadalcanal where members of the 1st Marine Division came aboard.

He was involved in the invasion of Okinawa with its heavy fighting and his work in the medical corps became more important in its care of the wounded. It required 430 ships and 182,000 personnel fighting for 82 days before the island was secured. But the worst was yet to come for Howard Smith.

On July 22, 1945 his ship was torpedoed while at anchor in Buckner Bay - 42 crew members died in their separate sleeping compartments, but he slept on deck and, it was his task to help remove and tag the bodies for burial on Okinawa.

The Japanese surrender on September 2, 1945 was most welcome. Later that month while on an R and R his ship was struck by a typhoon. He was safe because he hung on to the flag pole.

JOHN W. SMITH, World War II, United States Army, was born in Grassy Fork Township and spent his youth on the family farm. After his teenage years he was drafted and finally inducted into the army. In March of 1943 he was sent to Fort Leonard Wood, MO where he was to be trained and as an artillery man.

He was assigned to Headquarters Battery of the 898th Field Artillery attached to the 75th Infantry Division. Some time later he was transferred to train recruits of the newly-created 665th Battalion stationed at Camp Maxie, TX. He and the men were shipped overseas to the European Theater of Operations in 1945 to participate in the Rhineland Campaign.

He returned to the states and was stationed in California at the time of his discharge in April 1946. After returning home he attended barber college in Indianapolis and, for 41 years, he owned and operated his own barber shop in Seymour.

He and his wife, Mary Hamblin Smith, became parents of two children, Rhonda and a son, Timothy. They were later to be blessed with three great grandchildren.

John W. Smith is retired and lives in Seymour.

RANDOLPH J. SMITH II, World War II, United States Army, was born September 23, 1923 in Marion County, but moved with his family as a child when they relocated to Seymour. On May 8, 1943 he was drafted and reported to Ft. Harrison for induction into the army. He was sent to Camp Crowder for basic training and then assigned to the 189th Signal Repair Company. He received further training in communications and radio-phone repair.

He was shipped overseas to England in 1943 and based in Camp G-25 before leaving for France. His company was broken and he was assigned to an antiaircraft battery and later to the 36th Infantry Division which fought all through Germany. Following V-E Day he was slated for re-deployment to the CBI but the order was never issued because of

the Atomic Bombs which ended the war. He was then diverted to Belgium and finally back to the States.

He arrived at Camp Patrick Henry and was sent on to Camp Atterbury where he was discharged on January 16, 1946.

RAY T. SMITH, World War II, United States Navy, volunteered for the United States Navy during W.W. II and served from July 14, 1942 until honorably discharged on May 21, 1945. He was stationed at Norfolk, Virginia, Sampson, New York and Lido Beach, Long Island, New York during his service. Rating at discharge was Chief Specialist (A) (T), Service Number 626 63 20.

After service, Mr. Smith continued his career as a teacher. He taught and coached at Clearspring High School and retired from Brownstown Central School System in 1977. He was also a part time farmer. He was a member of Washington Masonic Lodge at Brownstown, Indiana.

He was born at Surprise, Indiana, on May 20, 1912, the son of William A.J. Smith and Dora Carter Smith. He married Marilyn Cummings Smith on June 11, 1948 and they had four children, Susan, Thomas, Jerry and Debra Smith. He died on November 5, 1988 in Seymour, Indiana and is buried at Riverview Cemetery.

THOMAS G. SMITH, World War II, United States Army, was a son of Frank and Oma Patrick Smith. He was a big, strong and one-eyed veteran who was an honor guard for MacArthur in Japan and who served in the South Pacific and in Korea.

Tom Smith retired from the army after 26 years of patriotic service. He re-enlisted after his first discharge because the government offered each veteran 52/20 allowance for adjustment to civilian life. That meant one year at $20 per week for substance. When he went to sign for the final check, he was not allowed to sign for the payment.

He re-enlisted in the army to make it a life career. During his service time he was awarded various medals and ribbons, along with 2 Purple Hearts for his being wounded.

WALTER A. "RED" SMITH, World War II, United States Army, volunteered for the United States Army during W.W. II. He was stationed in England, when he received a serious head injury when a German bomb hit the building where he was serving. After months in an English hospital, he was sent back to the States to continue his recovery at Camp Atterbury. He was awarded the Purple Heart for his service and sacrifice.

Prior to volunteering for the Army, Mr. Smith had been a school teacher. He was unable to return to his career after the war due to his injury. He was a member of the Washington Masonic Lodge at Brownstown, Indiana.

He was born in 1909 at Surprise, Indiana, to William A.J. Smith and Dora Carter Smith. He never married. Nephews and nieces were Susan, Thomas, Jerry and Debra Smith. He died in 1989 in Seymour, Indiana and is buried in Riverview Cemetery.

WAYLAND SMITH, World War II, United States Army, Company M, 119th Infantry, BSM & PH. Currently resides in Tampico, Indiana.

C. LOUIS SOMMERS, World War II, United States Navy, was born July 27, 1926 in Brownstown as a son of George H. and Essie Hurley Sommers. He attended and graduated from Brownstown High School with the class of 1944. Almost immediately, he enlisted in the U.S. Navy. After being assigned serial number #293 70 10 he was sent to Camp Perry in Virginia where he completed his boot camp training during mid-summer of 1944. He was assigned to the mine sweeper, the USS *Conqueror*. C. Louis Sommers was aboard ship until the end of World War II. His ship was then decommissioned.

Later, he was assigned to the Minesweeping Base located in Charleston, South Carolina. He was assigned duty as an aide to the Commander of Officer's Intake Station centered at that base until time for his discharge in July 1946 as Boatswain Mate 2nd Class.

Upon his release from the service, Louis Sommers entered Indiana Central College. He graduated and was granted his B.S. degree. He was awarded his M.S. degree from Indiana University. He was employed by the local school corporation as teacher, coach and administrator, retiring in 1988.

He married Helen Suzanne King (deceased) and they became parents of three sons, Gale, Mark and Brian. He later married Darline L. Nierman and they reside on Jodi Drive in Brownstown, Indiana.

G. HENRY SOMMERS, World War II, United States Air Force, 15th B-17 Flying Fortress Bomb Group, Distinguished Flying Cross. G. Henry Sommers was called to service in February 1943, shortly after he had married his high school sweetheart, a girl named Helen Otte. Assigned as a co-pilot on one of the B-17 Flying Fortress Bombers, he was shipped overseas assured the planes would be waiting for his squadron when they arrived in Italy at the port of Naples.

In the meantime, he and the crew members of his unit boarded train bound for Camp Patrick Henry located near Norfolk; Virginia. The men were herded onto a German-built ship named USS *Athos* sailing among a large convoy heading for an unknown destination.

Eventually his bomb group was stationed at a base located not far from Naples. From there he was destined to fly 35 missions over Germany, the Balkans, Austria and southern France. His plane was hit on one mission and he barely was able to make it back to his base. When he completed his tour of duty, he was the awarded the prestigious DFC. (Distinguished Flying Cross)

Henry Sommers returned home, completed his degree from Indiana Central College in 1949 and became a teacher in the Brownstown School Corporation.

ALVIE SONS

ALVIE SONS, World War II, United States Army, served in the United States Army from November 8, 1942 till September 2, 1945. Alvie was born July 24, 1921, in Medora to Nick and Mabel Sons. He attended school in Medora.

His basic training was at Camp Wheeler, in Macon, GA. Alvie earned the rank of Buck Sergeant.

He served during World War II with 39th Infantry, 9th Division, Company E. An editorial in the *Boston Globe* said this of the 9th Division: "If any unit has earned the right to be called Hitler's Nemesis it is the U.S. 9th Division. Here is an outfit that really thrives on tough opposition. America has reason to be proud of this superb fighting unit."

Alvie received the following awards for his services: 5 Bronze Stars, Purple Heart, Oakleaf Cluster and Good Conduct Medal. He was wounded June 24, 1944 in France and also October 26, 1944 in Germany.

Alvie served in five major battles: Tunisia, Sicily, Normandy, Northern France and Rhineland. His unit took 60,852 prisoners during the war.

Alvie was married to Betty Gallion, who is deceased. He is the father of 3 children: Carl of Brownstown; Charlotte of Columbus; and Carolyn, deceased.

Alvie resides in Medora where he is a member of the Medora Pentecostal Church.

JESSE F. SOVERN

JESSE F. SOVERN, World War II, United States Army Air Corps, was born October 18, 1923 and raised in the Clearspring area of Jackson County and later graduated from the local high school. He was drafted and inducted into the Air Corps February 27, 1943 at Indianapolis. He was sent to Louisville and then to St. Petersburg, FL for processing into five service schools for further training.

Two years later in 1945, he was sent to the Pacific Theater and arrived in Guam and assigned to the 24th Bomb Squadron of the 20th Air Force under

General Lemay. He served in 14 combat missions on a B-29 bomber and four additional supply missions. He flew as a tail gunner and radar operator on missions from Tinian over Japan and return which was a distance of 3,400 miles. On his final mission he flew cover for MacArthur receiving the Japanese aboard the *Missouri*.

His missions earned two Unit Citations, two Air Medals and a host of ribbons Including two Good Conduct Medals.

He was discharged at Camp Atterbury November 21, 1945 and returned to Jackson County where he married Helen Sherrill. They operated the Ashland Filling Station and distribution service in Brownstown.

ROBERT SPEER

ROBERT SPEER, World War II, United States Army Air Corps, was born in Seymour, Indiana, on July 25, 1922, to Gilbert W. Speer and Ethel Booker Speer. "Bob" had two brothers, Lloyd Speer and Gilbert Speer, Jr. He graduated from Brownstown, High School with the Class of 1940.

On November 4, 1940, in Indianapolis, he enlisted in the Army Air Corps and was immediately sent to Maxwell Field, Montgomery, Alabama, for basic training, to Chanute Field, Rantoul, Illinois for aircraft mechanic training, then on to Jeffersonville Barracks, St. Louis, Missouri to await assignment to air school. With the Class of 42-1 Robert E. Speer was graduated from Flight School at Air Corps Training Detachment, Brady Aviation School, Inc., Curtis Field, Texas.

Bob's next assignment was ferrying bombers from Natal, Brazil, South America, to North Africa. After nine months of ferrying bombers he returned home to Brownstown to marry Olive Huber. Lt. Speer then returned to active duty and lost his life in Natal, Brazil, when his plane crashed on June 7, 1944.

EDGAR SPRAGUE

EDGAR SPRAGUE, World War II, United States Army Air Corps, was born in 1906 at Freetown, the son of Thomas and Theresa Sprague. He later graduated from Freetown. High School. He earned his MA Degree from IU in 1952. He completed forty-six years as a teacher in Jackson County Schools. He was drafted into the armed forces even though he was married to Lois Fish of Clearspring on September 25, 1941. To them were born two daughters.

Edgar Sprague completed his basic training at St. Petersburg, Florida and was assigned to teaching math lectures to 800 other inductees at the same time. He tested and qualified for officer training, but elected to accept Weather School training so he could be stationed at Chanute Field, Illinois so he could be home for the birth of one of his children. Eventually

he was sent to Arizona as a weather observer plotting data of maps of various US Cities. Such information was critical and he was often at work 16 hours per day. He was always looking forward to shorter work time.

After two years and following Hiroshima, he received his discharge, and at the request of residents in Freetown, he returned to his original teaching position filled with memories of his service to his beloved nation.

JAMES W. SPURGEON

JAMES W. SPURGEON, World War II, United States Army, 230th General Hospital Corps, was born December 29, 1914 to James and Lillie Weathers Spurgeon. He graduated from Brownstown High School in 1933. He then completed his education and graduated from Indiana Business College in 1936, before becoming deputy clerk of the state treasurer's office under Joseph Robertson. He later became the chief licensing officer with the Indiana State Insurance Department.

In 1940 he purchased the Gunder Insurance Agency in Brownstown and operated it until he was drafted into the army in 1942. He completed basic training at Fort Harrison and was assigned to the 230th General Hospital Corps. His unit served overseas in France where he became company clerk. He was able to receive further training at Nice before returning to the States. He was discharged in 1946 and returned home to Brownstown to resume his insurance business.

Although married to Pauline Dawson, and with a family of 3 children, James W. Spurgeon was elected to the Indiana House of Representatives in 1947. He served four terms before being elected to the state Senate. In addition, he served as Lyons Club District Governor, and was a 50-year member of the local club, American Legion, Knights of Pythias, Scottish Rite, Masonic Lodge, Seymour Elks Club and the Seymour Country Club.

He was the recipient of various awards, including the Sagamore of the Wabash, named a Kentucky Colonel and served as the Parade Grand Marshal for the Brownstown Watermelon Festival.

RALPH L. SPURGEON

RALPH L. SPURGEON, World War II, United States Army, born June 20, 1926 to Earl and Nell Wheeler Spurgeon who lived not far from Brownstown. He attended elementary grades at the Honeytown school and graduated from Cortland Hugh School in 1944.

Six months later he was drafted and inducted into the army. He reported to Camp Joseph T. Robinson, Arkansas for his basic training. He arrived at Fort Meade, Maryland on May 27, 1945; nineteen days after V-E Day was declared.

Since troops were no longer needed in Europe, he was sent to Camp Howze, Texas and from there he would be shipped overseas to the Pacific Theater of Operations. Orders came July 18, 1945 and he left from Fort Ord, California bound for Manila in the Philippine Islands. His unit arrived just after V-J Day was proclaimed September 2, 1945.

He served 16 months with the 28th and 10th Special Services Companies before being discharged as a T/Sgt. on December 16, 1946.

He returned home to the family farm, and later married his high school sweetheart, Vivian Kuehn. Vows were exchanged January 28, 1951 and they became parents of three children, Paul, Jill Weber and Laura Lamb.

He entered the banking business and retired after 33 years.

ALVIN M. STAHL, World War II, United States Army, born in Jackson County to Nathan and Marie Stahl on a farm located in the Wegan area of Brownstown Township. He was product of the local schools and, at age 18 years, he was drafted into the army. He was sent to Camp Atterbury for initial processing before being ordered to Camp Lee in Virginia. It was there where he would complete his basic training.

He was then sent to Camp Bowie, Texas for further training before he was assigned to the medics. Upon completing specialized training, he was made part of the dental clinic staff at Camp Hood, Texas. His duties included treating the soldiers and the wives of officers assigned to the military post.

He was discharged in August 1946 with the rank of Sergeant.

He married Doris Darin in 1954; they became parents of 2 daughters named Patricia and Carolyn.

ERVIN H.A. STAHL, World War II, United States Navy, born 21 September 1924 son of Henry C.G. and Ruth (Mitschke) Stahl. Grew up on the Mitschke-Stahl Farm in the Wagen community. Graduated from Tampico H.S. 6 May 1943.

Entered active duty with the US Navy on 21 June 1943. After seven weeks of Boot Camp at Great Lakes, entered Class "A" Gunnery School, graduating 22 November 1943 as S1/c.

Transferred to Advanced Gunnery School at Treasure Island, California, graduating on 26 February 1944 as Gunners Mate 3rd Class. Reported to Anti-Aircraft Training Center, Shell Beach, Louisiana as an Anti-Aircraft Gunnery Instructor. This training facility had anti-aircraft practice firing 365 days per year, plus night firing on Tuesdays and Thursdays. Those receiving Anti-Aircraft Training

included Navy, Coast Guard, Army and Merchant Marine personnel from 46 different types of ships. Among foreign nationalities represented were British, French, Dutch, Russian and Norwegian. Weapons in use ranged from 50 caliber machine guns to 5" 38 caliber cannons.

On 20 April 1945 reported on board the USS *Roy O. Hale* (DE-336) as a Gunners Mate 2/c. Made a convoy run to Southampton, England and returned. Visited Guantanamo Bay, Cuba in July, 1945, followed by passage through the Panama Canal, and on to San Diego, and ultimately Pearl Harbor. Left the Hawaiian Islands 10 October 1945 for San Diego, another passage through the Panama Canal, and on to Norfolk.

The USS *Roy O. Hale* (DE-336) then made passage to Green Cove Springs, Florida in December 1945 for moth balling and decommissioning. He was discharged from the US Navy at Great Lakes on 8 April 1946.

ROBERT EDWARD STAHL, World War II, United States Army Air Corps, enlisted in the service on October 15, 1942. Selected to serve in the United States Air Force, he received training at Victory Field, Mississippi, Vernon, Texas and Blackland Army Airfield in Kansas. Robert graduated with the class of 44D on April 15, 1944. Subsequently he was commissioned 2nd Lt.

In June, 1944 Robert was sent to China, Burma, India Theater. As a pilot of a PBY airplane he was sent on a British gunnery mission near Bombay, India. He and his crew of 12 were killed on September 12, 1944.

Robert was born in Grassy Fork Township, son of Edward and Delia Stahl on July 14, 1921. He attended St. Paul Lutheran School and Tampico High School graduating with the class of 1939. Studied home-training courses from Patterson School of New York City and the Anthony Wayne School of Fort Wayne. He worked at Allison Manufacturing plant in Indianapolis and attended Roscoe Turner Aerial School in Indianapolis before enlisting in the service.

2nd Lt. Stahl is buried in the military cemetery at Fort Scott, Kansas. All members of the crew arranging from California to New York are buried together.

PVT. RALPH STEINKAMP, United States Army, First Jackson County Casualty in World War II, son of Fred and Ida Steinkamp, was born in Grassy Fork Township in 1920. He graduated from Brownstown High School with the class of 1939. He was then employed by Kieffer Paper Mill until he left for service with the United States Army. He was inducted January 16, 1943.

He completed his basic training at Camp Wheeler, GA and shortly thereafter, he was shipped overseas and assigned to the Italian Theater of

Operations. He was wounded in action and died November 3, 1943.

Ralph Steinkamp was survived by his mother, Ida.

HAROLD STUCKWISCH, World War II, United States Army, born June 30, 1924 in the Sauers area to William and Clara Benter Stuckwisch. He assisted his father on the family farm until joining the U.S. Army September 7, 1944. After completing basic infantry training in Fort McClellan, Alabama, he was assigned overseas to the European Theater of Operations, World War II.

He served with K Company, 276th Infantry Regiment, 70th Division as an automatic rifleman. He participated in the Rhineland Campaign in February and March of 1945 and in the Central Europe Campaign for the following seven months. At the end of that time he became an Administrative Non-Commissioned Officer for K Company. He held the rank of First Sergeant and supervised the staff in preparation of correspondence, payroll, and various military records and reports. After about eight months in this position, he returned to the USA and received an honorable discharge on June 29, 1946.

Military honors included the Combat Infantry Badge, Rifle Sharpshooter Badge, Good Conduct Medal, WWII Victory Medal, Occupation Medal/ Germany, and the E.A.M.E, (European-Africa-Middle Eastern) Theater Ribbon with two Bronze Service Stars, one for each of the two campaigns in which he participated.

In 1947 he married Myrtle Jean Wehrkamp and assumed operation of his father's farm. They have five children: one daughter, Sharon Rohr, and four sons, Tom, Max, Dennis and Jeff. Harold was later employed by the County Highway Department and then Jackson County Farm Bureau Co-op until his death in August 1974.

DONALD W. STURGEON, World War II, United States Army, residence is 5647 South State Road 39 Brownstown. Born January 1, 1925 near Brownstown, Indiana. Drafted and inducted April 3, 1943, 35701087, 3rd Division Recon Group sent to North Africa.

Saw action in Italy; on limited service; returned to the United States; transferred to the Air Corps. Discharged December 4, 1945.

THOMAS C. SUTTON, World War II, United States Army, son to George and Flora Gorbett Sutton.

Served September 3, 1943-October 17, 1945, European Theater of Operations. Discharged at Camp Atterbury. Awarded Word War II Victory Medal. Died January 18, 1992 in Tennessee

GERALD G. SWEANY, World War II, United States Army Air Corps, born December 11, 1922 at Seymour in Jackson County. Inducted December 2, 1942 at Fort Harrison. Completed basic training in Florida. Trained at Lowry Field in Colorado. Assigned as a tail gunner.

Shipped overseas to the CBI Theater of Operations Saw action flying over the hump. Discharged December 28, 1945 at Camp Atterbury. Awarded American Theater Ribbon, Pacific Ribbon w/4 Campaign Stars, WWII Victory Medal and Good Conduct Medal.

Returned to Seymour and employment at Arvin. Married Myrtle Hackman of Tampico. Parents of three children.

LESTER W. SWENGEL, World War II, United States Army, born July 24, 1922 near Reddington to Clyde and Flora Swengel. He attended elementary grades in the local school. Graduated from Shields High School in Seymour in 1940.

Enlisted in the army and was trained at Fort Lewis, WA. Selected to join the Air Corps, but it was canceled. He was needed at Fort Campbell as the chief gunner, 62nd Armored Infantry Battalion.

Shipped overseas to Marseilles and pushed northward. Stormed the Siegfried Line and crossed the Rhine River. Occupied southern Germany before being sent home. Discharged February 1946

Awarded the Bronze Star Medal for heroic duty at Bannstein Forest.

Returned to Reddington with his bride, Wilma. Became parents of three daughters.

Survived farm work and mail delivery until his death in 1986.

HUGH J. TANKSLEY, World War II, United States Army, born in Kentucky to Hugh and Sophia Hyden Tanksley. He was drafted into the army and inducted at Fort Harrison, Indianapolis on June 10, 1941. He was assigned to Company M, 143rd Infantry Division as a heavy machine gunner.

His unit was shipped overseas to the European Theater of Operations and he saw action at Naples, Rome/Arno, the Rhineland and Central Europe. He was wounded and received the Purple Heart in September 1943 and granted his discharge August 1, 1945.

He was awarded medals and ribbons reflecting his service. He returned home and lived with his uncle in Frankfort. Later he married Loretta Smallwood Tanksley and they became parents of a son. He lived in Tampico for a time and at the death of his wife he moved to Hamilton, Ohio.

DONALD L. TATLOCK, Indiana National Guard, Company B, 138th Tank Battalion, 38th Infantry Division, born at Mt. Sidney in Grassy Fork Township to Kerry and Marie Wolff Tatlock in 1930. He graduated from Tampico High School and later was married to Betty June Waskom.

Tatlock enlisted in the 138th Tank Battalion of the Indiana National Guard at Freeman Field. Later he was sent to OCS at Fort Riley, Kansas where he was commissioned a 2nd Lt. in the Armored Unit station at Fort Knox in Kentucky.

Donald L. Tatlock was past president of the Jackson County Historical Society.

ERVIN LLOYD THOMPSON, World War II, United States Army, born at Kossuth in Washington County in 1924, the son of Harry and Amanda Holsapple Thompson. Much later he was drafted into the army. After completing his basic training he was shipped overseas to the European Theater of Operations. During the winter of 1944 his feet were frozen while confined to a foxhole in Belgium.

He was evacuated to a field hospital in France and then transferred back to the states where he recovered at Camp McClellan. Four long months later, he was granted his discharge in August 1945, classified as a disabled veteran with a lifetime pension.

Ervin Thompson married Thelma Pauline McMahon at Salem in 1945 but they lived in Freetown. They became parents of two children. He retired from Arvin Industries in 1986.

BERNARD TIEMEYER, World War II, United States Army, born November 18, 1920 at Vallonia, inducted into army October 17, 1942 at Louisville. Trained as truck driver/mechanic, 5000th International Truck Regiment.

Shipped overseas to European Theater of Operations. Saw action in France, the Ardennes and Central Europe.

Awarded the EAME Ribbon w/4 Campaign Stars, WWII Victory Medal and Good Conduct Medal.

Discharged January 5, 1946.

LOUIS E. TORBORG, World War II, United States Army, born February 4, 1908 and went into the army early in 1942 and served honorably during the 2nd World War. Records verify he returned to his home and died February 22, 1972.

ELMER W. TORMOEHLEN, World War II, United States Army, born January 24, 1918 on a farm located between Brownstown and Crothersville. He attended grammar school in the area. He was drafted and inducted into the army at age 24 years when he reported for duty in Louisville on June 4, 1942.

He was trained as a field lineman and assigned to the 71st Joint Assault Signal Company. Following further training, his unit was shipped overseas to the southern Philippines and later back to French Morocco where he became part of the European Theater of American forces. He saw action at Normandy, Sicily and Naples/Foggia.

His ship was docked offshore at Omaha Beach and was sunk just after the men reached shore. They had only the clothes they were wearing and few weapons and equipment.

His unit was returned to the states in October 1944 for preparation to be shipped out to the Pacific Theater. He was among those who reached the destination on March 10, 1945. After the atomic bombs were dropped, he was returned to the states. He received his discharge October 3, 1945 at Camp Atterbury.

HERBERT L. TRIMPE, World War II, United States Army, born February 2, 1912 in Jackson County to Martin and Clara Schafstall Trimpe. After graduating from the local high school in Seymour in 1935, he was employed by Noblitt-Sparks Industries as a foreman until the war broke loose at Pearl Harbor in 1941.

He was inducted into the service shortly thereafter, and was sent to Fort Knox for basic training. He was assigned to one of the heavy tank units in the army then ready to be shipped overseas to the European Theater of Operations.

He was engaged in combat during the battles for Normandy, Ardennes, Rhineland and Central Europe. His discharge lists the medals and ribbons he was authorized to wear, reflecting the several campaigns in which his unit was a party.

Married to Elsie Schepman, he returned to his home as a farmer after receiving his discharge. He was quite active in various groups of the area, including his membership at Zion Lutheran Church and as a director of Camp Lakeview. He was the father of two daughters and had six grandchildren. He died early in October 1995.

LAWRENCE LEWIS TRIMPE, World War II, United States Army, Company E, 399th Infantry

Regiment, 7th Army, born September 19, 1924 to Fred and Mary Schafstall Trimpe of Seymour. He was the youngest of three brothers to be drafted into the army on September 7, 1944.

He completed basic training at Fort McClellan, Alabama, traveled to New York and was shipped overseas on the *Queen Elizabeth* to England. From there he was shipped to France where he spent nearly two months before crossing into Germany.

As a sergeant he spent 76 days on the front line, and was one of two men in his company who first crossed the Siegfried Line. Tom earned two Bronze Campaign Stars for his service. Somehow, all four Trimpe brothers returned home safely after the war.

He was discharged July 26, 1946 and returned to his home near Seymour. After becoming a farmer of note, he started his own excavation company which he operated for 45 years. In 1973 he constructed the Sandy Creek Golf Course which he opened to the public in 1976.

He has been active in community affairs, but now enjoys retirement with his wife, two Maltese dogs, six miniature horses, 3 grown step-children and three step-grandsons.

2ND LT. LEONARD H. TRIMPE, 741st Tank Battalion, United States Army, 35252567, D-Day Landing to V-E Day German Surrender, 5 Campaigns in the European Theater.

Silver Star Citation: "Sergeant Leonard H. Trimpe (ASN 35252567) of the 741st Tank Battalion, United States Army. For gallantry in action near Viervilla-sur-Mer, France, 6 June 1944. Sergeant Trimpe, commander of a tank recovery vehicle, successfully landed on the enemy-held coast of France with the initial assault wave of allied troops. Under heavy enemy machine gun, mortar and artillery fire, he dismounted from his vehicle and remained for several hours in full view of the enemy while he repaired an immobilized tank. By his service, valuable equipment was returned to combat, thus aiding materially in the successful establishment of the beachhead. This gallant action by Sergeant Trimpe reflects great credit upon himself and upon the Military Service. He entered the military service from Seymour, Indiana."

Awarded by Major General W.M. Robertson, U.S. 2nd Infantry Division.

OMER H. TRIMPE, World War II, United States Army, born in 1919, the eldest child of Fred and Mary Trimpe, and raised on a farm located east of Seymour. He was married to Thelma Kasting in 1941, and one year later was inducted into the army. He completed basic training in Wyoming and was first assigned to the 478th Quartermaster, but was later transferred to the 368th Engineers of the 3rd Army. He served in England, France, Belgium, Holland and Germany, constructing roads and bridges from Utah Beach during the advance of the Allied Forces.

Omer Trimpe had three brothers, including Leonard, Carl and Lawrence, serving in Europe at the same time. He was discharged in November 1945 and returned to the States and back to the farm, intending to resume work with his father-in-law, Ernest Kasting. But the family farm and two homes, including the new house he and Thelma had moved into in 1942, had been condemned in 1942 for the construction of Freeman Field. Indeed, Omer reached home to a different life because the Trimpe family was among other German-speaking families forced to move from their farms. Fortunately, the family salvaged what they could, stored materials and rebuilt a home on a farm located near Cortland following the war.

Omer Trimpe and his family maintained contact with an English family he met and he and his wife were able to visit them during their tour through England and Normandy in 1980. He was even able to locate the apple orchard where the 368th Engineers had camped during the winter of 1944.

He died on his farm in 1999 and his farm was later placed on the US Department of Interior's National Register of Historic Homes in 2003. His only child is Mary Elisabeth Trimpe Keller, and his only grandchild is Anne Keller.

ALVA TROWBRIDGE, World War II, United States Navy, born to Virgil and Amy Miller Trowbridge in 1923. He graduated from Vallonia High School and enlisted in the navy. Reporting to Great Lakes Naval Station, he completed boot camp training and was assigned to the USS *Warrington*. Later he was ordered to attend water tender school in 1944.

He was then ordered aboard the USS *Oklahoma City* and served in her until the end of the war in the Pacific Theater of Operations on September 2, 1945.

He returned to the states and was granted his discharge in October of 1945. He came on home to Brownstown and was married to Anna Wheeler and they became parents of three children. Both parents are dead, but the place of burial remains unknown.

LINDY TROWBRIDGE, World War II, United States Navy, born June 12, 1928 to Virgil and Ann Miller Trowbridge. He attended school in Vallonia and enlisted in the navy almost immediately.

Records show his service was rendered in the United States. He received his discharge at Great Lakes Naval Station and was issued a World War II Victory Medal.

JAMES W. TUNGEITT, World War II, United States Army Air Corps, born June 30, 1920 in Jennings County and later attended North Vernon High School. He enlisted at Fort Harrison December 9, 1941 and received training at Jefferson Barracks, MO and at Foster Field, TX and placed on general guard duty. Much later he volunteered for overseas duty. He was assigned to a Replacement Depot in Salt Lake City.

He was shipped overseas from New York to the European Theater of Operations. He arrived in England in April 1944 and on D-Day was sent to Omaha Beach. He participated and served in Normandy, Rhineland and Central Europe campaigns. When V-E Day came he was near the Austrian border with a detachment of Army Air Corps planes.

He returned to the states and was scheduled to be sent to the Pacific, but Japan surrendered and he was ordered to Camp Atterbury to receive his discharge on September 17, 1945.

KEITH ERNEST WAGGONER, World War II, United States Army, born near Freetown on April 9, 1918 to John and Josie Bowman Waggoner. He graduated from Freetown High School in 1936 and, as the youngest of three boys, he was inducted into the army on April 2, 1941 at Louisville.

He became a military police officer serving with Company A, 601st Tank Destroyer Battalion. His unit participated in Normandy, the Rhineland and Central Europe. After more than a year of service overseas, he was authorized to wear various ribbons and medals.

He was discharged at Camp Atterbury October 23, 1945. He was married to Leona Woodfill Wingham in 1947 and they became parents of an only daughter, Eileen Goss, who resides in Bloomington, IN. He took part in the D-Day invasion of Normandy and, at the 50th anniversary, he spoke very softly when he said "I was there."

WALTER JOHN WALDKOETTER, World War II, United States Army, born August 5, 1915 to John and Mary Altemeyer Waldkoetter. Graduated from Tampico High School. Employed by Noblitt-Sparks Industries.

Inducted into the army January 12, 1942. Completed basic training at Fort Knox. Further training in Louisiana, California and New Jersey.

Shipped overseas to England and trained as a tank driver. Company W, 741st Tank Battalion of 2nd Army. Killed in action during first assault on D-Day, June 6, 1944. Awarded Purple Heart and Good Conduct Medal. Buried at St. Laurent, France.

LEBERT B. WALKER, World War II, United States Navy, born in Jackson County August 8, 1916 to William and Rebecca Weddell Walker. He was drafted and inducted into the navy and reported for duty at Great Lakes Naval Station. After completing boot camp training he was assigned as a Motor Pool Auto Mechanic, Class 1.

Four years later on November 29, 1945 he was discharged from Great Lakes Naval Station. When he reached home he was married to Ruby Nichter but they were divorced later. He married Mildred Bridges and moved to Crothersville.

He had a collection of guns and knives which were always on display. He never became a father but was fond of telling stories about his forebears, Joab Scott and Scott Weddell, who fought in the Civil War.

LOYD A. WALLACE, WWII and Korea, United States Army, born September 27, 1923 in Indianapolis, Indiana and is the son of Floyd and Letha Wallace. At the age of 5 his family moved to rural Jackson County. He attended Tampico School.

On February 8, 1943 he was inducted into the United States Army. Loyd took his basic training at Camp Clayborn, Louisiana. Shortly after he was assigned overseas to the European Theater. He served in the 463rd Engineer Co. as a heavy equipment operator technician fifth grade. He was honorably discharged as a corporal on January 18, 1946.

He re-entered the United States Army December 7, 1948. He trained troops at Breckinridge, KY. He was assigned overseas to Japan with the 7th Infantry Division in the Headquarters Company as a heavy equipment operator and truck driver. He spent 11 months in Japan before the start of the Korean War. At the start of the Korean War he was with the ATC Amphibious Landing Company. He served 16 months overseas duty in the Korean Theater and was discharged as a corporal on June 3, 1952.

In 1953 he married Wilma R. Williams, and they have two children, Ellen Wallace of Crothersville and Donna Wallace of Seymour. He still resides on the farm in rural Jackson County where his family moved in 1928.

EDMOND E. WAYMAN, World War II, United States Army, born October 24, 1920 at Brownstown. His parents were Carl and Hazel Fountain Wayman. He was raised at the county seat and graduated Brownstown High School. He was employed as a fireman by the B&O Railroad.

Inducted into the army May 19, 1944 at Fort Harrison. Completed basic training near New Orleans. Shipped overseas to European Theater of Operations. Assigned to Hq. Co., 765th Railway Shop Battalion. Saw action during the Battle of the Bulge.

Returned to the states July 3, 1945. Discharged in Arkansas December 19, 1945. Awarded the EAME Ribbon with Campaign Star, Good Conduct Medal and American Theater Ribbon.

Returned to Brownstown and became a building contractor. Partner in Wayman Brothers Supply Company. Was married to Edith Dason. Parents of two daughters.

ROBERT CHARLES WAYMAN, World War II, United States Army, born at Brownstown November 23, 1924. Parents were Carl and Hazel Fountain Wayman. Graduated from Brownstown High School in 1942.

Inducted into the army October 7, 1944 at Indianapolis. Completed basic training in South Carolina. Shipped

overseas to the European Theater of Operations. Assigned to Company B, 55th Armored Infantry Battalion, 11th Armored Division. Saw action as a rifleman in the Rhineland.

Remained in the Army of Occupation after V-E Day. Discharged August 24, 1946

Awarded WW II Victory Medal, EAME Theater Ribbon w/2 Campaign Stars, German Occupation Medal, and Good Conduct Medal.

Returned home and started life as a farmer. Became a partner in a construction company. Salesman for Wholesale Electric Company.

Married Phyllis E. Mulberry July 11, 1947. Parents of three children.

ROBERT E. WEAVER, World War II, United States Navy, born February 9, 1924 to Ralph and Mattie Brown Weaver at Ewing, Indiana. He was raised in and around Brownstown. He entered the navy December 10, 1943 and received boot camp training at Great Lakes Naval Station.

He was assigned to the USS LST 988 in Boston, Massachusetts. His ship was sent to Oran in North Africa and later his ship was part of the Anvil Invasion of Southern France. He returned to the states and was sent to the Pacific Theater of Operations.

He was stationed in Guam when the war ended. Returned to the States and received his discharge April 30, 1946. He was authorized to wear appropriate medals and ribbons reflecting his long service to his country.

He was married to Roberta Fish, and they became parents of 3 sons, Dan, Don and Doug.

CLAYTON C. WEDDEL, World War II, United States Army, born February 5, 1915 to Samuel and Daisy Weddel. He spent all his life in Jackson County. On May 14, 1938 he married Dorothy Clampitt, and they had two children, Marshall and Barbara, both are now deceased.

Inducted into army at Camp Atterbury and assigned to Company K, 157th Infantry Regiment, 29th Division on March 5, 1944. Trained 17 weeks at Camp Wolters, TX and Fort Meade, MD.

Shipped overseas in June 1944, landing in England. He then was sent to France and later to Germany. He operated a walkie-talkie, a portable field radio-telephone and was five miles within Germany with his outfit when he was wounded and then died Nov. 20, 1944.

He received the Purple Heart for Military Merit and wounds received in action. He was buried in Plot G, Row 1, Grave 15 in US Military Cemetery at Margratin, Holland. Later his body was returned to Medora and buried in the Liberty Cemetery, November 12, 1948.

MARVIN HILMAN WEDDLE, World War 1947, United States Military Police, born February 10, 1917 to Harry and Alice Main Weddle. He attended Mt. Zion School before graduating from Clearspring High School in 1935.

He was drafted and inducted into the army at Louisville, KY, just after Christmas in 1942. He left Indianapolis for Camp Maxie, in Texas where he was assigned to the Military Police. His unit was assigned to pull guard duty of the oceanfront docks in and around New York City.

After the German prisoners were captured, many were returned to the states and the MP units were assigned to accompany them to specified camps. Most were moved by troop trains. Marvin was once directed to pick up prisoners in Scotland and return them on a navy ship which hit a severe storm in the north Atlantic Ocean.

He was discharged on February 8, 1946 at Camp Atterbury. He and his wife, Pauline Goss Weddle, were parents of two daughters.

MELVIN "BUNK" WEDDELL, World War II, United States Navy, son of Ralph and Mabel Brown Weddell, was born near Medora, Indiana in Jackson County. A 1942 Clearspring High School graduate, he joined the Navy in 1943 and went to Great Lakes Naval Training Station for Boot Camp. His next assignment was Radio School at Northwestern University, where he graduated in the top third of his class and was promoted to Seaman 1st Class.

He traveled on a troop train bound for California. To avoid possible sabotage, the train zigzagged across the country, taking five days to reach Camp Shoemaker. Next, he was assigned to his first ship, the USS ABSD3, one of only three reparation ships of its type. Located in the San Francisco Bay between Alcatraz and the Golden Gate Bridge, this ship headed for the South Pacific. Weddell was promoted to 3rd Class and given the assignment as Confidential Radioman and Armed Carrier. While in port, his duty was to carry messages from ship to shore and vice-versa. He was selected for officer's school, flew home, and then to Princeton University. After a few months, he resigned from school and was reassigned to the Philadelphia Naval Yard, where he played left field for the Navy baseball team (Coastal or East Coast League). Several major/minor league players were on the team. Weddell was sent to New York and assigned to his second ship, the USS *Taconic,* flagship for an Atlantic amphibious group. The USS *Taconic* had a 2-star Admiral in charge. Here, Weddell was made a Radio Supervisor for one shift, up until his time of discharge based on the point system. (One point was awarded for each month of duty in the states; two points awarded for each month on ship or overseas). He left this ship at Norfolk and went back to Great Lakes for discharge in 1946.

In 1948, he married Nellie Reynolds. They have two children, Brenda Weddell and Mrs. Larry (Janice) Claycamp, three grandchildren, and six great-grandchildren. Melvin joined the Indiana State Police, retiring after thirty-three years. He and Nellie now reside near Medora on the farm where he was raised.

ROBERT C. WELLS (on the right), World War II, United States Army, was born February 21, 1920 in Rensselaer, Indiana. Upon reaching the age of majority, he volunteered for the military service.

He reported for duty in Georgia and completed basic training. Being assigned to an ordinance unit, he was on immediate alert for overseas duty. He was shipped out to the European Theater of Operations and stationed in England.

On June 11, 1944 he was sent to Normandy and stationed behind the front not far from Caen. He turned out to be a card shark and often won. Consequently, he was able to loan the commanding officer money to buy supplies. Hence, the first lend-lease among the troops.

He was discharged in December 1945 and needed to take the bus home. The driver offered him free travel as a veteran but he declined; he was a civilian once again and paid his fare.

In February 1946 he married Anne Morrone; ten years later they moved to Brownstown and raised their four children.

GOVERNOR EDGAR D. WHITCOMB,

World War II, United States Army Air Corps, was born November 6, 1917 at Hayden in Jennings County to John W. and Louise Whitcomb. After he graduated from high school, he entered Indiana University at Bloomington. He attended classes until the outbreak of World War II following the attack on Pearl Harbor. He enlisted in the Air Corps.

He was trained and served as a navigator on a B-17 Fortress Bomber. Ed Whitcomb was captured by the Japanese, taken prisoner and remained under guard for nearly two years. Following V-J Day he completed his studies at Indiana University and was granted his degree in law. He then practiced law in Seymour and North Vernon before opening his Office in Indianapolis.

He was elected a state senator and, during the political campaign, he met and married Pat Dolfuss in mid-1951. Ed Whitcomb published a book entitled *"Escape from Corregidor."* The story evolved around his assuming the identity of another man. He was elected governor of the state of Indiana and served as the chief executive from 1968 to 1973.

Later he ran for state senator but was defeated by Richard Lugar.

REED WILLIAMS, World War II, United States

Army, was born near Spraytown in 1914 to Louis and Mae McKain Williams. He was employed by Cummins Engine Company during the years following Pearl Harbor, so he was granted several deferments. But he finally felt obligated to serve his country. He joined the army in 1943. After basic training, he was shipped overseas with Troop G, 12th Regiment of the 1st Cavalry Division. He fought and was wounded

in Manila and awarded the Silver Star for bravery and a Purple Heart.

Following hospitalization, he wrote home saying a metal plate had been placed in his head and he was waiting to be evacuated. But a second telegram was received indicating he had been killed in action. It stated that "on 2 April 1945 the men were attacking a hill on Luzon and Reed led host squad through pill boxes with the skills of a champion... and during the final assault Reed was hit by an enemy grenade and killed instantly... he was laid to rest with full military honors and buried in the US Army Cemetery .... while his friends stood at attention paying him last respects..."

After the war it was learned that 3 grandsons of Jackson County Civil War Veteran, George Williams, were on Luzon during WWII. Reed's family later received a citation signed by President Truman paying special attention to his bravery.

EMIL W. WINKLER, World War II, United

States Army Air Corps, was born and raised in Jackson County, a son of Clinton and Letha Winkler. He graduated from Freetown High School in 1935.

He was drafted into service in 1942 and was inducted in the Air Corps before being sent to Sheppard Field, TX for basic training. From there he was directed to various fields located in the far western states. He was then ordered to the Aleutian Islands and his tour of duty there.

After the war he was returned to Camp Atterbury and discharged January 13, 1946. He then married Gertrude Scott and to them were born two sons. Emil was in the reserves and worked at Bakalar until it closed. He transferred back to Grissom Field in 1970 and ten years later he retired. His widow lived near Peru.

ALBERT D. WOLKA, World War II, Company

B, 15th Infantry, 3rd U.S. Army, 1944-1946, a son of Daniel and Martha Borcherding Wolka of Driftwood Township, was born October 25, 1922 on a farm located three miles south of Vallonia. His youthful years were spent in Jackson County, until he was drafted into the Army at Indianapolis when he was 21 years old.

He was assigned serial number 25908075 and ordered to receive his basic training at Fort McClellan in Alabama. At completion, he was shipped overseas to the European Theater of Operations. His unit arrived in France in February of 1945. Albert Wolka participated in the Rhineland and Central European military campaigns.

Promoted, he served as a squad leader with Company "B" in the infantry and was authorized to wear the Combat Infantry Badge, along with the EAME Ribbon with 2 Bronze Battle Stars, two Overseas Uniform Stripes, the Army Occupation and Good Conduct Ribbons. Sgt. Wolka was honorably discharged at Fort Sheridan, Illinois August 1, 1946.

Albert D. Wolka returned home and was married to Gertrude Shoemaker. They became parents of six children, including 3 sons named Kevin, Brian and Terril. Their 3 daughters were named Debra Lambert, Jan Blomenberg and Susan Engelbrecht. Albert Wolka was an active member of Trinity Lutheran Church and helped organize Lutheran Central School in Brownstown. He passed away in 1988 and was buried in the Trinity Lutheran Church Cemetery.

GEORGE M. WOODSON, World War II,

United States Army, was born in Redding Township to Louis Woodson and was reared in Jackson County all of his life until he was inducted into the army October 12, 1941. Two months later the Japanese bombed Pearl Harbor.

He was shipped overseas in March 1942 and was made part of the troops going into Italy. He was killed in action November 4, 1943 and became the second Jackson County casualty of the war. Private Ralph Steinkamp of Brownstown preceded him in death, which was also in Italy.

Official word of his death was received by his sister, Mrs. Lucille Reichanba of Seymour on December 3, 1943.

ALBERT WRIGHT, JR., World War II, United

States Army. Genealogical background includes a long military heritage.

Henry and Elizabeth Shepman Claycamp arrived in the United States prior to 1840 from Venne on the Province of Hannover. They settled northwest of Tampico and purchased land in 1859. He erected a log cabin which was destined to be inherited by one of his great-grandsons named Henry Wright.

Four of the Claycamp sons served in the Grand Army of the Republic during the Civil War. Three of them never returned home from battle. William survived, returned home and his daughter, Jessie Claycamp, married Albert Wright and lived on the family farm.

Albert Wright, Jr. grew up there and graduated from Cortland High School in 1941 He was employed by Noblitt-Sparks before entering the army. He was assigned to Company H, 180th Regiment of the 45th Infantry Division. He was shipped overseas and served in Italy, but he was killed in action January 8, 1945 in Southern France.

On Memorial Day each year three American flags are placed at the Acme Cemetery honoring the military dedication of the families.

THE UNITED STATES AT WAR

WAR	CASUALTIES	COSTS
REVOLUTIONARY WAR	4,435	$100,000,000
WAR OF 1812	2,260	90,000,000
MEXICAN WAR	13,283	71,000,000
WAR BETWEEN THE STATES		
UNION FORCES	364,511	3,185,000,000
CONFEDERATE FORCES	164,812	2,000,000,000
SPANISH-AMERICAN WAR	2,446	285,000,000
WORLD WAR I	116,510	18,676,000,000
WORLD WAR II	405,399	263,000,000,000
KOREAN POLICE ACTION	54,246	67,000,000,000
VIETNAM WAR	561,480	140,825,000,000

BUT FOR THE GRACE OF GOD I COULD BE A CASUALTY

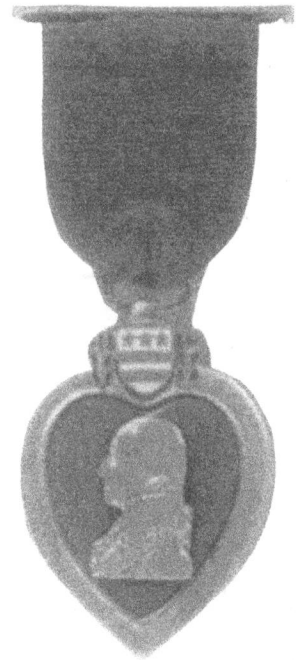

KILROY WAS HERE

THE KOREAN CONFLICT
UNITED NATIONS POLICE ACTION
JUNE 15, 1950 - JULY 27, 1953

During the five-year period of peace following WWII, unusual political events were transpiring in the United States. No one knew how this nation would deal with the outbreak of war once again! But, this was to be a different kind of war, because the world organization of nations was to play a major role in the fighting. The UN was just five years old when the North Korean forces attacked its southern neighbor in a struggle for control over the ideals of people. The bitter split of families created separate governments; the northern half was to be ruled by Communists and the southern nation was to be democratic and free!

THE TEN MOST DEADLY BATTLES

Pusan Perimeter	August 4	Sept 16, 1950	3,619
Chosen Reservoir	Nov 27	Dec 9, 1950	1,645
Kunu-ri	Nov 29	Dec 1, 1950	1,191
Naktong Advance	Sept 16	Sept 27, 1950	836
Hoengsong	Feb 11	Feb 13, 1951	773
Taejon	July 19	July 20,1951	638
Heartbreak Ridge	Sept 13	Oct 15, 1951	618
Kum Tiver	July 13	July 16, 1951	490
Unsan	Nov 1	Nov 2, 1950	454
Soyang River	May 17	May 20, 1951	406

Ecker: Database Research

THE MILITARY CASUALTIES

United States	54,246 Dead	103,284 Wounded	5,178 Missing
Chinese/Koreans	1,591,010 Dead	1,467,090 Wounded	124,082 Missing

The truce was finally signed July 27, 1953 and the fighting ended. A buffer zone two miles wide was created separating the two new nations. A military Armistice Commission was set up to enforce the terms of the truce. A permanent peace treaty has never been signed. To the loved ones of the casualties, the deadly fighting in Korea was nothing less dm all-out war. The political label of historians remains moot!

Korean Police Action
War By All Rights
Jackson County Roll Of Honor

The list of dead or missing in action during the conflict was recorded by the Adjutant General of Indiana and verified for release August 1, 1956 by John N. Owens

Name	Service No.	Branch Of Service	Home Address
ACTON, Floyd Neal	RA 23 047 724	A	R. No. 1, Cortland, Ind.
BEVERS, Lyneul	AO 1 908 996	AF	Brownstown, Indiana
BROCK, Joseph Henderson	RA 16 309 721	A	R. No. 1, Mcdora, Indiana
EDMONDS, Clarence Richard	RA 16 346 711	A	900 W. Oak, Seymour, Ind.
FARLEY, James E.	AF 15 253 731	AF	300 Jeffersonville Ave. Seymour, Indiana
HAWN, Roscoe L.	US 55 218 800	A	Crothersville, Indiana
HOLMES, John Ray Shields	US 55 178 412	A	425 Indianapolis Ave. Seymour, Indiana
KURTZ, Albert Joseph	S 906 843	A	672 Meder, Santa Cruz, Cal.
MCKAIN, Marshall Floyd	US 55 030 357	A	R. No. 1, Cortland, Indiana
ROSEMEYER, Earl George	RA 15 256 895	A	Crothersville, Indiana
SUTTON, Walter John	955 78 07	N	Box 104, Freetown, Ind-

DONALD ABNER, Post Korea, United States Air Force, was born May 19, 1934 to Robert and Maude Abner in Winchester, Kentucky. The family moved to the State of Indiana in 1935.

He entered the air force October 17, 1953 and one month later he was sent to Geneva, NY for basic training. He reported to Valdosta, Georgia for fire fighting instruction. He was assigned to the fire fighting crew at Moody AFB in Georgia, from whence he was discharged.

He returned home to the Brownstown area, was married to Mary E. Sirmans and they became parents of two sons. He retired from Keiffer Paper Mill after 39 years.

FLOYD N. ACTON, Korea, United States Army, 2nd Infantry Division, was killed in action during the Korean Conflict.

PAUL ADAMS, United States Army, Private, 8th Armored Infantry Battalion, enlisted at Indianapolis, Indiana, on the 19th day of March 1945 to serve in the United States Army. Paul "Ted" Adams was born February 14, 1920 at Norman, Indiana to James Monroe and Rosalie Cordell Adams. He married Elizabeth Williams, on December 31, 1939. They were the parents of five children: Martha Adams Killey, Mary Gail Adams Hanner, Edith Adams Hall, Harriet Jane Adams Starks, and Dennis Gene Adams.

Paul was a Marksman with the M-1 Rifle and received W.W.II Victory Medal at time of his honorable discharge on December 13, 1945. He received his discharge while stationed in California.

CARLIN J. ALLMAN, Korea, United States Army, 7th Infantry Division, was born near Acme in Hamilton Township in June 1927 and much later on September 9, 1950, he was inducted into the army with the first 13 draftees during the Korean Conflict. The group included Richard Reynolds, Marshall McKain, Charles Rucker, Bernard Bush, Paul Kilgas, Jack Haper, Raymond Vogel, Edward Ahlbrand, Jr., Chester Riley, Lynn Wehmiller, James Fox and Junior Smith.

Carlin completed his basic training at Ft. Leonard Wood, MO. He arrived in Korea in 1951 and was assigned as a rifleman in Company F of the 32nd Infantry Regiment. He and J. Herschel Forgey, a wireman with headquarters company, would see each other most every day.

Cpl. Allman returned to Ft. Leonard Wood for his final month of service as a cook in the mess hall. Before entering the service, he was employed at Arvin Industries. He and his wife, Marie Colwell of Austin, raised their family near Easyville. He is retired from Cummins.

WAYNE LEE ALLMAN, Post Korea, United States Army, born April 29, 1944 to Arnold and Mary Reynolds Allman. Graduated from Medora High School in 1962.

Entered military service in August 1965. Sent to Fort Knox for basic training. Transferred to Aberdeen Proving Grounds for advanced training.

Shipped overseas to European Theater aboard USS *Patch*. Assigned to Company C, 714th Battalion as shipping clerk.

On leave in Germany he attended Lutheran Church and was baptized.

Returned to the states in August 1967. Married Mary Johnson and became father of 2 children.

JERRY W. ARMSTRONG, born June 25, 1953 in Weisbaden, Germany as the son of George J. and Bernice Snyder Armstrong. The family returned to the United States the following year. His father was serving his military time as a career NCO and they lived close to wherever he was assigned until his retirement in 1964.

After the family returned to Jackson County, their residence was at Brownstown until 1974 when they moved to Columbus. But Jerry completed his elementary instruction at Immanuel Lutheran School in Seymour. He was graduated in 1971 from Brownstown Central High School.

Five years later in 1976 Jerry W. Armstrong enlisted in the Army and completed his basic training at Fort Leonard Wood, Missouri. He was selected to attend further training at Lowry Air Force Base located in Denver, Colorado. Upon graduation he was qualified as an Audio TV Specialist and assigned to Fort Benning, Georgia. He was shipped overseas to serve at Seoul, Korea until his time was completed. He received his honorable discharge in June 1979.

Following his military life, he entered Indiana Vocational Technical Center in Columbus and later graduated with a degree in Electronics in 1985. He then was employed by Crosfield Electronics with home offices located in England. In time he was promoted to a position of specialist as a Field Service Engineer. His responsibilities required constant movement.

Jerry W. Armstrong suffered a fatal heart attack July 31, 2002. He was buried next to his father at Immanuel Lutheran Cemetery in Seymour. He is

survived by his mother and his sister, Carolyn Sue Beck.

ANTHONY EUGENE "TONY" BAUGHMAN, Post Korea and Vietnam Era, United States Army, born September 7, 1959 in Seymour to Ralph and Inez Reedy Baughman. He was raised in the town founded by Meedy Shields. He was graduated from the local high school with the class of 1978. Two years later he was inducted into the army and completed basic training at Fort Knox, KY.

He was stationed at Fort Benning, GA for his training as a paratrooper and he graduated September 21, 1978. He was then assigned to "B" Company of the 508th Battalion of the Airborne Division. Six months later he participated in a jump to honor President Carter's daughter celebrating her birthday. One year later his unit was shipped overseas to Korea where he helped patrol the 38th Parallel line.

In 1981 Tony returned to the states and was stationed at Fort Bragg, NC until he was discharged in 1982. He was authorized to wear various medals and ribbons reflecting his service time. He returned home to Seymour and married Regina Montgomery in July 1984. To them were born two sons.

Tony Baughman died June 14, 1994.

HERSCHEL L. BAUGHMAN, Post Korea, United States Navy, joined the navy in 1958 and served aboard the USS *Robinson* (DD-562) until he was discharged in 1961.

He is married to Gloria Bane and they became parents of two sons, Ricky and Corey Baughman.

He owned and operated Baughman's Garage and Wrecker Service in Vallonia. He was fire chief of Driftwood Township and was active in organizations of the area. He was elected county sheriff and served from 1991-1999.

TEDDY L. BEAUCHAMP, Post Korea, United States Air Force. Served in the National Guard from 1957-1961. Enlisted in the Air Force on January 11, 1960, Lackland and Keesler AFB before assignment.

Tours of duty in Alaska, Philippines, Vietnam, Crete, Japan, Korea, Hawaii and Thailand Taiwan.

AF Overseas Ribbon with 5 Oak Leaf Clusters, Vietnam,

National Defense Medal, Longevity Ribbon, 5 Oak Leaf Clusters, NCO Professional Education Ribbon, Small Arms Expert Rifleman, DFC, Air Medal: 3 Clusters, Good Conduct, Presidential Unit Citation Award: 6 Clusters, Vietnam Gallantry Cross, Campaign Medal. Discharged November 30, 1986 as M/Sgt.

LLOYD L BOLDING, Army of the United States, 55178421, Corporal, Induction at Fort Harrison, Indianapolis. Discharged at Camp Carlson, Colorado, 1947-1953.

5th Army Area, 2nd Infantry Division, Company B, 15th Infantry Regiment.

"...dirty, unshaven and miserable, they stepped down, tried again, and groped upward only to slide, roll and crouch and grab for anything as they met the murderous fire amidst the blast of mortar fragments..." Lt. C.C. Munroe, Commander 2nd Division.

Combat Infantry Badge, Korean Service Medal, United Nations Service Medal and Army Occupation Medal.

FOREST R. BOLING, JR., The Cuban Crisis, United States Navy, born July 23, 1940 near Vallonia to Forest and Ethel Tuelker Boling. He was raised as a farm boy and later graduated from Brownstown in 1958. Three years later he was inducted into the navy at Indianapolis. He completed boot camp training at Great Lakes, IL.

He was assigned to the USS *Earl B. Hall* APD-107, later he was transferred to the USS *Kirwin* APD-90 and remained a member of its crew serving off the Cuban Coast until he was discharged.

He returned home and was employed by Kieffer Paper Mill where he worked for 35 years. He and his wife, Carolyn Ferguson Boling were parents of two children.

KENNETH BOSWELL, Korea, United States Air Force, born in Sharon, PA to Charles and Mary Ray Boswell. He grew up near Cortland, IN and graduated from the local high school in 1948. He worked for the B/O Railroad and for Dunlap & Company during construction of Redeemer Lutheran Church in Seymour.

He enlisted in the Air Force in 1950 and completed basic training at Lackland AFB in Texas. Later he completed language school at Monterey, CA.

and graduated in 1951. He was assigned to the 26th Radio Squadron and shipped overseas for Japan and volunteered to serve in Korea to shorten his tour of duty. He was attached to the 606th Squadron located on top of the Radar Hill overlooking Kimpo AFB located north of Seoul.

He was promoted to S/Sgt. in October 1952 and, following his overseas duty He was married to Lois Kuehn. They became parents of three children. He died in 1999 leaving a wife, two daughters, a son, and seven grandchildren.

ALFRED LEE BOWLING, Korea, United States Army, served in the army from 1957 to 1959 and was stationed at Fort Gordon, GA and Fort Riley, KS. He was assigned to the 18'h Infantry Battalion of the 4th Cavalry Division.

He was discharged as an E-4. He and his wife, Virginia

reside in Medora as the parents of a daughter, named Lori.

JESSIE L. BOYER, Korea, United States Army, born January 21, 1934 in Indianapolis to Stephen and Fannie Lowman Boyer. When he was only 3 years old his family moved to Waymansville.

On December 3, 1953 he was drafted in the army at Indianapolis where he was sent on to Fort Leonard Wood, Missouri for his basic training. He completed eight weeks of further training at Fort Eustis, Virginia. From there he was sent to Fort Lewis, Washington for processing. In April 1954 he was shipped overseas to Korea.

He was assigned to the 712th Railway Company as a conductor for the troop trains. His task was to take fresh troops to the front lines and return others headed for R and R or home. Following 18 months of such service, he was returned to the States and discharged October 20, 1955.

He was married to Carol Persinger in Brownstown in 1957. To them were born four children and they lived in Seymour.

WALTER BROCK, Korea, United States Navy, #482 8308, born January 22, 1934 and much later in December 1955, he was inducted into the United States Navy. He was assigned to and served on the USS *Helena.* He was eventually transferred from active duty to the Naval reserves on September 11, 1957.

He was discharged December 7, 1961, just twenty years after Pearl Harbor. Walter Brock was later married to Josephine Empson Martin on February 6, 1999. Three years later on February 20, 2002 Walter died. He was the father of five children by a former marriage. They are Tony, Tina, Tonya, Terry and Todd.

ALVIN BURCHAM, Korea, United States Army, son of Ben and Jessie Burcham, was born in 1928 and grew up on a farm located south of Vallonia on road 135. He graduated from Vallonia High School in 1948.

He worked on the family farm until he was drafted into the army in January 1951. He was assigned to Camp Breckinridge, KY for his basic training during which time he received a knee injury. He spent considerable amount of time in the hospital, and was released on a medical discharge August 2, 1951,

DONAL AND RONAL BURCHAM, Korea, United States Air Force, twin sons of Ben and Jessie Burcham, were born in 1931 on a farm located south of Vallonia on state road 135. Both graduated from Vallonia High School in 1950, and in August enlisted in the Air Force on the promise they would stay together.

Both received their basic training at Sampson Air Force Base, NY and From there they were sent to Aal-Aero Tech Institute in Glendale, CA, where they received training in aircraft maintenance. Then they went to Chanute Field, IL and from there they could enjoy passes to home,

In 1952 they were assigned to George Field in CA as crew chiefs and assigned to the 186th Bomb Squadron with the 21st Fighter Wing. Soon they were sent to Alaska and stationed at Eielson Air Force Base for a two-week Arctic indoctrination course involving C-119's.

Both boys had furloughs so they could be home for Christmas. They were alerted to overseas duty on Okinawa and Paul Stahl from Wegan drove them to Bakersfield where they took a train to Parks AFB. They left January 18, 1954 for duty in Okinawa, the Philippines and on to Japan.

Both boys received their discharges at Parks AFB and arrived home on August 2, 1955.

THOMAS D. CALLAHAN, born on a small farm in Carr Township of Jackson County, Indiana. After graduating from Medora High School, he attended Indiana University, for one year. Mr. Callahan enlisted in the Marine Corps in 1952, and completed his basic training at San Diego, California.

After Basic Training, Pfc. Callahan was assigned to Camp Pendleton where he was in supply, and later in accounting. When he entered the accounting unit, it was ranked 10 of 10 in the Marine Corps. He was put in charge of the unit and in 6 months it ranked 1 of 10 in the Marine Corps. After completing that challenge, Thomas D. Callahan was transferred to Kaneohe Marine Corps Air Station in Oahu, Hawaii.

Sgt. Callahan served as Stock Control Supervisor, and in late 1955 it was determined there may be a conflict with Laos. The Marine Corps did not have the proper personnel nor equipment aligned for that type of battle. The terrain was too rough for the battle units used in past conflicts or wars.

After encouragement by the 1st Sergeant, Captain, and the Colonel Battalion Commander, in early 1956 Thomas D. Callahan agreed to staff the Marine Corps Units with the Personnel and Equipment to wage the Laos type battle. After establishing the Personnel on paper, and ordering the Equipment for such a battle SSgt Callahan was allowed to tour the Islands until his tour of duty was completed.

Thomas D. Callahan was Honorably discharged from the Marine Corps in April 1956, and earned his degree in Industrial Engineering and Business Management from Indiana University in 1961.

Mr. Callahan was proud of his Marine Corps service, and had but one regret. It is thought the personnel organization he set up as well as the equipment he ordered was used in Vietnam because of the terrain. He never learned if it was what the troops needed. He assumed it was because he was told that if anything went wrong "they knew where he lived."

EARL H. CARR, Korea, United States Army, born in Austin, Indiana July 20, 1928 to Frank and Ebbie Carr. The family moved to Jackson County where Earl was raised. He graduated from Cortland High School in 1948 and he went to work for the Tool and Engineering Company in Seymour.

He was inducted into the army November 3, 1950 and reported for duty at Fort Harrison in Indianapolis, Indiana. He was sent to Fort Breckinridge, Kentucky and then on to Fort Bliss, Texas for further training. His unit was shipped overseas to Japan before landing in Korea on May 18, 1951.

He was assigned to Company B of the 116th Combat Engineer Battalion charged with building roads near the battle lines of the central and eastern Korean front. He was awarded the Korean Service Medal with two Bronze Campaign Stars.

After nine months in combat and more than one year overseas, he returned to the states and was discharged at Camp Atterbury on August 4, 1952. He was later retired from Cummins and he and his wife Mary Lou Gass Carr reside in Brownstown. They have two grown children and four grandchildren.

PAUL A. CARR, Korea, United States Army, 1953-1954, born at Medora July 14, 1932, the son of Louis and Marie Heidelbach Carr. He was raised on a farm and graduated from the local high school in 1950. Three years later he was drafted into the army and completed infantry training at Camp Chaffee, AR in May 1953. After 7 days leave he was sent to Fort Lewis, WA by troop train with buddies from Jackson County. They were Willie Davidson, Ralph Moberly, Carrol Fleetwood, Johnny Lawson and Russell Hall.

Shortly thereafter the troops were shipped

overseas to South Korea via WWII era ship. Stopping along the war, the men were issued combat gear, rifles an assigned to specific units. Carr and Davidson both went to Battery B of the 49th Field Artillery Battalion of the 7th Infantry Division, a 105th Howitzer unit. Upon arrival in Korea with this unit, Carr was assigned to a gun crew and Davidson went to the motor pool. Carr recalled later that the US infantry was dug in a mile forward of his Howitzer gun positions in the valley. He knew the Chinese and North Koreans were similarly entrenched less than one mile away.

Sometime later the opposing forces were in the process of negotiating a truce, but fierce military clashes continued daily until the papers were actually signed July 27, 1953. Sgt. Carr remembers that he was in the last battle for "Pork Chop Hill" during July 6 through 11, 1953 in which 115,000 rounds of artillery shells were recounted in the VFW Magazine published later in 2000.

After the truce, the 7th Division Infantry units were held in reserve, but the artillery was ordered to remain in position to support the 1st Marine Division. Carr remained in Korea until October 1954 and was released from active duty October 22, 1954. He returned home and helped his father with the farming, but eventually he became an operator of heavy equipment constructing parts of the interstate highway system.

During the winter months he attended Indiana University and graduated in 1963. He was then employed as a Special Agent with the Office of Naval Intelligence serving in Vietnam until 1966. He remained as an investigator for the US Department of Defense until he retired in 1993. He remained in the Indiana National Guard continuously from 1972 until 1992 when he retired as Sgt. 1st Class at age 60 years.

Carr is married to the former Jean Greathouse of Medora and they reside near Starve Hollow Lake located not far from Vallonia, IN.

DONALD EUGENE COCKERHAM, Korea, United States Army, born June 21, 1930 to Isaac and Dessie Baughman Cockerham in Jackson County. He grew up in the local area and loved to drive race cars.

He was drafted and inducted into the army August 1, 1951. He reported for duty in Indianapolis and was assigned to the infantry and sent to Fort Ord in California. He was shipped overseas to Korea to complete his service tour and was discharged May 1, 1953.

He was authorized to wear appropriate medals and ribbons reflecting his service assignments. When he returned home, he became an electrician and plumber. He and his wife, Deidra Sitterding became parents of five children, including Risa Jean, Jonathon Thomas, Steven Todd, Michael Joe and Leon Dale Cockerham.

After a divorce, Donald Cockerham married Frances Farmer.

NEAL COCKERHAM, Korea, United States Army, born June 11, 1933 at Medora in Carr Township. Parents: Henry and Mabel Baughman Cockerham. Graduated from Medora High School in 1952.

Inducted into the army June 1, 1953 at Indianapolis. Completed basic training at Fort Leonard Wood. Shipped overseas to European Theater of Operations. Assigned to Hdq. Company of the 7th Engineers Battalion as the mail clerk. Stationed in Germany more than one year. Discharged May 11, 1955.

Returned to Medora and on to Indianapolis. Retired in 1980 from the Monon Railroad. Married November 20, 1955 to June Stilwell. Parents of four children. Volunteer driver for Veteran's Van.

WILLIAM CHARLES COCKERHAM, Korea, United States Army, born November 6, 1928 to Isaac and Dessie Baughman Cockerham of Jackson County. He was raised in and around the local area until he was called to service.

He was drafted and inducted unto the army January 11, 1951 and not long after he completed basic training assigned to the ER 55091023 AMEDS. He drove an ambulance in Korea and was returned to the states January 19, 1953. He received his discharge in 1957.

He married Judy Glenn Cockerham in Alabama and, after his service days were over, they lived near Freetown. They became parents of 6 children including: Billie Faye, Rebecca Sue, Rhonda Gail, Larry Wayne, Ricky Lee and Elana Marie Cockerham.

William was an employee of Kieffer Paper Mill in Brownstown for many years. He died October 21, 1979.

EUGENE LEE COTTINGHAM, Korea, United States Marine Corps, born February 19, 1932 to Adrian and Ethel Ranson Cottingham. He graduated from Paris Crossing High School in 1950. He was raised with three brothers, all of whom were serving their country.

He went into the Marine Corps in December 1951 and was sent on to San Diego for basic boot camp training. He was directed to report to Camp Pendleton and assigned to be a clerk in the 3rd Marine Division.

He was destined to be promoted and was discharged as a corporal. He received his discharge at Cherry Point, NC in December 1953. He married Marry Frances Hoffman in 1954 and they became parents of four children.

LAWRENCE ADRIAN COTTINGHAM, Korea, United States Marine Corps, born October 15,

1929 to Adrian and Ethel Ransome Cottingham in Hayden, Indiana. Eventually they settled in Jackson County and he graduated from Paris Crossing High School in 1947. Three years later he joined the Marine Corps in Indianapolis.

Lawrence spent half of his time at Parris Island in North Carolina. He was selected to receive the Division NCO Leadership Course before his enlistment was up. He was discharged March 2, 1952.

After he had returned home on a furlough he married Norma Roth and she lived with him until he was discharged. They settled in Seymour where they became parents of two children, Dennis and Cynthia.

Lawrence retired from the postal department at Seymour

PAUL W. CRECELIUS, Korea, United States Air Force, 1952-1973, born near Knox, IN and later moved with his family to Seymour, IN. Later he enlisted in the US Air Force while living near Vallonia in Jackson County. After completing his basic training, he was assigned to Edwards Air Force Base in California. He received special training as a weather observer at Chanute Field in Illinois from 1963 to 1964. He was shipped overseas to Morocco, England and Taiwan and finally served for a time in Vietnam.

He was a part of a military family and had three older brothers who served in the Air Force. Two of those brothers gave their lives while on active duty. All three brothers were pilots in the US Air Force.

Paul W. Crecelius is proud of his military family and retains quite an interest in the well-being of the armed forces.

JOSEPH L. DAILY, Korean Era, United States Army, born July 4, 1936 in Seymour to Russell and Thelma Smith Daily. He attended the local schools and was graduated from Crothersville High School and employed by the Indiana State Highway.

He was drafted into the army and inducted October 15, 1959, and was authorized to wear various medals and campaign ribbons he was awarded during his service time at Hickam AFB in Hawaii as a driver for special dignitaries.

He was discharged January 30, 1962, returned to Seymour and was employed at Arvin Industries. Later he became a farmer and died of cancer October 15, 1996.

FESTUS DAVIDSON, United States Navy, 2nd Class Petty Officer, January 16, 1951-December 19, 1954, born July 8, 1931 to parents living in Manchester, Kentucky. Two years later he moved with his family into their home located in southern Indiana. It was there where he attended the elementary schools and Brownstown High School. After moving several times he finally lived in Dade City, Florida, but later graduated from high school in Austin, Indiana in 1950.

He enlisted in the Navy January 16, 1951 while in Florida. Shipped westward for his Boot Camp Training in San Diego and then received teletype instruction and was promoted to a petty officer.

He was eventually assigned to the USS *Essex,* and served at Yokosuka, Japan. Later he participated in the grand parade in downtown Tokyo. While he was stationed in Japan he was selected *the Personality of the Month.* Later on December 19, 1954, he was discharged from the service.

KENNETH DAVIDSON, Korea, United States Army, born to Meredith and Irene Davidson of Vallonia. Records fail to indicate date of birth, but he was inducted into the army in 1959. He was sent to Fort Leonard Wood in Missouri for his basic training.

He served in Korea as a Specialist 4th Class and was discharged in 1962. After returning to Jackson County, he married Carole and they became parents of three children. They now reside in Medora.

TAYLOR DAVIDSON, Post Korea, United States Navy, born to Luther and Sarah Bowling Davidson on February 16, 1925, in Clay Co., Kentucky. He moved to Indiana as a young child and attended schools in Jackson County.

He first joined the US Army during World War II and served his enlistment. After a brief time outside military life, he joined the US Navy, He was stationed in Germany.

He was killed in an automobile accident January 19, 1953, while serving in Germany. The US Navy escorted his body back for burial in March of 1954. He is interred at Blue River Cemetery, Salem, IN.

MILBURN D. DAVIS, Korea, United States Army, born April 27, 1929 at Medora to Roy and Edith Goss Davis. He graduated from the local high school in 1947. He was inducted into the army at Indianapolis February 1, 1951.

He completed basic training at Fort Lewis in Washington and assigned to the Hq. Battalion, 93rd Anti-Aircraft Battery. His unit was sent west to Oakland before shipped overseas to Alaska. He was a truck driver who delivered equipment of artillery pieces.

He was discharged at Camp Carson December 11, 1952 and returned immediately to the Medora Brick Yard where he worked for 43 years. He retired as a mail carrier. He and his wife, Rosie Lawson, became parents of two children.

TOM R. DAVIS, Post Korea, United States Army, born August 16, 1936 to Roy and Edith Goss Davis of Jackson County. He graduated from Medora High School in 1951 and four years later in 1955 was drafted into the army. He completed basic training at Fort Knox, KY and was assigned to Company B of the 23rd Armored Engineers which was part of the 3rd Armored Division.

He was a machine operator and was authorized to wear various medals and ribbons representing his service of nearly one years in Germany. He is married to Pearl McMahon Davis and they became parents of one daughter, Carla Jo, who became the mother of two grandsons, Jeremy and Justin Stuckwisch.

BILL DAY, Post Korean Era, United States Army, born at Boonville May 11, 1936 to Robert and Lenora Mae Bufkin Day. He graduated from the local high school in 1954 and enlisted in the military service the next month.

He passed the physical examination at Indianapolis and was assigned to Fort Leonard Wood, MO for basic training. He was then stationed at the Redstone Arsenal in Huntsville, AL for training on missiles. He was sent to Fort Bliss, TX for additional training on firing the missiles which took place at White Sands Proving Grounds in New Mexico.

He was shipped overseas to Germany and assigned to Ansbach for more than one year. He returned to the states, received his discharge and later graduated from Evansville College and Indiana University. He became a teacher and principal in Jackson County for 38 years.

He and his wife Sandy reside on Spring Street and they are parents of 2 children, Holli and Tony.

JAMES DAVID DECKARD, Post Korea, United States Army, born in Bloomington June 18, 1935 and later graduated from the local high school. Not long afterward he moved to Wichita and was employed in the aircraft industry. Almost 20 years later he was drafted into the army.

On January 16, 1958 he reported to Fort Leonard Wood to complete his basic training. While there he was assigned to Company "E" in 1st Battalion and the 2nd Regiment. He was then sent to Fort Knox where he was placed into Armored detachment so he could receive training in the tanks. He eventually became the personal driver for his colonel.

He was discharged January 15, 1960 and returned to his home in Wichita while remaining in the reserves. He moved to Jackson County in 1970 and became the Marathon Oil Distributor in Brownstown. He is survived by his wife, Barbara, and son, Jay.

WILLIAM K. DELK, Korea, United States Air Force, the youngest of three children, was born November 30, 1931 in Greenwood IN the son of Irene and Vertrice Delk. At a very young age the family moved to Kentucky to live during the depression years.

After the outbreak of WWII and new jobs becoming available, the Delk family moved to Columbus, IN where the Delks went to work at Noblitt & Sparks. Bill and his older brother Bob entered Columbus Jr. High school. After completing his sophomore year in high school, Bill joined the Air Force.

At 17 years of age on June 10, 1949 Bill entered the US Air Force. After completing basic training and radio mechanics school, Bill was shipped to Korea. For his duty there he received a Korean Service Medal, W/2 Bronze Stars, Presidential Unit Citation and a UN Service Medal. He was discharged September 9, 1953,

After his discharge Bill spent some time in western Jackson County on the farm of his sister and brother-in-law, Lela and Logan Cooper. Bill then went to work for Chevrolet at the Corvette factory in St. Louis, from there to McDonald Douglas. He then went to California to work for McDonald Douglas and Lockheed. In the late 1960's he went to work for Boeing Aircraft in Seattle.

His last project while working for Boeing was helping to build the new presidential airplane Air Force One, something that he was very proud of.

After retiring from Boeing, he returned to Western Jackson County where he bought a small farm. There he spent his time gardening, fishing, watching sprint car races and visiting his family.

William K. Delk never forgot the time he spent in Korea. He was very patriotic, he was a faithful blood donor, and took part in community activities. Bill knew the sacrifices we have to give for our freedom.

COURTNEY J. DOTSON, JR., Korea, United Sates Marines, born October 23, 1928 in Anderson to Courtney and Dorohy Owen Dotson. He graduated from Brownsburg High School in 1946. He went on to Purdue and received his degree in engineering and was employed by Link Belt in Indianapolis.

He joined the Marine Corps in October of 1951 and completed his boot camp training at Camp Pendleton in California. He was selected for OCS and was commissioned at Quantico, Virginia. After returning to Pendleton, his unit was shipped overseas to Japan and Korea. He was assigned Company D,

Engineers of the 1st Marine Division and was stationed near the DMZ line north of Seoul.

He was discharged in San Francisco in December of 1954, returned to Jackson County and was employed by the Medora Plastics. He retired from Krebsoge in 1994. He and his wife, Irene Dewar Dotson, currently reside in Medora.

DARREL DUFFY, Korea, United States Navy, born February 1, 1933 in Evansville, the son of Darrel and Effie Bess Duffy. He graduated from Bosse High School in 1950 and enlisted in the Naval Reserves, and at the same time he enrolled at Evansville College. One year later he was called to active duty. He reported to the naval training Station at Waukegan, IL in 1951 and completed his boot camp training. He was assigned to the troop ship USS *Pocono* in June 1952.

He was transferred to the aircraft carrier, USS *Wasp* which later in maneuvers, collided with the USS *Hobson*. The latter sunk November 26, 1952 with the loss of 126 seamen. The disaster was considered the worst in peace time. The USS *Wasp* returned to the states for repairs before departing for the Mediterranean Sea. Some 14 months later the ship had to return for major overhaul.

During his active duty he held the rank of PN3 and was later released from active duty in 1954. He then returned to Indiana State College to complete his education. He received his degree in July 1956 and was employed as a teacher in the Brownstown School System.

He and his wife, Rosemary Eisterhold Duffy, became parents of two children, Gail and Nicholas. In June 1972 his wife passed away. He later married Bonnie Lee Umphress Hansome Duffy. He taught in Brownstown for nearly 40 years before retiring in 1993.

ROBERT D. DUNNA, SR., Korean Police Action, United States Coast Guard, 1953-1975, long time resident of Seymour, served in the US Coast Guard for more than 20 years. During successive tours of duty most of which was in Alaska, he reached the rank of Chief Engineer. Upon retirement he attended the University of Texas and received his degree in science. He returned to Alaska and was employed by the Department of Corrections.

Robert D. Duffy, Sr. died in the Lutheran Community Home December 16, 2003 and, following

all military rites, his remains were buried at sea near Puget Sound from the Coast Guard Cutter *Mustang*.

KELLY LEE EISELE, Korean Era, United States Army, drafted on June 1, 1966 and inducted at Indianapolis on August 1, 1966 and ordered to report for duty immediately. After completing basic training, he was assigned as a Specialist 4E4 in the transportation corps of the army. His unit was shipped overseas to the European Theater of Operations where he was stationed in Frankfort, Germany from Nov. 13, 1968 until July 3, 1972.

He was sent back to the States and was discharged July 31, 1972 from the United States Army upon his honest and faithful service to his country.

FRANCIS HARVEY ELLIOTT, Post Korea, United States Army, born February 19, 1936 in Jackson County, Indiana. Completed academic high school course. Drafted May 13, 1959. Reported to Fort Harrison in Indianapolis. Completed basic training. Sent to Army Air Corps.

Completed training in Ordinance School, Aberdeen, Maryland. Assigned as Ordinance Supply Specialist. Shipped overseas to Fairbanks, Alaska. Served two years. Discharged at Fort Lewis, Washington March 9, 1961.

HOWARD EMPSON, U.S. Air Force, 3rd Air Force Headquarters, London, England, Korean Police Action, born February 1, 1926 on the family farm located along the Muscatatuck River in Grassy Fork Township. He was a son of Marion and Cora Mounts Empson. Later he graduated at Tampico High School with the class of 1944. He remained on the farm helping his father until he enlisted in the Air Force January 5, 1951.

He received his basic training at Lackland Base, assigned #AF16356241 and was sent to Arizona State College for additional training. Later he was shipped overseas and assigned to work for the Inspector General in London. Promoted to Sgt., Howard Empson was assistant office manager until he received his discharge in December 1953.

While stationed in England he met and married Doreen Smith, one of the nurses at a nearby hospital. After they reached the United States, they made their home in Columbus. Later he retired from Cummins Engine Company and Doreen retired from the Columbus Regional Hospital.

They are parents of three children. Sharman married David Wilmore and lives in Cincinnati where they became parents of three children. Son David married Sherree Hunt and with two children, they live in Hazelwood, IN. Neil lost his life in an auto accident and left several children, including a son, Stephan, who served in the Gulf War on the aircraft carrier, USS *Nimitz*. Daughters include Stacie Hamm, Christi DeMarco and Sara. Stepchildren are David, Shannon and Amanda Bain.

MAX W. ERNEST, Korea, United States Army, born July 21, 1930 in Seymour, Indiana and was the son of Henry and Gladys M. Ernest. He graduated from Seymour High School in 1948.

He was drafted into the army, inducted and completed his basic training at Fort Riley, Kansas and while there he played in the 10th Division Band. Later, he was shipped overseas to Korea and assigned to duty with the 7th Infantry Regiment of the 3rd Infantry Division Service Company.

He completed sixteen months of duty in Korea and earned the Combat Infantry Badge, Korean Service Medal with 3 Bronze Campaign Stars and the UN Service Medal. He was discharged at Camp Carson, Colorado with the rank of Sgt.

GARRETT G. FEE, Korea, United States Army, born October 27, 1928. Enlisted in the army in February 1948. Assigned to the 4th Infantry Division. Basic training at Fort Knox in Kentucky. Stationed near Fort Lewis, Washington. Military Duty at Mile 26 in Alaska.

BOB L. FERGUSON, Korea, United States Army, son of Clarence and Ruby Ferguson. Graduated from Freetown High School in 1950. Was inducted into the army in 1951.

Served in Korea and awarded the Purple Heart and Infantry Badge. In 2002 he received a medal for serving South Korea. Carried out duties as forward observer for Mortar Unit.

Assigned to the Ethiopian Imperial Guard. Returned stateside and assigned hospital duty at Camp Carson. Recovered from wound received in Korea. Discharged September 13, 1953. Married Ida Goble and became father of 4 children.

HAROLD GENE FLEETWOOD, Korea, United States Army, born August 4, 1933 in Hamilton Township to Hayden and Anna Anderson Fleetwood. He was raised near Acme, attended Surprise School and graduated from Cortland High School with the class of 1951. He began working at the Kroger Store and has made that his lifetime employment since 1951, with the exception of his time in the military service of his country.

He was drafted into the army July 7, 1951 and inducted at Indianapolis. He completed his basic training at Fort Leonard Wood, Missouri and on to Camp Gordon, Georgia to the signal school.

He was assigned to Headquarters Company, 2nd Battalion of the 17th Infantry Division during the time in Korea. He served as Field Wire Chief north of Seoul in the DMZ area for 18 months before being returned to the states for separation on May 10, 1956.

He and his wife, Dorene Fish Fleetwood, reside in the Madden Hill area after their three children became grown. He is still a part time employee of the Kroger Company,

MARVIN DEAN FLINN, Post Korea, United States Navy, born west of Medora December 16, 1933. Parents were Hubert and Flotilla Baker Flinn of Medora. Graduated from Cortland High School in 1951.

Entered the navy August 11, 1953 at Indianapolis. Completed boot camp training at Great Lakes Naval Station. Assigned to Aviation Supply Unit. Shipped overseas to Japan as a plane tester. Discharged medically March 30, 1959.

Awarded Good Conduct and National Defense Medals. Employed by Cesna Aircraft Industries at Hutchinson, Kansas. Married and raised one daughter.

ALFRED LOWELL FORGEY, Korea, United States Army, born October 13, 1928 to William and Nellie Brand Forgey of Freetown. He was graduated from the local high school in 1946 and went on to barber college before entering the service.

He was drafted and inducted into the army at Indianapolis December 4, 1950. He completed basic training at Camp Breckinridge, KY. He was sent to Camp McCoy in Wisconsin and then to Fort Sill, OK training for the artillery survey unit of the 469th Artillery Battalion in the Headquarters Division.

He remained at Fort Sill until he was discharged on December 3, 1952. He returned home and attended Tri State College at Angola, became a licensed surveyor and was elected the county surveyor for 16 years. Married to Patricia Bultman Forgey, they raised two children while residing in Brownstown.

Alfred L. Forgey died August 23, 1989.

JAMES HERSCHEL FORGEY, Korea, 7th Infantry Division, born August 28, 1928 to James and Edith McNiece Forgey and was raised on the family farm. He graduated from high School in 1946 and went to work as a lineman building the Rural Electric lines throughout southern Indiana.

He was drafted on November 3, 1950 and was inducted with the 3rd group of draftees into the army. Included in the group were Ray Abner, Arthur Ahlbrand Clifton Aynes, Wm. Bowman, Char Carpenter, Earl Carr, Carl Fish, Ralph Pardieck, Allen Pogue, Robert Pray, Chas Rebber, Robert Shffell, Alvin Sage, Melvin Sage, Melvin Taylor and William Willey. All completed basic training at Camp Breckinridge, KY.

Pvt. Forgey arrived in Korea in April 1954 and was assigned as a lineman in the 32nd Infantry Regiment. Some nine months of duty were spent on the east end of the Korean line. He left his company on February 13, 1952 and Cpl. Forgey spent his final three months at Fort Sill in Oklahoma.

After he was discharged, he worked more than 40 years for the REMC as a line man out of Brownstown. He and his wife, Berneice Barnett Forgey resided on Steinkamp and Main Streets in Brownstown.

JERRY JACK FORGEY, Korea and Afterward, United States Army, born November 4, 1956 in Seymour to Charles R. and Anna Mae Manuel Forgey. He was raised around Freetown but graduated from Brownstown Central High School in 1975. He was employed by the Arvin plant in Columbus until he went into the service.

He was drafted and inducted into the army March 3, 1979 and completed basic training at Fort McClellan, Alabama. He was assigned to the 525th Military Police Company at Fort McPherson, Georgia and eventually transferred to the 2nd MP Company while stationed near the DMZ line in North Korea. After that tour of duty he returned to California for a short R & R.

He volunteered for a second hitch in the 142nd MP Company at Seoul on October 1, 1981. He returned to the Hq Company at Fort Sill, Oklahoma and remained there until he was granted his discharge January 25, 1985.

He returned home and was employed by Sapp's Bakery in Columbus. He was the father of two daughters. Jerry J. Forgey died February 9, 2001.

JAMES ALBERT FOSBRINK, No Dates Available, Branch of Service Unknown. James Albert Fosbrink was born to Andrew and Carrie Fosbrink. He married Mary Lou Moore from Peoria and they became the parents of two sons. They made their home in Seymour most of their lives. When the astronaut

Grissom died they moved to Texas to be with Mary Lou's sister who was Mrs. Grissom.

JACK FOUNTAIN, Korea, United States Air Force, 16350327, born July 29, 1930, the son of Henry and Violet Parker Fountain. He graduated from Brownstown High School in 1948 and went farming and raising cattle on the family farm near Brownstown. He is married to Madge Gossman and they are parents of two children, Andy and Julie. They have four grandchildren.

He completed basic training at Lackland AFB, TX and was then assigned to George AFB, CA and from there he was sent to Hamilton AFB, CA where he served in the Air Patrol guarding the RADAR site in Mill Valley.

From there he was shipped overseas to the Erding AFB in Germany and was promoted to S/Sgt. He completed his service time in Germany in 1954.

OSCAR J. GOECKER, Korean Conflict, United States Army, born April 6, 1931 on a small farm located near Dudleytown, IN as a son of John W. and Sophia Goecker. He graduated from Seymour High School in 1949. Two years later he entered the Army and received his basic training at Schofield Barracks, Honolulu but graduated from leadership school at Camp Breckinridge, KY.

He was assigned duty during the Korean Conflict and joined the 279th Regiment of the 45th Infantry Division stationed in Japan before being shipped to Korea to relieve the 1st Cavalry Division. He served as an infantryman on the front lines. He was awarded the Combat Infantryman's Medal.

He was wounded in action May 29, 1952, recuperated in a field hospital located in Tokyo, Japan. He was returned to duty and rotated back to the States and awarded the Purple Heart.

He received his honorable discharge as a sergeant on March 25, 1954.

BERNARD GRAY, Korea, United States Army, graduated from Medora High School. Basic Training at Camp Picket, Virginia. Married and resides in Medora and is father of Sanda Wineinger and Andra Rainey.

LEONARD LEE GREGORY, Korea, United States Army, born January 26, 1933 to Theo and Allie Faulkner Gregory in Kentucky. He was raised in a large family and when most of children were grown the family moved to Jackson County and settled in the Maumee area.

He was a member of the Kentucky National Guard in 1950 and 1951 and on August 11, 1953 he joined the army and was stationed at several stateside bases. His unit was eventually shipped overseas to Korea. When his tour of duty was completed he was discharged April 6, 1956.

On December 17, 1965 he married Mona Kay Ratcliff in Brownstown. During the following years they were blessed with the birth of two daughters, Lori and Julia.

Leonard Gregory suffered many health problems and finally died of complications October 25, 2003.

JAMES, JACK & JERRIE GRIFFIN, United States Army, Vietnam and Korea. These boys are sons of Lawrence and Christine Bruner Griffin. All were raised in the Freetown area of Jackson County and each played basketball for the local high school. They all served in the army at the same time. Jim was in the Air Force as a radio operator flying over Vietnam. Jack was in the army in communications. Jerrie was in service from 1965 to 1974. One hitch was in Germany and the other in Korea.

CHARLES W. GRIFFITH, Korea, United States Air Force, born March 17, 1928, a son of Charles and Amanda McIntosh Griffith. He married Yvonne Sue Beldon in Tampico on September 3, 1950. To them were born a son and 2 daughters and 7 grandchildren.

He was in the Air Force, served in the Korean Conflict and continued with the Indiana National Guard as a chief warrant officer until he retired in 1988. During his wartime service he was awarded three army commendations and two meritorious service awards.

Following his discharge he was a member of several service organizations, including the Church of Christ at Edinburgh, Nineveh Masonic Lodge, Scottish Rite, Murat Shrine and a Kentucky Colonel. He also was awarded the Sagamore of the Wabash. He was a lifetime member of the Retired Officers Association and the Edinburgh American Legion.

CHARLES HACKMAN, Post Korea, United States Army, born November 30, 1933 and raised on a farm near Vallonia, Indiana. He entered the United States Army on June 14, 1956 and was assigned the Serial No. US55541546. He received Basic Training in Company D of the 10th Battalion 2nd Basic Training Regiment, Fort Leonard Wood, MO. After 8 weeks of Basic Training, he went to Fort Lewis, Washington where he was in the 8th Infantry for advanced training in Light Artillery. He was then assigned to Company A, 526th Armored Infantry Battalion, Ft. Knox, KY. There he was part of a group to test an experimental armored Personnel Carrier. He also served as Battalion Carpenter and for several months was assigned Temporary Duty to Ireland Army Hospital as an Elevator Operator and observer.

He was honorably discharged from active duty on June 14, 1958. He was in the U.S. Army Standby Reserve until he was honorably discharged May 31, 1962. He returned to the farm when he was discharged from active duty. On April 11, 1964, he married Laverne Lambring. They had three children: Thomas Hackman, who married Ruth Jones, Patricia (Scott) Butt, and Miriam (John) Lee. Over the years he fed 100 to 500 head of cattle to slaughter annually, and he raised corn, soybeans and wheat. He purchased land eventually bringing the farm up to 1,200 acres.

DONALD HACKMAN, Korea, was born on October 11, 1931, the son of Martin and Edna Nierman Hackman. He graduated from Tampico High School with the class of 1949.

Donald was the youngest of three brothers who served in their nation in times of peril. Edgar Hackman was in the U.S. Army while Martin, Jr. served in the U.S. Air Force. He also had two sisters and another brother.

Donald Hackman was stationed at Barksdale Air Force Base located in Shreveport, Louisiana. The impression was con sided, and while stationed in Louisiana, he married Betty Jane Whorton in Bossier City.

Most of his service time was spent while stationed there in Bossier City. Finally, they were married and she remained attached to the military life for 21 years while he continued as an auto mechanic. He was also involved as councilman, Boy School Troop 102 and a member of the Order of the Arrow.

Donald Hackman died at age 40 near Bossier City, LA, and the family crest was placed into the care of his brothers.

EARL HACKMAN, Korea, United States Army, served in the U.S. Army during the Korean Conflict.

Inducted into service Dec. 1, 1952 and discharged Aug. 31, 1954 with a rank of PFC. His serial #US 55-329-236.

He was born October 29, 1931 at Sauers in Washington Township to Amos and Katie (Duwe) Hackman. He graduated from St. John's Lutheran South District School only 1/4 mile from his family home place. He also graduated from Brownstown High School.

Cousin Orville Hackman and Earl were inducted at the same time. They left home and went to Indianapolis, IN. Buses took them to Indian Town Gap Pennsylvania for basic training. Traveled by train (3 days) to Fort Lewis, Washington. Then shipped out by boat from Seattle to Inchon, Korea (2 weeks). They then boarded a train to the front lines. They both were in Item Company, 3rd Battalion, 25th Infantry Division and 35th Regiment.

Earl received the Combat Infantry Badge, the Korean Service Medal, w/1 Bronze Service Star, Good Conduct Medal, United Nations Service Medal, and National Defense Service Medal.

Earl married Vera Joyce Goecker of Dudleytown on January 20, 1957. They have four children: Tracy Stam (Keith), Karla Thompson (Brian), Blake Hackman, and Kyle Hackman (Cher). They have lived their entire life on a dairy farm in Washington Township, God Bless America.

GLEN ROBERT HACKMAN, Korea, United States Air Force, born March 21, 1931 in Jackson County. Parents were Walter and Emma Hageman Hackman. Attended Tampico Elementary School. Graduated from Brownstown High School in 1949.

Inducted January 9, 1951 at Indianapolis. Completed basic training at Lackland AFB. Shipped overseas to Korea, 28th Field Maintenance Squadron. Discharged May 28, 1954 in South Dakota.

Awarded medals and ribbon reflecting his service. Re-enlisted and served another tour of duty. Retired again and returned home. Became an Insurance Adjuster with Farm Bureau. Married Connie Bryant of Crothersville. Parents of three children. Residents of Carmel, Indiana.

ORVILLE GEORGE W. HACKMAN, Korea, United States Army, born July 20, 1928 in Brownstown. Parents: Alva and Ora Hackman. Attended grade school. Graduated from Tampico. Farm.

Inducted December 1, 1952 with his cousin, Earl Hacksman (their services would run parallel). Both completed basic training at Indiana Gap, Pennsylvania. Both assigned to Company I, 35th Infantry Regiment, 25th Division. Both shipped overseas to Korea and

stationed in the central front. Both were riflemen and lager truck drivers

Each awarded Korean Service Medal w/1 Campaign Star, Combat Infantryman's Badge, UN Service Medal, Good Conduct Medal. Both returned to Fort Carson, Colorado. Each discharged August 31, 1954.

Each became a farmer until retirement.

Each was married and both became had three grandchildren

ROBERT H. HALL, Pre Korea, United States Army, born October 4, 1929 in Seymour where he was raised. Moved with his family to Freetown. Graduated from the local high school in 1946.

Enlisted in the army August 2, 1947 and sent to Fort Knox. Attended several service schools before being sent to Japan. Assigned to Military Headquarters. Volunteered for special duty in Korea. Discharged May 2, 1951.

Japan Occupation Medal, Korean Service Medal, five Campaign Stars, Bronze Star, Combat Infantry Badge.

Returned home and employed in Law Enforcement. City Police and Federal Drug Interdiction Officer. Retired in 2000.

Ridenour since 1980 and they have two children.

RUDOLPH HAMBLIN, Korean Era, United States Navy, attended grade school in Kentucky before moving to Tampico in Jackson County in 1946. He graduated from the local high school in 1952.

He joined the Navy in October 1954 and completed his boot training at Great Lakes Naval Station with Company 244. He was assigned to the USS *Cascade* AD-16, a destroyer tender at Newport, RI and served aboard for 2 years ending in 1956.

After being promoted to Radioman 2nd Class in 1967, and 1st Class in 1971 at Louisville, KY, he was assigned there until his retirement in 1994 for a total of more than 36 years of service time. He was authorized to wear various medals and ribbons reflecting his service.

ALLEN BAIN HARBAUGH, World War II and Korea, United States Army, Allen Bain Harbaugh was born near Freetown May 3, 1928 to Frank and Jessie McLean Harbaugh. He graduated from the local high school in 1946. He was drafted into the army and inducted at Fort Knox, KY September 13, 1946. He served more than eight months at Fort Lewis, WA, being trained for an engineering assignment.

He was shipped overseas to Japan

December 27, 1946 and participated in the army of occupation serving in Company "K" of the 35th Infantry Division. He returned to the states to receive his discharge June 3, 1947.

He was employed at Arvin Industries after he came home, but was recalled into the service on April 2, 1952. He was inducted at Indianapolis and then sent to Fort Knox, KY for basic training. He was finally assigned to the mail room in Irvine, California. Later he was shipped overseas to Germany where he served in Company "C" of the 4th Engineer Battalion in the 4th Infantry Division.

He returned to the states and was discharged on March 10, 1954 and authorized to wear various medals and ribbons depicting his military service. When he arrived home he was employed by Arvin and he assisted the county surveyor, sheriff and treasurer. He was elected county sheriff to an eight year term. He was later employed at the county garage. He and his wife, Betty Cockerham are residents of Brownstown where they became parents of twin daughters.

MARVIN L. HASH, Korea, United States Marine Corps, born September 4, 1937 at Indianapolis. Moved with family to Seymour. Attended Brownstown High School.

Joined the Marine Corps in September 1954. Completed basic training at San Diego, California. Received further training in Florida and Tennessee. Stationed at Edenton, NC. Assigned to the Air Wing. Sent to Puerto Rico but returned to South Carolina. Discharged in September 1958

Returned to Indianapolis and employed by Belt Railroad. Served as Insurance Agent. Worked for REMC for 30 years. Married Janet Dunipace of Ohio. Became parents of two children. Resides near the Jackson County seat.

FRANKLIN LEE HATTABAUGH, Korea, United States Air Force. On October 19, 1930 Franklin Lee Hattabaugh was born in Indianapolis to Merle E. and Belva Hattabaugh. He attended school in Indianapolis where he resided with his parents and two younger brothers; Ralph, currently of Vallonia, IN, and Keith currently of Salem, IN. In 1948 he and his family moved to a small farm at Rural Route 1, Vallonia, Indiana in Washington County. He then graduated from Salem High School in Salem, Indiana in 1948.

After graduation he went to work for ARVIN in Seymour, IN. In August 1951 he entered the United States Air Force to serve his country during the Korean War. He completed his basic training at Sampson Air Force Base in Geneva, New York. He was then assigned to the 3267th Training Squadron, 3250th Technical Training Group for Automotive Mechanics training. He was then transferred to the 3750th Squadron, Dallas Aviation School in Dallas, Texas for Engineering Mechanics Training. After he finished his schooling, he then went to Camp

Stoneman, CA. Prior to shipping overseas to Japan on the USS *Sitkoh Bay* in March 1952. He was assigned to the 374th Motor Vehicle Squadron until the end of his tour in June 1954. At this time he was shipped to the Naval Receiving Station at Seattle, Washington. From Seattle, he went to Moody Air Force Base in Valdosta, Georgia where he remained until his discharge in August 1955 with the rank of A1C.

Upon returning home to Indiana he was in the Air Reserves until October 1959.

During his service in the USAF he received the following medals and unit citations: KSM, UNSM, NDSK and the CCM ROK PUCE.

On October 19, 1956 he married Virginia Prather. He and his family moved to Seymour, Indiana in 1960. His life on earth ended on September 11, 2001 and he was laid to rest in the Vallonia Cemetery at Vallonia, Indiana, He was very proud to serve his country and to be a part of the United States Air Force. His family is very proud of him.

MICHAEL K. HAWN, Korea, United States Army, entered the army in 1971. Assigned to Company A of the 123rd Infantry. Completed tour of duty at Fort Polk, Louisiana. Served in Korea. National Defense Medal, Marksmanship Badge as Sharpshooter.

Married Vickie Bane and they became parents of two daughters. Employed by Cummins in Columbus. Resides in Brownstown.

ROSCOE LLOYD HAWN, Korea, United States Air Force, born November 3, 1929 to Willis and Nona Rucker Hawn. To those that knew him he was known as Lloyd or Little Nick. Lloyd attended Tampico School and was a member of Tampico Christian Church.

The only son, Lloyd helped his father farm. When he was old enough to drive a car Lloyd took on additional odd jobs to earn enough to purchase his own automobile. At the time of the Korean Conflict his father, a World War I veteran, encouraged Lloyd to join the National Guard. He was rejected because of a bad knee, but none the less was drafted into the army.

Lloyd reported for duty on October 25, 1951 and trained in the 101st Airborne Division at Camp Breckinridge, Kentucky. He left for the Far East on April 23, 1952 as a member of Company F, 279th Infantry Regiment. Lloyd volunteered for higher risk missions in order to secure a shorter tour of duty and return home sooner. In one such mission on July 10th near Hadokkom-gol, North Korea, contact was made with the enemy. Fragments from mortar rounds struck Lloyd a fatal blow. It was reported that he died instantly, spared suffering.

Lloyd's body was returned to the United States aboard the *Loma Victory* among 223 killed in Korea. He was awarded both the Purple Heart and Bronze Star posthumously.

Lloyd's love of autos allowed him to own many different cars in his short life, more than many a man who had more days. It was a sad time in Tampico when Roscoe Lloyd Hawn was laid to rest with full military honors at Russell Chapel Cemetery in the fall of 1952.

JOHN WILLIAM HAZZARD, Korea Era, United States Air Force, son of William and Cleta Hazzard, born February 22, 1930 in Vallonia, Indiana. Graduated from Vallonia High School. Service No. 1634 6532.

Entered active service October 31, 1950, Indianapolis, Indiana. Discharged October 30, 1954, Scott Air Force Base, Illinois.

Duty assignment 3320TT Sq. SAFB 111, Service Schools, Scott Air Force Base, January 1951 through March 1951, RAD FUND CRSE, Scott Air Force Base, March 1951 through June 1951, RAD. MACH, Scott Air Force Base, July 1953 through September 1953. TECH INSTR CREE. National Service Defense Medal, Occupational Medal of Germany, and Good Conduct Medal.

WESLEY ERNEST HAZZARD, Korea, United States Air Force, son of William and Cleta Hazzard, born May 28, 1931 in Vallonia, Indiana. Graduated from Vallonia High School. Service No. A-F 16 385-808 Rank SSGT(T).

Entered active duty July 31, 1951, Indianapolis, Indiana. Discharged July 30, 1955, Brooklyn Air Force Base, Alabama. Service School, Spartan School, Tulsa, Oklahoma from October 1951 to June 1952. National Defense Medal and Good Conduct Medal.

ROBERT DARRELL HEDRICK, Korea, United States Air Force, 1950-1954, born July 31, 1931 to Floyd and Cordelia Axson Hedrick of Houston. Attended the local school and graduated from Clearspring High School.

Enlisted in the air force December 29, 1950 at Indianapolis. Completed basic training at Lackland AFB. Trained

as a cable splicer at Warren AFB in Wyoming. Discharged at Camp Kilmer, NJ November 4, 1954.

Had been a barber in Seymour by trade. Married Mary Sue Stillwell Scott in November 1978.

NOBLE HEIMAN, Korea, United States Air Force, born August 30, 1931 to Howard and Esther Plump Heiman of the Pleasant Grove area. He was raised on the family farm and carried out the normal chores. He was later employed by Arvin Industries until he entered the service.

He was inducted into the air force December 9, 1950 at Indianapolis, IN but completed basic training at Sheppard Field, TX. He was assigned to the 567th Food Service Squad at McChord Field in Washington until he was discharged November 28, 1953.

He returned to Seymour and was employed by the Buhner Fertilizer Co. Many years later he retired from Schneck Memorial Hospital. Early in June 1957 he married Phyllis Wichman and they became parents of two sons, Douglas and Scott.

Noble Heiman died June 17, 2003.

RICHARD NEAL HUBER, Korea, United States Air Force, born April 25, 1931 to Oren and Ruth Whitcomb Huber of Brownstown. He was raised on the home farm and later graduated from Brownstown High School in 1949. He then attended Butler University.

He entered the air force December 7, 1951 in Indianapolis and was sent to Keesler Field in Mississippi for training in RADAR. He was a RADAR repairman and shipped overseas to Korea where he served nearly two years.

He returned to the states and was discharged December 6, 1955 at the airport in Knoxville, Tennessee. He was authorized to wear the appropriate medals and ribbons reflecting his military services.

He returned to make his home in Brownstown. He and his wife, Pat Able, lived in their farm home until his death October 29, 1981. They are parents of three children.

MARVIN H. HUFFMAN, Post Korea, United States Army, joined the army June 24, 1957. Basic training at Fort Chaffee. Shipped overseas to Europe. Assigned to 38th Artillery Division. Stationed at Darmstaadt, Germany. Returned to the states 6/15/59. Discharged May 31, 1953 and remained in the army reserves

CHARLES ISAAC HUTCHINSON, Post Korea, United States Air Force, born July 8, 1939 to

Cleatus and Audrey Hubbard Hutchinson. He graduated from Clearspring High School in 1957 and that fall he entered the air force.

He reported for duty at Lackland AFB, Texas for his basic training, then sent to Marsh AFB in California to complete his military instruction. It was from Homestead AFB in Florida where his unit was shipped overseas to the European Theater.

He returned to the states and was discharged from New Jersey early in May 1961. He elected to remain in the reserves until 1962.

He married Linda Waddell of Seymour and they became parents of one son, Ronald Keith Hutchinson. He married Shirley Keithley Hutchinson in 1972 and they became parents of three children.

He retired from Cummins in 1990 after 34 years of service.

RONALD K. HUTCHINSON, Korea, United States Air Force, born March 1, 1935 to Cletus and Audrey Hubbard Hutchinson. He graduated from Clearspring High School in 1953. One year later he joined the air force and was assigned to the 551st Periodic Maintenance Squadron.

He completed his training at Sheppard Field in Texas. Records fail to verify overseas duty. He was discharged at Otis AFB in Massachusetts on November 6, 1957 and elected to remain in the reserves until 1962.

He married Polly Ison December 21, 1954 and they became parents of five children. Many years later he retired from REMC.

DAVID LLOYD IMLAY, Post Korea, United States Army, born in Jackson County, Indiana, February 4, 1935, and graduated from Cortland High School.

Private First Class Imlay entered the U.S. Army at Indianapolis, IN, October 25, 1954; he was stationed at Ft. Leonard Wood, MO for his Basic Training. His Specialty was 111 Light Weapons Infantry, and attended Cooks School.

He was assigned to Co. D 746th Armored Infantry and stationed in Germany. He was in Germany 1 year 6 months and 25 days.

He was transferred to Ft. Sheridan, IL, October 17, 1956, and from there, he was transferred to the USAR Ind. Mil. Dist. until the termination of his Reserve Obligation October 24, 1962. He received the Army of Occupation Medal (Germany) and Good Conduct Medal.

He returned to his parents home on Route 4, Seymour and found work.

He attended Franklin College at Franklin, Indiana and received his Teaching Degree.

JOHN J. JACKSON, Berlin Crisis, United States Army, born in Owen Township October 7, 1938 to Thorn and Flossie Booker Jackson. They made their home near Strawberry Ridge. He graduated from Clearspring High School in 1956.

He entered the army September 18, 1961 and was sent to Fort Knox, Kentucky to complete basic training. He received some special instruction and was placed in line for an appointment as an intelligence specialist. Shortly thereafter he was instructing tactics in armor warfare.

Records fail to show if he served overseas in battle. It is now believed he completed his tour of duty at Fort Knox. He received his discharge September 18, 1963.

He married Cleo Davis January 11, 1964 and they became the parents of three children: Michelle, Michael and Monica.

ROBERT MELVIN JACKSON, Korea, United States Army, born July 15, 1929. Parents: Thornton and Flossie Booker Jackson. Grew up in Jackson County. Graduated from Brownstown High School in 1948.

Entered the army in 1950 and reported to Fort Bliss. Assigned to base in Michigan. Shipped to Korea. Discharged in 1952.

Married Della Jane Jackson in 1950. Parents of three children. Retired from Ford Motor Company. Residents of Charleston.

JOHN PETER JOHNSON, Post Korea, United States Army, born August 25, 1933 in Jackson County. Parents were Guy and Minnie Hurley Johnson of Ewing. Graduated from Brownstown High School in 1951.

Served in the air force reserve: 1950-52. Transferred to National Guard: 1952-55. Inducted into army August 10, 1955 at Indianapolis. Completed basic training at Fort Ord.

Assigned to Company E, 22nd Infantry Regiment, 7th Infantry Division. Shipped overseas to Korea and stationed at Pusan. Served on the DMZ Line north of Seoul. Played baseball for the 8th Army team in Korea. Returned to the states and stationed at Fort Sheridan. Discharged June 1, 1957.

Employed by Marion-Kay, then REMC for 37 years. Married Helen Gilsrap and has two children.

HAROLD DALE JONES, Korea, United States Air Force, born April 15, 1931 in Seymour and raised west of Brownstown in the Ratcliff Grove area. Enlisted in the air force in October 1951. Trained as vehicle operator after boot camp. Stationed at Bryan AFB in Texas.

Shipped overseas to Korea and stationed at

Kimpo. Served one year of foreign duty. Returned to the states and sent to Selfridge AFB. Discharged October 22, 1955.

JOSEPH H. KAMMAN, Korean Conflict, United States Coast Guard, 1952-1956, born to William H. and Nora Deppert Kamman in Brownstown on June 14, 1933. His forebear was one of the first German-speaking Lutheran immigrants to reach America in 1819 when a group of 15 young men from the Province of Hannover disbarked at Wilmington, NC. They walked all the way to Cincinnati where they found work through which they were able to save enough money to purchase land in Grassy Fork Township.

Many years later, Joseph H. Kamman graduated from Brownstown High School and almost immediately joined the Coast Guard. He completed basic training in Groton, Connecticut and then married Jane Odell. He then served at various ports at the direction of his superior officers. In due time he was assigned to a coast guard cutter patrolling the Gulf from its port in Texas.

Joseph H. Kamman received his honorable discharge in mid-1956, after which he returned home to Brownstown. He farmed while working at COSCO in Columbus. Other work took him to New Britain, CN where he was employed by Stanley Tool Company. He passed away while living in Austin, Indiana in 2002.

DONALD L. KELSCH, Korea, United States Air Force, Dates of Service: December 1951-December 1955. Completed basic training at San Antonio, Texas. Currently resides in Jackson County, Indiana. Married to Janet Smith.

JACK KENDALL, Korea, United States Army, born in November 1932, the son of Harold and Emma Steward Kendall. He was reared as a farm boy just north of Seymour. He completed his elementary instruction at Jonesville Lutheran School in 1948. He was later inducted into the army, he completed basic training at Fort Knox, KY. He also received truck drivers instruction to become qualified to transport troops.

He was eventually sent to Ft. Eustis, VA and was assigned to duty in the postal department delivering mail to the troops. Sometimes he hauled rations to the various mess depots.

He was discharged in September 22, 1930. He then returned home to Jackson County and resumed working on the Graessle Farm.

ROGER L. KILGAS, Post Korea, United States Army, born July 31, 1932 at Dudleytown, Indiana and was drafted from Jackson County January 31, 1954 and sent to Fort Riley, Kansas.

He became a tank commander and was assigned to the 18th Infantry Regiment which served overseas for more than a year.

He received his discharge January 31, 1956 and returned home. He was employed by King Industries in Seymour. He later became a well-known and respected registered auctioneer.

GLEN M. KILLEY, United States Marines, #1436924, Sergeant, October 19, 1953-October 18, 1957. Discharged at Camp Pendleton, CA. Combat Infantry Badge, Korean Service Medal, U.N. Service Medal.

Glen M. Killey enlisted in the Marine Corps when he was just 18 years old. From that time, his motto has been the traditional *Semper Fi.* He was inducted October 19, 1953 and completed his basic training before being sent to Camp Pendleton, CA. He was ordered to Korea and headed overseas in March 1954 where he was stationed until January 1955. Killey served in the 3rd Battalion, George Company of the 5th Regiment in the First Marine Division. When Army replacements arrived, Glen Killey was detailed back to the United States.

As an alternative to standing parade duty, Killey volunteered for Mess assignment. A few days later he was transferred to the 1st Marine Division at Camp Pendleton where he remained until March 1956. From there he was shipped out to the Marine Base at Adak in Alaska where he served in a guard company for another year.

Returned to Camp Pendleton, California, Killey was discharged October 18, 1957, after which he served in the reserves until 1961.

ALBERT L. KINWORTHY, Korean Police Action, United States Air Force, Far East and European Theater of Operations, 1951-1977.

Married Betty Jean McCasland April 12, 1952. Became parents of four children: Albert Jr., Vickie J., James E., Karl E.

MOSIER D. KIRTS, Post Korea, United States Navy, 1961-1965.

ROBERT D. KIRTS, Post Korea, United States Navy, 1963-1967.

CAROL DEAN KNOTT, Post Korea, United States Air Force, born in Brownstown June 7, 1934 to Joseph and Genevieve Boling Knott. He graduated from Brownstown High School in 1952 and was employed by Arvin Industries before entering the service.

He was inducted into the air force in January 1953 at Indianapolis but was sent to Lackland AFB to complete basic training. He reported to Sheppard Field and was trained as an aircraft mechanic. He elected to make the military his career.

He was shipped overseas to the European Theater but served in other sites around the world. His most active time was in Vietnam and Thailand during which time he was active as a maintenance line chief He was returned to the states and received his discharge at Columbus AFB in Mississippi October 1, 1973.

He returned to Brownstown and became a mail carrier. He became father to three children. He resides with a son near Gorbett's Chapel.

HAROLD A. KUEHN, Korea, United States Army, born January 15, 1929 in Jackson County to Martin and Stella Redicker Kuehn. He attended Honeytown Elementary School and graduated from Cortland High School in 1947.

He was drafted into the army February 1, 1951 and inducted at Fort Sheridan, Illinois. He was sent to Fort Lewis, Washington for his basic training with emphasis on anti-aircraft artillery.

After completing specialized training in computer operations, he was assigned to the 746th AAA Gun Battalion and sent west to San Francisco, California for the air defense.

He was appointed range section leader and was instrumental in the design and fabrication of electronic pictoral consol depicting gun emplacements and their field of fire. It was used in the command post so officers could view the aircraft location and determine if guns were in the right quadrant of fire.

In 1952 his unit was shipped overseas to Alaska and stationed on the "dew line" where they built an air defense around the AFB at Fairbanks. He was discharged at Camp Carson, CO December 12, 1952.

He married Janet Cross of Brownstown and became the father of three children, Karen, Jerry and Kathy.

LESTER L. KUEHN, Korea, United States Air Force, Radar Operator, born at Honeytown in Jackson County on August 19, 1933, a son of Martin and Stella Redicker Kuehn. He matured as a member of a large family and graduated from Cortland High School in 1951. He worked on the farm during the following two years.

In January 1953 he and three friends joined the US Air Force, and sent to Lackland Air Base in Texas. After completing his basic training, he received special training and became a radar operator, but he requested a different assignment. Sent on to Keesler Field in Mississippi, he was trained by Leland Hackman a friend from home. He was assigned to the 670th AC&W Squadron based on San Clemente Island in California. Promoted to S/Sgt he served as a radar operator on the island.

He enjoyed the sights of both San Pedro and Long Beach but later he was assigned to the 700th AC&W Squadron then based at Two Rivers in Wisconsin where he served as the NCO in charge of radar operations. It was there where he received his honorable discharge in December 1956. When he returned home he received his degree from Ball State University in 1964 and became a teacher at Nineveh, Indian Creek and Howe Military School. He married and became father of two sons. He is presently retired and lives with his wife, Ethel, near Reddington.

LOWELL H. KUEHN, Korea, United States Army, born July 27, 1931 near Brownstown. Parents: Martin and Stella Redicker Kuehn. Attended Honeytown Elementary School. Graduated with twin sister from Cortland High School in 1949.

Entered active duty in the army January 17, 1952. Completed basic training before being shipped to Korea. Served as Personnel Management Specialist. Discharged as T/Sgt. at Camp Carson, Colorado. Awarded Commendation Ribbon, Korean Service Medal w/3 Campaign Stars.

Returned home - employed at Nierman & Kuehn Store, Dunlap Building Supply Company.

Married May 22, 1955 to Shirley Nehrt. Residence at Crothersville, Operated Home Furnishing Store. Lowell H. Kuehn died February 6, 1983. Survived by wife and six children.

ORVELLE LUBKER, JR., Korea, United States Army, was the fifth child born to Orville H. and Lottie Lubker in 1929. He graduated from Brownstown

High School in 1948 and from Purdue University with a degree in Agriculture in 1952. He was soon sworn into the army and sent to Camp Chaffee, AR where he completed his basic training and leadership training. He and 25 other men were then shipped overseas to Korea. He was assigned to Charlie Battery of the 9th Field Artillery near Kumwha.

Shortly thereafter the Communists broke through the South Korean troops stationed to the east and the entire 3rd Infantry and supporting artillery was sent for support. One of his buddies received shrapnel and was pulled out and in a few days he was also sent to the center. He was on duty during the final hours before the Armistice took effect in July 1953.

Within a few weeks his unit was moved south of Chorwon in Korea. For another year he served as Troop Information Non com teaching classes in army defense of South Korea. He was mustered out of service as a S/Sgt in 1954 after which he returned to Brownstown and the farm. He entered the teaching and guidance program at Brownstown Central High School.

On Christmas Day in 1957 he married Laura Rose Burcham and they became parents of three children, Rise, Jeff and Sharon.

PATRICK M. MACKEY, Korea, United States Army, born on August 10, 1952 in Seymour, Indiana. He graduated from Seymour High School in 1970.

Within the first year after graduation, Pat received induction papers from the draft board notifying him to report for his physical and induction into the Armed Forces. Pat, with his wife, Mary W. Frazier, of Freetown, made the decision for Pat to go ahead and enlist in the United States Army, instead of waiting for the draft induction.

On October 16, 1972, Pat began his military career with Basic Training and Advanced Training at Fort Knox, Kentucky. Upon completion of training Pat received orders to report to Fort Campbell, Kentucky. Pat was assigned to Headquarters Company, 1st Battalion of the 501st Infantry, 2nd Brigade, 101st Airborne Division.

Pat received orders in May 1974 to report to 8th Army Headquarters in Seoul, Republic of Korea. After arriving at the 8th Army, Pat was then assigned to A Battery, 1st of the 38th Field Artillery, 2nd Infantry Division at Camp Stanley. While stationed in Korea, Pat extended his time in service.

After 13 months in Korea, Pat was reassigned back to the United States. He was ordered to report to the 101st Airborne Division at Fort Campbell, Kentucky. When Pat arrived at the Division Headquarters, he notified the Commander of the 1st of the 501st Infantry Division that he was at Division Headquarters awaiting assignment. Within 10 minutes of the phone call, Pat received written orders to report to Headquarters Company, 1st Battalion of the 501st Infantry, 2nd Brigade, 101st Airborne Division. In 36 months Pat had gone full circle and back to his original unit. On December 15, 1975, Pat's tour of duty in the military was expired. While serving Pat was decorated with an Army Commendation Medal, Meritorious Service Medal and the Army Commendation Medal with first Oak Leaf Cluster.

Pat currently resides in Clearwater, Florida with Mary and his two daughters, Lauren and Sarah. He is manager of Industrial Projects with Essilor of America.

VICTOR MARCOTT, No Date, United States Army. Two months of basic training and four months at AME school at Fort Lewis, Washington. Assigned shop foreman duties, transferred to Fort Belvoir, Virginia. Helped organize a detachment of troops to be attached to the Canadian Army for cold weather testing of military equipment in temperatures of 38 degrees below zero.

Following six months of such weather he was returned to Fort Belvoir where he received his discharge.

GENE ROLAND MARSH, Korea, United States Air Force, born March 15, 1929 at Seymour to Charles and Ruth Simmons Marsh. He was raised in Reddington and attended the local School and graduated from Seymour High School. He was then employed by Gerwin Shoe Company until he entered the service.

He was inducted into the air force December 26, 1952 at Indianapolis. He completed basic training at Lackland Field, TX and sent to school at Camp Polk, LA. He transferred to Kelly Field, TX and was assigned to the 75th Airborne Wing of the 2851st Hq. Squadron.

He was discharged just before Christmas in 1955. He returned home and to the shoe factory in Seymour. Twenty years later he was employed by Reliance Electric for six years before opening his own business.

He and his wife, Pailone Jones Marsh moved to Easyville. He is the father of two step-sons.

ROGER B. MATLOCK, Korea, United States Army, Meteorologist, born August 2, 1932 at Honeytown in Jackson County, IN. He was a son of Joel Burton and Helen Reedy Matlock and was reared with a brother, Herschel, and a sister, Alta, on the family farm. He graduated from Cortland High School with the class of 1950.

Three years later he entered the US Army and was assigned number 55359502. He completed his basic training at Camp Stewart in Georgia. He was selected to receive Meteorology instruction, and upon graduation he was assigned to Thule Air Base in Thule, Greenland.

After completing his tour of duty of 8 months, he was rotated back to the States and sent to Carswell Air Base in Texas. He was promoted to S/Sgt. and served as meteorology specialist. He was named the "NCO of the Month" and was presented the "Key to the City" of Fort Worth before being honorably discharged from the service in March 1955.

Roger Matlock returned to Jackson County in 1955, married and became the father of four children born on the farm near Reddington. He was employed for 30 years by Cummins Engine Company before retiring as Office Manager in 1985. In 1996 at age 64 years, he was stricken with cancer and died December 27, 1996.

MARSHALL FLOYD MCKAIN, Korea, United States Army, born June 2, 1926 at Spraytown, IN as the first child of Louis and Nellie Weekly McKain. He spent his entire young life in the Spraytown area. He attended both Freetown and Spraytown schools. He attended the Spraytown Free Methodist Church where he sang with the mixed quartet with his bass voice. He was a member of the I.O.O.F. Lodge in Freetown. His first job was at the Berry Sawmill in Seymour, Indiana. He went to work later at Arvin Industry in Columbus.

With the outbreak of war in Korea in June 1950, he was one of the very first draftees inducted from Jackson County. His serial number was 55030357. He completed his basic training at Fort Knox and was able to be at home for Christmas, but in early 1951 he was directed to report to Seattle. He then boarded the ship *Marine Phoenix* headed for Etta Jima, Japan. After the 3 week voyage he received further training before being sent into action in Korea.

Stationed near Pusan with the 858th Ordinance and Ammunition Company, he awaited the time for his rotation back to the United States. Sometime on October 21, 1952 he was killed by a sniper while riding in an open Jeep.

His remains were shipped home aboard ship *Marquett Victory,* and he was laid to rest February 7, 1952 near his home in Spraytown, Indiana. He was survived by his sister, Lois, and his parents.

ERNEST L. MCMAHAN, Korea, United States Army, 1951-1953, born October 23, 1928 in Illinois, the son of Herman and Lona McMahan. He grew up in Medora and attended the local high School. He was inducted into the army in January 1951. He completed basic training at Fort Bragg, NC.

Shortly thereafter he was shipped overseas to the European Theater where he served in Company C of the combat engineers. After receiving his discharge he returned home and was employed by Cummins Engine Company. With 30 years of service, he retired.

He was married to Mary Peek Miller and he became step-father of 3 children, David, Sharon and Roger Miller.

RAY N. MEAHL, Korea, United States Army, born in January 1938 in Jackson County. Later on in 1961 he was ordered to report to the induction center in Indianapolis to be drafted into the army. He was sent to Fort Leonard Wood for his basic training. During that time he was granted secret clearance necessary to attend the Intelligence School in Maryland.

He was ordered to report to the army transportation terminal in Oakland, California. He was assigned to service in South Korea. He went overseas on the USNS *General Hugh Gaffey* for a 23-day run across the Pacific to Inchon Harbor.

He was assigned to the 7th Division, 6th How Bn., 28th Arty. located at the edge of the DMZ. While stationed there he fired the highest score in the Artillery Division so was assigned to the rifle team. In June 1963 he returned to the states for separation from the army.

After being discharged he was assigned to the reserves in Michigan. Later he was transferred to Scottsburg, Indiana where, when released he could attend IU and seek his associate degree.

JOHN C. MONTGOMERY, Post Korea, United States Army, entered the army in June 1955. Completed basic training at Fort Leonard Wood. Sent to Fort Bliss, Texas for special training. Anti-aircraft Artillery RADAR Division.

Assigned to Battery B, 501st AAA Battalion. Stationed at Camp Hanford, Washington. Served as Computer Operator Specialist. Promoted to Sergeant 1st Class. Received honorable discharge.

POERCE C. MOSS, JR., Korea, United States Army, born July 4, 1932 in Spartansburg, SC. High school graduate 1950. Enlisted in the army and completed basic training at Fort Knox, KY.

Shipped overseas to Korea with Co. D of 21st Regiment of the 24th Division as machine gunner until wounded. Completed tour of duty assigned to motor pool before being returned to South Carolina.

Discharged July 8, 1953; returned; married and settled in Seymour. Employed by Cummins Engine in Columbus from 1956 to 1988. Retired and now enjoys traveling, camping, boating and fishing.

MILTON LEO NEHRT, Korea, United States Navy, born December 9, 1933 near Crothersville to Paul and Thelma Nehrt. He graduated from the local high school in 1952 and joined the navy almost immediately.

He completed boot camp training at Pensacola, Florida and was assigned as a mechanic on trainer aircraft. His duties included repair and maintenance preparing the aircraft for flight testing. His unit was sent to Iceland where he was on duty for more than a year before he was returned to Florida.

He was discharged from the NAS at Jacksonville. He returned to East St. Louis where he enrolled at Parks Air College. He was awarded his commercial license.

He was employed by the army as an instructor for cadet training at Savannah, Georgia. Finally, he was employed by AMP, Inc. as a corporate pilot for more than 20 years before retirement.

ROBERT DALE NEHRT, Korea, United States Air Force, born December 11, 1931 in Crothersville to Paul and Thelma Pheral Nehrt. He was raised as a farm boy and graduated from the local high school. He was employed as Tool and Engineering in Seymour before entering the service.

He was inducted into the air force January 9, 1951 at Indianapolis and was directed to Lackland AFB for basic training. He received instruction at Sheppard Field and was trained as a machinist at George AFB in California. He was stationed at Hamilton AFB before being shipped to Tule in Greenland for one year.

He was discharged from Shaw AFB located in Sumter, SC.

He returned to Jackson County and continued his work as a tool maker at King Industries in Seymour. After working at the American Can Company, he opened his own Quality Tool Company near Brownstown.

He married Ileen Schneider of Vallonia January 1, 1955 and they became parents of four children.

RICHARD NEAL NEHRT, Post Korea, United States Air Force, born September 6, 1940 in Crothersville to Paul and Thelma Pheral Nehrt. He graduated from the local high school in 1958. He was employed at the US Shoe Factory for a time before entering the service.

He entered the Air Force at Louisville February 1, 1959 and was directed to Lackland AFB to complete basic training in Texas. He was assigned to the 4138th Food Services Squadron stationed at Turner AFB in Georgia.

He was discharged February 1, 1963 from his home base. He returned home to Crothersville and was employed by Cummins in Columbus. He is currently serving as the County Recorder.

GERALD MARVIN OATHOUT, Korea, United States Air Force, enlisted November 13, 1961 at Denver, Colorado. Released July 19, 1965 at Offutt AFB in Nebraska. Carpenter Assignment. Air Force Reserve Center in Colorado. Returned to Corland, Jackson County.

CHARLES PATRICK, Korea, United States Air Force, Stateside Air Traffic Control Operator, 1951-1955.

JOHN BRADLEY PATRICK, Korea, United States Air Force, Stateside Service, 1952-1953.

JOE PETERS, Korea, United States Air Force, born October 1, 1930 not far north of Vallonia to William and Helen Smith Peters. He attended the local school. On February 12, 1951 he joined the Air Force and was trained at several AFB, including Lackland Field, Embry Riddle, Chanute Field and Grumman Aircraft in New York.

Because of high scores on the qualifying tests, he was assigned as an instructor of operations, maintenance and control of various aircraft parts. He was sent to different schools located across many states. He was discharged at Lincoln, NE on February 11, 1955.

He was married June 7, 1953 to June Craigmiles of Crothersville and became parents of 3 children, Joe Mark, Michael Kent and Jana Kay. Joe Peters has been a farmer, trucker and salesman. He is now retired.

RICHARD WILLIAM PFERRER, Post Korea/Pre Vietnam, United States Air Force, born March 1, 1937. Parents: Charles and Opal Davis Pferrer. Raised in Brownstown and graduated from the local school. After his parents died he was raised by his grandparents.

Entered air force in November 1958. Stationed in Texas, Minnesota before going to Alaska. Shipped to Vietnam. Returned to Texas. Appointed recruiter. Discharged December 19, 1978 with 20 years service time. Residents of Florida

ALLEN D. POGUE, Korea, United States Army, was drafted into the army November 3, 1950 and completed his basic field training at Camp Breckinridge, KY. He was then sent to Ft. Sam Houston, TX where he received training in the care for the wounded. Eventually he was shipped overseas to Korea. He was assigned to the 8076th Mobile Army Surgical Hospital. (MASH) in which he served until rotated back to the States.

He was authorized to wear several ribbons and medals. He was eventually returned to Camp Atterbury where he received his discharge on August 4, 1952,

KENNETH R. POLLERT, Korea, United States Army, born January 17, 1934 to Martin and Mary Redicker Pollert. After the sudden death of his father, he was reared on the family farm by his mother and two sisters. He graduated from Vallonia High School in 1952.

Kenneth Pollert was inducted into the army July 20, 1956 at Fort Leonard Wood, MO. He was sent to Fort Hood, Texas to complete his basic training. He was then assigned to Fort Chafee, AR to attend radio school.

In 1957 he was shipped overseas to Korea in the 4th Armored Division but was transferred to the 43rd Construction Engineers. He carried out his duties as a radio operator during his tour of duty in Korea.

He was discharged in March 1958, returned to Fort Sheridan, IL and came home to Driftwood Township. He was married to Elsie Schroer in Bartholomew County. To them were born 3 children, now all grown. Kenneth Pollert currently resides on the farm where he was born located south of Vallonia.

JUNIOR L. PORCH, Korea, United States Air Force, enlisted in the Air Force on May 7, 1950. Stationed at Lackland Air Base in Texas. Stationed at Rapid City, South Dakota. Stationed at Sidi Slimane, Ft. Morocco.

Returned to Barksdale AB in Louisiana. Discharged in May 1954, unknown base.

Junior Porch was the son of Dayton and Mary Porch of Norman. He graduated from Clearspring High School in 1950. He was married to Phyllis Crider and they became parents of two sons. Phyllis died in 1955.

EARL J.C. POTTSCHMIDT, Korea, United States Air Force, born August 7, 1934 to Alfred and Lillian Melloncamp Pottschmidt. He was raised as a farm boy and later graduated from Brownstown High School in 1952.

He was inducted into the Air Force at Indianapolis, completed basic training at Lackland AFB and sent to Keesler AFB for additional training. Other stations of training included Warren in Wyoming, Ent in Colorado before he was assigned as an office clerk. He was authorized to wear the appropriate medals and ribbon reflecting his service.

He was discharged December 6, 1956 from McClellan AFB and returned to the home farm near Brownstown. He married Mary Freeman of Medora and they became parents of two sons.

HAROLD POTTSCHMIDT, #55091030, Sergeant, induction at Ft. Breckinridge, KY, January 1951-October 1952. Discharged at Camp Atterbury, IN.

The military Memoirs of Harold Pottschmidt, a sergeant in the Army of the United States during the Korean Conflict; a war by other standards! Assigned a serial number of 55091030, Harold served from January 1951 to October 1952.

He was born April 3, 1928 not far from Brownstown, and was the son of Alfred and Lillian Melloncamp Pottschmidt. He was reared as a farm boy on the family homestead. He was a graduate of Brownstown High School in 1947.

After his induction, he completed his basic training at Camp Breckinridge, Kentucky. Shortly thereafter, he was assigned overseas duty in the Korean Theater. He served in George Company of the 35th Regiment in the 25th Infantry Division as a rifleman. He first received his Combat Infantry Badge, but later became mess sergeant of his unit.

Harold Pottschmidt completed eleven months of foreign service, and spent most of the time with troops assigned to the center of the Korean battle line. Along with Herschel Forgey of the 32nd Regiment, he eventually rotated back home to Camp Atterbury in 1952.

Harold's father, Alfred Pottschmidt had been one of the prisoners in WWI in 1918. Having been able to speak fluent German, he spent much time behind enemy lines. Harold Pottschmidt was proud of his military heritage in defense of the American freedoms!

JOE DALE RAMP, Korea, United States Navy, born August 26, 1928 not far from Brownstown to Frank and Addie McMahon Ramp. He was raised northwest of the County seat and later graduated from Cortland High School in 1947.

He joined the navy not long after graduation and was inducted at Great Lakes Naval Station, Illinois and reported for training August 25, 1947. He was sent to San Diego, California for further training before being assigned to the destroyer, USS *Eversole* BD-789. He served three and one half years aboard ship.

His ship was sailing in the Pacific Theater of Operations and saw action along the Korean coastline in 1950-51. He was discharged in August 1951 at San Diego and returned home to Brownstown where he found employment with Kieffer Mills. He remained with the company for 39 years until his retirement.

Joe and his wife, Georgia Estes Ramp, were married in 1955 and reside in the Pleasant Grove community. They have three grown daughters.

GLEN DALE RATCLIFF, Post Korea, United States Air Force, born August 26, 1941 in Ewing to Howard and Gladys Baughman Ratcliff of Freetown. They became parents of three sons, Ronald, Randy and Robert.

Glen Dale Ratcliff joined the air force August 10, 1960 after graduating from Brownstown High School. He served four years and was then discharged August 7, 1964.

During his time in the service, he was stationed at several air bases in the states. He was trained as an electrician and assigned to a line crew. One of his jobs was to change the light bulbs in the mountain warning lights. He was taken to the mountain top, climbed down a rope ladder to the ground. Then he climbed the tower, changed the bulbs and went back down to catch the helicopter for the flight back to the base.

He completed his tour of duty in Klamath Falls, Oregon. He met and married Patty Van Dyke October 16, 1965.

ALBERT WEIR RAY, Korea, United States Army, born October 21, 1929 in Jackson County. Parents were John and Hester Bridges Ray of Cortland. Raised as a farm boy. Graduated from Cortland High School in 1947. Employed by the Sinclair Oil Bulk Plant.

Inducted into the army November 15, 1951 at Indianapolis. Completed basic training at Indian Gap, Pennsylvania. Assigned to the 11th Regiment, Prisoner of War Service. Shipped overseas to Koje Island. Discharged in Colorado October 30, 1953.

Awarded Korean Service Medal, UN Service Medal, Presidential Unit Citation and National Defense Medal. Returned to Cortland and employment with Sinclair. Married April 8, 1951 to Genevieve Flinn. Became parents of three children.

CHARLES ALBERT RICHARDS, Korean Police Action, United States Navy, USS *Paiute* AFT-159, 1948-1952, born June 16, 1929 to Clarence and Effie Reedy Richards. He entered the naval service at the Great Lakes Naval Station near Chicago. He received his honorable discharge at Norfolk, Virginia after having served in the Mediterranean Sea and the Greenland area.

After returning home he married Dorothy Jane Empson who was reared in the Tampico area. They became parents of three children while their father was superintendent with Public Service of Indiana. Charles Richards died July 1, 1980 in Noblesville. His wife, Dorothy, retired later from Washington Township Schools in Indianapolis as Media Technical Services Manager.

Their son, Charles James, along with his wife, Janice, live at St. Joe, Michigan. He is the father of two daughters named Danielle and Jillian Richards.

Joy Annette and her husband John D. Ickes live in Tampa, Florida. She is the mother of two sons, named Michael Ryan and Christopher Todd Harley.

Jan Anita and her husband Frank P. Padula live in Panama City, Florida and are the parents of four children, named Frank Joseph, Erica Jane, Charles Albert and Cassandra Caroline Padula.

HERBERT HOOVER RINER, Korea, United States Army, born in Kingsport, Tennessee on January 11, 1929 to Charles and Addie Riner. Moving to Clearspring, Indiana in 1936 with his family, a very young lad entered and attended school there in the hills of Jackson County, Indiana.

In 1948 he was married to Alice Winslow Hilderbrand, one of the residents of Norman, Indiana. Four years later he was drafted and inducted into the Army. In mid-January 1952 he reported to Indianapolis where he was assigned the number of US 55-233-334. He was directed to Ft. Belvoir in Virginia where he completed his basic training.

Shortly after that he was shipped overseas with Company A of the 1092nd Combat Engineer Battalion. He was promoted to S/Sgt. on July 15, 1953. Herbert Hoover Riner was rotated back to the states and sent to Camp Atterbury, Indiana where he received his discharge October 17, 1953.

He made his home near Brownstown, Indiana until he died November 17, 1987. His widow has since remarried and resides in rural Norman, Indiana.

ERNEST DALE ROBERTS, Korea, United States Army, enlisted in the army August 1, 1951 and completed basic training at Fort Riley, Kansas. Was shipped overseas to Korea and assigned as a truck driver to transport ammunition to the front line troops. H

He was assigned to Company L of the 87th Infantry Division. Was authorized to wear several medals and ribbons awarded him during his overseas service.

CLAIR DEAN ROBISON, Korea, United States Army, Poky, as he was known by his family and friends, was born to George and Myrtle McKinney Robison on November 7, 1930, in Ewing, IN. He graduated from Brownstown High School in 1951. He excelled in sports. He married Marcia Hanners in 1952 in Brownstown.

Poky went on active duty in the US Army on July 24, 1953, in Seymour, IN. He had been a member of a National Guard unit in Seymour, IN. He entered the US Army active duty with a rank of sergeant. He soon joined Company C, 370th Armored Infantry as a Squad leader in Fort Riley, Kansas. He then was deployed to Germany. He was awarded the National Defense Service Medal and the Army of Occupation Medal for the time that he had served in Germany.

Upon returning from the military, Poky returned to his job at Marion-Kay for a time. He became actively involved with Marion-Kay's athletic programs as a coach and player for their fast pitch softball teams and as a coach and player for their basketball teams. He was very successful and produced many winning teams. Upon leaving employment with Marion-Kay, he continued to have a close relationship with MK sports teams. He refereed local basketball games for many years. He owned and operated Poky's Tavern and Robison Trucking in Ewing, IN, for several years before retiring.

Clair Dean Robison died June 13, 1998, in Brownstown, IN. He had 2 sons, Kevin Dean Robison and Bradley David Robison.

WILLIAM P. ROLLINS, Army of the United States, #55 340 601, Corporal, February 2, 1953-December 7, 1954.

CHARLES GALE RUCKER, Korea, United States Army, born October 26, 1927 near Acme in Jackson County. Parents were Ralph and Josie Goss Rucker. Attended Surprise elementary school. Graduated from Cortland High School in 1945. Employed by Hamilton COSCO

Inducted into the army September 9, 1950. One of the first group of county draftees called to service. Completed basic training at Fort Knox. Assigned to the 858th Ordinance Ammo Company.

Shipped overseas to Korea to complete his tour of duty. Discharged August 1, 1952. Awarded Occupation Medal, Service Medal w/3 Campaign Stars. Earned the United Nations Medal.

Returned to Surprise and assumed employment at Hamilton. Married Carole M. Carmichael of Freetown. Became parents of four daughters. Died January 16, 1970.

DAVID W. RUST, Korea, United States Army, born March 25, 1925 to Walter and Lillian Schafstall-Rust in Seymour. He was raised by his family who provided inspiration and training from his grandparents. It was with them that he helped operate the farm, even at his early age. His elementary instruction was completed in the Myers school and he graduated from Cortland High School in 1943. He continued his studies in an Agriculture short course at Purdue University.

He was drafted into the army in January 1951 at Fort Sheridan, Illinois, but was sent to Fort Lewis, Washington to complete his basic training. He was with a medical company, but was later assigned to an artillery unit stationed near the Golden Gate Bridge in California. While there he was ordered to attend Officer Candidate School so he could participate in the Leadership Training School at Camp Roberts. Upon graduation he was assigned to the faculty to train more then 100 other men. He received a letter of commendation from General Wedemeyer.

David W. Rust transferred to Santa Monica and received orders to report to the Signal School at Fort Monmouth, NJ. He was assigned to Fort Leslie McNair where he pulled guard duty at the Tomb of the Unknown Soldier and funeral services at Arlington National Cemetery. President Truman ate with the men of his unit every two weeks. Later, David was assigned guard duty for the inauguration of Eisenhower as President of the United States.

He was granted a letter from the Secretary of Defense to use military transportation on a "space available-non priority basis" to study the agricultural situation in Europe and North Africa. He was discharged January 31, 1953 and returned home to organize his egg business.

Once home following the war, he raised a large family. With his first wife, Lois, were born seven children: Anthony, Marcus, Ruth Ann, James, Karen, John and Robert. With his second wife, Sylvia were born six children: Victoria, Alexander, Regina, Solomon, David and Joseph.

David W. Rust died January 30, 2004.

IVAN LEE SCHNEIDER, Korea, United States Air Force, born January 11, 1928 in Vallonia. Parents were Oscar and Freda Shoemaker Schneider. Graduated from Vallonia High School in 1948. Employed as a truck driver for Bundy Brothers Mill.

Enlisted November 29, 1948. Completed basic training at Lackland AFB in Texas. Stationed at San Antonio and Warren AFB in Wyoming. Trained as a clerk/typist. Assigned to 814th Police Squadron Provost Marshall. Stationed at Fairchild AFB in Spokane to complete his tour of duty. Discharged November 28, 1952.

Married Ann Kruger and became parents of three children. Employed as manager of a J.C. Penny Store.

JOSEPH F. SCHRINK, Korea, United States Navy, born February 3, 1934 in Seymour to Louis and Mary Engleking Schrink. He attended the local schools and graduated from Seymour (Shields) High School. He then became employed by Sears Tire Store.

He enlisted in the navy in June 1952 and later served aboard the LST ISS 527 and completed two tours of duty during the Korean Police Action. He was authorized to wear various medals and campaign ribbons denoting his military service.

He was discharged July 13, 1956 at San Diego, CA and returned to Jackson County. He was employed by several concerns before retiring from Cummins in 1999.

He was married to Carol Daily and to them were born two sons and several grandchildren. He also enjoys one great grandson.

RALPH MARVIN SCOTT, Korea, United States Army, born near Medora January 25, 1928 to Morton and Myrtle Brown Scott. Ralph later graduated from Medora High School in 1945. He was one of nine drafted during the 2nd call for the Korean Conflict, including George Merrill, Bussy Smith, James Sutherland, Harold Scifres, Louis Weinhorst, Jr., Harlan Oringenburg, Gordon Kelley, Robert Patrick and Frank Griffin, Jr.

He was sent to Camp McCoy, WI for training and was assigned to Company B, 114th Combat Engineers of the 5th Army. He served on a railroad bridge crew and was named foreman over bridge construction back in the states in Kansas following the floods in 1952.

He was discharged at Camp Atterbury on October 3, 1952 and returned to work for the B&O Railroad. He then was employed at Hamilton COSCO and Cummins in Columbus. He married Pat Eastin and they reside in Medora.

DONALD DWIGHT SHEPARD, Korea, United States Army, was raised in and around Medora and graduated from the local high school in 1948. He was married to Eva Nethercutt and they became parents of two sons named Steven and Billy.

Dwight Shepard was inducted into the army sometime in 1951 and, after completing his basic training at Camp Breckinridge in Kentucky. He was shipped overseas to Japan and he served there and in Korea until 1954.

Records verify he died in 2001.

ERMAN SHOEMAKER, Corporal 55419507, Company A, 76th Battalion, 11th Airborne Division, United States Army, born September 7, 1932 near Vallonia, Indiana. He graduated with the class of 1950 from the local high school. He helped his father on the farm until he was drafted into the army shortly after the Korean Conflict ended.

He started his basic training with the Airborne Division at Fort Campbell, Kentucky, and upon completion, he received specialized training in the operation of an M-47 tank. He became skilled in the various operational positions of the tank. He remained with the unit and became part of the "combat-ready" 11th Airborne Division, on call for deployment at any time to defend the national freedom.

Eventually he was assigned work in the orderly room as Company Clerk, and part of his duties included making out the morning report as part of the clerical functions. He reached the rank of corporal by the time of his discharge in June 1955.

He returned home and resumed the farm work. He is married to the former Betty Jane Hansen and they became parents of four children; Kisa Lohmeyer, Carol Delph, Bruce Shoemaker and Julie Dietrickkh.

JAMES R. SHOEMAKER, Post Korean Era, United States Army, born January 21, 1937 to Louis and Leah Otting Shoemaker of Driftwood Township. He was raised on the family farm and graduated from Vallonia High School in 1955. Three years later he was drafted into the army and was inducted November 10, 1958.

He completed basic training at Fort Leonard Wood, MO and was assigned to the 5th Battalion, 2nd Regiment of the Military Police. He was transferred to Fort Lewis and then to Camp Hamford, WA. He served on special assignments at various locations while serving as a Military Policeman.

He completed his tour of duty and was discharged in August 1960 and then returned to civilian life on the farm. He married Carolyn Grelle and they became parents of four daughters who produced ten grandchildren. James has remained active in retirement, community affairs and Trinity Lutheran Church located south of Vallonia.

ARCHIE SMITH, Korea and Vietnam Era, United States Navy, born in Bartholomew County December 20, 1930 to Hoyt and Clara Mitchell Smith. The family moved to Seymour where he attended the local schools. Following his graduation in 1946 he was employed by Cummins until he joined the navy.

His duty stations from October 18, 1948 to May 15, 1970 included assignments on the USS *Curtiss* AV-4 to 1950, USS *Princeton* CV-37 to 1952, USS *Oriskany* CVA to 1953, USS *Salisbury Sound* AV-34 to 1955, NAVRECTA to 1958, USS *Buck* - DD 761 to 1960, and others until assigned to the Naval Reserve Fleet in Philadelphia to 1968. His final assignment was on the USS Sterett (DLG) to 1970.

Commendations included the National Defense Service Medal, Good Conduct Ribbon, Expeditionary Korean Medal, Vietnam Service Medal with one Silver Campaign Star and one Bronze Campaign Star and the Vietnam Device.

He was married to Kyoko Maeda while stationed in Japan and they became the parents of two sons who now live in Poway, California. He died of cancer in San Diego December 10, 2003.

GEORGE MERRILL SMITH, Korean Conflict, United States Army, born in Medora, IN May 13, 1928, the son of William H. and Olean Nicholson Smith. His father was a blacksmith and his mother a school teacher. Bussie graduated from Medora High School in 1946 and went to work on the B&O Railroad in Lawrenceville, IL for a time. Later he was employed by Arvin Industries.

He was inducted into the army October 3, 1950 at Fort Sheridan, Illinois and then sent to Camp Atterbury for basic training. In April 1951 he was shipped overseas to Korea with the 10th Field Artillery Battalion, made part of the famed 3rd Infantry Division. He was assigned to the Ordinance units responsible for transporting materials to the front line soldiers.

Bussie returned to the States in April 1952 and was discharged from the service as Sergeant 1st Class at Camp Atterbury. He was authorized to wear the Service Medal with a Bronze Star with his Unit Citation. He continued to serve until the Army Reserve status was restored at Fort Benning in 1956.

He was employed by the US Postal Service in 1953 and later approved by the Postmaster who, with a battle star component, was appointed permanently and he continued his service time for another 35 years.

He married Caolynn Jo Airhar in 1955, and to them were born 3 children including Greg, Leslie and Tiffany. He lived in Medora and finally passed away after completing more than 38 years of service to his country. He was buried at Beem Cemetery located near Medora.

ALFRED B. SPURLOCK, Korea, United States Army, born in Lafayette to Alfred and Mary Lynch Spurlock. He was raised with three brothers and until he was 13 years old, he lived in Frankfort and Bloomington. He graduated from high school before entering the University of Dayton.

He finally settled in Jackson County but never married. He later resided in California and worked for Lockheed. He was inducted into army January 18, 1953 and discharged in February 1957 with the Hq Company of the 8068th AU.

His father was in the army and completed separate tours of duty and became the county veterans service officer.

HOWARD L. SPURLOCK, Korea, United States Army,

Howard L. Spurlock was born August 28, 1930 to Alfred and Mary Spurlock in Dayton, Ohio. He joined the army September 10, 1951 at Fort Riley, Kansas and was assigned to the 10th Infantry Division and sent to Elmendorf AFB at Anchorage in Alaska. He was discharged August 20, 1953.

ALBERT LEO STAHL, Korea, United States Army, ERC AMEDS, 1951-1953.

PAUL J. STAHL, Korea, United States Air Force,

born August 29, 1931 near the Wegan community in Jackson County to Edgar and Rachel Hallow Stahl. He was reared on the family homestead and later graduated from Tampico High School in 1949. He joined the National Guard and served 2 years before being inducted into the service.

He reported for duty, and was stationed in England during the Korean Conflict as a dental lab technician after receiving training at Manhattan Beach Base in Brooklyn, NY at the Weisbaden Hospital in Germany for two years, 1954-1955. He was discharged on December 12, 1955.

Following service he was married to Marie Franke on May 13, 1956 at Cortland. He attended Franklin College and graduated in 1960 before entering his graduate training at Indiana University. Paul J. Stahl then went into dental practice in Franklin. He and his family of four sons remained residents for more than thirty years.

Paul J. Stahl died September 10, 2003 and was buried at Riverview Cemetery in Seymour, Indiana.

STEVEN D. STARR, Korea, United States Army, 1965-1971, Company B, 1st Battalion, 151st Infantry Division, Seymour, Indiana.

MORRIS J. STOUT, DCG3 - 403-86-44, USS PCS 1385, United States Navy,

born June 26, 1932 on a farm located east of Brownstown. He is the son of Otis Lee and Estella Voyles Stout and one of nine children born to them. On June 26, 1952 he enlisted in the U.S. Navy for four years.

He completed his basic training at the Great Lakes Naval Base in Chicago, Illinois. After thirteen weeks of training, he was assigned to the USS PCS 1385 at Key West, Florida. That ship was equipped to locate submarines. It was used to teach sonar detection. Morris was on that ship during his four years of duty.

In 1955 the ship was de-commissioned and beached along the St. Lawrence Seaway near Cleveland, Ohio. The Navy reserves maintain the ship there. Stout was awarded the Commissioning Pennant from 1942-1956. His duty was completed in Philadelphia as a brig chaser. He received his discharge in August of 1960, returned home to his wife, Patricia Soladine and their six children. He was employed by the Jackson Brick and Holloware for more than twenty years. He retired from Cummins Engine Company on October 1, 1987.

GERRY JOE SULLIVAN, Korea and Afterward, United States Navy,

17 years of service from 1962-1986. Engineman 1st Class, awarded a host of medals and ribbons reflecting his service record. Served aboard the USS *John F. Kennedy* and USS *Sumpter*. Married December 21, 1986 to Peggy S. Shaver. Retired in Austin.

ROBERT G. TATLOCK, Post Korea, United States Marine Corps, 1953-1959,

born and raised on a farm near Tampico to Kerry and Marie Wolff Tatlock. In 1955 he graduated from Tampico High School. During those years he helped on the farm, played basketball and joined the National Guard. He reported for duty in 1953 and remained a member until he enlisted in the Marine Corps in 1956.

He was assigned number 1601798 and completed his boot camp training at San Diego. His platoon was composed of all volunteers from Indiana and were called the "Medal of Honor" company. His tour of duty took him through campaigns in Okinawa, the Philippines and Japan. He completed his call to service in North Carolina in April of 1959 and was honorably discharged as a Corporal.

After discharge he returned home and was employed by a neon sign company and introduced to the world of electricity. During the following 20 years he helped build high line and substations throughout several states. In 1983 he returned to the farm and is retired and lives in Grassy Fork Township. His log home, built in 1866, has been completely updated for him and his second wife. He is the father of 2 daughters and has four grandchildren.

GERALD TERRELL, Korea, United States Air Force,

born in 1931 at Scottsburg to Jack and Loretta May Terrell. He lived in Crothersville during the early years of life and married Millie Baughman in 1951. They became parents of three sons.

He joined the air force in 1952 and was assigned to the supply division refueling jet air planes. He was a member of the base band when going from base to base entertaining the troops.

They lived in California for more than 14 years before moving to Brownstown. He was a truck driver. He died May 17, 1996.

CHARLES ALLEN THOMPSON, Korea, United States Army.

He was inducted into the military September 10, 1951, and he was discharged August 12, 1953.

He received his basic training at Fort Riley, Kansas. He was in the 10th Infantry Division, Company K, 87th Infantry from September 1951 to January 1952.

After his basic training he went to the Basic Parachute Training Co. I, Fort Benning, Georgia. He attended the school from January 1952 to March 1952.

After he became a paratrooper, he went to the Quartermaster School at Fort Lee, Virginia. He took a twelve weeks course in Parachute Packing, Maintenance, and Aerial Supply. He took this course from March 19, 1952 to July 24, 1952.

He was a Parachute Maintenance Inspector in the 8081st Company in Japan, from July 1952 to August 1953. He supervised the maintenance work on all air type items. He supervised 150 Japanese workers. He also made numerous parachute drops.

He was discharged at Headquarters 5022, ASV Transfer Center, Camp Carson, Colorado, on August 12, 1953.

GLENN LOUIS TORMOEHLEN, Post Korea, United States Army, was drafted and inducted into the army at Indianapolis February 15, 1962. He completed basic training at Fort Leonard Wood and was assigned as a truck driver for the center at Fort Knox, KY.

He served out his hitch in the United States, was discharged but remained in the army reserves until February 1968.

WAYNE H. TORMOEHLEN, Korea, United States Army, born August 4, 1929 to Louis and Lena Wessel Tormoehlen who lived in Grassy Fork Township. He attended St. Paul Lutheran Church and school at Wegan and he graduated from Tampico High School in 1948.

He was inducted into the army at Battle Creek, Michigan on March 19, 1951. He completed basic training at Camp Breckinridge, KY and received further instruction with the 101st and 4th Divisions. His unit was shipped out of Camp Kilmer, NJ bound for Germany where he attended clerical school. He was assigned the company clerk during his overseas service.

He was discharged from Camp Atterbury in February 1953. He returned home and was employed by Arvin and Cummins, but retired from Moorman's Manufacturing Company in 1994.

KENNETH WEHMILLER, Korea, United States Army, the military memoirs of Lynn Kenneth (Kenny) Wehmiller who served in the Korean Conflict was assigned a serial number of US55030352. Kenny was born on June 6, 1927 to Walter and Hilda (VonDielingen) Wehmiller, and graduated from Seymour High School in 1946.

He served in the U.S. Army from September 1950 to September 1952, After his induction in the U.S. Army, he completed his basic training and eight weeks advance infantry training at Carson, Colorado.

The next phase of his service was at Salzburg, Austria unassigned. When arriving in Austria Kenny was assigned to the 63rd Signal Battalion as a wireman. The last year of his service was a non-commissioner officer in charge of installation and maintenance at Camp Roeder. At the end of the Auto-Baum in Austria, he returned to the United States in September 1952 with an honorable discharge.

He resumed his employment with the Indiana Telephone Corporation where he had worked 5 years as a cable splicer before entering the service. He retired from Contel Telephone company in 1983.

He married Ida Marie Roettger in 1954 and they have two children, Roger (Susan) Wehmiller and Rebecca (Barry) Stuckwisch, and four grandchildren: Julie and Greg Wehmiller and Kelly and Cory Stuckwisch.

LOWELL F. WESSEL, Korea, United States Air Force, born December 8, 1931 on a farm located in Jackson County. He completed his elementary grades at Wegan Lutheran School, but graduated from Brownstown High School in 1950. He was employed by the county REMC before joining National Guard at Freeman Field.

He enlisted in the air force June 6, 1952 and completed his basic training at Lackland AFB, TX. He was sent to Keesler AFB, MS for training in electronics. Upon completion he was selected for special duty requiring high security. He was granted leave and en route to Brooks AFB, he was married to Rosalyn Stuckwish who accompanied him to his assigned base. He was transferred to March AFB, CA where he helped install new equipment.

He was shipped overseas to Elmendorf AFB, Alaska where he completed his tour of duty in electronics. Returned to the states and discharged June 5, 1956 as a S/Sgt. He maintained his role in the Reserves until 1959.

He retired from the county REMC in 1996 and currently resides with his wife of 50 years on a small farm near Brownstown.

WILBERT WESSEL, JR., Korea, United States Army, born March 1, 1930 to Wilbert and Viola Steinkamp Wessel of Tampico. He was raised on the family farm and graduated from Tampico High School in 1948.

He was inducted into the army at Indianapolis on May 3, 1951 and completed basic training at Fort Custer at Battle Creek, Michigan. He was assigned to the 804th Station Hospital Unit before being shipped overseas to Germany.

After receiving his discharge April 24, 1953 he returned home to Jackson County and resumed his work at Brownstown Hardware. Two months later he was married to Donna Meahl. They became parents of three daughters: Jo Gail Ross, Kim Loree Lucas and Dena Hutchinson.

PAUL R. WHEELER, Korea, United States Army Air Corps, born March 7, 1931 in Green County, Ohio to James and Orpha Harris Wheeler. He was inducted into the air corps August 28, 1946 and completed basic training at Lackland Field, TX. He was released from service due to his age.

Later, he was drafted into the army at Indianapolis. He was sent to Fort Leonard Wood, MO, Fort Meade, MD and Camp Pickett, VA. His unit was shipped overseas and arrived in Korea April 1, 1951. He was assigned to Company B, 64th Field Artillery of the 25th Division. He served nine months in Korea and returned to the states to be discharged at Camp Atterbury July 18, 1952.

He returned to his home near Vallonia and was later employed by Kieffer Paper Mill for 38 years. He resides near the Medora Junction in Jackson County.

JAMES F. WILDE, Korea, United States Army, was drafted into the army January 16, 1953 and reported for duty to Camp Chaffee, AR where he completed his basic training. He then went to the service leadership training course and remained as an instructor until he received orders for overseas duty in Korea.

His troop ship had engine failure on the way over and was diverted to the Hawaiian Islands. After spending 10 days there he was sent to Japan for further training. Two weeks later he was ordered to Korea where he was assigned to the 15th Field Artillery of the 2nd Infantry Division.

He remained with that unit until November 1953 when he was returned to the States for discharge on December 24, 1953. He had served more than seven months overseas.

HAROLD L. WILSON, Korea, United States Army, graduated from Seymour High School in 1953 and entered the army immediately. After he completed basic training, he was sent to the Pacific Theater of Operations.

He served in the far east and was discharged in November 1955. He was married to Sharon D. Wilson.

EARL WOLKA, Korea, United States Army, born March 17, 1930 to Sim and Lydia Otte

Wolka and graduated from Tampico High School in 1948. He entered the army three years later on July 3, 1951.

He completed his basic training at Ft. Leonard Wood, MO and was soon shipped overseas to Japan. He arrived on January 1, 1952 and was assigned the money order clerk with the 20th Army Postal Unit stationed at Camp Drake in Japan.

He was discharged in June 1953. He married Alberta Hinnefeld in 1960. He retired from Midway Supply in 1996 and is currently employed part time at Bridgepoint Goodwill Store.

DEAN ZIKE, Korea, United States Army, born December 20, 1930 at Freetown to Dayton and Bertha Zike. Graduated from the local high school in 1948. Was drafted and inducted into the army October 1, 1951 and completed basic training in Pennsylvania. His unit was shipped overseas to Korea in February 1952. Assigned to Company H, 27th Infantry Regiment as forward observer for 81 mm mortars.

Was rotated back to the states in January 1953, served at Fort Knox and discharged June 30, 1953.

Married Jane Mullen and became father of two children.

Graduated from Indiana Central College and became a teacher at various Jackson County Schools.

KOREAN WAR VETERANS

THE VIETNAM WAR

1957-1975

Each day for more than twenty-five years, many American citizens have taken time to recall the sacrifices of those Vietnam War veterans who fought bravely in an unpopular conflict. In historical retrospect, those service men deserve the belated label of heroes. The records herein, attempt to remember their deeds. But such thoughts are hardly enough! It is only now that Vietnam veterans have earned the respect of a new generation of thoughtful Americans. Records of their bravery, as told by their family accounts, complement the Wall of Memory dedicated to 58,000 American casualties. Included in RECALL are records which enables readers of generations to come may pay their personal tribute to those Jackson County Veterans of the Vietnam War The rightful honor due them is certainly never-ending!

THE EMERGING OF A NEW NATION
A UNITED VIETNAM

1894-1975

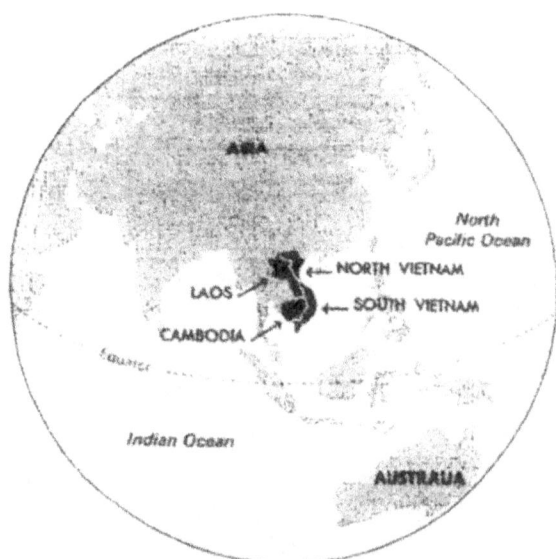

Indochina, in black, was a French colony for about 60 years. Four independent countries–Cambodia, Laos, North Vietnam, and South Vietnam–were created in the region in 1954. North Vietnam conquered South Vietnam in 1975.

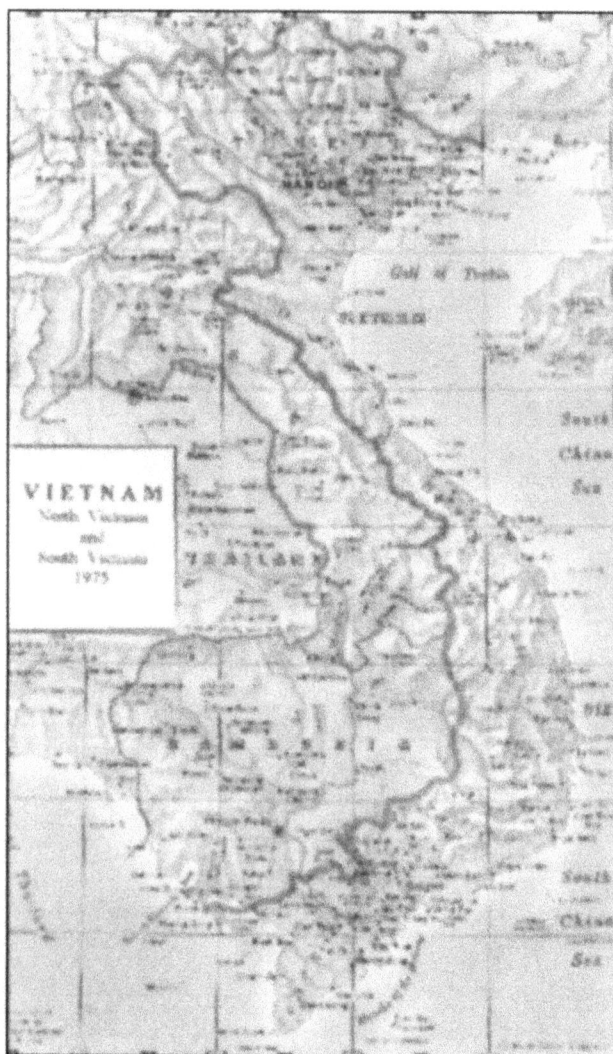

IMPORTANT DATES OF THE VIETNAM WAR

1963 South Vietnam government overthrown
1964 US Congress passed Resolution to support UN
1965 US bombs military targets in North Vietnam
1966 US Marines landed to protect South Vietnam
1967 Elections held in South Vietnam for President
1968 Communists launch Tet Attack on South Vietnam
1969 President Nixon ordered withdrawal of US troops
1970 US Senate repeals Gulf of Tonkin Resolution
1973 US, North & South Vietnam sign cease fire pact
1973 Last American troops evacuate South Vietnam
1975 South Vietnam eradicated by Communists

THE VIETNAM WAR
1957-1975
JACKSON COUNTY ROLL OF HONOR
SERVICE MEN KILLED IN ACTION

The list of dead or missing in action during the conflict was compiled by the
U.S. Military Casualties Commission and later recorded by the Adjutant General of
Indiana and verified for immediate public release by John N. Owens

BRANCH	NAME	RANK	SERIAL NO.	DOB	DOD	HOME
Army	BRANAMAN, Kenneth Merle	PFC	55823170	10 Jan 45	19 Jul 66	Seymour
Army	ROTHERING, Howard Earl Jr.	PVT	55823143	26 Nov 44	14 Apr 66	Crothersville
Marine	REYNOLDS, Jackie Dean	LCPL	2043827	01 Nov 44	04 Mar 66	Seymour
Marine	LARAWAY, William Dean	LCPL	2210088	26 Jan 43	11 Apr 67	Seymour
Marine	HARRELL, James Elmore	LCPL	2267220	29 Sep 46	29 Mar 67	Seymour
Marine	CARMICHAEL, Dale Eugene	PFC	2152040	05 Dec 45	25 Apr 67	Seymour
Army	HAWS, Homer Howard	CPL	16945506	01 Sep 48	15 Apr 68	Seymour
Army	STEVENS, Thomas Arthur Jr.	SP4	55944072	16 Sep 42	28 May 68	Seymour
Army	GUTHRIE, Thomas Leon	SSGT	16606398	10 Jul 40	19 Jul 68	Medora
Army	CLEVENGER, William Henry	MAJ	35168175	30 Aug 20	06 Jun 69	Seymour
Army	*CLARK, Gary Lee	SP4	67159101	19 Dec 49	24 Jun 69	Seymour
Marine	DAULTON, William Manson	LCPL	317544964	29 Apr 50	24 Oct 70	Medora
Army	GOEN, Martin Douglas	SP4	304569588	27 Feb 52	06 Apr 71	Medora

Died not as a result of hostile action, other causes.

JACKSON COUNTY VETERANS
A PARTIAL LISTING

Steven Bode	Bill Caudill	John Wetzel	Mark Darlage	Gary Clark
Marvin Ratcliff	Carl Hounshel	Donald Zink	Randy Zink	Steve Scarlett
Kelly Bowling	Charles Wheeler	Jim Jones	Samuel Spray	Robert Lkuen
Lonnie Wilson	Robert Beaty	William Knott	Phillip Trimpe	Tom Snyder
John Shelton	Robert Torborg	Louis Hallett	Dale Nay	Robert Black
James Darling	John Nolting	Steven Gray	Delbert Field	Terry Skaggs
Bill Boughman	Lee McCorey	Kenny McCory	Dennis Dill	Tom Coleman
Elmer Stidham	Max Spencer	Ray Reynolds	Ricky Roberts	Rik Greenwood
Wayne Minton	Bill Nagle	Ralph Mobley	James Bowling	Gil Carpenter
Leon Carpenter	Donald Mulder	Tom Robertson	Jim Frederickson	Jack Griggin
Wil Frederickson	Jim Griffin	Steve Forgey	John Schafstall	Charles Darkis
Ken Perry	Larry Rollins	Floyd Bottorff	Robert Kirts	Don Perky
John Gambrel	Charles Stahl	Daniel Rollins	Otis Freeze	Charles Owens

SPECIAL HONORS
AND RECOGNITION

TO THE BRAVE MEN AND WOMEN WHO FOUGHT IN VIETNAM

SURVIVING VETERANS
OF THE
UNPOPULAR VIETNAM WAR
1961-1975

Robert L. Carr   Brownstown
US Army: E-4 1965-1967
541st Transportation Company
Wife: Georgetta and one son and daughter

Thomas W. Cooley   Seymour
Marine Corps: Cpl. 1961
Wife: Darlene and 2 children

Marshall Davis   Nashville
Brownstown High School
US Army: M/Sgt. 21 years
Wife: Patricia and 5 children

Gary W. Dyer   Seymour
US Army: Sgt. 1967-1968
Wife: Flecia and 6 children

Arnold Huntchinson   Brownstown
Green Berets   1970-1971
Wife: Alice and 3 children

Warren Lucas   Seymour
23rd Infantry   1967-1969
Two Purple Hearts
Four Bronze Stars
80% Disabled

Micahel McElfresh   Brownstown
US Army E-4   1970-1971
Wife: Georgetta and one son

Toby V. Milroy   Seymour
US Army   1967-1968
Three children and one brother

Raymond Oathout   Seymour
US Army   1969-
Purple Heart Commendation
Wife: Anita and two children

Charles Owens   Seymour
US Army E-4   1968-1969
Wife: Kathy and two children

Ronald Pray   Seymour
US Army   1968-1969
Three children

Ricky Roberts   Kurtz
US Army E-4   1970-1972
Wife: June and two children

Ernest A. Smith   Seymour
US Army   1953-1967
Wife: Kitty and six children

John Stakamp   Seymour
US Army E4   1965-1967

Herbert Zumhingst   Seymour
Air Force Major   Career
WWII, Korea and Vietnam
71st Special Services Squadron
Indiana Certificate of Merit
Clyde Sherrill   Squire Riley
Albert Hall   Donald Jerrels
Paul Olmstead   Orville Smith
James Stuckwisch   Ray Stein
Dick Hehman   Ron Coleman

DENNIS G. ADAMS, Post Vietnam, United States Marine Corps, was born in Seymour to Paul and Elizabeth Williams Adams. He was raised in a family of four sisters: Martha, Mary, Edith and Harriet. After graduating from Brownstown Central High School, he enlisted in the Marine Corps in 1973 and Completed recruit training in San Diego. He attended Ordinance School at Aberdeen Proving Grounds, Maryland and was assigned to 3rd Battalion, 4th Marines on Okinawa.

Upon his return to the states in 1974 he was assigned to a Division unit at Camp Lejeune in North Carolina. In 1975 he was assigned to Aberdeen Proving Ground, Maryland where he became a Master Instructor. In 1978 he was selected to attend Drill Instructor School in San Diego, CA, pushed eleven recruit platoons, was promoted to S/Sgt and ended a successful tour. In 1981 he was again returned to the 3rd Marine Division on Okinawa and assigned as an Inspector. He was selected for Warrant Officer in 1981 and returned to the states to attend Basic School, which he completed in 1982.

He was assigned to 10th Marines as a Battalion Ordinance/Maintenance Officer. In 1984 he was selected for the Limited Duty Officer Training Program and promoted to 1st Lt. In 1985 he was assigned to 2nd FSSG as Commanding Officer, Ordinance Maintenance Company. In 1989 he was assigned to the 7th MEB at Twenty Nine Palms, CA as Brigade Maintenance Officer. With the Brigade he was deployed to southwest Asia with the 7th ᴹᴱB on August 10, 1990 for Desert Shield and Desert Storm. He served as Brigade and MEF Ordinance Officer. In 1992 he returned to the 2nd Marine Division and assigned as Division Ordinance Officer. He was promoted to Major in 1994. In 1996 he returned to Okinawa and assigned as the Commanding Officer, Ordinance Maintenance Company, 3rd FSSG. In 1997 he returned to Camp Lejeune and was assigned to the 2nd Marine Division. He was promoted to Lt. Colonel in May 2001 and transferred to 11th MSF where he is currently assigned. He holds the Meritorious Service Medal, Navy Commendation Medal and Good Conduct Medal.

In 1975 he married Judith Olsen of Baltimore and they became parents of two daughters, Lisa and Erica. He became a veteran at retirement in February 2004.

MICHAEL RAY ALLMAN, Vietnam, United States Army, born April 13, 1948 in Jackson County. Graduated from local high school in 1966. Drafted into army May 22, 1970 at Indianapolis. Assigned to Administrative Center in St. Louis. Discharged January 16, 1972 at Oakland, California.

RALPH ALTEMEYER, Vietnam, United States Army, 1964-1970 Indiana National Guard, Company B, 1st Battalion, 151st Infantry, Truck Driver. Assigned to Fort Knox. Discharged January 4, 1970. Returned to Seymour and employed by Cummins.

ROBERT ANDERSON, Vietnam Era, United States Army, moved to Jackson County as young child with his parents, Harley J. Anderson and Frances Boxman Anderson, and his older brother, Karl. After graduation from Seymour Senior High in 1970, he attended Indiana University in Bloomington. Enlisting in the Army in 1973, Bob received basic training and advanced schooling at Ft. Knox, KY, graduating as a PFC. His first duty assignment was as a personnel records specialist for HHC USAREUR, stationed in Frankfurt, West Germany. He later was accepted as a bass singer for the V Corps Command Chorus, based in Fulda, with the 11th Armored Cavalry at NATO's post of honor on the East German border. The all male Chorus traveled throughout Germany, entertaining US, British, French, and West German troops, as well as performing for Warsaw Pact dignitaries and German civilian functions.

When the VCCC was disbanded, Anderson was reassigned to the TASCOM Entertainment Showcase, barracked in Worms. He played trumpet for this group whose history dated back to the early Allied occupation of Germany. The Showcase performed contemporary pop music for NATO troops and dignitaries, visiting Greece, England, Italy, and Belgium. In 1975, Bob was named Director of the re-designated 21st Support Brigade Entertainment Showcase and made acting sergeant.

During his service with the Showcase, Bob met his future wife, Adele Akin, a fellow soldier and member of the group. In 1975 he had the opportunity to visit St. Lo, France where his father, "Andy," was wounded in 1944 while serving as a machine-gunner for the 79th Infantry Division. Adele and Bob were married on December 28, 1975. While Adele finished her tour of duty, Bob worked as Assistant Director of the Kaiserslautern Army Theater Center.

Bob and his wife returned to the US in 1976. They have two children, Seth and Geneva. Bob received a BA, cum laude, in Visual Arts from Columbia University in 1982. The Andersons moved to Nashville, Tennessee in 1983. Bob and Adele were especially grateful in November of 1989, when the Berlin Wall finally came down, bringing the opportunity for freedom once again to all those for whom they, and so many before and after, served.

Since 1993, Bob has been employed by nationally renowned Vintage Millworks in Nashville, Tennessee, where the family still resides.

JAMES R. AULT, Vietnam, United States Army, born near Medora and graduated with the class of 1964. Served in the army from 1966 to 1968 after completing basic training at Fort Knox, KY and Fort Ord, CA. Sent overseas to Vietnam in the mortars and infantry of the 1st Cavalry Division.

Earned various medals and ribbons during his tour of duty. Returned to the states and stationed at Fort Knox training new recruits. Was discharged and returned to Medora and employed by General Motors in 1968. Was married to Brenda Kay Couch in 1970 and became father of two children. All reside near Medora.

STEPHEN ROY BACHMANN, Post Vietnam Era, United States Marine Corps, was born July 4, 1958 to Raymond and Annette Bachmann before they moved to Jackson County in 1974. This "Yankee Doodle Dandy" boy was enrolled in Brownstown Central High School and, while still a junior, he enlisted in the Indiana Army National Guard. He was assigned to the 3658th Maintenance Company stationed at Bedford. He was to be trained as a mechanic and later was honorably discharged in May 1976 so he could join the Marine Corps.

Following his graduation from high school, he was ordered to complete boot camp training. He was then assigned MOS number 3521 as a second echelon mechanic. From there he attended a service school at Camp Lejeune, NC and he was sent overseas to Okinawa. For one year he was assigned to the 12th Marines, 3rd Division and stationed in Japan. He was then returned to the states and stationed at Cherry Point, NC.

He was returned to Okinawa and completed his tour of duty with an honorable discharge in August 1979. He returned to Jackson County briefly before moving on to Indianapolis. He was then employed at various Ford dealerships before settling in Kokomo in 1984. He works as an ASA Master Auto Technician and Ford certified powertrain master mechanic.

He was pleased to have served his country and signs off "Semper Fi."

ROGER DALE BAUGHMAN, Vietnam, United States Army, born to David and Goldie Cockerham Baughman on December 10, 1939. He was raised in the local area and attended the Medora schools. He was drafted and inducted into the army May 16, 1963 for a two-year term. He was sent to Fort Knox, KY for his basic training.

He was assigned to Company "D," 8th Battalion, 3rd Regiment. After further training he was shipped overseas to Darmstadt, Germany. While stationed there, he became a mechanic on heavy equipment.

He was returned to the states and received his discharge April 30, 1969.

JAMES E. BEDEL, Vietnam, United States Army, born August 9, 1943. Served in the army from 1967 until 1968, Company B, 6th Support Battalion, 11th Light Infantry Regiment, American Division.

Returned home and was employed by Cummins. Retired August 1, 200_. 5th Generation on family farm in Vernon Township. Raised Appaloosa Horses. Married to Emma Bedel.

STEVEN W. BODE, Vietnam, United States Army. The military service of Steven W. Bode took place during the Vietnam War. He was a PFC (Private First Class) in the United States Army. Assigned the serial number of 55845032, he served from February 9, 1966 until February 9, 1968.

Born on August 31, 1946 in Seymour, Indiana, he was the younger of two siblings, Glen Bode and Bettie Bode (Burbrink). The son of Orville and Edna Bode, he grew up in Bobtown and graduated from Cortland High School in 1963. His hobbies included reading, mostly historical literature, and auto mechanics. After graduation, he worked at Nolting's Supermarket on Tipton Street in Seymour and also at his brother's Sunoco service station on the corner of Fourth Street and Broadway, also in Seymour.

On February 10, 1966 he was inducted into the U.S. Army and stationed at Fort George G. Meade in Maryland. Shortly thereafter, he was assigned to the 976th SUP & SVG Company and sent overseas. He served in infantry and also as an Ammo. Rec. Clerk for his division. Following two years of service, he was honorably discharged on February 8, 1968. He received the following decorations for his service: Vietnam Campaign Medal w/60 SVC, Vietnam Service Medal w/1 Bronze Star, 2 O/S Bars, Marksman Badge Rifle M14 and the National Defense Service Medal.

After returning home to Seymour, Indiana in 1968, Steve pursued his interests in reading, auto mechanics and also enjoyed drag racing. On April 3, 1971 he married Sandy Y. Sparks. A short time later they had a daughter, Stephanie R. Bode (Starr). He was employed with George's of Seymour as an auto mechanic until 1994 when he was diagnosed with terminal lung cancer. Although he won the fight for his life on the battlefield, it was sadly lost to his illness on November 23, 1996. His wife, daughter, and granddaughter remain in Jackson County.

WALTER LOWELL BURKE, Post Vietnam, United States Army, was the son of Harold and Eva Butler Burke and was graduated from Shields High School in Seymour in May 1977. The next year he went into the army and earned the rank of Specialist.

He was assigned to the Military Police and trained as a dog handler at Fort McClellan, Alabama where he was stationed until June 10, 1978. He returned to Seymour and served as a recruiter for one month and was then shipped overseas to Germany where he was stationed from October 15, 1978 until February 17, 1981.

He was discharged at an unknown post.

GREGORY DALE COCKERHAM, Post Vietnam, United States Marine Corps, born July 24, 1957 to Neal and June Stilwell Cockerham. Graduated from Brownstown High School in 1975. Joined the Reserves November 20, 1974.

Inducted into Marine Corps June 11, 1975. Stationed at San Diego. Attended Administrative School in Virginia. Limousine chauffeur during Carter Inauguration, January 20, 1977. Discharged September 5, 1978.

He married Carley Hammonds in Washington. Residents of Clearspring.

LARRY WAYNE COCKERHAM, Post Vietnam, United States Marine Corps, born March 23, 1957 to William and Judy Glen Cockerham. He was raised in Jackson County around Freetown but attended school in Brownstown.

He was drafted and inducted into the Marine Corps June 26, 1974 at Indianapolis. He was sent to Camp Lejeune in North Carolina and was in the service for more than two years.

When he received his discharge November 12, 1976, he was authorized to wear appropriate ribbons and medals representing his campaigns. Also, he was charged to be in good behavior.

After he reached home he married Sharon Gambrill in 1982 and they became parents of two children, William Isaac and Jessica Evona Kay. Larry Cockerham and others live in Seymour and records show the details of his military life.

THOMAS C. COLLINS, Post Vietnam Era, United States Navy, born in Morganfield, KY. Entered military service April 23, 1987 at Indianapolis, IN. Basic training at Naval Reserve Center in New Orleans. Assigned aboard the USS carrier, *Dwight D. Eisenhower.* Completed service school classes of 11 weeks in aviation. Passed exam for Navy wide advancement in Navy per law.

Awarded: Sea Service Deployment Ribbon, National Defense Service Medal, Meritorious Unit Commendation, Navy E Ribbon and Good Conduct. Separation Date/Transfer to Naval Reserve: April 22, 1991. Honorable Service at Discharge

Was married to Kathleen J. Noblitt of Brownstown. Parents of two children, Tyler Noblitt and Karolyn Nicole. Residence in Norwalk, Connecticut. Employed at Pfizer and Veterans Administration of NY.

GARY L. COOLEY, Berlin Crisis, United States Army, 1960-1962, born January 13, 1942 in Seymour, Indiana, son of Albert and Elsie May Cooley. He graduated from Seymour High School in 1960. He entered the Army in August, received his basic training at Fort Leonard Wood in Missouri. Following that training he was sent to Fort Sill, Oklahoma as an artillery gunner. From there he was sent to Fort Dix in New Jersey for processing before being assigned overseas duty in Germany where be became a truck driver and gunner in the artillery service.

While in Germany, he was a specialist in the 73rd Artillery Battalion of the 3rd Armored Division. While stationed there the Berlin Wall was erected. He served 18 months overseas and after active service, was in the Reserves of the Indiana National Guard holding the rank of Black Belt Karate and serving as an instructor.

In June of 1964 he married Betty L. Robinson in Seymour and they became parents of two children, Shelley and Gary. He was employed at Kruwell Block Company as a machine operator, but later was promoted to the manager's position.

STEVEN L. COOLEY, Vietnam, United States Army, was drafted in the Army in January of 1971 with the lottery number of 252. He was pleased his number was so high and thought he was safe for some time. He received his call to duty by a letter from President Nixon and was forced to leave a new wife, family and unfinished college behind and incompletes.

He received his basic training at Fort Knox, KY during the cold wintertime, but found the weather much warmer in Vietnam during the summer month. He was flown overseas to the Vietnam Theater of Operations. From the time he stepped off that plane until he returned home, he felt abandoned by his country. Within a few days after his arrival at Phu Bai with the 101st Airborne Division, he was assigned a bunker with two other green recruits.

None of the men had much training on weapons, a grenade launcher or anything else. By the time darkness had fallen, they had cleaned three clips of usable shells for their M-16's His MOS training was finance, but he was to every other experience which could be imagined. He learned the number of American casualties in Vietnam was as great as the population of all of Jackson County.

THOMAS WAYNE COOLEY, Vietnam, United States Marine Corps, was born January 21, 1940, son of Albert and Elsie May Toberg Cooley in Seymour. He attended Rockford, Riley, Brownstown, Clara Carter and Seymour Schools. On September 8, 1958 he enlisted in the U.S. Marine Corps and was sent to San Diego, California recruiting depot. It was there he was promoted to Pfc.

In January he received infantry training at Camp Pendleton and then assigned to the 1st Marine Division. He received several months of training necessary for becoming an Ammo Technician. He spent one month at sea on the USS *Paul Revere,* made one amphibious landing at San Clemente Island and promoted to Corporal.

The 3rd Marine Division was sent to Okinawa and, after one month at the Ammo Dump, he was transferred as an expert Rifleman to Camp Hansen and then on to Camp Schwab as a rifle coach. Six months later he was transferred back to the Ammo Dump where he taught hand-to-hand combat. Before he left the island, he completed his training and received an Instructor Grade Black Belt. He also made one cruise with the 5th Marines to Vietnam dispensing ammo on the beach to the Vietnamese and their advisors.

He was then sent to the 2nd Marine Division where he embarked on a six months cruise making amphibious landings on Corsica, Sardinia and Crete before enjoying R and R in Spain, Italy and Greece. He was discharged at Camp Lejeune and Fort Bragg on September 7, 1962. In 1970 he married Darlene Nielson and they became parents of two children. He retired from Cummins with 40 years of experience as an Industrial Electrician. Currently, he is an active member of Zion Lutheran Church in Seymour, Indiana.

RANDY RAY DARLAGE, Vietnam, United States Army, born February 13, 1949 at Seymour. Parents were Orval and Mayme Hobbs Darlage. Raised near the Jackson County seat. Graduated from Brownstown High School in 1967. Employed by State Highway before entering the service.

Enlisted and inducted into the army October 14, 1968. Reported to Indianapolis but completed basic training in Missouri. Received further training at Fort Gordon. Shipped overseas to Ethiopia for his tour of duty. Returned to the states for a furlough. Shipped overseas to Vietnam and stationed near Saigon. Discharged January 14, 1972 in California.

Returned to Brownstown and employed by the REMC. Married to Brenda Oberman. Became parents of two daughters.

MICHAEL L. DAVIDSON, Vietnam, United States Navy, born April 21, 1961 to Festus and Elinor Davidson. Grew up and attended school in Brownstown, IN. Completed high school in Brownstown. Joined the navy October 26, 1979, served faithfully.

MICHAEL E. DEATON, Vietnam, United States Air Force, born at Jeffersonville but raised at Charlestown. He graduated from the local high school in 1981 and entered the Air Force June 1, 1981 at Louisville, KY. He was sent to Lackland AFB in Texas for basic training.

He received further training in combat missile launching at Sheppard Field, TX and Vandenburgh AFB, CA. He was assigned to the 374th Strategic Squadron, 308th Wing of the 8th Air Force stationed at Little Rock, AR.

He was later discharged on December 3, 1983 after having served in Granada during the Lebanon period.

He and his family reside on Redding Road near Seymour and he is employed at Cummins at the Walesboro plant. He is the son of Curtis and Joyce Featon Duncon Napier.

RAYMOND GERALD DISMORE, Vietnam, United States Navy, 1954-1967, born June 22, 1935 in Washington County on a small farm located near New Salem, Indiana. He was a son of Earnest Glen and Edna Mae Woods Dismore, and later graduated from Vallonia High School with the class of 1954.

He completed his boot training at Great Lakes Naval Station and later was assigned to various bases in Maine, Newfoundland, Morocco and Vietnam with the U.S. Navy Seabees, MCB, 4 as a Petty Officer, 2nd Class.

He married Jean A. Dunham in 1938 and they became the parents of one son, Raymond. He married 2nd to Betty Jean Waddell Brock in 1967 at Brownstown. He then became father to two step-daughters, Mary and Brenda.

Upon completion of his military service, he became a postman in Brownstown. He retired in 1990 and he and his wife currently reside in Citra, Florida.

RICHARD DEAN DISMORE, Vietnam, United States Navy, 1971-1975, born February 11, 1952 in Seymour, IN. He was a son of Ernest Glen and Edna Mae Woods Dismore. Much later he graduated from Brownstown Central High School with the class of 1971.

He completed his boot training at Great Lakes Naval Station, IL and was sent to "A" school in Lakehurst, NJ. He was then stationed in A.I.M.D. aviators equipment division at the NAS in Albany, GA. He received his honorable discharge from the Naval Station at Norfolk, Virginia as a 2nd Class Petty Officer.

Upon completion of his military service, he was employed by Ben Franklin Distribution Center in Seymour. He is currently driving for Wal Mart Center also in Seymour, Indiana.

He married Elrita Thomas in Jamaica in 2001 and became a father to her two daughters, Jodi Ann and Rusheen. They presently reside on State Road 235 near Vallonia, Indiana.

RONALD H. DIXON, United States Navy, #6854021, 1943-1966, Vietnam Service Medal.

ROBERT EMPSON, Vietnam, United States Air Force, was the son of Robert and Fay Pemberton Empson. The loyalty to his country was more than evident because he served 10 years in the reserves during the Vietnam War.

THOMAS EMPSON, Vietnam, United States Navy, was the son of Robert and Fay Pemberton Empson. He was inducted into the military service of his country when he entered the navy on June 23, 1967. He was later discharged on March 15, 1973.

TERRY E. FIELDS, Vietnam, United States Army, Warrant Officer Helicopter Pilot, born in Seymour in 1947 and graduated from Seymour Senior High School in 1965. In October 1967, he enlisted in the U.S. Army Warrant Officer program for training as a helicopter pilot. After completing basic training in Ft. Polk, LA, Terry began his helicopter training at Ft. Wolters, TX and graduated as a Warrant Officer helicopter pilot from Ft. Rucker, AL in September 1968.

After graduation, Mr. Fields was assigned to the 3/17 Air Cavalry Squadron of the 1st Aviation Brigade in Dian, South Vietnam in October 1968. Later, he was transferred to the 2/17 Air Cavalry Squadron of the 101st Airborne Division in Camp Eagle, Phu Bai, South Vietnam. During his tour in Vietnam as a UH-1 "Huey" helicopter pilot, Terry flew over 2,000 hours of combat missions, such as combat assaults, resupply missions and search and rescue. He was awarded several commendations including the Air Medal and Bronze Star.

Upon concluding his Vietnam tour in October 1969, he was stationed at Ft. Hunter, Savannah, GA as an instructor pilot. His primary duty was the training of Vietnamese student pilots in the UH-1 Huey helicopter. While at Ft. Hunter, Terry was promoted to 1st Lieutenant and subsequently to Captain.

Terry concluded his active service in February 1972 with the rank of Captain and graduated from Indiana University in 1974. Mr. Fields now lives in Atlanta, GA and is an active member of the American Legion and Veterans of Foreign Wars.

DONALD M. FREDERICKSON II, 1976-

1980, United States Marine Corps, was the youngest son of Donald and Myrtle Ballard Frederickson. He was born in 1956 in Jackson County and later graduated from Brownstown Central High School in 1975. Following the footsteps of his brothers, he enlisted in the Navy in 1976.

He completed his boot training in San Diego, CA. He was then stationed at Cherry Point, NC with the 1st Marine Aircraft Wing. He held the rank of Sergeant when he was discharged in 1980.

He joined the Reserves in June 1980 as a maintenance supervisor He holds the rank of sergeant and he and his family live in the County seat of government at Brownstown, IN.

JOHN B. FREDERICKSON, Vietnam, United

States Marine Corps, 1963-1967, born in 1945, the son of Donald and Myrtle Frederickson, and he arrived to their home in Jackson County. He graduated in 1963 from Brownstown Central High School and enlisted in the United States Marine Corps.

He was sent to San Diego where he received his boot training. He was then assigned to Camp Pendleton for further training. C & E Battalion at San Diego became his new home. It was attached to 1st Air Wing in Da Nang, Vietnam.

After returning to the States, he was stationed at Beaufort, SC until he received his honorable discharge in 1967. He and his family currently reside at Sparksville, Indiana.

WILLIAM A. FREDERICKSON II, Vietnam,

United States Marine Corps, 1962-1982, was born in Jackson County to Donald and Myrtle Myrtle Ballard Frederickson. He graduated from Brownstown High School in 1962 and immediately enlisted in the Marine Corps. He completed his boot training in San Diego, CA. By September he was assigned to "F" Co of the 5th Marines at Camp Pendleton as an office clerk. Six months later he received electronic training and was reassigned to Camp Lejeune, NC.

In 1966 the 3rd Marine Corps Division moved from Okinawa to Da Nang in Vietnam. Two years later he was part of the Electronic Maintenance Battalion and in July he was assigned temporary duty

in Vietnam. In 1969 he received training in communications and reported for duty as a teletype instructor and repairman.

In March 1972 he attended the recruiting school at Parris Island, SC and later was assigned to the recruiting station in Warsaw, IN. Two years later he was back in Okinawa with the 1st Marine Air Wing. By 1980 he was in Denver, CO learning meteorology.

He retired as a gunnery sergeant and was transferred to the Reserves. He moved to Denver and worked for the Department of Safety, and later he moved to Missouri, and was employed by the state university as a senior electronics technician. He and his family reside in Waynesville, MO.

ODDIS LEE FREEZE, Vietnam, United States

Army, was the son of Glen and Wilma Roberts Freeze. He was drafted into the army March 18, 1970 and sent to Fort Knox, Kentucky. He was sent to Fort Sill, Oklahoma in May.

After a furlough, he reported to Oakland, California so his unit could be shipped overseas to Vietnam. He spent 15 months before being returned to the states. He was discharged from Fort Lewis, Washington October 18, 1971. His mother picked him up when he reached Seymour.

Currently he is employed at Fort Hood, Texas with the National Guard. He is married and the father of a son, Dana.

DONALD GENE GARDINER, Vietnam,

United States Navy, born November 24, 1942 at Odin, Indiana. Parents were Orin and Doris Grafton Gardiner. As a young lad, moved to Brownstown with his family. Graduated from the local high school in 1961. Re-located to Florida. Employed as apprentice pipe fitter Entered the navy in February 1965 at West Palm Beach. Completed boot camp training at Great Lakes. Assigned to the carrier, USS *Intrepid*. Flown Norfolk to the ship at sea. Deployed off the coast of Vietnam. Returned to the states and discharged in November 1968.

Married Jane Browning of Brownstown. Parents of one daughter. Employed by REMC.

JOHN STEPHEN GILL, Vietnam Era, United

States Army, born in Seymour February 6, 1940 to John Howard and Doris Fox Gill. As a lad he worked part-time helping his father operate the Elm Street Grocery Store until he graduated from the local high school.

He was inducted into the army in June 1963 and completed basic training at Fort Knox, KY. He was dispatched to Fort Bliss, TX where he received training in artillery as a launcher on the Ajax and Nike Hercules missiles in the 34th Artillery Detachment. He was shipped overseas to Vicenza, Italy for nearly two years and during that assignment he distinguished himself as an exceptional marksman.

He was selected to compete in the 1965 US Army, European Small Arms Championship matches

at Grafenwohr in Germany. As a member of the five-man skeet shooting team, he won many awards, including the Expert Rifle M-14 Medal, and the Infantry Trophy Match under SETAF in Italy.

He returned to the states on the General Wm. O. Darby to receive his discharge on May 31, 1965 in Hamilton, NY. He has been employed by Cummins Engine Works since 1959. He and his wife, Janet, reside in Seymour and are co-owners of Gill Enterprises, along with their sons, Fred and Toby. He has served four terms as Jackson County Commissioner.

HAROLD L. GARLAND, Vietnam, United

States Army, 1965-1971 Indiana National Guard, Company C, 2nd Battalion, 152nd Infantry Division, Salem, Indiana. Company C, 1st Battalion, 5th Infantry Division, Fort Carson, Michigan.

JERRY L. GOBLE, Vietnam, United States

Army, 1965-1967. Inducted into the army October 14, 1965. Completed basic training at Fort Knox. Sent to Fort Gordon for training as an MP. Assigned to Company A, 504th MP Battalion. Shipped overseas to Vietnam.

Returned to the states October 1967. Married Cathleen Neal in July 1968. Became father of three children. Retired from Cummins April 1995.

RALPH W. HAMBLIN, United States Army,

Lifetime Career, 1972-1999. Retired as Major, born January 18, 1954 at Ft. Knox, KY. He was the first child and only son of Ralph and Ann M. (Ruppert) Hamblin. His father was a career soldier and the family moved on average every three years. Despite the relative stability, Ralph W. went to seven schools in 12 years, graduating from high school in Heidelberg, Germany in 1972. He spent a year in college in Illinois and enlisted in the Army on October 16, 1973 in Kaiserslautern, Germany. He was immediately returned to the states and began basic training as a PVT at Ft. Dix, NJ.

Following basic training, he was sent to Ft. Polk, LA for advanced individual training as an infantryman. In 1974, he was assigned to Germany where he remained until the completion of his three-year commitment. He was a SGT when he was released from active duty on October 8, 1976 He returned to the US and began college studies using the GI Bill at the University of Colorado. While in school, he was a member of the 7th Special Forces Group, a National Guard unit based in Denver, Pueblo, Golden and Ft. Collins.

In January 1982, Ralph re-enlisted in the Army and was required to again complete basic training at Ft. McClellan, AL due to the length of his separation from active duty. He reported to Ft. Benning for Officer Candidate School in March 1992 after the basic training stint. He graduated in June 1982 and was commissioned an Infantry Second Lieutenant.

Ralph remained at Ft. Benning for training until January 1983 when he reported to the 4th Infantry Division in Ft. Carson, CO.

In June 1986, Ralph was ordered to the 2nd Infantry Division for a one year unaccompanied tour.

In July 1987, he returned to Ft. Leavenworth for training and was thereafter sent to the 6th Infantry Division in Ft. Richardson, AK where he remained for three years.

In November 1990, he was ordered to the Defense Language Institute for a one-year program of study for Mandarin Chinese. Upon graduation, he was sent to Honolulu, HI to enroll in the Masters program a, the University of Hawaii to complete a course of study in Asian Studies.

After earning the M.A., he was sent to Frankfurt Germany in December 1993 for an assignment with V Corps. In December 1994, he was assigned to Hanau, Germany for duty as a Battalion Executive Officer.

In December 1996, Ralph was assigned to Ft. McPherson, GA as an Inspector General.

He retired from the Army as a Major on February 28, 1999. His total active service was 20 years, one month and 27 days. Included in the active total is overseas time of 10 years, 4 months and 9 days. If his inactive time is counted, he had 24 years, 9 months and 1 day. Among his awards and decorations are the Meritorious Service Medal (4th award), the Overseas Service Ribbon (5th Award) and the Parachutist Badge.

He moved to Topeka, KS in 1999 and graduated from law school with a J.D. in May 2001.

In June 2003, Ralph moved to Grand Junction, CO to begin work with the Department of Homeland Security as an Assistant Federal Security Director with the Transportation Security Administration.

Ralph has been married to Judy Ridenour since 1980 and they have two children.

DAVID A. HAMILTON, Post Vietnam, United States Navy 1978-1984.

JACK D. HANNER, Army of the United States 1966-1968. Vietnam Service Medal.

LELAND RUSSELL HARRISON, Vietnam, United States Army, born February 27, 1944 to Harry and Juanita Sherrill Harrison. Lived in Jackson County and attended the local school. Graduated from Clearspring High School in 1962.

Joined the army July 26, 1965 at Fort Knox. Assigned to Company A - Special Troops, Administrative Specialist and Driver for Commanding General. Discharged July 25, 1971.

Married Karel Ann Isaacs December 26, 1965. Became parents of three children: Kay, Beth and Todd.

LARRY L. HARTOG, Korea and Vietnam, United States Air Force, Chief M/Sgt., born in Lake County, Indiana. When he was a small boy he moved with his grandparents, Elmer and Rena Phillips Sutton, to a home located on State Road 135 only a short distance north of Freetown. He attended the Freetown and Cortland schools but matured not far from Spraytown, Indiana.

In August 1954 when he was not yet 18 years old, he enlisted in the Air Force. He received his basic training at Sampson Air Base in New York. Attendance at technical schools followed when he was sent to Keesler Field, MS, to receive instruction in Ground Control Approach Radar Maintenance.

Before shipping out to Saudi Arabia he was granted leave to return home to Spraytown in 1955. He married Lois McKain, daughter of Louis and Nellie Weekly McKain. Following his return to base he served at Dhahran. Upon his return from overseas, he was assigned to Castle Air Base, Wright-Patterson Air Base and then back to Keesler Field. He was discharged in 1962, but in 1967 he joined the Air Reserve Technician Program at Bakala Air Base located near Columbus. He was reactivated to duty in 1968 for Vietnam. He was stationed at Nha Trang and from there he completed his active duty in 1969. He continued to serve at Grissom Air Base, and Barksdale Air Base, and Wright-Patterson Air Base where retired in 1997.

He and his wife, Lois, make their home in nearby Fairborn, and they are parents of a son, Gregorya, and a daughter, Rhonda, who is a disabled veteran of the Air Force. Her husband, Capt. Frederick Clare, is currently serving his country in the Air Force. Both children have presented them with one grandchild each.

LARRY L. HATTON, Vietnam, United States Army, born February 19, 1945 in Seymour to Howard and Eve McKain Hatton. Was raised in family of three brothers and a sister, including his identical twin. He graduated from Seymour High School in 1964.

Inducted into the army in October 1965 and was assigned to the 196th Light Infantry Brigade, Company C, 2nd Battalion. Completed basic training, earning Expert M-14 Rifle Medal, the 45 Cal Pistol Medal and Automatic Rifle Medal.

Shipped overseas to Vietnam and served at night on ambushes as well as other tasks in major operations at Attleboro. Two buddies lost - one to a land mine and the other to a sniper.

Was rotated to Company A, 4th Battalion, 23rd Infantry Division during 1967 Operation Junction City. Also took part in Mekong Delta area. Discharged and authorized to wear the Combat Infantry Badge, Vietnam Campaign and Service Medals w/two campaign Stars, Good Conduct Medal and Army Commendation Medal.

Returned home and was employed as an auto mechanic. Married to Linda Royalty Hatton 1975 and became father of 3 children.

DENNY JOSEPH HAZARD, Vietnam, United States Army, born to Hubert and Betty Beavers Hazard in 1948. Years later in 1968, he was drafted into the army and inducted at Indianapolis. He was sent to Fort Knox, Kentucky and assigned to 11th Battalion, 4th Regiment and served out his hitch in the USA. He was discharged April 14, 1974.

He married Judith Marie, Fosbrink in 1969 and they became the parents of one child. Judith married second and became mother of two sons named Zachary and Zane Lucas. The photo shows Dennis holding his daughters when he was yet in the service.

JOHN ROSS HILL, Vietnam, United States Coast Guard 1971-1974, born November 25, 1952 in Cincinnati, Ohio, the son of David and Glenna Ross Hill. He was raised in Seymour and graduated from Shields High School with the class of 1971. Shortly thereafter, he was inducted into the Coast Guard. He completed his basic training at Camp May, NJ and then was sent to Elizabeth City, NC for training to become an Aviation Machinist Mate.

He was then assigned to the USCG Air Station located in Traverse City, MI and was promoted to 3rd Class Petty Officer. He became Search and Rescue on the HU16E fixed wing and HH53Q Rotary winged aircraft. He served the remainder of his career as a flight mechanic and search and rescue air crewman flying SAR missions over the Great Lakes.

He left the Coast Guard in 1974 to become a police officer on the Seymour Force where he still serves. He married Rebecca Gaiter in 1973 and they became parents of three children: Sandon, David and Johnni.

STUART L. HINNEFELD, Vietnam, United States Army, born December 4, 1952 in Brownstown to Lynn and Wilma Melloncamp Hinnefeld. He graduated from Brownstown Central High School in

1971 and entered Hanover College that fall. Changes in the draft law brought selection based on the birthdays and the lottery for those born in 1952 was held in 1971. Stuart's number was one. He completed classes for that year, but was drafted and he reported for duty June 21, 1972.

At that time draftees were no longer being sent to Vietnam, and Stuart completed basic training at Fort Knox, KY then sent to Fort Gordon in Georgia for advanced training. He volunteered to serve as company clerk and was assigned to Company "A" of Battalion, Brigade of the Signal School. He remained there until his discharge in June 1974.

He returned home and re-entered Hanover College and graduated with a degree on physics in 1977. He went on and was awarded a master's degree in radiation from Purdue University in 1979. He now works for the National OSHA in Cincinnati, Ohio.

DALE HOPPER, Vietnam, United States Air Force, joined the Air Force March 7, 1966 and was sent to Lackland AFB in TX for basic training. He was then ordered to Keesler AFB in MS for training as a radar operator. With a leave of absence he returned to Jackson County and was married to Brenda Ault. They moved to Iowa where he was assigned to the 788th Radar Squadron.

Two years later he became a father to a daughter named Lori and one week later he was ordered to report to Korea. Taking his family back to Jackson County, he proceeded overseas. After he arrived he was promoted to S/Sgt. training ROK troops to control aircraft. He was awarded various medals and ribbons before returning to the States.

He was discharged January 23, 1972.

GARY LEE HUBBARD, Vietnam, United States Army, born November 6, 1943 in Jackson County, Indiana. Entered the army June 23, 1965. Reported to Camp Atterbury, Indiana. Completed basic training at Fort Riley, Kansas.

Trained as Radio and Relay Carrier Radio Mechanic. Assigned to Company C, 57th Signal Battalion, Fifth United States Army. Shipped overseas to Vietnam and Okinawa.

Discharged January 1977. Awarded National Defense Medal, Vietnam Service Medal and Sharpshooter Badge.

LARMIE D. HUBBARD, United States Air Force, #16465214, S/Master Sergeant, May 7, 1954-May 1, 1981. Discharged N.W.S.C. Crane, Indiana.

The unusual military career of Larmie D. Hubbard spanned 26 years of service in the U.S. Air Force. After graduation from Clearspring High School in 1954 he enlisted and was inducted at Indianapolis. He completed his basic training at Sampson AFB in New York. He received more than one year of training in electronics at Keesler Field which was followed by further training in air traffic control before being assigned to Barkssdale AFB in Louisiana.

After being transferred to Little Rock, Arkansas, he married Cherry Fay Beard at her foster parent's home. The military base Chaplain performed the ceremony. More than one year later Linnie Gene Hubbard was born at Shreveport. After a daughter entered the family, Larmie D. Hubbard was trained in the Crypto field to meet the requirements of the Federal Aviation Authority.

By 1962 he was stationed at Guam where a son was born and one year the Cuban Crisis erupted. Three years later he was ordered to Hickam AFB in Hawaii where he was assigned to special communication projects for the Airborne Command. In July 1976 he graduated from the non-commissioned officer training Academy in Alabama and assigned to supervise the installation of special equipment Five years later in 1981 he retired from active duty with the U S. Air Force.

TROY F. HUTCHINSON, Vietnam 1957-1975, #35584331 Communications Specialist, November 3, 1965-August 1, 1967, was inducted into the military service on November 3, 1965 at Indianapolis. He received his basic training at Bowman Field in Kentucky. He was then assigned to Fort Knox before being sent to Fort Gordon in Georgia. It was there where he became a teletype operator in the Signal Corps. Not long afterward he was ordered overseas and was stationed in Thailand. There he was surrounded by a security fence and guards on duty at all times.

After thirteen months of service, he was redeployed back to Oakland, California and then was discharged August 1, 1967. One month later Troy Hutchinson learned that South Vietnam held their first elections under their new constitution. Less than ten years later, they surrendered to the communists.

LEWIS W. IMLAY, Post Vietnam, United States Navy, was born in Jackson County, IN and still resides in Jackson County.

Lewis W. Imlay entered the U.S. Navy at Indianapolis, IN and his basic training was at Great Lakes Naval Training Center. He was transferred to Millington, TN for A School. In 1983 he was stationed at LeMoore Naval Air Station for further training in preparation for his duty station with the Navy.

ATAN Imlay received an Honorable Discharge from the U.S. Navy in 1985 at Portsmouth, VA.

RICHARD D. KEITHLEY, Vietnam, United States Army, was born November 10, 1944 to Wm. and Geneva Fish Keithly. He graduated from Clearspring High School in 1963. He went into the army February 8, 1966 at Fort Harrison in Indiana. He was later stationed at Fort Knox, Kentucky before he was transferred to the 6th Battalion of the 32nd Armored Division.

He served three years as an auto mechanic, was listed in the reserve reinforcement unit and sent to St. Louis, Missouri. His obligation to the military expired February 7, 1972. He was authorized to wear appropriate medals and ribbons reflecting his service.

His family included three children and several grandchildren. He was married to Dorothy Legere May 15, 1993.

PAUL KERKHOF, Vietnam, United States Navy 1966-1970. Basic training at Great Lakes Naval Station. Was on duty in Japan and served in the Philippines. Stationed in Hong Kong, Australia, Okinawa and Hawaii. Attained rank of Seaman E/5. Discharged and employed by Cummins, Seymour, Indiana.

ROCKY LUCAS, Vietnam, United States Army January 21, 1969 to September 9, 1971. Basic Training completed at Fort Knox, Kentucky. Assigned to the Infantry in training at Fort Polk, Louisiana.

Served in Vietnam from April 1970 until September 1971. Assigned to 1st Aviation of the 61st Assault Helicopter Company. Stationed in Anson, Vietnam. Received Honorable Discharge while placed on limited duty

WARREN LUCAS, Vietnam, United States Army, enlisted in October 1967 for a three year tour of duty and completed basic training at Fort Campbell, KY. Shortly thereafter he was assigned to Company "A" - 3rd Platoon in the 196th Lt. Infantry Brigade. Not long after that his unit was shipped overseas to South Vietnam. They arrived in May 1969 when the combat deaths were at their peak.

By July of 1968 they were involved in an assault on the HUEP-DIC Valley. Their mission was to find and destroy any of the VE-WVA Forces. But everyone was tired and literally exhausted from the sporadic sniper fire. Then the 8 inch guns worked over the slopes and the GIs all around hit their holes. In the morning they witnessed the corpses. Many of the men were never seen again.

After recovering from wounds, he eventually was returned stateside ready for his discharge. He was awarded two Purple Hearts, an Army Commendation, four Battle Bronze Stars and the CIB Badge. But the scars of body were not all; he was destined to suffer for years by thoughts which haunt one's subconscious.

Records verify he was 80% disabled from land mine wounds and being shot by an AK-47 communist assault rifle. He returned to his home near Seymour, Indiana.

STEVEN RAY LYNCH, Post Vietnam, United States Navy 1978-1982, United States Army Reserves 1989-1990. Recruit training at Orlando, Florida 1978. Entered tech training program in Tennessee: Graduate 1979.

Assigned to aircraft carrier USS *Coral Sea.* Served 102 days of duty in the Persian Gulf. Stationed off coast of Iran 1979 to 1980. Sent to Persian Gulf again for 82 consecutive days. Protected shipping through the Suez Canal. Stood by to defend against Libyan hostilities.

JAMES RAY MARSHALL, Vietnam, United States Navy, was born in Seymour August 7, 1947 to James A. and Rebecca Oathout Marshall. He was raised in the Surprise neighborhood of Jackson County. He graduated from Cortland High School in 1965. He was employed by Cummins in Columbus before his service days.

He joined the navy as a machinist and completed his boot camp training in California. In just a few weeks of further instruction, his unit was shipped overseas to Da Nang in Vietnam. He was assigned to one of the navy construction battalions. He served his complete tour of duty and was returned to the states for discharge.

After his separation from the navy he returned home and picked up his work at various garages in Seymour. He was later employed by L.C. Farms near Brownstown.

He died September 29, 1997.

TOM MARTIN, Pre-Vietnam, United States Air Force, 1961-1965. Graduated from Brownstown High School, Lackland AFB and Lowry AFB. 48th Fighter Squadron, Air Defense Command, Langley Field at Hampton Roads, Virginia. Presidential Citation and Good Conduct Medal. Parents: Herbert and Ilene Pogue, Freetown.

LEE P. MCCORY, Vietnam, United States Army, Lee was drafted and his basic training took place at Ft. Benning, GA, Ft. Dix, NJ and advance training at Ft. Lewis, WA. He was a heavy vehicle driver.

Lee was sent to Viet Nam and spent 9 months and 16 days. He served there as a heavy vehicle driver with the transportation company, hauling supplies to different places in Viet Nam. Hauling ammunition, food, petroleum, etc. out of Cam Ranh Bay, until the last five months. His company then was taken by boat

to the DMZ for the rest of his tour of duty. Lee was discharged March 15, 1968 SP5 (T).

Lee is the father of three daughters, Renee, Jamie and Judy. Lee and his wife, Jill, live close to Sky Line Drive in Jackson County.

RAYMOND MCINTOSH, Vietnam, United States Navy, was born to Carl and Mary McIntosh and later joined the navy in January 1970. He completed boot camp training at San Diego, California and was transferred to Memphis, TN and assigned to the Naval Aviation Administration.

He was shipped to the naval air station in Agana, Guam where he was stationed for eighteen months. He later returned to the states for further training and later sent to the Philippine Islands before taking a supply ship. He then boarded the USS *Midway* off the coast of Vietnam.

The *Midway* headed toward home in 1973 and followed a detour across the equator and had a brief stay in Hawaii. It then headed for the Golden Gate Bridge and he spent the remaining months in Miramar Base. He received his discharge January 28, 1974.

After returning home he graduated from Purdue and was employed by IBM in Tucson, Arizona. He was assigned to different plants of the company and is currently the Business Office Manager in Phoenix. He lives with his wife Penny Dugdale and they became parents of one child, Justin.

DAVID K. MILLER, Vietnam, United States Army, born October 17, 1948, the son of Clifton and Mary Miller. He graduated from Brownstown Central High School in 1966. The next year he was married to Mary Brewer and they became parents to a daughter named Julie Michelle. A divorce resulted before he went into the service.

When he reported for duty he was sent to Ft. Knox, KY but later on he was sent to Fort Riley, KS and assigned to the 1st Infantry Division and trained as a mechanic. On May 2, 1970 he was killed in an automobile accident at Abilene, Kansas.

WALTER E. MILLER, United States Air Force, #3687865, 1971-1988. NCO Graduation Ribbon, AF Longevity Ribbon, Vietnam Service Medal.

DAVID W. MYERS, Vietnam, Sergeant, "B" Company, 2nd Battalion, 508th Parachute Infantry, 82nd Airborne Division 1972-1975.

Ancestors were American Patriots during the Revolutionary War who fought with Daniel Boone at Blue Licks in Kentucky.

Father was 1st Sergeant Arnold Myers who served during World War II, 9th Infantry Division, wounded October 1944 at Hürtgen Forest in Germany.

Son, Royal D. Myers, served in the U.S. Navy aboard the LST USS *Frederick.*

David W. Myers served as Past Commander of the American Legion, Post 112. Currently a life member of American Legion, Post 24 in Columbus, Indiana.

JAMES E. MYERS, Vietnam, United States Army, Sp-4 7th Squadron, 1st Air Cavalry, graduated from Seymour High School in 1965 and started to work for Cummins Engine Company trying to earn enough money so he could enter Indiana University during the spring semester. Something intervened and he joined the Army and left for Fort Polk. His enlistment indicated his patriotism and also the need for the GI benefits so he could return to complete his education.

He was assigned to the new Air Cavalry Unit being formed at Fort Knox in Kentucky. His unit was called the Blackhawks and it left for Vietnam in January 1968. Several days before they left he was granted a pass to go home and marry Linda Carol Buescher.

His united reached Vietnam on a troop ship sailing from Long Beach, CA. While en route on January 23, 1968 the USS *Pueblo* was attacked by the North Korean naval vessels and MIG jets. The Blackhawks were not diverted to North Korea but continued onto Vietnam and arrived just after the Tet Offensive. They were assigned to cover much of the Ho Chi Minh Trail. A few months later they relocated into the Delta area. Myers served as the expediter in locating items and supplies needed by other than by official channels.

Upon release from active duty, James Myers returned to Indiana University and graduated in June of 1971.

JOHN LLOYD NOLTING, Vietnam, United States Army, was born in Seymour February 12, 1946 to Harvard and Marguerite Newkirk Nolting. He was raised there and graduated from Shields High School in 1964. He helped his father operate the grocery market store until it was time for him to go into the service.

He enlisted and was inducted at Indianapolis December 20, 1966 and sent on to Fort Knox, KY

for basic training. He received further training back at Fort Harrison. He arrived in Vietnam August 19, 1967 and was then assigned to Hq. Company in the e Infantry Division at Pleiku as an intelligence specialist. He helped plan the operations during TET Offensive. He was ordered back to the states August 19, 1968.

He returned to Fort Riley, KS in Company A of the 1st Battalion, 34th Regiment of the 24th Division. His unit was shipped overseas and stationed at Augusburg, Germany during the Soviet invasion of Czechoslovakia in 1968. He returned to the states, then sent back to Vietnam in 1969 with 1st Field Artillery. Later he returned to Fort Lewis where he received his discharge November 20, 1969.

He and Helen Layton Nolting currently reside in Brownstown as the parents of two grown daughters.

DANIEL PATRICK, Vietnam, United States Navy, Mediterranean Sea Theater of Operations, 1959-1960.

ROY RATLIEFF, Vietnam, United States Air Force, Strategic Air Command 1963-1984. M/Sgt. Roy Ratliff (16790236) completed his military career in the US Air Force with the Strategic Air Command. He was born in 1941 in Columbus, IN, the son of Roscoe and Gladys Pedicord Ratliff. The family moved to Jackson County in 1945 and eventually, he graduated from Brownstown High School in 1959.

He completed his basic training at Lackland Air Base, Texas and continued training in communications at Keesler Air Force Base, MS. As a ground radio operator he was assigned duties between units of the 601st Tatical Control Squadron based in Germany. That assignment was followed back in the States in South Carolina.

In 1969-1970 during the Vietnam War he served a tour of duty at Nha Trang Air Base in Vietnam. Back in the States at Malmstrom Air Base in Montana he served as First Sgt. of the 341st SAC and in Naples he worked as communications security monitor and programmer for the NATO. At Castle Air Force Base in CA and Plattsburg, New York he trained and certified air crews of the SAC.

ROY Ratliff returned to Jackson County where he retired.

RICHARD RIGSBY, Vietnam, United States Army, was drafted into the army on August 25, 1969, but decided to enlist for a 4 year tour of duty. He enlisted in the U.S. Army Security Agency as a Criticom Center Specialist - 72B20D1.

He went to Ft. Leonard Wood, MO for Basic Training and then off to Ft Gordon, GA for AIT. After that he was sent overseas to Herzogarnaugh, Germany near Nurnberg in May 1970. He was there for about five months when he volunteered to go to a remote listening post called Det J, Mt. Schneeberg; it was at the Fulda Gap and a

very active area. After several months there he was sent to Augsburg, Germany to man a new commcenter for Headquarters USASAEUR. Since the war in Viet Nam was winding down he got a years early out, so on August 25, 1972 he was Honorably Discharged from Active Duty.

Once back in Seymour he started to work at Cummins Engine Co. on Sept. 25, 1972, also several months later he joined the Indiana National Guard in Seymour. But in 1982 after being laid off from Cummins he decided to join the Navy. He entered the Navy the day before Thanksgiving 1982; he went through Navy basic training at 32 years of age down in Orlando, FL. After basic he went to Corry Station in Pensacola, FL for "A" School. He enlisted for 5 years to be a CTO - Cryptologic Technician Operations. He was honor graduate of his class so he got his pick of his first duty assignment, he picked assignment to the staff of COMSUBLANT in Norfolk, VA.

His job was to provide secure broadcast communications to forward deployed submarines; it was like working in a bank vault. It was on the CINCLANTFLT compound and you sure saw a lot of gold braid. He left there in 1987 and went back to work at Cummins. He retired from Cummins in 2002. He was married to Susan in October 30, 1998 and has a stepson living at home named Jonathan.

COLONEL RICHARD R. "PHIL" ROBERTSON, Commanding Officer, 434th Combat Support Group, Tactical Fighter Wing, U.S. Air Force, received his commission in the US Air Force upon graduating from Kansas State University in 1956. Called to active duty the following year, he was sent to pilot training at Marana Air Base in Tucson, Arizona and Malden Air Base, Missouri. In 1957 he married Ruth Horstman.

Upon completion of training at Tyndall Air Base, Philippines in 1957, he was assigned to the 6207th Control and Warning Squadron at Clark Air Base. His wife joined him a few months later, and their first child was born there. Not long after that he was returned to the United States in February 1960 and left the service, returned home to work in the family milling company in Brownstown.

He was recalled to active duty for the Cuban Crisis in 1962 and served with the 434th Troop Carrier Wing then stationed at Bakalar Base in Columbus. Robertson was transferred to the Reserves and remained at Bakalar. In 1969 his reserve unit was transferred to Grisson Air Base located near Peru, Indiana.

Major Robertson then became comptroller of the 930th Combat Support Squadron of the 434th Special Operations Wing. In 1974 he was promoted to deputy commander. Upon further completion of training at Wright Patterson and, in May 1976 he assumed command of the Combat Support Group. While commander he was promoted to Colonel in March 1978.

In 1979 Colonel Robertson retired from the Air Force, returned home and devoted full time to his executive position in the Robertson Corporation.

RICHARD J. "DICKIE J." ROBISON, Vietnam, United States Army, the youngest son of George and Myrtle McKinney Robison, was born April 26, 1940. He was the fourth son to serve in the military forces of the United States. He graduated from Brownstown High School in 1959 after compiling an admirable record in basketball, baseball and track.

He was inducted into the army August 15, 1965. Following his basic training he later was promoted to the rank of Corporal. He was trained as a gunner on the 105 Howitzer and the 155 Howitzer. He was assigned to the 2nd Battalion, 9th Artillery in the 25th Division. While serving in the South Pacific Islands, he was selected to represent both his Battery and then his Battalion as a member of their basketball teams.

That was his duty assignment until the Vietnam War escalated and the basketball program was terminated. He was then re-assigned back to his unit.

After he was discharged he returned home and was employed by Public Service of Indiana, later to be known as Cinergy. He retired after 32 years of service. He was associated with Swifty Farms hauling horses, and he has raced horses at various tracks throughout the United States. He won several stake races, including the All-America Congress.

He is married to Carolyn Brooks.

JAMES MICHAEL ROSS, Vietnam, United States Army, was born in Seymour to Manville and Louise Henry Ross. He was raised in the local area and completed his instruction locally. He was drafted into the army May 23, 1966.

His induction took place in Indianapolis but he was sent to Fort Knox for basic training. While there he lived in a barracks along with Larry Rollins of Jackson County. Together, they passed the time singing western songs.

He was sent to Fort Lee in Virginia for training before being shipped overseas to Vietnam where he was stationed at Cam Ranh Bay. The trip on the high seas required 21 days because they stopped at the Philippine Islands. He survived all kinds of hardships and, on return he stopped in Japan and Alaska before reaching the states. He received his discharge in Washington before going on home to Brownstown.

On January 6, 1973 he was married to Jo Gail Wessel and they became parents of two sons, Michael Brant and Shawn Aaron.

MELVIN RANDOLPH ROUSE, Vietnam, United States Army, was born February 9, 1948 to Henry T. and Elma Opal Tedder Rouse. The family resided near Freetown, IN. He was married to Katsuko Miyagi "Marty" Rouse in October 1969. They became the parents of a daughter named Michelle Elma Rouse and she was married to Damon Dale Davers II.

Melvin Rouse graduated from Brownstown Central High School in 1967. He was drafted into the army on February 28, 1968. He completed his basic training at Fort Campbell, KY and was assigned to Company B of the 25th Infantry Division which was sent to Vietnam in August 1968.

He was wounded September 15, 1968 and a citation read "Pfc. Rouse distinguished himself with heroic actions ... while serving with Company B when it came under intense enemy fire. His platoon was pinned down and although wounded, Pvt. Rouse, with complete disregard for his own safety, placed heavy suppressive fire on the enemy which enabled his comrades to withdraw safely. His valorous actions contributed to the success of the mission and defeat of the enemy ... his personal bravery and devotion to duty are in keeping with the highest tradition of the military service and reflect great credit upon himself, his unit, the 25th Infantry Division and the US Army."

He was hospitalized in Japan and later assigned as a supply clerk. He was authorized to wear a variety of medals and ribbons, along with the Purple Heart. He Was discharged February 1, 1974 and currently resides in Congress, Arizona.

JACK L. SHIRLEY, Vietnam, United States Army, was born. on December 16, 1949 in Seymour, Indiana to Rawland and Ada (Maxie) Shirley. He grew up in Jackson County and attended School at Tampico and Brownstown, graduating from Brownstown Central High School in 1967. In the fall of that year, he began a long career with Cummins Engine Company in Columbus, IN. In August of 1969, prior to his military service, Shirley married Ellen R. (Williams) of Berea, Kentucky.

Shirley entered the U.S. Army on May 21, 1970 at Fort Knox, Kentucky. He served there, with Company D, 15th Battalion, 4th Training Brigade. His deployment to Vietnam came on October 19th of the same year. While serving in Vietnam, he was assigned to the 192nd Aviation Company, Assault Helicopters, as a Spec 5. He returned to the states and was honorably discharged from the United States Army on November 26, 1971.

He was awarded many honors while in the U.S. Army, including Vietnam Service Medal, Vietnam Combat Medal, Army Commendation Medal for Meritorious Achievement, Expert M14 Medal, Expert M16 Medal, Two Overseas Bars, and was named "Soldier of the Month" by the 10th Combat Aviation Battalion.

He returned to Cummins Engine Company shortly after his discharge from the Army, working at many of their locations throughout the next several years. While employed by Cummins, he earned a degree in accounting and finished his career with that company as a supervisor in the claims department. Shirley retired from Cummins in 1997 and he and his wife now reside in Lakeland, Florida. He has two children, Jennifer Shirley-Mellencamp of Jackson County and Blake Shirley of Florida.

LLOYD STEVEN SILENCE, Vietnam, United States Air Force, was born in Seymour, Indiana on March 4, 1949, and was raised in Brownstown, Indiana. He enlisted in the United States Air Force on May 27, 1968, during the Viet Nam War era. He was stationed at Lackland Air Force Base for basic training. He was then transferred to Keesler Air Force Base, Biloxi, Mississippi, for electronics training.

After a year of training, he was transferred to Wildwood Air Force Base, Kenai, Alaska. He was a microwave and tropospheric communications specialist. He was responsible for maintaining communications for the Alaska White Alice System and the Dewline Early Warning System for the Northern Hemisphere. Lloyd also helped with the communications from Viet Nam to the lower 48 states through telephone and teletype communications.

Silence was honorably discharged on December 13, 1971, from Elmendorf Air Force Base, Anchorage, Alaska, after achieving Sergeant status. Since that time he has been in Industrial Electronics using his talents for electrical maintenance, combustion engineering, and instrumentation technology.

Lloyd had a grandfather, Charles Peter Silence, who served in the United States Army during World War I. He also had two uncles, Robert Silence, and Melvin Silence, who served in the Navy during World War II.

STEVEN SILENCE, Vietnam, United States Air Force, Records of Steven Silence are almost non-available but they do verify that he was married to Derenda Silence on June 11, 1971 while on leave from the military service of his country.

The family was blessed with the birth of a son named Chad who was later married.

RANDOLPH J. SMITH III, Vietnam, United States Army, was born in Seymour July 6, 1947 and later graduated from Seymour High School in 1965. He was drafted August 1, 1966 and reported to Ft. Harrison with a friend. Both were sent to Fort Knox for basic training. He was made a squad leader which promoted him to Pfc.

He was then sent to Ft. Sam Houston for advanced training as an army medic. He reported to Ft. Hood and was assigned to the 1st Battalion of the 50th Infantry Division which was deployed to Vietnam. His unit left San Francisco on the troop ship, USS *John Pope,* and after 3 weeks at sea, they reached Vietnam. His battalion formed a forward observation base where Smith was assigned to Delta Company as senior medic providing aid to the casualties. He was awarded various medals, the

Purple Heart and Bronze Star for valor during the TET offensive.

He was ordered from Vietnam to Japan in 1968 and was reassigned to the 420th Medical Company stationed on Okinawa. He was in charge of the Serology lab until July 1968 when he was flown to Oakland. He was discharged and returned home to Seymour.

SAMUEL J. SPRAY, Vietnam, United States Army, was born December 31, 1948, in Medora to William L. and Marian Day Spray. He grew up in Medora and graduated from Medora High School in 1967.

He was inducted into the United States Army in 1970 and completed his basic training at Ft. Knox, Kentucky. He was then stationed at Ft. Polk, Louisiana for eight weeks, then assigned to overseas duty in Chu Lai, Vietnam in October 1970. He was in the infantry and was a Specialist 4th Class. He was stationed on Fire Base 4-11 and spent his time patrolling the jungles and river valleys in that area.

Sam received a Combat Infantry Badge, a Vietnam Service Medal, and various other routine medals.

He returned to the United States in October 1971 and was stationed for a short while at Ft. Carson, Colorado. He was discharged in December 1971, when President Nixon issued an early discharge for troops returning from Vietnam.

Sam graduated from Indiana Central College (now the University of Indianapolis) in in 1975 and obtained his Master's Degree from Indiana University in 1978.

He presently teaches at Medora High School. He is married to the former Diana Frazier and they have two children, Seth Andrew and Carrie Suzanne.

CHARLES STAHL, Vietnam, United States Army, was born January 4, 1940 in Grassy Fork Township to Edgar and Rachel Hallow Stahl. He grew up in the local area on the family farm and he graduated from Brownstown High School with the class of 1940.

He was inducted into the army in 1962 and completed basic training at Fort Knox, Ky. He was then sent to Fort Rucker, AL where he was assigned to maintenance on multi engine repair of transport aircraft. He was assigned to the 61st Aviation Company at Fort Bragg, North Carolina.

His unit was shipped overseas to Vietnam where he was stationed at Vangtau Airbase. Upon the end of his tour of duty he was discharged and returned home to the family farm in Jackson County.

JOHN LISTON SULLIVAN, Vietnam, United States Army, born December 2, 1940 at Seymour in Jackson County. Parents: William and Elsie Snider Sullivan. Graduated from Shields High School in 1968. Employed by Cummins in Columbus.

Inducted into the army October 1, 1963. Reported to Indianapolis. Completed basic training at Fort Knox. Trained as Military Police at Fort Gordon. Assigned to 720th Military Police Battalion. Completed tour of duty at Fort Hood. Discharged September 30, 1965.

Returned to Seymour and employment at Cummins. Retired with 31 years.

JERRY LEE THOMPSON, Vietnam, United States Army, was born in Washington County to Ervin and Thelma McMahon Thompson. He moved with his family when he was only a child and they settled in Freetown. Later he was a member of the last graduated class from the local school which was then consolidated with the Seymour Consolidated Corporation.

He was employed by Cummins in Columbus but, in October 1965 he was drafted into the army. He completed his basic training at Fort Knox. From there he was sent to Ft Leonard Wood where he was assigned to the 4th Special Training Brigade. In 1966 during the peak of the Vietnam War he was shipped out to Yokahama, Japan where the wounded were all airlifted for treatment. Thompson drove the ambulance carrying them to the hospital.

After he was promoted he was assigned to the administration office and when Camp Drake closed, he was returned to the states and discharged in September 1967. He remained in the Reserves and was awarded his discharge in 1971.

He married Bonita Lou Daab of Spratrown in St. Peter Lutheran Church in Waymansville. They became parents of twins, and much later he retired from Cummins in 2002. The Thompsons were residents of Spratrown in Jackson County.

ROBERT L. TOBORG, Vietnam, United States Army, was born March 5, 1946 to Louis and Josephine Rittman Toborg in Seymour, Indiana. He has lived in Jackson County most of his life. He graduated from Seymour High School in 1964, worked at Thompson Dairy 1960-1965 and went to work at Cummins Engine Co. He was drafted in to the U.S. Army in December 1965, spent basic training

at Ft. Knox as E1. (His father Louis did basic there in 1945 and his brother William did basic there in 1955). In February of 1966 he was sent to Ft. Bliss, TX for A.I.T. (Advanced Individual Training) and was E3 PFC. In May 1966 he married Donna Mulder of Seymour and together they spent until October at Ft. Bliss, coming home on a 15 day pass as an E4 (Spec 4) before shipping out on the US *Geiger* ship to Viet Nam. (It took 18 days).

Bob's base camp was Long Binh. In January 1967 he went to Cu Chi Base Camp with the 25th Infantry Division. (There is a book called *"The Tunnels of Cu Chi"* that describes the complex of tunnels running below their camp).

The Red Cross notified Bob in April, that he was a father of a little boy born April 4th. (Timothy Donald).

In a vicious attack June 26, while serving with the Battery D (Machine Gun) 71st Artillery, serving on a perimeter defense of an isolated-fire support base, his sergeant, Kyle Smiddy was killed, along with Spec 4 Carl Holbrook, Spec 4 Lawrence Mayberry, PFC Joe South, and Bob were all injured. He received the Purple Heart from wounds received in action, and Bronze Star Medal with Valor from that attack. In July he became Sergeant E5. Arriving home to the United States in late October, to be united with his wife again and little boy, 7 months old. He got to see his first steps 2 weeks later!

Bob is father to Tim, Tammy (Claycamp), Tisha (Krueger), and Doug. He is the grandfather of 9. Their families live within 12 miles of them. He retired from Cummins in February 2001.

RICHARD A. TRIMPE, Vietnam, United States Army, a son of Virgil and Alberta Trimpe of Route 2 in Seymour, was drafted August 19, 1965. He completed basic training at Fort Knox, KY. He was assigned to Headquarters Company ASATCA at the fort. He was stationed at the Ammunition Depot until he was discharged August 18, 1969.

He was married to Linda Gill Trimpe and they became parents of three daughters, Teresa, Jennifer and aira.

KENNETH G. WAGGONER, Post WWII, Korea and Vietnam, United States Air Force, 1954-1974, born in 1934 near Houston in Jackson County, IN. He graduated from Freetown High School in 1952 and attended college for one year before entering the military service. He completed his basic training at Samson Air Base in NY, then was ordered to Wyoming for special instruction in teletype maintenance.

Following came a series of assignments across the United States before he was sent to Vietnam. His service records indicate he was awarded several medals, including the National Defense Medal, Vietnam Service Medal as well as Unit Commendations.

Tech Sergeant Kenneth Waggoner (16478094) received his honorable discharge in October 1974. By that time he was able to celebrate 20 years of married life with Nellie K. Wright. To them were born 3 children including Roger, Yvonne and Cynthia. Currently they have eight grandchildren.

JOHNNE DEAN WETZEL, Vietnam, United States Air Force, was born in Seymour February 23, 1947 to Donald and Delcia Isaaks Wetzel. He was raised locally and graduated from Cortland High School in 1965. He was employed by the JC Company until he was to enter the armed forces.

He was inducted into the Air Force at Indianapolis and sent to Lackland AF Base for basic training. He received further instruction on aircraft mechanics at Sheppard AF Base before being assigned to the 375th MAC 4-star General's planes and then he was shipped overseas to Vietnam.

He arrived November 10, 1967 near Da Nang and was stationed with the front line missiles launching group covering the DMZ line. He left Viet Nam and returned to Scott AF Base where he worked on official's planes during the long working hours of each day. He retired and was discharged without ceremony.

He and his wife reside near Surprise. They have five grown children.

DONALD ZINK, Vietnam, United States Army, enlisted in the US Army in 1965. He was discharged in 1967, but didn't receive his final release papers until 1971.

He received his basic training at Ft. Knox, KY. From there he was sent to Ft. Bliss, TX for missile training. Then he was sent to Germany, where he was sent to many different cities. From Frankfort he was sent back to the States to Ft. Eustis, VA for special training as a Stevedore. From there he was sent to Viet Nam. He was discharged as a 16D 40 Stevedore - Sergeant E5.

During his term of service he also served at Ft. Hamilton, NY.

Donnie and his wife, Diane, now reside in the Medora area. He has one son, Ricky Joe.

Vietnam War Veterans

THE PERSIAN GULF WAR
DESERT STORM TO IRAQ
1991–2004

A PARTIAL LISTING OF JACKSON COUNTY SERVICE PERSONS WHO PARTICIPATED

Nathan Barlow: US Navy–Seymour
Tracy Fleetwood: US Army–Brownstown
Steven Scarlett: US Army–Brownstown

Kurt Douglas: US Army–Seymour
Joseph M. Robertson: National Guard
Darrel WIlliams: US Navy–Seymour

Jeannie Wright: US Army–Brownstown

LUCAS ALEXANDER ACTON, Desert Storm, Indiana National Guard, after graduating from Seymour High School in 1999, Luke attended Indiana University taking pre-requisites for the nursing program. He joined the Indiana National Guards and attended basic training in Fort Benning, Georgia. He then attended AIT to become a medic at Fort Sam Houston, San Antonio, Texas. He was assigned to Company A, 205th Medical Battalion at Camp Atterbury.

He continued at IU to obtain a BS in nursing, but was removed from nursing school in February 2003 to train for Operation Enduring Freedom and became federalized by the Department of the Army. In May he was then deployed to Camp Arifjan, Kuwait, where he worked as a medic in the troop medical center. The medical center treats over 200 people a day with assorted medical illnesses such as camel spider bites, scorpion bites and heat exhaustion. He worked 6 12-hour days per week and gained experience in suturing and working with the trauma team. At the time of printing, he remains in, Kuwait.

Luke is the son of Steve and Sally Acton who live in the Clear Spring area with a sister, Elizabeth.

MANDY LANE BANTHER, Iraq, United States Army, graduated from West Point Military Academy, born November 10, 1970 to Tom and Jeannie Trimpe and James M. Banther of Seymour. She is the first woman from Jackson County to graduate from West Point Military Academy. After graduating from Seymour High School, she entered the academy and graduated in 1993 as a 2nd Lieutenant with honors in law.

She served in the 24th Infantry Division when deployed to Cuba in support of Operation Sea Signal. She was promoted to 1st Lieutenant at Fort Stewart in April 1996. Leaving active duty, she joined the Arizona National Guard and served in the 855th Military Police Company. She was promoted to the rank of Captain in 1999. She served in the Ohio National Guard before moving on to Massachusetts. Her unit was activated and stationed in New York until deployed to Iraq with the 211th Military Police Battalion. She served as the operations officer.

Attached to the 4th Infantry Division, Mandy was awarded the Bronze Star for meritorious service. She returned home with her unit in September 2003 and currently resides in North Quincy, Massachusetts.

MATTHEW BANTHER, Desert Storm, United States Navy, is the son and step-son of Tom and Jeannie Trimpe and James M. Banther. He was born April 26, 1968 and enlisted in the navy right out of high school.

He reported to Great Lakes Naval States July 9, 1986 and was trained as machinist on aviation equipment. From Millington, Tennessee he was sent to Norfolk, Virginia and then transferred to the Naval Air Station at Jacksonville, Florida as helicopter mechanic until 1999.

He served in Desert Storm and Shields while assigned aboard the USS *Eisenhower*. He returned to the base in Florida for 16 years and is now stationed at Great Lakes Naval Training Center where he serves as an instructor.

He is married and the father of three sons. Upon retirement in 2006 he plans to operate his own boat repair marina in Florida.

FOREST R. BOLING, JR., The Cuban Crisis, United States Navy, born July 23, 1940 near Vallonia, to Forest and Ethel Tuelker Boling. He was raised as a farm boy and later graduated from Brownstown in 1958. Three years later he was inducted into the navy at Indianapolis. He completed boot camp training at Great Lakes, IL.

He was assigned to the USS *Earl B. Hall* APD 107, later he was transferred to the USS *Kirwin* APD 90 and remained a member of its crew serving off the Cuban Coast until he was discharged.

He returned home and was employed by Kieffer Paper Mill where he worked for 35 years. He and his wife, Carolyn Ferguson Boling were parents of two children.

WALTER LOWELL BURKE, Pre-Desert Storm, United States Army, born in Jackson County to Harold and Eva Butler Devine Burke raised in Seymour and graduated from high school in 1977.

Inducted into army February 21, 1978. Assigned to Fort McClellan. Trained for Military Police.

Returned to Seymour as Recruiter in 1978. Deployed overseas to Munchenwiler, Germany: 1978–1981. Discharged February 17, 1981.

Married Carolyn Jo Stahl in 1982; parents of 2 daughters.

STEVEN TODD CAMPBELL, Iraq, United States Army, born December 6, 1979 to Rhonda Cockerham Campbell. He was raised in Seymour and attended school there. He joined the army in July 1998 at Fort Harrison in Indianapolis. He was later stationed at Fort Knox, Kentucky and Fort Benning, Georgia.

Records fail to show any overseas duty and he was discharged in 2002 But he elected to remain in the national guard reserves.

He came home to his family of three children.

TONY WAYNE CLARK, Desert Shield, United States Navy, son of Melvin and Mary Lucas Clark. Enlisted June 21, 1989, basic training at Great Lakes. Assigned to the USS *Saratoga* scheduled for Mediterranean.

Returned to the states for fire fighting training August 1990. Ordered to Mediterranean to support Desert Shield, 21 shipmates perished in ferry boat accident in Israel. Became Electronic Equipment Repairman.

Awarded a host of medals and ribbons reflecting his service. Received discharge June 18, 1993.

Married Melissa Hubbard of Austin, became parents of two children.

MARY COTTERMAN, Iraqi War Period, United States Air Force, Airman, daughter of Joe and Helen Cotterman of South Walnut Street in Seymour, completed her basic training at Lackland Air Base in San Antonio, TX. She graduated from Seymour High School with the class of 2003. She has been selected to receive special credit toward an Associate degree from the Community College of the Air Force.

Mary Cotterman completed studies in rifle marksmanship, human relations and military organization.

STEPHAN NEIL EMPSON, Persian Gulf War, United States Navy, 1993-1997, born to H. Neil and Pamela Empson on March 27, 1975. He graduated from Hope High School with the class of 1993. Four months later on September 19, 1993 he enlisted in the Navy.

He completed his boot training in Orlando, Florida and was sent to the Corryfield Naval Base at Pensacola for specialized training. He was ordered aboard the Aircraft Carrier USS *Nimintz* where he was assigned work in cryptology. He was promoted to Technician 3rd Class and later was discharged in September 1997.

Stephan Neil Empson is the grandson of former Jackson County residents, Howard and Doreen Empson.

DONALD M. FREDERICKSON II, 1976-1980, United States Marine Corps, the youngest son of Donald and Myrtle Ballard Frederickson. He was born in 1956 in Jackson County and later graduated from Brownstown Central High School in 1975. Following the footsteps of his brothers, he enlisted in the Navy in 1976.

He completed his boot training in San Diego, CA. He was then stationed at Cherry Point, NC with the 1st Marine Aircraft Wing. He held the rank of Sergeant when he was discharged in 1980.

He joined the Reserves in June 1980 as a maintenance supervisor.

He holds the rank of sergeant and he and his family live in the Ccounty seat of government at Brownstown, IN.

JAMES M. HASH, Desert Storm, 1988-1992, United States Air Force, born November 20, 1969 in Indianapolis. Parents are Marvin and Janet Hash of Brownstown. Graduated from high school at the County Seat in 1983.

Entered the air force in August 1988. Completed basic training at Lackland AFB.

Assigned to the Air Police. Shipped overseas to Italy where he served for two years.

Returned to the states and stationed in Michigan, discharged in August 1992.

Returned to Brownstown and enrolled in night classes. Became a journeyman pipe fitter and plumber.

JUSTYN D. HAWKINS, Iraqi War Period, United States Army National Guard, Private, son of Paula Hawkins of Sunset Lane in Seymour, Indiana, graduated from basic combat training at Fort Knox in Kentucky. He ranked high in the weapons and rifle marksmanship instruction. He specialized in tactical exercises and chemical warfare training. He was singled out for recognition in Army traditions and care values.

CRAIG ARTHUR HOEVENER, Enduring Freedom, Army National Guard, CW2, was sworn into the Army National Guard on May 14, 1979 by his father, Leon Arthur Hoevener who retired from the Guard on October 31, 1994. The son was then promoted through the enlisted ranks and finally became eligible to attend the Warrant Officer College located at Fort Rucker in Alabama in April 1997.

Once again, he was sworn into the officer ranks by his father in June 1997 but this time as a Warrant Officer. Called into active service as part of operation "Enduring Freedom" he served until October 21, 2003.

LEON A. HOEVENER, Korea to Desert Storm, Indiana Army National Guard, 1952-1994, was married to Loretta Beldon and they became parents of three children, including a daughter Debbie and sons, Greg and Craig.

Leon was called to active duty in 1991 but retired October 31, 1994.

He had served to support Operation Desert Storm and Desert Shield.

GREGORY F. HUTCHINSON, Arabian Gulf to the Present, United States Army.

February 1987, entered the Army, conducted Basic Training, Advanced Infantry Training and Airborne Training at Ft. Benning, GA.

May 1987-February 1990, Riflemen-Squad Leader with 5th Bn. 502nd Infantry; Berlin Brigade; Berlin, Germany. Member of the last platoon to conduct the Changing of the Guard and to stand guard at Spandau Prison; Rudolf Hess (Hitler's next in charge) died during their watch; prison was immediately closed and destroyed. His platoon was on Wall Patrol the day the Berlin Wall came down.

March 1990-July 1993, Squad Leader with the 2nd Bn. 505th Parachute Infantry Regiment; 82nd Airborne Division; Ft. Bragg, NC, one of the first units to enter and conduct Combat Operations in Saudi Arabia and Iraq during Operation Desert Shield and operation Desert Storm. Deployed to Panama and Honduras.

August 1993-August 1994, Special Operations Sergeant; 2nd Infantry Division; Camp Red Cloud, Korea. Worked for COL Chamberlain III, grandson of the Civil War, COL Chamberlain.

September 1994-November 1997, Drill Sergeant and Senior Drill Sergeant; 1st Bn. 38th Infantry; 1st Infantry Training Brigade; Ft. Benning, GA.

November 1997-November 2000, Platoon Sergeant and First Sergeant; 1st Bn., 21st Infantry Regiment (GIMLETS); 25th Infantry Division (LIGHT); Schofield Barracks, Hawaii. Conducted Operation Cobra Gold; Kurrat, Thailand.

December 2000-December 2001, First Sergeant and Battalion Sergeant Major for HHC, 2nd Bn., 503rd Infantry Airborne; 173rd Airborne Brigade; Vicenza, Italy.

January 2001-UTP, J3 Special Operations Sergeant; Southern European Task Force (SETAF); Vicenza, Italy. Conducted Operations in Monrovia, Liberia as part of Joint Task Force-Liberia.

Military awards and badges include: 4x Meritorious Service Medals, 1x Joint Accommodation Medal, 3x Army Accommodation Medals, 7x Army Achievement Medals, 1x Joint Meritorious Unit Award, 1x Meritorious Unit Award, 1x Army Superior Unit Award and Combat Infantrymen Badge.

RONALD KEITH HUTCHINSON, Desert Storm, United States Army, born to Charles Hutchinson and he attended and graduated from Brownstown High School in 1980. He joined the army August 13, 1981 and was assigned to the Field Artillery.

After basic training he was stationed at the McClellan AFB, AL. He was later sent to Fort Lee, Virginia and then to Fort Sill, OK as a records and parts specialist. He spent

two years in the service and discharged from Fort Sill August 12, 1983.

He married Dena Wessel February 1, 1985 and they became parents of two children, Jesse and Tessie.

LEWIS W. IMLAY, Post Vietnam, United States Navy, born in Jackson Co., IN and still resides in Jackson Co.

Lewis W. Imlay entered the U.S. Navy at Indianapolis, IN and his basic training was at Great Lakes Naval Training Center. He was transferred to Millington, TN for A School. In 1983 he was stationed at LeMoore Naval Air Station for further training, in preparation for his duty station with the Navy.

ATAN Imlay received an Honorable Discharge from the U.S. Navy in 1985 at Portsmouth, VA.

WILLIAM J. MIDDENDORF, War in Iraq, Company "A" Engineer Battalion Baghdad, Iraq 2003, the only son of Dr. Max and Eva Middendorf of Brownstown, graduated from Brownstown Central High School. He is currently serving his country in the War in Iraq and is stationed in downtown Baghdad as the Executive Officer: Company "A" of the 40th Engineer Battalion. He expects to be re-assigned to Germany in mid-2004. Upon his discharge he will assume his membership in the American Legion, Post 112 of Brownstown, IN.

BYRON S. MYERS, Iraq, United States Navy, graduated from Seymour High School in 1990. Joined the navy and completed boot training in Orlando, FL. Trained in technical services on metals and fire fighting. Promoted to Petty Officer status, assigned to USS *Canapus*.

Stationed in Georgia he was assigned to the pope repair shop. Performed maintenance on Navy Submarines.

Reported aboard USS *Yorktown* in Mississippi. Assigned duties in the Pacific and Atlantic Oceans.

Promoted to Chief Petty Officer. Transferred to USS *Emory S. Land* in Italy.

Remained on active duty and is currently stationed at Norfolk, VA. Resides nearby with his wife and 3 children.

PERRY A. MYERS, Desert Storm, United States Navy, enlisted in the Navy in February Of 1988. He took basic training at the Great Lakes. After basic he was transferred to Charleston, South Carolina where he served on the USS *ELROD*, which is a fast frigate. He was deployed to Bahrain two times in the four years he served. The last time during Desert Storm.

His ship also served as part of a drug force operation in Cuba. He was discharged in February of 1992. He then served one year active reserve and three years inactive. He's married to the former Jodi Shake and they have three sons, Blaine, Dalton, and Nigel. They reside in Brownstown and he works for REMC.

ROYAL D. MYERS, Iraq, United States Navy, born at Jackson Co. Hospital in March 1976, Royal D. Myers graduated from Crothersville HS in 1994. Myers enlisted in the U.S. Navy and completed boot camp at Great Lakes Recruit Training Command serving as divisional yeoman.

In the fall of 1994 Myers attended Electrician's Mate Class A School and served as division's yeoman and mail carrier. From EM Class A school Myers received the honor of Distinguished Military Graduate and was ordered to duty aboard the "Great Ship Frederick" USS *Frederick* LST-1184 (Landing Ship Tank), where he would serve until June of 1999. The duties of the Frederick were to transport Marines, Marine equipment, and to train reservists.

Aboard the USS *Frederick,* Myers achieved the rank of Electricians Mate 2nd Class Petty Officer (E-5) in September of 1996 and earned his Enlisted Surface Warfare Specialist (ESWS) pin in April of 1998.

Myers' duties were as Electrical Safety Program Manager, Electric Plant Operator, LST Bow Ramp Operator, and finally Electrical Division Supervisor.

During Myers' "hitch," the USS *Frederick* visited America Samoa, Tonga, Japan, Malaysia, Mexico, Indonesia, Thailand, Singapore, and Australia.

The USS *Frederick* successfully completed 3 separate "at sea" rescues of civilians during Myers' time aboard. The first rescue was a New Zealand man, Mark Sheffield, who was bitten by a barracuda while swimming around his sailboat at the Christmas Islands. After steaming for nearly 10 hours at a full bell to reach Sheffield's boat, the crew of the USS *Frederick* working together, rescued, treated and then transported Mark to Hawaii for medical care.

The other two rescues occurred off the coast of Hawaii. A man and his young grandson, sailing from Washington State to New Zealand, were stranded at sea with a broken mast following a storm that also sank a sailboat and left a group of 11 friends and a child stranded several miles from shore. They swam in the ocean for half a day until the crew of the USS *Frederick* found them. All were safely returned to their families.

RICHARD WILLIAM PFERRER, Post Korea/Pre Vietnam, United States Air Force, born March 1, 1937 to parents, Charles and Opal Davis Pferrer.

Raised in Brownstown and graduated from the local school. After his parents died he was raised by his grandparents.

Entered air force in November 1958. Stationed in Texas, Minnesota before going to Alaska. Shipped to Vietnam.

Returned to Texas. Appointed recruiter, discharged December 19, 1978 with 20 years service time. Resident of Florida.

DARYL L. POGUE, Pre-Desert Storm, United States Air Force. Parents: Larry and Jean Pogue of Brownstown. Graduated from Brownstown Central High School in 1982.

Joined the air force September 1982, Lackland AFB and Charlestown AFB, 437th Civil Engineering Squadron, Grissom AFB.

Discharged May 1986. Reserve in Kentucky National Guard 1987, discharged 1992.

JEFFREY PORCH, Desert Storm and Desert Shield, United States Navy, enlisted in the navy July 7, 1986 and completed boot camp training before being sent to the naval air station located in Fallon, Nevada. He was assigned to Coronado Air Station in California. He was later placed into the Helicopter Squadron #8 at North Island.

He was deployed to serve on the aircraft carriers, USS *Constellation* and USS *Independence* before receiving his discharge. When he arrived home, he entered the Indiana National Guard and served with the 181st Fighter Wing at Terre Haute from 1992 to 1995. He re-enlisted again in the Indiana National Guard and served with the 150 Field Artillery stationed at Danville, Indiana to the present time.

He was married to Lisa Abbett and they became parents of a son.

JAMES D. PREWITT, Iraqi War Period, United States Air Force, 39th Security Forces Squadron, Airman 1st Class, son of Stephanie Prewitt of Sugar Street in Brownstown, has arrived for duty at Incirlik Base in Adana, Turkey. He will be stationed there and assigned to the Security Forces after serving in the United States during the past two years.

Airman 1st Class Prewitt graduated from Brownstown Central High School with the class of 2001.

JILLIAN PAIGE RICHARDS, Iraq War, United States Army, Enlisted July 9, 2003, in the army and completed basic training at Fort Jackson, South Carolina. She was selected for special training and sent to Fort Gordon, GA. Following several weeks of intensive instruction, she will be ordered to Fort Campbell, Kentucky,

Her parents are Charles Richards of St. Joseph, Michigan and Ron and Betty Wachoviak of Wrightsville, Pennsylvania. She has a sister Danielle who graduated from Western Michigan University.

Jillian is the granddaughter of Charles and Dorothy Empson Richards. She is able to trace her lineage in a direct line through her great, great, grandfather Daniel Empson, who was a veteran of the Civil War, and on through successive patriots of every American conflict. Her oldest ancestral forebear, Cornelius Empson was a soldier who served under General Anthony Wayne at Brandywine Creek and who participated in the Battle of Yorktown.

Jillian Richards may be proud of her military heritage. It represents a long-standing family record of patriotism.

CHARLES DANIEL SCHEIBLE, Iraq to the present, United States to the Line, joined the Army in Columbus, Indiana.

Basic training at Fort Jackson, South Carolina, F-Co/28 INF BN 11/ 2001-2/2002.

AIT (advance individual training) Fort Gordon, Georgia D-Co/ 447th SIG 2/2002-4/ 12002. Where he was an Honor Graduate, 2nd in his class.

A-Co/501th SIG BN 101st Airborne Division (Air Assault) Ft. Campbell, KY 5/2002-Present.

Daniel was deployed to Iraq with the 101st ABN DIV (AASLT) in support of Operation Iraqi Freedom 3/1/2003-2/9/2004. As a 31R, Daniel was responsible for maintaining communications throughout the Division. Allowing for fast and accurate reports and orders to be given through the Division.

Daniel was born in Clarksville, Tennessee on July 6, 1979.

Daniel is a graduate of Seymour High School Class of 1997. His parents and siblings still remain in the area.

Daniel married Elisha Troxell of Seymour. They have one child, Charles Ethan Paul Scheible, born while his father was in Iraq.

While in Iraq, Daniel completed the Air Assault School training. He also was qualified as a Combat Life Saver. Daniel's goals are to remain in the military and continue his educcation.

CHARLES MARTIN SCHEIBLE, Vietnam to Iraq, United States Army, was drafted during the Vietnam War, April 1972 in Columbus, Indiana.

Charles' Basic Training was at Fort Knox, KY D-Co/2/5.

Charles attended Jump School at Fort Benning, Georgia (paratrooper).

AIT (advance individual training) at Fort Campbell, KY with the 3/187. Rakasans 101st Airborne Division.

After a short tour in Vietnam, Charles transferred to medical corps in 1974.

Medic 91B Fort Sam Houston, TX, 91C (Nursing) Fort Bragg, NC, 42nd Field Disaster Hospital Fort Knox, KY.

After leaving active duty Charles transferred to the Indiana National Guard at Camp Atterbury, IN. He has held the position of Medical Supply Technician and 91C until just recently. The army has converted all 91Bs and 91Cs to EMTs.

Charles will celebrate 32 years in the service come April of this year.

Charles is married to Dori Mahon of Clarksville, Tennessee. They have 5 children. Christina Michelle, Tesa Danean, Charles Daniel, Amanda Erin and

Thomas Benjamin. He has 3 grandchildren Charlcie, Rachel and Ethan.

Charles has lived in the Seymour area for 10 years, but is originally from Columbus.

Charles was reactivated November 02, in support of Operation Enduring Freedom. He remains stationed at Camp Atterbury, IN processing troops for deployment.

Charles' goals are to retire in about 5 years and to enjoy his grandchildren.

CHRISTINA MICHELLE SCHEIBLE-HEARN, Iraq, United States Army, born in Fort Campbell, Kentucky June 13, 1974. She joined the Army in Nashville, Tennessee 3/1998.

Her basic training was completed at Fort Jackson, SC. AIT (advance individual training) completed Fort Jackson, SC. E-Co/396th Finance Unit.

C-Det./176 Finance BN Tague, Korea 9/1998-9/1999 At this station Michelle earned Soldier of the Year for all the Finance Units in the Army.

A Co/101st SSB Finance Corp/ 101st Airborne Division (Air Assault) Fort Campbell, KY 10/1999-6/2001. A Co/208th Finance BN Mannheim, Germany 6/2001-present.

Michelle was deployed to Iraq with V Corps, in support of Operation Iraqi Freedom 3/2003-5/2003, Michelle had to return to Germany due to the open-heart surgery of her youngest child.

She is presently still serving in Mannheim, Germany, with 6 months left before she returns back stateside.

Michelle is married to Jon Hearn of Georgia and has two girls: Charlcie Denise and Rachel Elizabeth. Her husband and children live in Clarksville, Tennessee presently.

Michelle's parents and siblings still live here in Jackson County. Michelle was employed a short time before entering the service at Jackson County Hospital in registration.

TRACY EUGENE STIDAM, Desert Storm, United States Air Force, born September 6, 1971 in Jackson County.

Parents: Howard and Cheryl Stidam. Raised at Vallonia and graduated from high school. Entered Indiana National Guard July 30, 1989. Transferred to the Army at Indianapolis October 16, 1990. Assigned to Co. D, 2nd Bat., 505th Para Inf., 82nd Div. Deployed overseas for operation Desert Storm, discharged July 29, 1997.

Married to Reene Stidam: Parents of 3 children. Residents of Vallonia, Indiana.

GERALD WAYNE TERRELL, Pre-Desert Storm, United States Army, born to Gerald and Millie Terrell in California but the family moved to Brownstown in 1968. He completed his high school education there.

He joined the army in 1981 and was sent to Alabama to complete his basic training at Fort Ord in California before being shipped overseas to Hawaii for the remainder of his tour of duty. He was discharged in 1986 and returned to the states for discharge.

He married Kandra Winchester and they became parents of three sons. He was a truck driver for the rest of his working days.

MATTHEW G. WILSON, Desert Storm, United States Army, born in Seymour to Harold and Sharon Wilson on February 3 1966. He graduated from Shields High School in his home town in 1984. He enlisted in the army that November and was soon shipped overseas to Germany.

From there he served in Desert Storm and was awarded the Bronze Star for bravery in action. He was then discharged in 1994 and currently works for the U.S. in Germany.

JOHN M. WISCHMEIER, Iraq, United States Army, born July 15, 1982 in Jackson County,

graduated from Seymour High School.

Received degree from Northwestern Iowa in 2003. Enlisted in the army November 16, 2003. Reported to Fort Jackson, Wyoming for basic training. Scheduled for additional training in South Carolina.

Will report to Fort Benning to be trained in Field Communications.

JEANNIE S. WRIGHT, Desert Storm, 1979–2000, United States Army, graduated from Brownstown Central High School in 1979 and immediately enlisted in the army. She completed basic training at Fort Leonard Wood, MO, then received further training as a still photographic specialist at Lowry Field in Denver, CO. Her assignments included Fort McPherson in Atlanta; Yongsan, Seoul, Heidleburg and Stuttgart, Germany.

In 1985 she was transferred into the transportation field and, as an operator specialist she drove tractor-trailer rigs cross country for the 62nd Transportation Company stationed at Fort Bliss, TX. She was shipped overseas as a VIP driver for Lt. General Colin Powell.

Other assignments included Korea, Panama, NC, Saudi Arabia. and back to Fort Leonard Wood, MO. She was selected by the army for a 3-year tour of the Defense Equal Opportunity Management Institute in Cocoa Beach, FL. She has been authorized to wear dozens of medals and ribbons after she retired.

She retired with more than 20 years of service at Virginia Beach in Virginia. She is married to Duane Cottle, also a Navy veteran and they reside in Somerset, KY with their two children.

IN MEMORY OF JACKSON COUNTY VETERANS

1776 – 2004

VETERANS OF FOREIGN WARS

KENNETH BRANAMAN POST 10807

BROWNSTOWN, INDIANA

THEY ANSWERED TO CALL TO ARMS
AND
DEFENDED OUR LIBERTY

A Tribute to Jackson County Veterans
1776 – 2004

The American Legion

Camp Jackson Post 112

Brownstown, Indiana
-Since 1919-

That They Shall Not Have Died in Vain

THE AMERICAN LEGION
POST 112
BROWNSTOWN, INDIANA
THE PAST COMMANDERS

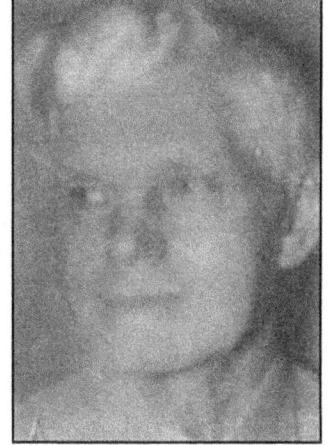

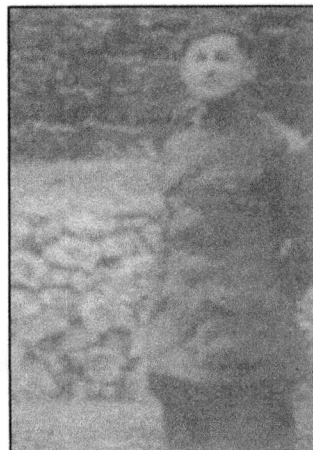

THE AMERICAN LEGION
POST 112
BROWNSTOWN, INDIANA
THE PAST COMMANDERS

THE AMERICAN LEGION

POST 112

BROWNSTOWN, INDIANA

THE PAST COMMANDERS

THE AMERICAN LEGION

POST 112

BROWNSTOWN, INDIANA

THE PAST COMMANDERS

IN MEMORIAM

WORLD WAR I DOUGHBOYS OF THE AEF
SOISSONS, FRANCE

PRIVATE CARL JOHN HENRY FOSBRINK (LEFT)
AND HIS BUDDIES
115TH INFANTRY DIVISION
NOVEMBER 2, 1918

We pause with uncovered heads to honor the brave men who gave their lives that the world might be made safe for democracy, and for the sake of their country and humanity they were faithful unto death, itself.... "Greater love hath no man than this, that a man lay down his life for his friends!!!

FREEMAN FIELD

SEYMOUR, INDIANA

JACKSON COUNTY TRAINING CENTER
1943 - 1946

M/Sgt. Morris W. Durham

VETERANS REMEMBER

The grades of enlisted men and their rates of monthly pay as authorized by Congress by the Act approved September 16, 1940 are shown below

Private	$30.00
Corporal	$36.00
Sergeant	$60.00
Staff Sergeant	$72.00
T/Sgt. and 1st Sgt.	$84.00
Master Sergeant	$126.00

THE GET RICH PLAN OR G.I. BLUES

TAPS

AN
ETERNAL TRIBUTE

GRAND LODGE
KNIGHTS OF PYTHIAS

BROWNSTOWN LODGE #60

OUR TRIBUTE
JACKSON COUNTY VETERANS
1776-2004

TOGETHER AGAIN

Chesapeake and Ohio Railroad
Troop Trains

1946

A
MEMORIAL
TO

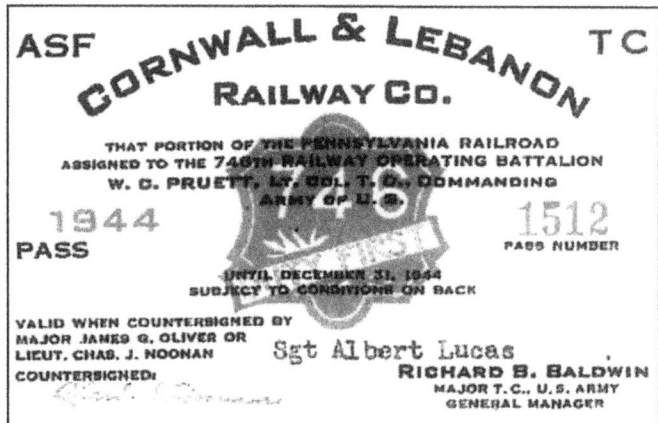

ASF   **CORNWALL & LEBANON**   TC
RAILWAY CO.

THAT PORTION OF THE PENNSYLVANIA RAILROAD
ASSIGNED TO THE 746TH RAILWAY OPERATING BATTALION
W. C. PRUETT, LT. COL. T. C., COMMANDING
ARMY OF U. S.

1944   **1512**
PASS   PASS NUMBER

UNTIL DECEMBER 31, 1944
SUBJECT TO CONDITIONS ON BACK

VALID WHEN COUNTERSIGNED BY
MAJOR JAMES G. OLIVER OR
LIEUT. CHAS. J. NOONAN   **Sgt Albert Lucas**
COUNTERSIGNED: **RICHARD B. BALDWIN**
MAJOR T.C., U. S. ARMY
GENERAL MANAGER

THE
746TH RAILWAY OPERATING BATTALION

Sara Marling Lucas

INVASION OF SICILY

AIRBORNE ASSAULT

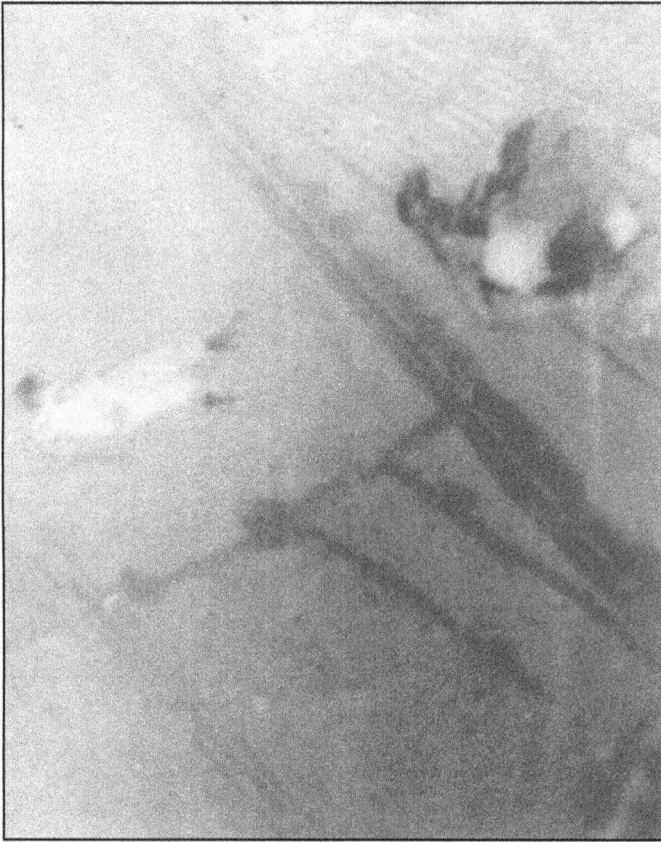

Landing near the railroad

On our way from the plane

OPERATION HUSKY

"H" HOUR PLUS THREE
8:20 AM
10 JULY 1943

In Memoriam

....to the flying crews who perished
and to
those who survived in their parachute jump to safety....

B-24 LIBERATOR BOMB GROUP
LOW LEVEL OIL FIELD RAID
AUGUST 1, 1943
BENGHASI, LYBIA – PLOESTI, RUMANIA

....we are to destroy those oil field refineries in a single day, and it will shorten
the war and we will knock out this target, or die trying....John R. Kane, Commander

JACKSON COUNTY INSURANCE AGENCY, INC.

John Wm. Spurgeon – J. Andy Fountain
Brownstown, Indiana

DEATH AT MALMEDY

1944

BATTLE OF THE BULGE

THE PRICE OF FREEDOM

THE AMERICAN CEMETERY AT NORMANDY

www.ingramcontent.com/pod-product-compliance
Lightning Source LLC
Chambersburg PA
CBHW080403270326
41927CB00015B/3336